# A
# NEW
# ISRAEL

Also by the author

*The Tragedy of Zionism*

# A

# NEW

# ISRAEL

## Democracy in Crisis
## 1973–1988

## Essays

---

## Bernard Avishai

TICKNOR & FIELDS
NEW YORK 1990

For information about permission to reproduce selections
from this book, write to Permissions, Ticknor & Fields,
215 Park Avenue South, New York, New York 10003.

Library of Congress Cataloging-in-Publication Data

Avishai, Bernard.
A new Israel : democracy in crisis, 1973–1988 / Bernard Avishai.
p.    cm.
ISBN 0-89919-966-6
1. Israel — Politics and government.   2. Mifleget po' ale Erets
Yiśra 'el.   3. Likud (Party)   4. Jewish-Arab relations — 1973–
5. Jews — United States — Attitudes toward Israel.     I. Title.
DS126.5.A914   1990   89-20674
320.95694'047 — dc20   CIP

Printed in the United States of America

HAD 10 9 8 7 6 5 4 3 2 1

Most of the chapters in this book were originally published in the *New York Review of Books*. "Israeli Nerves After Camp David," "Zionist Colonialism: Myth and Dilemma," and "Breaking Faith: *Commentary* and the American Jews" were published in *Dissent*; "Wounded Spirits: Shipler's Israel" was published in the *Boston Globe*; "To Praise Zionism and to Bury It" was published in *Moment*; "The Arts in Israel: Rebirth" was published in *Vogue*; "The Forty Years' Crisis" and "Sacred and Secular" were published in *The Nation*.

For Benjamin, Elisheva, and Tamar

# Acknowledgments

Most of the essays in this book were written for the *New York Review of Books* between 1973 and 1984. I was barely twenty-four years old when the *Review* accepted my unsolicited first article. For ten years thereafter, Robert Silvers, the editor, encouraged me, instructed me, many times rewrote me, and took a cheering (somewhat astonishing) interest in my perceptions and my work. This kind of thing changes your life.

Many people taught me about Israel, too many to mention here, though it is probably obvious that a great number of the experts cited in the pieces are also friends. I am grateful to Irving Howe for professional indulgences at *Dissent* and for almost every other kind of indulgence.

Thanks to my agent, Mildred Marmur, for making this book happen, and to John Herman, my editor, for agreeing that it should happen. Finally, thanks to Susan, who lets me happen.

# Contents

PART THREE / IMAGINING THE NEW JEWISH PEOPLE:
ISRAEL AND AMERICA

# Introduction

Israel is a home; too often it is thought of as a cause. It is a fact still defended as if it were an experiment.

Israel is the product of a socialist Zionist revolution whose residual socialism is now a drag on the country's economy and whose Zionism is a fetter on its democracy.

Israel's unique achievement is in building a secular Hebrew culture. Most Israelis take Hebrew for granted and instead celebrate their country for being a state "like any other." The point of that state was independence: Jewish national power. Yet Israel's economy is profoundly dependent on external assistance; and no matter how great the country's military power, Israeli Jews seem unable to feel their own strength.

Israel's state apparatus declares itself in the service of the Jewish people and Judaism, though nearly 20 percent of its citizens are not Jews, most Jews are not its citizens, and its parliament dares not decide precisely who Jews are. Most Israelis claim to know what a Palestinian state will look like, but they cannot say just what a Jewish state should look like.

Israel's Jews live mainly in modern cities; their heroes are pioneering settlers and Old World rabbis. Israel's national origins are in Eastern Europe, its majority's roots in North Africa. Its dominant political party dreams of Greater Israel while, in smaller Israel, the prospect of an Arab Galilee looms.

These heartbreaking ironies, all too evident in the second year of the *Intifada*, first impressed themselves on me during the grim but comparatively calm days following the October war of 1973, while I was living in Jerusalem. As I look over the essays and reports collected in this book, it is sobering to recall how grudgingly they took shape on the page and how cocky they seemed in print.

In those years, to use the word "Palestinian" without qualification—worse, to ask whether Israelis and diaspora Jews still needed classical Zionist myths—was to risk infuriating people you admired. It was as if the Sabbath could be desecrated only by writers. After I wrote the election report whose title serves for the book, one childhood friend, now a well-known columnist living in Washington, broke relations with me. He was incensed by my claim that Menachem Begin's victory in 1977 was rooted in solid and disturbing political trends; that the occupation forces were meanwhile making enemies of Palestinian youth. Alas, I have not heard from him since. When it comes to Israel, prescience was never much of a pleasure.

I hasten to add that what prescience there is in these essays is largely the result of the exhausting education I got from a great number of Israeli friends and colleagues before the October war: teachers, moshavniks, furniture dealers—people who were more nervous and open-minded than the Canadian Zionists from whose company I had ingenuously emerged. In retrospect, that w as a more pivotal time than anybody fully realized: Labor Zionism was dead, the new Israel was not yet born. One could imagine Israel's becoming a more perfect democracy as easily as a more repressive state committed to the "unity of Eretz Yisrael."

One piece of luck, after I started writing about Israeli affairs, was my coming across Arthur Koestler's *Promise and Fulfillment* —just when Golda Meir's Labor coalition began to break apart in 1974. Koestler had wrestled with the potential failures of Labor Zionism back in 1949; his book provided a historical context for what might have seemed ordinary headlines. He also made nice distinctions: between a Jewish culture and a Hebrew one, socialism and the conceits of a labor aristocracy, durable political power and the temporary pleasures of aggression. It was difficult though necessary to see such distinctions in the middle of war, political scandals, and terrorist attacks. It has not become easier since.

Though the essays in this book began as journalism, I believe
they amount to an increasingly coherent line of thinking. Some
essays introduce polemics and narratives that ultimately found
their way into *The Tragedy of Zionism*, but this new book completes
a different task: it chronicles the previous generation of Israeli
politics and asks what Israeli leaders have done with opportunities for peace. In standing up to military threats, have they
realized liberal democratic standards? It seemed to me that too
many diaspora Jews blushed over the question.

Like Koestler, I looked at the political and economic forces
shaping Israeli culture and diplomacy. I also tried to get under
rather obscure ideological principles—deriving from the debates of classical Zionism—that nuanced political discussion before and during the Begin era. These debates have more or less
evaporated under the brutal pressure of the *Intifada*.

If there is an obtuse angle of criticism in this book, it points
to the self-defeating ways so many Israeli peace activists have
shied away from the strictures of liberalism and the logic of
federalism during the past twenty years. In my view, the rather
barren conception of democracy one finds among left intellectuals, particularly in the Labor Party, explains the Israeli right's
success in setting the terms of national debate—even now, as
Europeans reconsider the value of full national sovereignty and
when the risks of maintaining the occupation are so obviously
greater than the risks of peacemaking.

It may seem like carping, now that the leaders of the Labor Party
are struggling to move the peace process forward, to analyze
Labor's historic failure to project a vision of a just society distinct
from Likud's. But it is this very failure that plagues peace efforts
at every turn. Labor periodically threatens to leave the National
Unity government when Likud seems intent on obstructing negotiations. But to what end? Polls show that Labor—in spite of
its closer associations with the United States and Egypt—would
do even worse in the next election than it did in the last.

Since 1973, Labor's leaders have put forward nothing more
creative than a "return" to the little Israel of 1948. So they have
been reduced to reacting to initiatives taken by the right. In the
face of Arab hostility, the religious parties and younger voters

take for granted that Likud rhetoric about Jewish historic rights in Eretz Yisrael captures the essence of what Israel can be. Labor, in contrast, comes off as something of a scold.

Nor do Shimon Peres, Yitzchak Rabin, and others in the top ranks of Labor show any signs of grasping how desperately Israelis need a radically positive alternative vision to the revolutionary Zionism of 1948. "We have become morally ill," writes Czech President Vaclav Havel, "because we are used to saying one thing and thinking another." The post-1967 generation of Israelis affirms democratic standards but actually thinks them a mortal danger to their parents' national ideal. They think of violence as preempting democracy; they do not see that it is the other way around.

After the 1988 election, for example, Peres blamed his party's defeat on a terrorist attack: Palestinian violence "cost Labor three seats," he said. But think this through. Is Peres right that the course Labor proposes — Palestinian self-government, territorial compromise, binational cooperation, a democratic Israel — can be discredited by Arab violence? Do Israelis have to "trust the Arabs" to vote for his notion of a democratic Israel?

Peres has obviously assumed, with some justice, that Israeli voters do not for the most part think of the word *democratia* when they imagine ways to settle disputes. By his logic, civil liberties and representative government are the *reward* for civility, not the means to achieve it. He has been articulate about reasons for ending the occupation. But he has been at a loss to show why liberal democratic institutions, not force, presuppose peace.

And whose failure of imagination is this if not Labor Zionism's? True to their tradition, Labor leaders want "partition" but are fuzzy about association. They want Israel to be an open society but have always been deeply skeptical of the open cultural field this implies. They want a liberal society but not a plural one; they want to live in a community of people who look pretty much like themselves, though Israel is actually a country that includes, among other groups, many Arabs and Christians.

If the very point of politics is to preserve, in effect, a Jewish state defined as a society exclusively for Jews and a state apparatus devoted to the Jewish people, how does long-term peace with the Palestinians really make sense? Palestinians are everywhere. You can either expel them or build a political system that contrives to ignore them.

Make no mistake, leading Palestinian intellectuals are often no better. They, too, speak in solemn voices about self-determination, as if it weren't Israelis shuddering at the thought of what Arabs would do if they *could* simply determine their future that helped to get the occupation going in the first place. One hears from Israelis and Palestinians humane defenses of the principle of a "two-state" solution. Almost nowhere does one hear reasonable proposals to put federal principles to work, though it is impossible to imagine a single jurisdiction either state could exercise without presupposing the guaranteed co-operation of the other—and Jordan's. A Palestinian state might have a passport and a flag. But could it make laws about water, Jerusalem, transportation, labor, land reclamation and access, voting rights, immigration, tourism—anything—without ne-gotiating in advance reciprocal laws in Israel? Could it even have its own currency? Is it any surprise that, in the absence of trans-national ideas, Israeli and Palestinian youth trust nothing but power?

What both sides seem to miss is painfully simple: this conflict is not going to be solved by more pious sanction for the principle of national self-determination. The Palestinians have always con-sidered Zionism a movement that excluded them, first from lands purchased by Zionist settlers, then from jobs in the Tel Aviv economy, then, after 1948, from much of their country. Under occupation, Palestinians have felt excluded from civil so-ciety, during the *Intifada*, from the human community. And so when they get carried away by slogans such as "Zionism is rac-ism," they are really voicing doubt about the democratic char-acter of Jewish nationalism.

At the same time, Israelis take stock of the religious intensity that purported to justify Palestinian terrorism since 1929 and the Mufti's alliance with fascism. They look at the PLO's militarist command structure and aesthetics through the 1970s, at the brutal ways it has silenced, in many cases assassinated, Palestinian dissenters during the 1980s. They see the logic of totalitarian minds in all of this; and Palestinian illiberalism is not mitigated by the fact that Palestinians are currently the main victims. As

Yael Dayan has observed, if there is asymmetrical suffering right now it is only because of asymmetrical power.

What Israeli and Palestinian peace activists really need to offer each other is democratic hope, proof that each side sees human equality as a *universal* value — not respect for each other's nationalism. Both nationalisms have had more respect than they've earned for three generations. Peace activists need to insist on, and offer each other, serious ideas about sharing democratic political institutions — insist, certainly, that all citizens of either a Jewish or Palestinian state will live under a fully democratic regime constitutionally committed to mutual cooperation.

If Israeli intellectuals carry a disproportionate share of the responsibility for propagating a democratic vision at this point, it is because the state of Israel does indeed exercise a disproportionate share of the political power. How have Israeli peace intellectuals responded?

Understandably, the memory of the 1948 – 67 partition has had a certain charm in this context. Many Labor intellectuals hold on to it fiercely. The writer Amos Oz told an American Jewish audience recently that he is seeking not a marriage to the Palestinians but "a fair and decent divorce." He wants good relations with individual Arabs, he said, but seeks most of all a "painful separation of assets and real estate" — "no matter how small the apartment."

The alternative to national self-determination for the Palestinians, Oz insisted, is endless bloodshed. His criticism of annexationists is harsh; he is for elections. Yet Oz has little inclination for searching out pluralist institutions *with* Arabs, such as maverick peace activists Meron Benvenisti and Ezer Weizman have advocated. No, Oz believes, peace proposals do not mean love: he doesn't really care what kind of state the Palestinians have so long as it doesn't threaten Israel. He wants a democratic Israel because he cares about the Jews. Israelis and Palestinians cannot leap from sixty-five years of conflict into a "honeymoon."

But here, in a nutshell, is the Israeli left's contribution to Israel's political trap — a subtle contribution, though not an inconsiderable one. National self-determination is good. Pluralism, in contrast, is too good. And democratic federalism is something else again — a somewhat exalted luxury, something only the most privileged societies can afford. Democrats, presumably, do not know how to deal with the dirty, gritty facts of ambition and hatred. If *democratia* means that different peoples are supposed to share the same political institutions, it is naiveté — something Zionist grandparents, who had lived through European fascism, knew better than to trust.

Where if not in the vision of a liberal democratic society *with* Palestinians — two secular democratic states sharing a federated structure and economy with Jordan — is to be found Oz's hope for sharing those assets that cannot, and should not, be separated? Jerusalem, for example? Wherein lies his hope for an open society for all of Israel's citizens, Arabs included, as opposed to the theocratic principles espoused by Moslem fundamentalists and Israeli religious politicians?

The hope, apparently, is *his* Zionism. To have a liberal Israel, Oz replies, American Jews should come en masse and "steal the show." But why, if he thinks liberalism works, would he imagine that liberal American Jews would leave their homes in America? Why, if American Jews *would* come, could he have any faith in the liberalism he is paying lip service to? What Americans *are* coming to Israel — or, more usually, to the West Bank — if not people cynical about pluralism? And if "divorcing" the Palestinians is the point of the exercise, what about the Arabs who will remain inside Israel? What about Jews on the West Bank?

Oz and others in the peace camp show great courage in acknowledging the national claims of their historic enemies. But what does national self-determination portend divorced from the strict liberal and federal principles Israeli young people need so badly if they are to make sense of their future? If Israel is lucky, it will one day look something like Quebec. Yet even Israel's most prominent peace activists stoke the dream of living in something like Japan.

One gets a particularly strong sense of this conundrum when one hears Israeli doves speak of the so-called demographic problem. I've had to consider this matter especially carefully in coming to terms with some unexpectedly vexed criticism of *The Tragedy of Zionism* by some close friends in the Israeli peace camp.

Professor Avishai Margalit, a philosopher at the Hebrew University and a founder of Peace Now, writes in one review essay that it was wrong of me (or any American, presumably) to focus on old Zionist obstacles to liberal democracy in Israel when the real challenge in his country is the one presented by the rise of Meir Kahane, whose supporters want to solve the demographic problem—i.e., the problem of a potential loss of a Jewish majority in the state of Israel—by expelling Arabs.

"On this point," Margalit asserts, "Kahane's support goes well beyond a lunatic fringe that won him his parlimentary seat, and this is crucial for understanding the current Israeli scene—much more so than the issue of whether or not the state is a democracy according to the liberal theology of Avishai."*

Theology. Margalit's point, presumably, is that Western writers often tend to use the word "democracy" in an inappropriate way, idiosyncratically American. In its place, Margalit advances the idea that democracy is to be measured either "by free expression or by free participation of citizens in public life"—a rather malleable definition one often finds in Israel, though he obviously means to imply by it some more classical version of democracy—"rule by the people," "majority rule," "mass participation," something along these lines.

In fact, Margalit adds, "the history of Israel is one of increasing democratization." One infers that it is the very efficiency of Israel's democracy that is a part of its problem; that the views of "hoi polloi" have democratically prevailed. He does not say so, but he is obviously anxious about the rise to prominence through the Likud of, say, less well educated North African immigrant groups, people who disproportionately favor expulsion of Arabs.

Now, a moment's reflection would reveal the contradiction in this analysis. Like many other Israelis, Margalit objects to taking democracy in its liberal, pluralist sense at the same time as he sincerely appeals to liberal sensibilities. Underlying his own repugnance for the expulsion of Palestinians are the same liberal nuances he accuses me of insinuating into the discussion from America. And yet the American model seems disturbingly presumptuous to him.

*New York Review of Books, October 23, 1986.

If "free expression and free participation" were the only values at stake, then a majority of Israelis might feel justified choosing freely to repress or expel a minority. In this vein, the Israeli right keeps insisting that it is *democratia* that determined Jewish expropriation of West Bank lands would go on.

But if expulsion and Jewish expropriation of Palestinian land are wrong, then democracy is *best* measured, surely, by the social patterns of liberty guaranteed by law and reinforced by the institutions of the secular state. Democracy is to be judged by whether or not citizens live by public institutions that accommodate differences of faith and opinion and culture, whether or not they regard each other *essentially as individuals* and support a state apparatus that protects a dissenting view, an artistic departure, or a nonconforming style of life. Liberal protections keep majority rule fair and tend to ensure that minorities will fight for their part of the truth without resorting to violence.

Majority rule and opportunities for participation are necessary conditions for democracy, but they are hardly sufficient. Indeed, when Israeli Jews argue that Israel cannot be a democratic state unless Jews remain in a strong, absolute majority, they are greatly oversimplifying Israel's challenge.

Actually, the argument in behalf of a "Jewish majority" amounts only to a restatement of classical Zionist goals long achieved. The Hebrew nation, whose consolidation once depended on a Zionist majority in parts of Mandate Palestine, is no longer a theoretical nation. Neither is the Hebrew language in danger. Whoever comes to work in Tel Aviv will speak Hebrew. Tens of thousands come from Gaza.

Israelis and Palestinians inhabit a world in which America's biggest export is communications and entertainment, Western Europe gropes toward 1992, Eastern Europe bloc gropes toward Western Europe, and Motorola and Toshiba cut deals that dwarf in importance anything the governments of small countries can do. Abstract talk about national self-determination, or academic disquisitions on the surprising strength of nationalism in the twentieth century, do not do justice to the opportunity of living in the new world order.

And just what *is* a "Jewish majority" two generations after the founding of the state? What about an Arab boy who speaks (and perhaps thinks in) Hebrew, who is a citizen of the country, and who wants to shape Israeli identity in a way that clashes with the will of, say, Orthodox Jews? What about Christian theologians who want to wrestle with the Jewish tradition in the Jews' own language, as Martin Buber once wrestled with Christianity in German? How to protect, teach, and learn from such people? How to extend, equally, the burdens of citizenship? *How to avoid civil violence?*

Margalit is right to imply that, since 1967, new groups have been empowered by the Israeli electoral system. Certainly, commercial and artistic freedoms developed in the country as the Labor Zionist settler society gave way to urban, middle-class life. I believe these facts come through strongly in this book of essays.

But his claim that the history of Israel is thus one of "increasing democratization" is seriously misleading. Greater "populism" is not the same as democratization. Electoral laws that give disproportionate power to the *apparat* of old Zionist parties have not changed during this time, and civil laws have made new concessions to Jewish orthodoxy. And if social attitudes toward individual liberty are indeed critical (e.g., the attitude toward expulsion), then the other side of the story is that of a perceptible growth in intolerance in Israel, of an increasing willingness all around to resort to sheer force.

Consider the polarization between Jews and Arabs *within* the 1967 borders — also the growing tendency among Orthodox Jews to push secularists around. Most significant, perhaps, is the evolution of a huge electoral bloc, potentially the majority, which has adjusted to occupation of the West Bank and Gaza, though occupation obviously means that Israel must evolve — to borrow Benvenisti's term — as a *Herrenvolk* democracy.

This is the heart of the matter. It is becoming difficult to discuss the problem of democracy in Israel as if Israelis lived in a country separable in imagination from Greater Israel. Liberal and federal ideas, laws, and protections are urgently required, not only because they are just, but because they alone can help mitigate the divisions of nation, class, and religion. They are not the honeymoon, as Oz would have it, but the contract. It is not too late to start laying out its terms.

Israeli Jews and Palestinian Arabs cannot avoid sharing a common political life in one form or another. There is no going back to an Israel of kibbutz fences, water towers, and guard huts. Indeed, by the time this book is published, indirect negotiations between Israelis and Palestinians may be under way in Cairo. If they have any chance of succeeding, simple, classical conceptions of statehood will have to be abandoned. As the late I. F. Stone wrote some twenty years ago, the alternative to new forms of association is a binational state torn apart by violence — and continued talk of mutual expulsion.

To what extent are the self-segregating patterns of historic Zionism still embedded in Israeli government practice and official ideology? To what extent is this a burden on Israeli democracy or on the evolution of liberal democratic convictions among Israeli citizens? Is the choice really either democracy *or* Zionism? Indeed, are Kahane and the parties of the West Bank settlers winning support because, in spite of their repellent racism, they are given credit among young people for posing the choice honestly?

The answer seems plain by now. There *is* an institutional legacy to Zionism that makes a more liberal democracy impossible and lasting peace unlikely, whatever the Palestinians do, and I am not referring to such trivial (and admittedly touching) symbols as menorahs on state buildings or a state holiday on Passover.

Young Israelis have grown up with a state apparatus that may be democratic in many essential respects (with regard to press freedom, for instance) and yet routinely discriminates in favor of *individual* Jews, who are legally designated "Jewish" on state identity cards. Israel is legally the state of the Jewish people, not a state of its citizens.

Israelis who travel the agricultural heartland know that an Arab citizen cannot bid on an adjacent farm if it is part of a Keren Hayesod collective — and it usually is. Israelis hear national politicians exhorting young Jews to take Jewish Agency loans and state tax concessions to "Judaize the Galilee." They know that religious schools and movement schools are in large measure publicly funded. It does not even cross their minds that their democracy might benefit from an integrated system of public education.

Young Israeli Jews know that they cannot legally marry a non-

Jew in Israel, owing to the status quo that David Ben-Gurion negotiated long ago with religious Zionists. They know that the Law of Return gives immediate citizenship to virtually any Jew on request—not, say, landed-immigrant status to refugees from anti-Semitism but citizenship. And in consequence of having to make policy for such institutions, the Knesset debates "Who is a Jew?" as if a definition were the business of any parliament.

Discrimination of this kind does not affect many people directly. However, everybody feels it as a cultural ambiance, a moral education. Koestler once referred to it, gently, as "claustrophilia." For centuries, ghetto Jews were made to feel that if they got close to goyim they'd eventually have to give up being Jews. What's left of Zionism teaches young Israelis—Jews and Arabs alike—that the Jewish state is something analogous to the embattled Jewish family, and Kahane spins off from this illusion a *Kehilah* with an army.

Again, the most striking thing about Israeli Jews who toy with the idea of expelling Arabs is their youth. The arguments for tolerance do not occur naturally to children.

Why not concentrate, as Margalit and Oz urge, on the demographic problem? Why not struggle for the separation of the West Bank and Gaza from the state of Israel rather than for the positive standard of liberal democracy for all the inhabitants of Israel and Palestine?

The answer is that anybody who wants peace and a new flourishing of Hebrew culture *would* try to end the occupation. But even if Israel were to revert to the 1967 borders, it would remain with a huge Arab population. Three quarters of a million Arab citizens (surrounded by millions more outside Israel) do not pose less of a challenge to the notions wrapped up in that suffocating phrase "demographic problem" than the million and a half Arabs of the West Bank and Gaza. By itself, partition does not look like peace, and young Israelis know it.

Many Israeli doves speak of dividing the land of Israel as a way of making the Arabs disappear from their midst, as if living in a pluralist state is a betrayal of the trust of Israel's founders. Meanwhile, the Israeli right points out, acutely, that Israel without the West Bank and Gaza would still be something less than the Jewish state Zionist thinkers had in mind. Is it not time to say that an Israel with a substantial Arab minority federated with

Palestine—a country liberal, scientific, urbane, and Hebrew—might be something *more* than any Zionist had in mind?

Israelis are living in a new Israel, but they are perceiving it through the strong wishes of the past. Violence, grieving, and the fear of loss explain some of their impulses, but these things do not shape the imagination by themselves.

The key to self-determination, national or otherwise, is to see old wishes plain and to distinguish them from the realities they would otherwise distort. It is hard for people in the heat of a fight to know what they need. Israelis need most of all to understand the anachronistic political structure they live with and how it reinforces obsolete wishes. They are under pressure. They exert pressure in return.

Not long ago, Daniel Pipes, a neoconservative, wrote to *Tikkun* magazine to criticize certain observers, myself included, who in his opinion see Israel "in a vacuum." He says: "Like a host of American critics of Israel (Bernard Avishai comes first to mind) they focus so intently on the Israeli policy that they lose sight of the larger context in which Israeli actions take place."

Pipes will not easily understand why I consider this high praise. If these essays will help Israelis to see themselves "in a vacuum," they are doing their job.

The book is divided into three sections. The first looks at Israel's politics by means of a series of essays and election reports. Driving the analysis was my growing sense after the October war of the Israeli right as a juggernaut. The last piece looks at the right's continuing triumph during the early days of the *Intifada*.

The second section looks at the Israeli-Palestinian conflict directly. On the whole, I don't think there is much about these essays that needs changing, though I have taken the liberty of fussing with my prose. I would also have liked to have spent more time thinking about the evolution of the international PLO, less about reconciling the Palestinians to Israel by means of Jordanian diplomacy. I wish it had dawned on me earlier that partition was not enough. I also made the mistake of taking the Reagan administration seriously. That was a case of my own wishful thinking getting the better of me. I hope the Bush administration will be more tough-minded.

Yet I would not change my view that Israel's confrontation

with the Palestinians remains a triangular one that includes Jordan. The Camp David process and the Reagan plan will look better to historians than they look to observers right now. And if Israeli Arabs are what shatter contented Zionist myths of a Jewish state, so too will the people of Jordan, with or without the King, shatter Palestinian myths of a united Palestinian people.

In the last section, I've included a number of essays on seemingly diverse subjects — Israeli popular culture, *Commentary* magazine, Michael Walzer's reading of the Book of Exodus — but all are bound by a single thread. This is my sense that Zionist ideas take many forms, as do the ways of seeing beyond them.

*"Der mensch tracht, und Gott lacht,"* my father used to say. "Man plans, and God laughs." There is a Jewish sensibility here that predated the Zionist revolution and will no doubt outlast it. And if this is "liberal theology," then more power to it.

PART ONE

# THE POLITICAL TRIUMPH OF THE ISRAELI RIGHT

# Three Months of
# Yom Kippur

*Jerusalem, late December 1973*

The aftermath of the October war is still very much before us, but Israeli society is already gripped by the urgency of "drawing conclusions"—*hasakat maskanot*, words at the center of the new political lexicon. Indeed, the name Yom Kippur War, tentatively assigned by the Israeli press, seems to have stuck fast for reasons transcending the actual day of attack. For the pain, introspection, and grim self-criticism that Jews so vigorously exercise on Yom Kippur have become, for the present at any rate, a way of life. This is a society facing its shortcomings; the achievements can wait.

Internal political criticism has become stormy among a citizenry recognized not only for its insatiable political appetite but also its generally patronizing approach to its own political leadership—even during the most tranquil periods. It is precisely the Israelis' sense of social interdependence, the "for better–for worse" resignation characterizing the relations between Israelis and their governments, that has made this intensity of critical debate possible. The disenchantment here is with policies, decisions, and deciders, not with the Jewish national project.*

*

*A recent public opinion survey conducted by the Communications Institute of the Hebrew University reveals, among other things, that a full 84 percent of those questioned believe that a meaningful cut in their living standards is "ac-

Premier Golda Meir, Defense Minister Moshe Dayan, and Minister Without Portfolio Israel Galili, a special adviser on security affairs, are obvious preliminary targets, for they bore, indeed usurped, complete civilian responsibility for defense. The defense watchdog committee of the Knesset has long been starved into paralysis, and the government as a whole was not consulted or advised about the deteriorating condition on the borders until four hours before the outbreak of hostilities. No doubt Meir, Dayan, and Galili presided over a remarkable victory by military standards, but Israelis have other standards. Two thousand five hundred killed is a staggering setback. And what comfort is there in inflicting greater losses to the other side?

There is, moreover, dissatisfaction with the state of the country's defenses at the outbreak of the war. Israelis get their "real" news from their husbands or sons at the front, and the stories filtering back from the Syrian front suggest that only the skill and sacrifice of Israeli soldiers—the "sons," *barcinu*—coupled with Syrian logistical incompetence prevented destructive incursions into northern heartlands. On the Egyptian front, furthermore, there appears to have been such a shocking breakdown of communications that the General Staff's "full alert" was not executed by the Southern Command. General "Goordish" Gonen, the officer in charge of the South, has been demoted and replaced by Assistant Chief of Staff Tal, an acknowledged architect of the counteroffensive. But many see this demotion, although perhaps justified, as scapegoating.

That Israelis draw inspiration and confidence from the idealism of the Israel Defense Forces only increases their skepticism about what the disgruntled ex-Laborite Shulamit Aloni has dubbed "Golda's Defense Kitchen" (*ha'mitbach*), which had smugly dictated defense policy, operation, and expenditure for the last five years. Dayan, who had placed himself above criticism on defense matters, is generally suspected of having forced an

---

ceptable" and that almost 20 percent insisted that cuts were "necessary." Over 83 percent have already purchased war bonds or will be doing so. The net average Israeli income is, by the way, roughly only two thirds that of the American with regard to purchasing power. Moreover, during the war period, public volunteering *exceeded* demand although all men between eighteen and forty-five years of age were conscripted.

intransigent line on the ruling coalition of Labor Alignment—against the explicit opposition of Mapam—by threatening to bolt the party to form a government with the coalition of right-wing parties, the Likud. The State List, a new member of the Likud and remnant of Rafi, of which Ben-Gurion and Dayan were leaders, had gone to the Histadrut elections explicitly claiming that every vote for them would help chip Dayan away from the Alignment.

Dayan is paying a double price, not only for his apparently faulty command but for having flaunted his political indispensability. There has been very strong opposition to his remaining as Defense Minister in the next government, although his charisma, albeit tarnished, and his very close ties to Golda Meir still compel one to see his political future as uncertain. Shimon Peres, Minister of Transport, erstwhile Rafi member and close associate of Dayan, is now expounding the argument that Israel has in fact been *at war* since 1967, and that one ought to appreciate Dayan's competence during the *whole* of his tenure. But it will not wash. After all, it was Dayan's claim to have provided a *stable* "no peace–no war" that had justified his hard line prior to October.

Israel Galili, on the other hand, faces more immediate political challenges. His name has become synonymous with the government's lethargy in making peace initiatives because of his leading role in producing the "hawkish" and now unofficially defunct "Galili Document," and then, in cooperation with Dayan, grafting it onto the Alignment. The "Galili Document" was a patchwork of plans for selective settlement of the occupied territories and indifference to Palestinian national aspirations, and was predicated on a Dr. Pangloss view of Israeli deterrent power. It has now been superseded by a highly syncretic but decidedly more dovish "fourteen-point program," which emphasizes territorial concessions and recognition for Palestinian Arab self-determination. I shall refer to this new document later, but the extent to which its acceptance compromises Galili's position in the government is unquestionable.

A longtime friend of Golda Meir (her translator into "nice Hebrew") and de facto leader of the Achdut Ha'avoda faction in the Alignment, Galili has lost his constituency, it would seem, to Vice Premier Yigal Allon. Allon has been an outspoken "dove," and his newfound political courage makes him a strong candidate to form a new government should Mrs. Meir step down or, though this is unlikely, be forced out by the party machine. Allon called for Dayan's resignation and suggested that Mrs. Meir form a projected government *before* the elections so that the Israeli voter would know for what he or she is voting.

Mrs. Meir seems to be the only member of the "kitchen" whose position remains stable. It now seems indisputable, nevertheless, that Israelis are no longer prepared to tolerate Golda's "democratic centralism" when the IDF, their most precious national asset, is involved. The Foreign Affairs and Security Committee of the Knesset appears now to have a greatly augmented responsibility, and academic think tanks have been commissioned to prepare contingency plans for the Geneva talks.

General "Arik" Sharon's openly critical remarks to the foreign press caused quite a stir—not so much for their content, with which many agreed, but because they were correctly taken as a symptom of serious, politically motivated malaise among the IDF's senior officers. It is clear, by the way, that Sharon's Likud political affiliations are intimately connected with the fact that he was passed over for Chief of Staff, although it is not certain which preceded what. There is a vocal public nostalgia for the days of Ben-Gurion, when, or so it is presumed, the IDF was not run by the fiat of folk heroes but by rigorous standards of merit, noninvolvement in politics, and efficiency.

To be sure, an IDF completely free of political intrigue may be a somewhat idealized view, but one that all seem eager to believe in the wake of Ben-Gurion's recent death and the memories of a noble epoch that a three-day national mourning aroused. It is widely felt that the extent of the Arab surprise in the last war, in planning and execution, was, by comparison, caused by a withering of vigilance, which often accompanies arrogance and elitism. The first surge of public outrage directed at the "failures" (*ha'mechdalim*) of government leaders and senior officers, and their practices, has temporarily been stifled only by the appointment of a Judicial Commission of Inquiry, unprecedented in its prestige, independence, and discretionary power.

Included on the commission are Lieutenant General Haim Lasko, who, as Chief of Staff when the "Lavon crisis" broke in 1960, maintained a political neutrality beyond reproach, and Professor Yigael Yadin, the first Chief of Staff, a gadfly in the establishment, whose agitation for electoral reform, complemented by his personal "pioneering" example at the excavations of Masada, endows him with respect. The latter, by the way, was highly touted to become Defense Minister in 1967 but was passed over for Dayan for reasons that are not clear.

However, it would be simplistic to suppose that Israelis, or at least a significant number of them, will now be satisfied with merely a clarification of purely technical failures when the very political and strategic assumptions that these techniques were intended to serve are seriously eroded. Over these assumptions a decisive political battle has been taking place within the Alignment since mid-October. Maverick doves such as Yitzchak Ben-Aharon, who resigned from the powerful Histadrut leadership to get closer to the action, and Arie ("Lova") Eliav, an ex–general secretary of the party who has been waging his fight against the kitchen out in the open for two years, have been pressing the initiative, and Mapam has also been stirring.

But what now seems even more significant is that moderate ex-Mapai power brokers — the "fire extinguishers" — such as Finance Minister Pinhas Sapir and Tel Aviv Mayor Yehoshua Rabinovitch, and even steady *apparatchiks* such as Party Secretary Aharon Yadlin and election campaign chief Avraham Ofer, seem all to be committed to a new style and substance of leadership. The "fourteen-point program" was *their* victory, and Sapir seems to have tamed Eliav at the marathon central committee convention that adopted it, with a secret promise of a cabinet post for a committed dove. Mrs. Meir, it is true, will probably remain leader, however modulated, out of deference to her magnetism. A mid-December poll revealed that Golda still held a hefty plurality, 46 percent, as the "people's choice" for premier, but now Allon ranks second in the Alignment, not Dayan. But the political wind sniffers broke openly with her at this meeting.

The writing on the wall is, after all, printed in block letters. In mid-December the polls showed the Alignment and the Likud running neck and neck, each with about 30 percent of the vote, with a huge 30 percent undecided. Shulamit Aloni's Civil Rights faction showed surprising strength. Moked, the left-wing splinter party, drew unprecedented crowds (two thousand in Tel Aviv on a Friday night) and seemed to be making real inroads in the kibbutzim with its pragmatically dovish program. Further, over 46 percent polled agreed that at least "some territorial concessions" are now necessary, and only 20 percent insisted that no territory should be returned.

Granted, "territorial concessions" seems a rather superficial solution to a complex problem. Nevertheless, the term has become an accepted litmus test of a willingness for diplomatic flexibility. The Alignment Party machine churned out election propaganda claiming that it is the only *strong* peace party and that a vote against it will "split the left." This has worked before. But, at least this time, the machine has felt pressured to deliver more than empty socialist rhetoric; some leaders will go, or, as it is more commonly claimed, they "will fly"—an expression revealing the almost comic relish with which so many Israelis anticipate the cashiering of government ministers.

Meanwhile, during November and December the press and the articulate public set a very peppery tone of debate. Petition campaigns flourished, led by hitherto politically inactive but extremely influential men: distinguished scholars (Talmon, Rottenstreich, Avineri, Shamir), writers (A. B. Yehoshua, Amos Oz, Amos Elon), ex-generals (Mati Peled, Meir Pa'il), actors (Hannah Maron), and, of course, kibbutz leaders (Dan Sion, Muki Tzur) and hundreds more. And if there was a common theme to the various petitions, it was that *all* peace initiatives must now be attempted, with due regard to fundamental national security. The most impressive campaign was an abortive attempt to force all parties to reopen their "election lists" so that a *new* leadership, such is the implication, might have been chosen more democratically to deal with the "new" situation.

What *is* new? Is there not a depressing familiarity about conflict and war between Jews and Arabs? Yes, but the catchwords "new situation" refer not to the supposed constancy of Arab enmity, or to the chilling specter of "Jewish fate," but to the real and now more evident strategic alternatives that appear to have existed all along for the Israeli government to explore, but to which Golda and her leadership addressed themselves only with unambiguous claims that no such alternatives had existed.

For a start, the notion that the Israeli army has had no choice (*ein breira*) but to sit on the Suez Canal and dig in on the heights overlooking the road to Damascus until Egypt and Syria respectively agree to direct negotiations *with no preconditions* appears to have been a poor strategic decision even under the very worst of scenarios which would reflect the very worst of Arab intentions. The sorry fact that nobody ever called Sadat's peace bluff, if it was a bluff (he did, after all, make clear rumblings about "recognition" and "peace" if Israel would agree, *in principle*, to return the whole of Sinai), is only coincidental to the more central point that a unilateral withdrawal from the Canal, with strongholds left to, say, a UN Emergency Force, might have ironically *served* Israel's strategic interest.

The elegant image of "security borders" was blown apart by two thousand artillery pieces. A preemptive first strike was ruled out. General David Elazar, Chief of Staff of the IDF, asked for it to be begun exactly two hours before the Arabs eventually attacked. Golda refused. He asked her if she knew what it meant. She replied that she did. She didn't.

Dayan himself contended in a wholly plausible response to early criticism that the IDF, being four fifths a *reserve* army, could not sit eyeball to eyeball with professional, standing, continuously mobilized Arab troops. Israelis have a country to build, he rightly observed, and simply couldn't sit at the front in numbers sufficient to repel a massive first strike. Also, it would have been impossible to mobilize the reserves at any sign of smoke for the practical reason that Sadat's threats and maneuvers could have turned the IDF into a gigantic yo-yo—at forty million Israeli pounds a spin. Thus the inescapable conclusion must be that "security borders" were *rather short on security*—particularly and tragically for the five hundred to six hundred boys who manned the Bar-Lev Line when hostilities broke out.

Granted, the war was fought on the Golan and in the Sinai, not near Israeli populated areas. But in an age of missiles, only a mutual balance of terror precluded greater devastation. In the early hours of the fighting, a SKUD missile from Egypt was headed for Tel Aviv when it was, incredibly enough, shot down by an Israeli Phantom; a Syrian FROG missile leveled the children's quarters of Kibbutz Gvat, but the children were in shelters. Massive retaliation bombing by the IDF in the early days apparently ended the missile activity, but the missiles are, of course, still in their silos.

Besides, as Mati Peled and Meir Pa'il, both reserve generals, have pointed out, a new war should not have to be fought near Israeli cities in the future, for surely this at least is a durable consequence of the Six-Day War. The extent of Israel's territorial sovereignty is not the point. The real question, they continue, is whether the cease-fire lines offer more security than *demilitarized zones*, the latter being a possibility that the government had steadfastly opposed, conjuring up the image of fleeing UN troops in 1967.

But, the generals argue, was *that* situation strategically so bad? Any military infringement by Arab armies upon another UN-controlled buffer zone would be an immediate and mutually understood *casus belli*, would provide the Israeli command with a clear and unambiguous signal *cum* time for calling up the reserves and would impose on invading Arab armies precisely that kind of fast-moving, wide-open battle at which the IDF excels and in which Israeli air superiority can be far more decisive. The upshot of their arguments is that, on the contrary, "security borders" invite battle on the worst possible terms. The loss to Israeli society of so many of its finest young men — breadwinners and fathers — is incalculable; their deaths in bloody slugging matches on Mount Hermon or on the Canal is particularly bitter.

For what now seems clear in all of this is that Dayan, Meir, and Galili understood "security borders" to mean, not borders that are properly defensible, but merely borders so radically disadvantageous to enemy Arab states that the latter would not *dare* to attack Israel again. In other words, borders that are secure because they are *unlikely* to be attacked but that are paradoxically anything but secure as soon as they are. One is tempted to recall Abba Eban's description of the UN Emergency Force in 1967: "an umbrella which is removed as soon as it begins to rain."

Dayan's borders seem to have withstood the test even less successfully. The government's contention that Israel must not permit the re-creation of those conditions that invited war in 1967 now appears to be a remedy far more fatal than the disease. And it is a remedy that in the process closed off any chance for a meaningful Israeli peace initiative.

It is, of course, anything but clear that Israeli peace initiatives might have led to a productive response from the other side. Internal Arab propaganda is still virulently anti-Zionist, and no one would want to test Arab claims that this war was fought only to "liberate territory" and that they would have stopped at the cease-fire lines of 1967. But, as Professor Shimon Shamir, head of Tel Aviv's Shiloach Institute and the country's main Arab watcher, has recently claimed, whatever the beneficial results of aggressive peace-probing, it is certain that Israeli intransigence did not merely spar with a stable Arab enmity. Instead, this intransigence transformed the very nature of Arab struggle; that is, from the quixotic and periodic outbursts of 1967 and before to a full-scale national effort in which all domestic and international resources were mobilized — from a "holy war" of pan-Arab pretensions to a war of "just liberation."

The continued and explicitly indefinite occupations appear to have been a political blunder, moreover, for the latter seem to have forged a national unity in Syria and especially Egypt (we must deal with the Palestinian question separately), which was certainly unprecedented — and all the more remarkable in view of the stunning class divisions that had to be overcome — and which was bound to erupt in acts of what Golda Meir calls "lunacy."

This brings us to a final point about "security borders." The policy presupposes that in the final analysis the only dependable *political* weapon at Israel's disposal is the IDF invincible. The "final analysis" was consequently acceptable. Not only would a tough posture supposedly discourage Arab attacks, but it had turned out, or so the government understood, to be the vital link that guaranteed American backing despite, and ironically *in service of*, very real American interests in the Arab world. America, predictably, was ready to acquiesce in a powerful IDF

periodically knocking out fully equipped Soviet clients—
burned-out Soviet tanks cannot assault the Persian Gulf.

The actual dynamics of the Arab-Israeli conflict are, for American interests, quite irrelevant. After all, where were American
arms from 1948 to 1967, when they were no less necessary and
when American Jews were no less restless? But as Kissinger
pointed out on a visit here in 1969, American support is not
unconditional. Israel must maintain its dominance in the area
"alone" and cheaply, for America can neither risk alienating the
Gulf states beyond the breaking point nor see its projected détente with the Soviets deteriorate beyond repair.

Consequently, as her policy unfolded, Golda was required to
prove Israel ever more invincible to her American patron in order to keep open Israel's only source of arms. Nor did she ab-
stain from the cold war rhetoric that was music to Nixon's ears,
including implied support for American intervention in Vietnam, which shocked all but the most "realpolitikal" of Israelis.

Israel thus became committed to a policy which ironically made
both its genuinely pacific political objectives and the continued
support of its only powerful external assistance dependent on
an almost naked military superiority. As Americans rediscover
their traditional neutrality, many Israelis are understandably
perplexed.

For Israel has sacrificed its relations with the Afro-Asian bloc
and the Soviet bloc, and its romance with the international left,
out of the conviction that these were all unimportant in comparison with the fundamental strategic need to keep the IDF
sitting in strongholds and "in the game." The most frustrating
lesson of the last war seems to have been, however, that the IDF
may defeat the Arab armies a score of times without achieving
Israeli political objectives. For the relative military power of each
side is far from the only determinant of political outcomes in
the Middle East; at least, that is, for the Arab states, who enjoy
the support of the Soviet Union (war has been the latter's entering wedge) and a quantity of oil.

There is for Israelis, however, a more painful point. The IDF
is a people's force. It is not a foreign legion. Sadat can cold-
bloodedly threaten to sacrifice a million Egyptian soldiers in
order to achieve his objectives, but Golda Meir cannot. The IDF

is not a political card that can be continually played; it is not a political card at all. It is a civilian *defense* force—highly motivated, highly trained, and highly efficient, but its morale and willingness to sacrifice must never be abused. In the long run, cynicism within the IDF about cavalier or shortsighted political decisions will threaten it far more effectively than SAM missiles. And there is a vague, retrospective uneasiness here that the government's use of it in the last five years may have overstepped this pragmatic and moral limit. The Prime Minister of Israel is not authorized to endanger a single soldier's life in order to prove Sadat a lunatic.

The Palestinian issue is, of course, more tricky. Maximalist Palestinian nationalist aspirations still require the dismantling of Jewish national existence. No Jew in Israel faults the government for remaining vigilant against terrorism. But there is a growing sentiment, nevertheless, that the stubborn reluctance of Israel to recognize the principle of Palestinian Arab self-determination and thereby help to cultivate a politically independent group of Palestinian leaders and organizations within the occupied territories was a badly wasted opportunity. Surely this might have complemented Israel's comparatively humane policies of normalizing productive and social relations there.

Instead, despite open borders with Jordan and a healthy abstention from press censorship, Israeli authorities severely curtailed fresh or dissenting political activity in the territories and relied on the traditional Jordanian elites and political institutions. My own conversations with the Arab merchants of Jerusalem suggest that the prestige of Arafat, and even of Habash, has never been higher, and it is gallingly clear that this is mainly by default.

The educated and prosperous Palestinian bourgeoisie of the West Bank and in the Persian Gulf "corporate refuge" make up a natural constituency for a moderate nationalist regime, progressive with regard to rapid economic development, expansion of social services and utilities, and even progressive toward labor relations, since they would still have to compete with the high standards for working conditions set by the Israeli Histadrut. Moreover, the members of a moderate regime of this sort might be reasonably expected to reconcile themselves to Israel's existence, however much they resent it, for the reparations and the attraction of enhanced future prospects that such an approach would bring.

But neither the political potential of the resident Palestinian bourgeoisie (there is no developed working class) nor their reasonable suspicions of the terrorist groups have been given growing space. A political elite requires more than an appropriate ideology or a power base to assume leadership; it requires some history of political success, organized cadres, and a recognized appeal—who should know this better than the Labor Zionists? —but among Palestinian Arabs today there is a serious poverty of choice.

Hussein remains unlikely to inspire the loyalty of Palestinians. He is hated by them for his excesses of "Black September" 1970; moreover, Egypt and especially Syria would not want to settle the Palestinian issue by turning it over to Hussein. But Israel is now boxed in to a pro-Hussein solution, along the lines perhaps of the federation that the Hashemite King had proposed last year but that had hitherto been rebuffed. Israel must now *grasp* for an accommodation with Hussein because any development of indigenous political leadership among the residents of the "territories" was narrow-mindedly thwarted amid Golda's sanctimonious and esoteric arguments that *she* was a Palestinian and that there can be no "third" Arab state in the area.

One must only hope that the situation can still be salvaged and that the power that Arab extremism and the Israeli government's inertia have bestowed on the *fedayeen* does not torpedo Israel's chances for an overall settlement. As of this writing, the Algiers conference and the Soviets have sanctioned the PLO under Arafat as the only legitimate representative of the Palestinians, and Hussein has about-faced and agreed to attend a peace conference even if the PLO is there; but the Alignment's new "fourteen-point program" is absolutely *opposed* to anything short of a Palestinian-Jordanian federation. For although the Israeli government officially and belatedly recognizes that no settlement can be possible without accommodating sensible Palestinian national demands, it understandably cannot contrive to overlook Arafat's murderous escapades. Yet who else is there?

These words are being written in late December. Before us lie bitter Israeli elections, a peace conference, more great-power jostling, and fully mobilized armies. Yet despite the turbulence there is timidly hopeful talk: about a Druse buffer state to separate Israel from Syria; about a reconciliation between Palestinians and Israelis in a way worthy of the Jerusalem experience; about staged withdrawals leading to joint Egyptian-Israeli patrols of a demilitarized, repatriated Sinai; of cultural exchanges and trade; of peace. It strikes one as so utopian precisely because it all sounds so reasonable.

The conclusion of the Yom Kippur liturgy heralds the messianic age with a robust sounding of the *shofar*, as if the single-minded introspection of the preceding day can in some way help to bring about the millennium. This motif is not absent from Israeli society as it emerges from three months of Yom Kippur.

### POSTSCRIPT: JANUARY 2

The December 31 elections will likely produce a flurry of assessments presuming a clear rightward shift among Israeli electors. But closer analysis confounds this picture. Recent events have strained mechanical party loyalties to the breaking point, and even in retrospect there is nothing to suggest that the great number of voters who declared themselves undecided (some 30 to 35 percent) were insincere.

The Alignment did indeed present itself as the party of peace initiatives, and it dangled before the voters the image of a new collective leadership untainted by October's failures. But the Likud is still more than anything else the party of protest. Likud gained eight seats but did not gain them all at the Alignment's expense. In the light of the way votes were scattered in municipal elections, I am not persuaded that the Likud could have deprived the Alignment of three or four of its seats had the voters' desire to punish the government been satisfied, i.e., had a new Alignment leadership, which paradoxically promised to be a good deal more dovish than the present one, actually taken over before the elections. Moreover, we should not ignore the four or five seats that the Alignment lost to left-wing splinter parties such

as Shulamit Aloni's Civil Rights group and Moked, whose supporters are politically energetic and can be counted on to give
these seats disproportionate significance.

The most dramatic result of the elections was not that the
Alignment declined but that it recovered. For its late rally depended on a large number of Israeli voters being ready to swallow the contradiction of supporting the Alignment in order to
repudiate the very policy that an Alignment government followed during the last four years. Labor's peace strategy seems
to have been rewarded.

Still, the final distribution of seats leaves the formation of a
stable "peace" cabinet no easy matter. An implicit coalition of
the left remains a seat or two short of a simple majority; and
Rakah, the pro-Moscow communist party depressingly popular
among the Israeli Arabs, would never be invited to hold the balance with its four seats.

Labor's present coalition partner, the National Religious Party,
won its predictable ten seats, which have usually been added to
Labor's plurality in the past. It has incorporated into its platform
opposition to territorial concessions in "Judea and Samaria," i.e.,
the West Bank. The NRP's influence may thus strengthen the
*present* government leadership and force the competing factions
within the Alignment into an insufferable deadlock.

So it would seem that, short of a major rift within the religious
parties, the election has provided only a mandate for Israel's
participation in Geneva's first phase, having to do with a disengagement of forces; a coherent policy on more complex issues,
especially on settlement with the Palestinian Arabs, will almost
certainly require another round of elections.

# The New Struggle
# for Palestine

Your duty is to beat off attacks, but the smell of blood must
not go to your heads. Remember that justice is in our name,
defense [*Haganah*]; our aim is to provide security for creative work. Your organization is subordinate to this ideal
—not its master.

—*Havlagah (Self-restraint)*
Haganah pamphlet circa 1937

*Jerusalem, February 1974*
January's disengagement pact between Israel and Egypt understandably conjures up more than it immediately promises to
deliver; how can one resist anticipating the taste of peace? Dis-
trust and hatred still smolder, but a cynicism about the prospects
of peace has come to seem frivolous. Israeli TV recently released
a remarkably poignant documentary film dealing with the many
hundreds of contacts between Israeli and Egyptian soldiers on
the Suez front even during the period of "attrition." Thousands
of gifts, addresses, and words of commiseration were exchanged
among the shells.

Far more important than this new atmosphere, however, is a
new political certainty. Whatever the concealed, perhaps sinister,
designs of either side, were Cairo and Jerusalem to commit themselves to an overall settlement sincerely and unambiguously,
their first bilateral pact would not look different from the one
they signed and executed with meticulous care.

The two main features of the agreement, i.e., the unilateral Israeli withdrawal to the Gidi and Mitla passes, and the Egyptian commitment to reopen the Canal (the east bank of the Canal being partially demilitarized) and to rehabilitate Canal cities, may superficially appear to favor the Egyptians. But this appearance was an important element of the agreement itself and no doubt helped President Sadat with his internal problems. His firing of his hawkish Chief of Staff, General Shazli, and, more recently, of Hussinein Heykal, the Nasserite editor of *Al-Ahram*, and their replacement by pro-Western moderates (respectively, Gamsi and Amin) reveal that Sadat's internal challenges have not been puny. His mass victory celebration in February, to which even Qaddafi came, did not strengthen Sadat's war potential, only his power to conclude a binding peace.

At any rate, the December agreement has clearly served the strategic interests of both parties. Israel's lines at the close of the war would hardly have been desirable as a long-term defense perimeter. If the fluid situation in the field hardened into a political border, the Israelis would have faced a continuous war of attrition or been subjected to wholesale attacks by the reinforced First Army to the west of the bulge and the Second Army to the north. Moreover, so long as the IDF continued to threaten Cairo directly or to maintain its siege on the Third Army, the Israeli government would have had to contend with both the possibility of direct Soviet intervention and growing American resentment as Kissinger was dragged into another diplomatic confrontation with his partner in détente.

Finally, and by no means the least of Israeli calculations, was the severe strain on Israel's citizen army and already disrupted economy caused by full mobilization. Morale was withering while political disillusionment was running high. The army voted more heavily for the opposition Likud than for the Alignment, and double the national average for the leftish parties. The sandy winds and sobering poverty of "Africa" were abandoned emotionally by the IDF but with little regret.

Nor did Israel's strategic gains in withdrawing prove to be greater than those of Egypt. A final Israeli strike could never be discounted, and Sadat surely knew that this would cripple Egypt's diplomatic leverage and put an end to his own political career — this quite apart from what appeared to be his very real concern for the entrapped soldiers of the Third Army.

The more sensitive point, however, is whether Israel was bullied by the United States into giving up an important bargaining card by returning effective sovereignty over the Suez Canal to Egypt and acquiescing in the reconstruction of civilian life in the area. This was the substance of the right-wing Likud's criticism of the pact. General Sharon attacked the plan, claiming that by giving up the heights, which command the Canal ten kilometers to the east, Israel "loses the all-important *deterrent* to a massive Egyptian crossing." The Likud demanded at least a declaration of "nonbelligerency" in return for the withdrawal (although they usually admit in the same breath that such a declaration would not be worth a damn, particularly as long as Sinai remains largely occupied).

This mechanical argument ignored what should have been obvious: that Israel has a positive interest in Egypt's economic and social reconstruction of the war zone. What might be called a Cobdenite spirit dominated the Israeli government's enthusiastic response to Egyptian Foreign Minister Fahmy's announcement that rebuilding on a large scale would be begun even before the pact was fully implemented.

Furthermore, the immediate risk Israel has taken by repatriating the Canal should not be exaggerated. Control of southwest Sinai remains in Israeli hands; and this includes both Sharm al-Sheikh, the point from which a blockade on the Gulf of Suez (not just the Gulf of Aqaba) might be introduced, and the billion-dollar-a-year Abu Rodeis oil fields.* In fact, one might bluntly contend that it is Sadat who has taken the biggest gamble, and this can be appreciated by imagining his deteriorated military position should progress on a general settlement be seriously stalled.

---

*This oil is sold to Europe to earn the foreign exchange that helps to pay for the high cost of war. It is not an impressive "vested interest" and will be no impediment to any settlement that, at least partially, stifles the arms race now bleeding the Israeli economy white. (See Evans and Novak's suspicions to the contrary, *Washington Post*, January 14, 1974.)

Sadat, moreover, has openly committed himself to de-Nasser-izing Egypt's economy—selling off state enterprises to private capital, overturning land reform, cutting down the political influence of students and labor unions. He has made it clear that he badly wants foreign capital and corporate technology to develop Egypt's production; he has been fending off bitter political opposition within the Arab Socialist Union by crowing that his diplomacy has been getting results. It is therefore not surprising that he has engineered so remarkable a rapprochement with Dr. Kissinger—and has publicly called for immediate diplomatic solutions at every opportunity. He has been told, after all, that in two years he might be facing President Jackson.

Yet the deal with Egypt is still a risk for both sides and remains vulnerable, above all because of the other disputes that can affect it. The Syrian front is much more prickly than the Sinai. The Golan is a stretch of heights and high plains forty to eighty kilometers deep, which both the Israelis and Syrians proved could be traversed in about fifteen hours by large numbers of assault vehicles. Control of these heights by either army menaces the vital heartland of the adversary; the IDF now threatens Syria's cultural and industrial center in Damascus while for twenty years the Syrian army harassed the Hula Valley, in which lie many of Labor Zionism's most important settlements.

The "obvious" solution, i.e., a staged withdrawal combined with demilitarization, would therefore have to be based on a buffer zone so slender that Israel would enjoy little "strategic depth," a concept that, as used by Israel's general staff, refers simply to the ability to absorb an attack and remain capable of retaliation, a sine qua non for a citizen army. To succeed, such a solution would seem to require the kind of goodwill that has been worked out, for better or for worse, with Jordan; but Syrian-Israeli relations are so utterly poisoned by ideological antagonisms and atrocities that a settlement on the Suez model would be remote if the superpowers are not willing to impose it.

Kissinger, at least, is trying to do this. Gromyko has seemed more concerned to maintain a tense situation in which Soviet diplomatic and military assistance will be indispensable. The Israeli paper *Yediot Acharonot* (March 7, 1974) claims that he was instrumental in fanning Ba'ath radicalism against President Assad, a development which heated up the front with Israel, and that he cautioned the Syrian president against overchumminess with the Americans. With Soviet influence declining in Egypt, the USSR can be expected to hold on to what it can in Syria while continuing to advocate negotiations in Geneva and détente generally.

General Assad had precariously maintained his floundering prestige within the ruling Ba'ath Party* before October by outdoing the party's radicals in his extremism and, unlike Sadat, hinging his political fate upon a Soviet-sponsored "anti-imperialist, anti-Zionist, pan-Arab revolutionist," etc., strategy; the first main achievement of this strategy was to be the "Liberation of Palestine."† True, Assad has now moved off this position slightly, releasing the Israeli POW list and sending a negotiating team to Washington in defiance of the hawk faction led by Foreign Minister Khaddam; but his choices are limited by his own precedents and by Soviet machinations.

For its part, the Israeli government has responded to the Syrian threat with comprehensible but, in view of its own often brutal retaliations, somewhat sanctimonious shudders. In fact, Israeli policy on this front has evolved into a nonpolicy, with little diplomatic flexibility. The Golan was de facto annexed to Israel when it was captured in 1967, and has since been dotted by almost twenty kibbutzim and other settlements (about two thousand people) whose undisguised purpose is to establish the

---

*The composition of the Syrian Ba'ath is most revealing of its "radicalism." It is mainly a party of petit bourgeois, bureaucrats, teachers, and professionals, with few peasants and workers, and many army officers. Its leftish rhetoric ought not to obscure its protofascist tendencies—it is xenophobic and totalitarian, conservative in its Moslem orthodoxy, elite and exclusivist, organized around the army, and "socialist" only in the sense that the state bureaucracy is considered vital to economic development. A captured Syrian document from the October war revealed something about its socialism when it forbade the evacuation of wounded below the officer rank.

†This "liberation" in no way suggests clear-cut support for Palestinian self-determination in a conventional sense. The Syrian Ba'ath promotes the Palestinian "revolution" through the Saika, a Palestinian "guerrilla" organization attached to the Syrian army and committed to the virtual annexation of Palestine to Syrian sovereignty as under the Turks.

facts of this annexation; settlers here are already stirring up opposition to withdrawal. The tragic death of a young mother last month at Ramat Hamagshimim testifies to the sheer stupidity of removing Syrian guns from the Hula Valley in 1967, only to bring new settlements under the Syrian guns after 1967. But the government persists. A new town is being planned and Mrs. Meir has recently declared the Golan to be "inseparable from the state of Israel." The claim made in Israel that this is merely a bargaining position is hardly a convincing one.

Nevertheless, the Americans, Egyptians, and Saudi Arabians (Faisal wants to see Jerusalem before he dies, not Damascus) are bringing pressure on Assad to approach the disengagement talks seriously, and correspondents in the Syrian capital have claimed that he is reconciled to a cease-fire and troop separation based on the existing situation in the field. Damascus, we should remember, is still within the range of Israeli artillery. Nor would there be opposition in Israel to a unilateral withdrawal to pre-October lines by the IDF in exchange for demilitarization. But can this formula really be expected to satisfy Assad, whose suspicions that this first pact may be his last appear more justified than those of Sadat?

Some hope for a more lasting diplomatic solution may exist with respect to the Syrian city of Kuneitra, on the Golan's south-easternmost tip, occupied by Israel since the 1967 war. Perhaps the rehabilitation of this torn-up city and the return of the 60,000–80,000 refugees who lived in or near it (the Syrians claim 150,000–175,000 for the entire Golan) could prove to be the first positive step toward the kind of peacemaking represented by the Canal reconstruction. The prospects would be even more encouraging if both sides could also grant some degree of municipal autonomy to the approximately 10,000 Druse villagers who before October 1973 made up the remainder of the Golan's non-Jewish residents—and if there were also a declared freeze on Jewish settlement subject to future negotiations.

So far, however, the Israeli government has unanimously taken an intractable stand toward territorial concessions on the Golan, and it will start any negotiations by opposing the return of Kuneitra (so as to leave this card for a "final" settlement); like the Syrian murder of Israeli POWs, this attitude could sour the climate of the talks before they even get under way. Kissinger's impressive talent for courting the enemies of "imperialism" appears to be in for its most strenuous performance.

The closer we come to talks on Syrian-Israeli disengagement, however, the clearer it becomes that disengagement is really not the main point. In fact, it is on the most tranquil military front where the difficulties are intimidating; for Jews and Arabs have been plainly fighting all this time about something more real, if less tangible, than the consequences of their most recent round of war. And it is a bitter irony that the fundamental national-political struggle within, and for, historic Palestine is only emerging into full view after Israel's savage battles with other nations have been grudgingly tamed.

The long-obscured Palestinian question has now sharpened into a triangular conflict among the government of Israel, the Hashemite monarchy in Jordan, and the Palestinian Arabs, whose growing national consciousness now seems inextricably linked to the fortunes of the Palestine Liberation Organization. The Moslem summit meeting in Lahore during late February seems to have iced Arafat's cake by bestowing upon the PLO (and Arafat personally) recognition as the *only* legitimate representative of the Palestinian people — a decision which, unlike that of the Algiers conference, Hussein has been forced to accept. The *Financial Times* (March 5, 1974) reports, moreover, that the Soviet Union has officially recognized the PLO; should the PLO set up a government-in-exile after the Syrian disengagement (as was decided at the PLO Damascus conference), the latter could probably expect to enjoy the recognition of 103 countries, including the whole of the Soviet bloc.

The Israeli government's overriding and irreducible concern remains and will remain the proximity of *any* Arab means of making war on the Jewish state's heavily populated coastal plain (Ashdod, Tel Aviv, Netanya, Haifa) and on Jerusalem.* I do not

---

*Jewish settlement on the West Bank, outside Jerusalem, has been sparse and mainly concentrated near Hebron at Gush-Etzion–Qiryat Arba, where Jews had lived prior to 1948. This presence should not be incompatible with a political arrangement there any more than in large Arab towns, such as Nazareth, which fall within Israel.

mean to ignore the far more demanding claims of the Likud opposition—a subject to which I will return. But no Israeli government, no matter how dovish, will agree to anything short of a full and effective demilitarization of the West Bank and Gaza Strip—not even the most accommodating Israeli leaders could risk the reintroduction of the siege that prevailed until 1967. But here the problem thickens.

The Israeli government still insists that the "Palestinians" be lumped together with the Jordanian regime. The Alignment's "fourteen points" of last December, for example, call for a negotiated settlement with a "Jordanian-Palestinian" state. This is a self-defeating casuistry which promotes a very distorted image of real possibilities. Most Palestinian Arabs now living under Israeli occupation (and how much more so those in "Fatahland" refugee camps) regard Hussein as a treacherous and bullying conqueror, who by virtue of his fanatically loyal and Bedouin following (disproportionately concentrated in the senior ranks of the army) had maintained a twenty-year regime of cultural and political repression and economic exploitation of the West Bank. Reimposing Hashemite sovereignty in the occupied territories would invite a desperate and concerted wave of terrorist-guerrilla activity by the PLO,* almost certain to have popular support, which might very well crest in another prologue to "Black September"—once more raising the specter of Israeli-Syrian and perhaps even superpower confrontation.†

The King seems eager to deal with Israeli leaders and they with him. But he is a fossil of His Majesty's Colonial Office, of T. E. Lawrence and Glubb Pasha and their soaring yet simple-minded imperial visions. And although Hussein now seems capable of handling internal threats from the understandably cautious and generally traditionalist Palestinian Arabs who make

---

*Eduard Saab of *Le Monde* (January 25, 1974) reports that the PLO has already taken a decision, now an open secret, that the "neutralization of Jordan's claim to the West Bank (and Gaza) is the first in its hierarchy of priorities."

†A Jerusalem Arab acquaintance put it this way to me: "Every young mother in her kitchen *hates* Hussein." Mati Peled has pertinently recalled in his *Ma'ariv* column that the tanks that eventually attacked Israel in 1967 from the West Bank were originally introduced by Hussein, with American diplomatic backing, to control the Palestinian population, not to threaten Israel.

up 80 percent of Jordan's population (how many divisions do they have?), it seems an absurd folly for Israelis to stake their security hopes upon an exclusively Hashemite solution while claiming that they are indifferent to internal Arab affairs. All moral considerations aside, Israelis are historically bound to Palestinians in a cycle of tragedy and cannot afford the luxury of self-righteousness.

Nor should one assume automatically that cautious and realistic overtures from Israel to the PLO will be fanatically rebuffed. Some of the most experienced and informed Arab experts in Israel believe that it would be both timely and opportune—and no greater risk to security—if Israel now took the initiative by (1) inviting the PLO to begin negotiation; (2) declaring unilaterally that satisfaction of Palestinian national construction will be a favored principle of Israeli policy; (3) offering to participate unconditionally in a tripartite body (Israel-PLO-Jordan, under the American-Soviet sponsorship set up for the Geneva talks) to resettle Palestinian refugees on *both sides of the Jordan*; and (4) acquiescing in the formation of a Palestinian national council *including West Bank and Gaza residents*.

Instead, as Professor Shimon Shamir, perhaps the most respected of the experts, pointed out in *Ha'aretz* (February 22, 1974), Israeli's West Bank administration (i.e., Dayan) has even forbidden a delegation from the territories to attend the Damascus conference of Palestinian leaders. But who, as Shamir observed, might better bridge the yawning gap to the PLO than West Bank moderates, merchants, and intellectuals, with good connections on both sides.

The PLO itself now appears in the midst of a fateful internal struggle reminiscent of the vicious one between moderates of the Haganah and extreme nationalists of the Irgun when the Zionist settlers were faced with Partition. By all accounts, Arafat, and recently Hawatmeh—supported by Sadat, Algeria's Boumédienne, and the Soviets—are leaning strongly toward a strategic compromise whereby the construction of an independent Palestinian state would be begun on the West Bank and Gaza; it is further reported that this faction has gained the upper hand on the hard-line PFLP led by George Habash.

Even the so-called moderates in the PLO still couch their conciliatory line in talk of a "staged struggle," presumably saving the liquidation of Israel for some future date. But the PLO's transparent sophistry, which called for a "democratic, secular *Arab* state" in historic Palestine, is now dead, and with it, we can hope, a primitive, purely irredentist nationalism.

Some of the recent PLO statements go farther than ever before in asserting that an Israeli-Palestinian "partnership" must begin by coexistence of two states.\* The name of Anwar el-Khatib, the moderate former governor of Jerusalem who has retained the respect of both Hussein and the PLO, has been often mentioned as a possible leading minister in a regime led by Arafat. Factions within the PLO are now openly discussing the challenge of creating national economic and social projects. At least a significant part of this still-evolving movement seems to be realizing that fruitful fields and factories engender more dignity than a thousand noble deaths. Most West Bank Arabs will support this approach wholeheartedly; and it is an ideological tendency that Israelis can encourage particularly by proposing bold and imaginative solutions to the plight of refugees.

But any eventual coexistence of Hashemites, Palestinians, and

---

\*See the article by the PLO representative in London, Said Hammami, in the London *Times* (December 17, 1973): "We are well aware of the fact that a state in partnership can be constructed only if and when the two parties genuinely want it and are ready to work for it. Past decades of enmity do not provide a good ground for an immediate realization of a state in partnership.

"I believe that the first step towards that should be a mutual recognition for the two respective parties. The Israeli Jews and the Palestinian Arabs should recognize one another as peoples, with all the rights to which a people is entitled. This recognition should be followed by the realization of the Palestinian Arab entity through a Palestinian state, an independent full-fledged member state of the United Nations."

More recently, on March 22, the radical Palestinian leader Naif Hawatmeh gave a special interview to *Yediot Acharonot* in which he called openly for a separate Palestinian state and no longer for a democratic *Arab* state in Palestine. He retains as his ultimate goal a unified state of sorts but now seems clearer and more convincing than before in advocating binationalism. Instead of aligning himself with the extreme radicals of Matzpen, he praises such prominent doves as Arie Eliav, the former secretary-general of the Labor Party, and Yitzchak Ben-Aharon, the former head of the Histadrut. See also David Hurst's report in the *Guardian*, January 18, 1974.

Arabs suffers from a chronic danger. A PLO regime in a newly independent Palestinian state is the least likely to agree to demilitarization. We are not dealing here with the Rhineland or the Sinai. Even the most congenial relations between the Israeli government and the PLO would not dispel the fact that the latter sees itself as a militant, vanguard party, the sole authentic embodiment of Palestinian nationalism. Moreover, the PLO depends on its military command system for coherent political organization and must establish its rule within a comparatively traditional Islamic society, in which the force of arms has been perhaps the principal basis for political legitimacy.

The PLO's expected resistance to demilitarization could topple any diplomatic house of cards before it could be reinforced by economic development and face-to-face contacts. This very prospect underlies the Labor Alignment's contention that Israel's security demands no more than *one* Arab state straddling the Jordan River. But the Labor Alignment will not be able to dictate to the Palestinians what leaders will represent them. Nor will Hussein. So that as long as the replacement of Hussein seems unthinkable for the State Department and no significant thaw in Hashemite-PLO relations is imminent, then Palestine appears headed for yet another doomed proposal for partition into Jewish and Palestinian-Arab entities.

On February 22, *Ma'ariv* reported that Arafat claimed to have been offered the prime ministership of Jordan by Hussein. More interesting than the validity of the claim was Arafat's denigrating and negative response. More plausible is *Ha'aretz*'s report of March 8 that Hussein will shortly inform Kissinger that he forgoes his claim to the West Bank—which would serve only to intensify the quandary of Israel's leaders.

Moreover, when one realizes that an improvement in Israeli relations with the rest of the Arab world (and the Soviet bloc)
—no matter how propitious—will probably not proceed at a much more vigorous pace than the one set by the original parties to the conflict—i.e., Jews and Palestinian Arabs—then Israel seems cursed with very little room in which to maneuver. However impatient Sadat may be privately with the PLO, he cannot ignore its rising prestige and its pressures.

Little room is more than no room, however, and every inch ought to be explored by Israeli planners. Therefore the question that begs for urgent consideration is elementary: Who or what group will emerge from Israel's murky politics to assess the Palestinian challenge and make Israel's diplomatic response? Alas, it is highly improbable that political success inside Israel will depend on the vital Palestinian question.

# Golda Meir's Last Hurrah

*Jerusalem, early April 1974 (before Golda Meir's resignation)*
No historical struggle, no cultural revival, has been more deliberate and self-conscious than that of the Jews in Israel. They are
fanatics about individual liberty and personal independence—
often to a point of being impudent and undisciplined—and in
bearing immense burdens they have evolved a comparatively
sophisticated egalitarian spirit. No doubt Israel is and had to be
a "free society"; but it has become a very poor democracy.

The Jewish settlement in Israel—the Yishuv—was carried to
statehood by clumsy and often contrived political institutions that
have never been overhauled. The authority of these institutions
is crumbling as the fervid appeal of the Zionist movement continues to fade for the "new" Israeli public, mainly young, native
born, and reluctant to accept ideological conformity. The older
leaders have already used up most of the large reserve of prestige
upon which they have long been nourished. But the recent dis-
crediting of Israel's leadership, particularly acute since the October war, may ironically prove to be a great advance for Israeli
political life, which has consistently been demeaned by despotism, however benevolent or self-sacrificing.

For David Ben-Gurion, Jewish political construction depended
on a cohesive, organized, and visionary labor movement. Nationalism implied the creation of such national facts as Jewish

industry, Hebrew language, and housing; and these required both direction and cooperation. Guided by this strategy, the socialist leaders who in 1920 organized the Jewish workers of Palestine into the super labor federation called the Histadrut brought the labor movement and, not just coincidentally, the entire Jewish community here to political, economic, and military preeminence. But these people never had much time or inclination to ponder how their own power would or ought to be checked. They were the stepchildren of Russian revolutionary movements and themselves presided over conspiratorial, subversive, and underground groups; when it came to conflicts with the Arabs, the British, or intrigues with their allies in fighting the Nazis, orders had to be given and followed.

The socialist parties, to their credit, maintained a lively dissenting spirit, but Israel's veteran Labor leaders have spent most of their lives flaunting or fighting legal (Turkish, then British) authority and doing what was politically expedient for the sake of their single-minded dream. That's the stuff of which revolutions are made; but the revolutionary leaders have understandably clung to arbitrary and paternal and conspiratorial practices when dealing with the new problems raised by success.

For Israel, at least, the "revolution" ended in October. The traditional political system has been badly crippled and now appears to be merely superimposed upon a much-changed and troubled society. In the euphoria that followed the 1967 war, the Labor Alignment was opportunistically patched together from tired factions of the Labor establishment that had been bitterly contending with each other for years. These old conflicts have become much worse since the October war and are now paralyzing the Israeli government. Although some of these disputes are by no means irrelevant to the country's crisis— particularly disagreements on security strategy and economic policy—the most pressing problem for Israel's discouraged and disillusioned public has been the deterioration of the political process itself.

A healthy society, Plato observed, needs laws no more than a vigorous body needs medicine. Israel, however, has neither health nor law. It has no formal constitution, no developed tradition of parliamentary ethics and ministerial responsibility, no serious checks on executive authority, no routine contact between elector and elected, no Bill of Rights. And although the parties are publicly financed, no laws govern internal party democracy or organization; the bosses of the old Mapai (Ben-Gurion's moderate Labor Party)—called the Gush—came to run their organization with Tammany Hall insolence and transformed it into a well-greased machine with immense political leverage and economic power. As Prime Ministers, Ben-Gurion, Sharrett, Eshkol, and Golda Meir have all relied on the Gush apparatus to hold their coalitions together. In short, there is no strong traditional democratic procedure that can carry out the public's vigorous demand for change and yet help to keep changes orderly.

Quite the contrary; within the limits of conventional Israeli politics there was no effective way to resist what became a conspiracy of indifference by Alignment politicians to the outrage, both in the public and in the party, over the creation and composition of the "new" government. Golda Meir's most recent "last hurrah" was undertaken in the face of near unanimous opposition from the press and when her personal popularity was at an all-time low. It astounded even her most generous supporters for its lack of public conscience. But more to the point, her return indicated that the exhausted and ideologically bankrupt elements of the Labor Alignment would be giving themselves another chance. It is not surprising that many Israelis are now taking "to the salons and to the streets."

No fewer than three new citizens' organizations have been formed in the last few weeks to rally the public behind the cause of more accountable and democratic government. Israel's present system of proportional representation greatly enhances the power of party "list makers," who have transformed their parties into pyramids of privilege controlled from above. A British-style constituency system, or variations upon it, has often been proposed, but this of course is in itself no panacea. Laws governing procedures inside the parties themselves are urgently required.

The most successful and exciting group thus far has been founded by a core of war-hardened reserve armor and paratroop officers as well as reservists from other divisions in the IDF. The leaders of this group themselves come mainly from the Labor Zionist settlements. They have organized in support of a strict constitutionalist and social democratic charter, and in March they carried out an impressive demonstration in front of the Prime Minister's offices in Jerusalem.

Some six thousand to eight thousand citizens came to this rally, and far from engaging in demagoguery, the young leaders (including Captain Motti Ashkenazi, a war hero on the Sinai front who had earlier campaigned against Dayan) spoke quietly and soberly of democratic ethics and parliamentary reform. The movement, now called simply Change, had originally named itself the Union for Governmental Responsibility. More directly, its leaders called for the resignation of Mrs. Meir and her leading ministers and for an immediate election of new leaders within the Labor Party and the dissolution of factions within it. They will shortly be organizing a national conference and are clearly enjoying the momentum of having captured the imagination of large sections of the "younger" generation (which in Israel usually means those up to the age of forty-five, when active army service ends). They are getting wide and sympathetic coverage in the press.

A somewhat stodgier academic movement, pressing for essentially the same demands but with more refined political ambitions, is the Movement for Social and Political Renewal. Led by the *Ha'aretz* columnist and Tel Aviv University law professor Amnon Rubinstein, the group hopes to be the nucleus for a constitutionalist, technocratic, and "Westernist" political party, drawing its members from the universities and the free professions. They have the implicit intention, furthermore, of chipping heretics away from the Alignment (such as the "nevertheless Alignment" group) as well as the center liberals from the Likud. But unless they successfully recruit some of Israel's academic superstars from the Hebrew University, or at least win the support of some other prominent journalists and professional trade union leaders, they seem inevitably headed toward some marriage of convenience with Shulamit Aloni's Civil Rights Party, which has three seats in the Knesset.

Jerusalem's more prominent academics and former generals who have closer connections to the government bureaucracy have been reinvigorating their own constitutionalist lobby, founded before October by the archaeologist-general Yigael Yadin. Yadin is a self-styled independent and is still sitting on the Agranat Commission. But under its new leader, Meir Amit, this lobby is becoming more partisan. Its sole aim is ostensibly parliamentary and constitutional reform, but it will likely serve as a "rank-and-file" base for a power play by the new generation of "Mapai" cabinet ministers, mainly former IDF commanders (Yitzchak Rabin, Chaim Bar-Lev, Sharon Yariv). These men see themselves as the natural heirs to the old Gush machine *after* Golda is finally forced out, ideally along with the two leading old guard political bosses, Finance Minister Pinhas Sapir and Housing Minister Yehoshua Rabinowitz. Rabinowitz earned his place in the cabinet by taking a trouncing in the Tel Aviv mayoralty election — a clear and stunning rejection of the Gush.

In fact, Meir Amit, himself a former general and now director of the Histadrut's largest industrial complex — Koor — has simultaneously been meeting in private with Rabin and the other "young" cabinet members. They have dubbed their timidly Thermidorian but decidedly more dovish and pragmatic faction Challenge. The "generals" can be expected to be more dovish precisely because they are unencumbered by the veteran Zionist leadership's blinkers with regard to Palestinian Arabs. Although in fact they usually avoid the issues of a separate Palestinian state on the eastern front, all, especially Rabin, their "leader," are convinced that Israel must rely on negotiations and international (mainly American) guarantees, more than on territory, for durable security. Naturally enough, they speak not of wholesale changes but of "refreshing" the leadership. This group (along with Achdut Ha'avoda's Yigal Allon) would have the inside track in any conventional political race.

Yitzchak Rabin's popularity within both, the intellectual and the military establishments, however, now transcends that of the group, and he is often being mentioned as the next Israeli Prime Minister. His aloofness within the party prior to October may prove a more important political virtue than his reputation as a general and as ambassador to Washington.

*

Finally, there remain older radicals of the Labor Alignment whose names are by now familiar abroad because of their protests against Israel's rigid policies on the occupied territories—Yitzchak Ben-Aharon, Lova Eliav. These men must be distinguished from the new citizens' associations because they seem unwilling to bolt the party, although they had the temerity not to vote confidence in the new government. They are obviously reluctant to forgo orthodox Labor coalition politics in favor of testing their strength independently in new elections. Unlike Challenge, they claim to want a veritable revolution within the labor movement; but despite their obvious courage and integrity they are wary of mass politics in modern Israel and of the new protest movements trying to stir up the population.

The same is true of Mapam, the party of the old leftists, which was generally sympathetic to the Soviet Union until the revelations of the early 1950s. Periodically in and out of government as an independent party, Mapam joined the Labor Alignment when it was formed in 1969. Although still socialists and dovish in foreign policy, they sided with the well-connected Gush machine in opposing democratization. Mapam is fearful, perhaps justifiably, that their slim constituency in the left-wing kibbutzim will be insufficient to guarantee them anything near the political influence they enjoy under the present Alignment. Mapam's leaders have already begun discouraging the activities of the small radical peace party called Moked on their kibbutzim (where the Moked won a remarkable 10 percent of the vote in the last elections). And in the worst tradition of coalition politics, Mapam has been demanding a third minister in the government to "make up for" the extra one "granted" to both the National Religious Party and the Independent Liberals. This would, by the way, bring the Israeli cabinet to twenty-three members, i.e., one third of the votes that the coalition controls in the Knesset would have found their way into the cabinet.

The arrogant way in which the government coalition was put together in February was itself one of the most revealing and demoralizing political events to have happened here recently. Following the December elections, there was a deceptive lull which lasted through the mid-January disengagement pact with Egypt and which was finally disrupted when negotiations over the formation of a new cabinet were undertaken in earnest. Only then did it become clear that the changes that the Alignment had promised during the election campaign—both in politics and leadership—were merely bait thrown out to quiet the public's anger in November. Furthermore, in attempting to punish the Alignment government, protest voters seemed to succeed in punishing only the rest of the electorate. With the Alignment down to fifty-one seats (fifty-four with the cooperative splinter Arab lists) the National Religious Party's ten votes (a drop from twelve) became essential for a stable, albeit unpopular, Knesset majority.

The NRP's Machiavellian rabbis wasted little time in laying it on the line to Sapir, the Alignment's chief power broker: the Law of Return, already a contentious document, would have to be changed so that only converts made under the Orthodox law would be able to enjoy the special privileges given Jewish immigrants to Israel.

This was not merely a point of theological significance. Israel's Orthodox rabbinate has used its advantage in coalition politics to fashion a formidable, profitable, and widely resented monopoly on all clerical functions—marriage, funerals, divorce, supervision of Kashrut, etc.—by blocking competition from secular authority or other streams in Judaism. All of which led to the now infamous debate on "Who is a Jew?"—and a depressing spectacle it was. In the midst of a crisis of survival, Israelis were forced to watch their chief ministers pandering to obscurantist principles of religious fundamentalism, an exercise that moreover threatened to weaken the already feeble status in Israel of the Conservative and Reform movements, to which most American Jews at least formally belong—and this at a time when American Jewish support was being strained to its limits.

Golda, mainly because of American Jewish pressure, would not budge, and neither would the NRP, which was encouraged (perhaps illegally) by Israel's two chief rabbis, its own young radicals, and Orthodox leaders abroad. A suggestion by the NRP and Likud that they form a "national coalition" government, in which the Gush would be a minority and Mapam would likely not care to sit, was also rejected by Mrs. Meir, and there the issue stood for over three weeks. While Israel's leadership was trying to blend the Talmud with party patronage, by the way, 21 percent of Israel's young men (between eighteen and twenty-nine) were "weighing the possibility" of emigration, or so a subsequent poll revealed (*Ha'aretz*, March 26).

The NRP finally rejoined the coalition when Dayan returned, but the pious politicians are still arguing among themselves; and with one of their leaders, Michael Hazzani, the Minister of Welfare, threatening to resign from the coalition, the entire storm might blow up again, with the NRP reviving its demand for a new Concordat.

However, debate over "Who is a Jew?" was but a symptom of more ominous ailments to which the Israeli government has become prone. Indeed, as Arie Eliav put it to me, "leadership has been replaced by cover-up." During this period, Golda and Dayan in fact imposed an astonishingly strict discipline upon the party, which kept dissent under wraps until the middle of February. Only then did the lonely and enigmatic struggle of Motti Ashkenazi to unseat Dayan finally gain steam.

As Dayan's popularity dropped (*Ha'aretz* showed him at 50 percent, as against 90 percent last summer), party members began pecking away at him openly. David Shacham, editor of *Ot*, the Labor Party's eclectic magazine, ran critical editorials. Mapam joined in, as did Ben-Aharon and Eliav, and finally a young protégé of Sapir, Yossi Sarid, began asking Dayan embarrassing questions in the Knesset. Sarid told me that he was still apprehensive that Dayan might bolt to the Likud, a possibility greatly underlined by Dayan's transparent cease-fire with General Ariel Sharon. Sharon left the army calling David Elazar incompetent and demanding his resignation as Chief of Staff, and vilifying Bar-Lev for "politicizing" the army. But for Dayan, who appointed both, Sharon had only praise.

On February 19, Dayan finally "resigned," declaring that under existing conditions he would not take a post in the next government and unleashing his own tough-minded followers — the Rafi faction — to bring pressure on the Alignment to reimpose party discipline. If they did not get their way, they were ready to demand a "national coalition," to which Dayan would be indispensable, or, a last resort, new elections and internal "democratization."*

Faced with the prospect of a minority government without Rafi or, worse yet, new elections, the Gush bosses who would otherwise have been glad to see Dayan fall proved themselves to be paper tigers. With the demise of the Alignment at hand, they loudly and humbly begged Dayan to return and decided to reimpose discipline at least in the Gush; they secretly promised to fire David Shacham and suppress *Ot*, which, after all, Golda did not like any more than Dayan did. Thus, as the chorus of pleading from the Gush grew deafening, and as Golda's threat to retire was greeted with relief by the public—revealing the political wasteland that awaited them both—Dayan and Mrs. Meir seized upon one of many Syrian mobilizations to rejoin the fold. They returned "for the sake of the national interest." (*Ot* was closed down.)

But the December–February "cover-up" had a more sinister side. Not satisfied to stifle criticism within his own party, Dayan tried to "discipline" the public as well through the IDF bureau of information and censorship (Dover Tzahal). By arrogating to itself responsibility for the public's "morale," the bureau began going far beyond the bounds of censorship established by twenty-five years of precedent. Deaths at the front were reported abstractly (no names were given and no circumstances); the real cause of the costly fire at Abu Rodeis, an errant Israeli Hawk missile, was not reported until the story was broken independently by an NBC reporter who filed the story outside the country. Dayan himself took on the academic establishment, impugning their loyalty and the propriety of their attacks on the Defense Ministry during "wartime."

The inner cabinet as a whole went along with this attempt to project an image of "normalcy": it opened the universities with

*Rafi, the list formed by Ben-Gurion after he left Mapai in 1963 during the aftermath of the Lavon crisis, includes Dayan, Shimon Peres, Yitzchak Navon (the second choice for president last time around), and others of the new generation who promoted themselves as democrats and technocrats. Rafi, however, had shrewdly opposed opening up the party lists last November, fearing a revolution against Dayan. The rediscovery of its democratic principles probably means that Dayan believes he has nothing to lose, and he is probably correct.

more than half the students at the front and refused to take
strong emergency measures to reorganize the ravaged Israeli
economy. But of course both decisions, added to the public's
fear of not being told the truth about the war, backfired. Public
morale is low. The new Ministry of Information, to be headed
by Rafi's Shimon Peres, which has been given authority over
radio and television, is not likely to raise spirits either. Peres has
been talking about "too much coverage" being given to marginal
political groups.

Nevertheless, the pressure on Golda and Dayan to resign is
now building up once again. Confidence in the Defense Minister
suffered another blow in mid-March with the surprise resignation of General Israel Tal—the army's assistant chief of staff
and one of its most respected and reliable officers. For it has
been revealed (by UPI, since the military censor quashed the
story in Israel) that while Tal was commander of the southern
front in December and January, Dayan had given him an order
to "heat things up." Tal, a tactical genius who takes a moderate
position on the question of the occupied territories, demanded
that Dayan put the order in writing. Dayan refused. However,
when Tal subsequently returned to the General Staff, he found
that the northern front's General Yitzchak Chofi had been appointed to his old post (chief of the General Staff). Tal was left
with little option but to resign. The dovish reserve general Mati
Peled fears that this resignation will be only the first of many.

Furthermore, Dayan's hard line on the territories will not gain
him any more popularity than will his political maneuvers. No
matter what the Agranat Commission of Inquiry into last October's "mistakes" has to say about Dayan's responsibility for
military failures, support has greatly dwindled for his views on
security. A *Ha'aretz* poll (March 5) revealed that 67 percent of
Israelis favor substantial territorial concessions as part of an effort to win a political settlement, while 77 percent among the
more highly educated and professionals support this policy of
diplomatic flexibility. Dayan's constituency has therefore been
slowly evaporating; but his pet issue is essentially his only issue,
and unless Dayan brings off some unanticipated feat in foreign
policy—Kissinger seems strangely eager to supply Dayan with
a personal triumph—he is not likely to be a force in Israeli

politics except in the struggle of the present government to survive. He undertook to serve under Golda precisely and merely because he shied away from alternatives.

However, in view of internal party cleavages and the persistence of external criticism—particularly since it is directed against a prime minister who is proving increasingly thin-skinned—it is difficult to conceive of this government lasting much beyond disengagement talks with Syria. And unlike disengagement, the Palestinian challenge is not an issue likely to keep Mrs. Meir's government together; in fact, it can be expected to blow the cabinet apart. Mapam and the Independent Liberals will favor diplomatic initiatives. The Challenge group, including Yigal Allon, will at least keep an open mind to whatever schemes for a Palestinian role Kissinger proposes. Golda and the Gush old guard, on the other hand, will favor only a Hashemite solution, as they are skeptical of all Palestinian national rights. The Rafi (Dayan and Peres) and the NRP will not agree to any substantial withdrawal from the West Bank whatsoever. In short, this is hardly a stable alliance, and it will become less so as historical options narrow.

But unlike Dayan, Likud, the bloc of right-wing opposition parties, does have other issues; and this explains the paradox that its strength increases while its pronouncements remain "hawkish." In fact, there is no small danger that Israel's opportunity to reach a political settlement with its neighbors, especially with the Palestinians, will be compromised by further Likud gains in the next elections. Should the Alignment continue to tumble into scandals and fail to change the current leadership, a Likud victory would be at least a distinct possibility.

POSTSCRIPT, APRIL 11

After this article was completed, two major and related events forced the various factions of the Alignment to the moment of decision, well before the knotty Palestine issue could do so: the release of the interim report of the Agranat Commission, followed by Golda Meir's resignation. At this writing, the government is still wallowing in crisis.

The members of the Agranat Commission were not empowered to consider failures of diplomacy or to assign ministerial responsibility, only to analyze the operational and technical failures leading up to October 6. Their recommendations were nevertheless devastating. The Chief of Staff, David Elazar, was forced to resign, although firmly repudiating any inference that Dayan stood apart from the army's operations, and the competence of some other high IDF commanders was seriously questioned. To the public's chagrin, the commission cautiously avoided assigning responsibility directly to ministers—the Tel Aviv University law professor Amnon Rubinstein pointed out in a careful analysis that this was an overtimid interpretation of its powers (*Ha'aretz*, April 9). But the commission's report clearly implied that the efficiency of decision making on defense had deteriorated significantly as a result of the secretive and unscrutinized consultations of the "kitchen"—Meir, Dayan, and Galili.

According to Dayan's own pronouncements on ministerial responsibility, he should have resigned forthwith. But Rafi's leaders were not prepared to permit Dayan to be lopped off the government so neatly, and are openly flaunting their friendliness to the Likud. Mapam and Achdut Ha'avoda, whose members regarded Elazar as one of their own, threatened to vote "no confidence" in any government in which Dayan was Minister of Defense, while the Gush politicians, fearful of having the rug pulled out from under them should any of the other factions leave, generally favored having Dayan reassigned with as little abrasion as possible. However, abrasiveness has become a way of life with Israel's political leaders.

With Alignment radicals and the articulate public once again demanding her resignation—and with her saving prestige no longer capable of bridging the factional disputes—Golda Meir resigned in exasperation. She is an old woman who indeed had come, as she put it, to the end of her road, perhaps well beyond it.

But Mrs. Meir's resignation has only served to intensify the confusion. The Gush bosses will now certainly occupy the center of the political stage here, but their ability to write the script is no longer assured. Their power has always rested on both the basic consensus among the factions on ruling together and on the trusting indifference of the public—and both have now disappeared. Sapir and his cronies have already come up with a self-serving compromise: a Gush prime minister (perhaps Sapir himself), with Dayan reassigned to a new post. Failing this, the Gush leaders, according to some rumors, might attempt to join Rafi and the Likud in a national coalition, leaving the Alignment's left wing to fend for itself. After all, Mrs. Meir was the decisive opponent of such a national coalition last month and now she is gone. But this last possibility would require an act of cynicism beyond the capacities of perhaps even the Gush bosses.

The late Levi Eshkol, a champion of the Gush, was once offered the choice between tea and coffee, and, so the story goes, he replied, "Well, I'll take half and half." Now that the left wing of the Alignment has summoned up the courage to force a showdown with Rafi, it will be up to the Gush leaders to choose sides. But if new elections *and* serious reform of the Alignment's party arrangements are not forthcoming, it will be a sure sign that the Israeli public is being served up some such repugnant beverage.

# The Threat from
# the Right

*Jerusalem, mid-April 1974 (just before Yitzchak Rabin's election)*
Ever since the December elections, the right-wing coalition in
Israel—the Likud—has been a looming presence here and one
often misunderstood abroad. The Likud now commands thirty-
nine seats in Israel's Knesset (roughly a third of the total). It
is often mentioned as a possible partner in a national coalition government with the embattled Alignment (such as the
one formed after the 1967 war).

This growing prestige has not been lost on Likud leaders; they
are presenting themselves as united, confident, and capable of
exercising power. They have taken Mrs. Meir's resignation as a
signal that new elections are in the offing and are already working on their campaign. In short, they are behaving like a plausible
political alternative, and this is something new in Israeli political
life.

The foreign policy pronouncements of the Likud have certainly remained hawkish. It essentially opposes any territorial
compromises beyond the return of half of Sinai to Egypt and
the return to Syria of the new bulge in the Golan Heights taken
by Israel in October. Likud's augmented strength has therefore
been interpreted abroad as resulting from despair among Israel's
public over peacemaking, and pessimism about the state's security.

This analysis is completely false. Politics in Israel did not begin
when the Western press discovered it. The Likud's success, if

anything, is an indication that Israelis are more convinced than ever of their staying power — the October war confirmed nothing if not Israel's ability to survive. They are now becoming increasingly preoccupied with the problems of daily life and with those social rifts and political divisions that have been plaguing Israeli society for many years but which had always been shunted aside by defense priorities and collective insecurity. The Likud is gaining because, like the Alignment left opposition, it is raising questions of domestic reform.

The Likud, like the Alignment, is dominated by ideas and factions whose history goes back to the early days of the Jewish settlement in Palestine. The most important of the factions are the Herut (Freedom) Party and the Liberals, who had combined to form the right-wing Gahal bloc in 1965. Herut is a direct political outgrowth of Irgun Zvai Leumi, the fanatically anti-British terrorist group, which had been itself a stepchild of the Zionist Revisionist movement. The Revisionists seceded from the left-dominated World Zionist Organization in 1933. Their animating force was the fiery Vladimir Jabotinsky, surely one of modern Jewry's stormiest figures, who, although himself Russian-born (in Odessa — a contemporary of Trotsky's), was deeply influenced by the Italian *risorgimento*. As the chief advocate of Jewish armed resistance, founding the Jewish Legion during World War I and then the paramilitary youth organization called Betar, Jabotinsky, it is said, thought of himself as the Jewish Garibaldi.

Jabotinsky's romantic nationalism and brooding sense of Jewry's doom in Europe (he died in 1940) blended, not always harmoniously, with his abiding admiration for Western modernization and liberalism. The latter aspect of his thought (he had even pressed for the latinization of the Hebrew alphabet) was not easily passed on to the desperate and immensely bitter post-Holocaust conspirators of the Irgun. Under Menachem Begin, the Herut Revisionists have taken a chauvinist and decidedly illiberal direction.

Begin grew up among the Polish Jewish bourgeoisie before World War II and still has about him, or so say those close to him, some of the foxy elegance of the Polish aristocracy.

He is always correct and courtly, but he is also a didactic and usually unconvincing orator whose real power is maintained by surprisingly brutal back-room power plays. This can be attested to by such ambitious young right-wing reformers as Ezer Weizman, who finally left Herut in disgust, and Shmuel Tamir, who was drummed out of Herut for his liberal views, but who has now rejoined the Likud as leader of the Free Center.

There is little doubt that Likud's overall chances for an electoral victory would be greatly enhanced by Begin's ouster. The younger and more moderate elements in the Likud are leaning toward the proposal of General Ariel Sharon of the Liberal Party to abolish factions and "overhaul" the leadership; and it is generally assumed that Sharon himself would benefit personally from such a development — not only because of his exploits in October's war but because Likud was Sharon's brainchild in the first place. Sharon's electoral strength has never been tested, however, and he gives the impression of being abrasive and egotistical. It is difficult to see how he would make inroads where Begin could not. Likud's major chance for success might come in the unlikely event that the leadership went to a more moderate figure such as Weizman or Tamir or the new mayor of Tel Aviv, Shlomo Lahat.

Herut's traditional battle has been, nevertheless, the same as that of Revisionism before it — a continuous vilification of Labor Zionism (which still considers Revisionism "fascist") and of the plodding socialist strategy of Ben-Gurion and Ben-Tzvi, which Jabotinsky claimed discouraged immigration of the predominantly petit-bourgeois Jews of Europe and America.

Begin usually carries this criticism to absurdity by charging the Labor Zionists with some of the responsibility for the Holocaust; by failing to plan a revolution against the British in 1936–39, they thereby denied European Jews a refuge. Between Hitler and the British Colonial Office (remember the White Paper?), Begin's "plan" would probably have led to the snuffing out of the Yishuv then and there.

Herut's social and economic theory has repudiated working-class solidarity and institutions ("Jewish nationalism cannot afford the luxury of class struggle"). It proposed instead a kind of corporate state that would arbitrate wage demands, abolish restrictions on the use of Arab labor,* and encourage a fully capitalist economy.

This implies, of course, the effective dismantling of the Histadrut. It also implicitly opposes the principle that Jews must do their own work in the fields and factories, without hiring workers from the less demanding, politically disorganized, and easily exploited Arab population — the twin pillars of the Yishuv's socialism and the industrial strategy, which prevented the emergence of a Jewish "colon" class.

But Herut, like Revisionism before it, is not wholly reactionary. It enthusiastically advocates the populism, egalitarianism, and ambitious self-discipline of the petit bourgeoisie. It is suspicious of big capital, big empires, and monopolistic impediments to "free enterprise." Moreover, it leans toward a sentimental and heroic political nationalism that, aside from a well-sharpened moral snobbery toward the goy (e.g., Begin's recent statement, "The world doesn't care about slaughtered Jews, only armed ones"), now translates itself into an oblique "historic" claim upon, roughly, the whole territory of ancient, tribal Israel under King Solomon. (Herut's ideologues wisely do not choose another epoch, which would, say, lop off Tel Aviv and Haifa.)

The other major faction of the Likud is the Liberal Party, whose prestate movement, the General Zionists, led by Chaim Weizmann, combined the pragmatic diplomacy of Theodor Herzl with a rather phlegmatic ideological pluralism and cosmopolitanism. Zionism was for the General Zionists more an answer to gentile racism than a positive cultural ideal. (The early publicist Achad Ha'am was less kind: he believed the Zionism of Herzl to show the greatest ignorance of Jewish culture and its modern possibilities.)

---

*Labor's historic scruples with regard to Arab labor are now greatly compromised. Seventy thousand Arabs work in the Israeli economy — mainly in agriculture and construction — and although labor exchanges still formally guarantee wages equal to Jewish wages, many menial jobs now held by Arabs no longer have Jewish counterparts. Hence wages in agriculture have, for example, *fallen* 16 percent (*Jerusalem Post*, February 15, 1974).

At any rate, the General Zionists (as now the Liberals) generally served to organize the middle-class Jews in Europe and America, who usually preferred to contribute money and influence rather than their own futures to Zionism. The Liberals still draw support and financial backing mainly from Israel's haute bourgeoisie, which more and more seems to be developing an authentic class consciousness. For example, Mark Moshevitz, president of Israel's Association of Manufacturers and perhaps the most important of the Liberal Party's backers, recently served notice that the postwar wage hikes demanded by the Histadrut (to cover *only partly* the abolition of staple subsidies) would be the "last time" the government forced the "productive class" to pay for the "war burden." (His firm, Elite Foods, last year made a 50 percent gross profit.)

The Liberals attack maladministration and inefficiency and aspire to a formal liberal state apparatus that would eliminate the stranglehold of Israel's Orthodox rabbis on civil institutions. They recently defied the Herut faction and supported, in principle, an electoral reform bill certain to cut back the power of smaller parties, such as the National Religious Party. But they would no doubt dispense with their anticlericalism if they, with the rest of the Likud, came close enough to power and an alliance with the National Religious Party became feasible.

Herut, on the other hand, finds its main support today among poorer Sephardic communities, the *sans-culottes* of Tel Aviv and Jerusalem, whose social outlook is now not very different from the one they had in Casablanca or Algiers before 1950. Their leaders and intellectuals drifted mainly to Paris (e.g., the writer Albert Memmi), leaving them to be buffeted by Israel's devoted yet often condescending political establishment and the inevitable dislocations of settling in a country largely run by immigrants from Eastern Europe. Apart from those few who were incorporated into the Labor machine from the frontier towns to which many Sephardic Jews were dispatched (Migdal Haemek, Yerucham, Qiryat Shemona, Dimona), they have found their main chances for economic success and social recognition through small—then larger—business enterprises in the cities.

Fear and hatred of Arabs are understandably more wide-

spread in the Sephardic neighborhoods—Sephardic Jews are
refugees from Arab states—but it is not Herut's chauvinism
that wins over so many Sephardic voters. Large sections of the
Sephardic communities regard the Histadrut economic establishment and the Labor Party, with some justice, as an elite
patronage system for veteran bureaucrats. In fact, only 3 percent of high-level government positions (Israel's bureaucracy is
large—and cumbersome) are held by Sephardic Jews, who make
up 50 percent of the population. Herut rides high therefore on
its populist demagoguery, arguing for a "freed" market economy
and an end to the tyranny of Israel's "socialist-bureaucratic des-
pots."

Both as an employer and as a union representing well over
80 percent of Israel's workers, the Histadrut can take much of
the credit for building a workable Jewish state. The Histadrut
and government-owned or -controlled enterprises make up
roughly 50 percent of Israel's productive forces. Their dominant
or monopoly position in virtually every key sphere of Israeli
industry and banking gives this "public sector" decisive economic
power.

But it is hard to deny that particularly in the last decade the
Histadrut leadership and Israel's socialist parties have preferred
to develop the profit margins of "public" industries within a
market economy—and themselves as a labor aristocracy—rather than to evolve the industrial democracy and planning that
were supposed to serve as a base for a more classless society and
more equally distributed social benefits.

The industries run by the Histadrut (Hevrat Ovdim)—including light manufacturing, banking, insurance, retail trade,
construction, heavy industry, etc.—make it Israel's biggest capitalist. These enterprises were established, often at great immediate sacrifice, with the intention of combining economic
growth and social welfare. But the executives who now run their
operations appear to have appropriated the sterile pragmatism
of Western "managers," and they have been more intent on
fitting Israel's public corporations into the pecking order of European multinationals than on carrying out bold experiments in
industrial relations.

Furthermore, Labor Party bosses and conservative union leaders have provided Hevrat Ovdim managers with a congenial setting in which to operate. They were instrumental in pushing Yitzchak Ben-Aharon, the former radical secretary-general of the Histadrut, out of office last fall, and show little interest in such elementary issues as conservation and air pollution where the immediate profits of Hevrat Ovdim plants are at stake (e.g., their abortive attempt to extend the polluting operations of the Nesher cement factory in Haifa by further encroaching on the Carmel Mountain National Park).

Most striking is the Histadrut-Labor attitude toward health care. After running their own sick fund for two generations, the Labor leaders are the major *opponents* of a national health insurance scheme, which, although improving the quality of health care, would deny the Labor establishment a comfortable pocket of patronage. All of this makes them easy targets for Herut's self-congratulatory criticism.

Worse still, Pinhas Sapir, Israel's high-handed "socialist" Finance Minister, has personally presided for the last seven years over a program of huge subsidies to "development" capital. He has virtually challenged the Israeli bourgeoisie, and the Histadrut and kibbutz industrial planners, to compete for these lucrative "incentives" in an openly political fashion. Playing sugar daddy in turn to private and public corporations, Sapir often subsidized undertakings that turned a quick profit which distorted economic growth and guaranteed private enrichment at government expense. Apparently without any interest in social equality himself, he has painstakingly cultivated Israel's haute bourgeoisie and, particularly, Jewish investors from abroad (his "millionaires club").

Sapir has replied with a Benthamite petulance to recent demands from Moshe Zanbar, governor of the Bank of Israel (and no socialist), for controls on capital ("It would be inefficient"). Instead he has attempted to meet the crushing war expenses by abolishing government subsidies for food, fuel, and transportation: a hard blow for most Israeli wage earners.*

---

*It is instructive that Likud joined the parties of the left (and Ben-Aharon and Eliav) both in opposing the abolishing of subsidies and in calling for an end to easy loans to big business. But Likud's eighteenth-century faith in "free enterprise" would be a further dose of poison rather than an antidote.

This is Sapir's idea of a "war economy." Nor is he apparently capable of appreciating the damage such measures do to Israel's social cohesion—condemning increasing numbers of families to elaborate and demeaning welfare programs, intensifying growing class divisions, and giving full run to Israel's *nouveaux riches*, who set an unrealistic standard of expectations for the majority of Israelis ("Put a castle next to a house and the house becomes a hut"). Israel's unabashed consumption binge and social uneasiness of the last five years owe a great deal to Sapir's shortsightedness, and so ironically do Labor's current political difficulties.

Begin scores very well by exploiting thwarted hopes for more equality—and by railing against the widening "social gap" (*ha'pear ha'sotziali*) that has emerged under forty years of Labor's continuous rule. Although Begin's populism must rankle his Liberal Party allies in Likud, one understands nothing in fact about Israeli politics until one realizes that the Labor Party and not the right-wing bloc is broadly perceived to be the party of privilege—the party of the "new class."

This was graphically confirmed only last week after the brutal terrorist attack on Qiryat Shemona. The mainly Sephardic residents of this "development town" received the Labor ministers who came to the funerals there with an open antagonism that almost led to a riot. A few hundred of them subsequently held a rowdy demonstration at the Knesset and would not be appeased, even by some very impressive promises from the government—e.g., Sapir will be "giving" them 250 million Israeli pounds in additional aid. When they finally broke into the Knesset, only Begin was able to quiet them. He assured the demonstrators that the security arrangements for the town would indeed be tightened, as the government had pledged.

But I suspect that Likud's approach to foreign affairs, dominated by Herut's proposals for annexation, will be the strongest obstacle to its taking power during the next few years. For Likud usually persists in relying on euphemism—calling the West Bank "Judea and Samaria"—and trying to ignore the Arab civilization that lives on top of this soil. Its plan to offer

West Bank Arabs full Israeli citizenship—like the old PLO "secular" state—would, at best, result in another Algeria. True, it offers the standard hawkish arguments on security, especially the Liberals and Free Center, who generally shy away from esoteric nationalist exhortations but hardly need to since Likud's own flamboyant military wizard, Ariel Sharon, has emerged as a leading Liberal. However, Likud as a whole does not devote much energy to fresh thinking on security and foreign policy and depends rather on the nationalist fantasies of Begin (and of Moshe Shamir's Movement for the Whole Land of Israel). These fantasies extend now to the Palestinians as well. Recently in the Knesset Begin attacked Golda's now defunct "throne speech" for including the word "Palestinian." "No wonder," he claimed, "the whole world now believes there is a Palestinian nation."

With regard to the Palestinian issue, Jabotinsky himself was far more astute than Likud is proving to be today. Assessing the moral dilemma posed by the Jewish claim on Palestine, which of necessity conflicted with the claim of Palestinian Arabs, Jabotinsky contrasted the "hunger" of the Jewish Yishuv to the "appetite" of the Palestinian Arabs. Like the right wing of the Labor Alignment itself, Likud leaders refuse to recognize that increasing numbers of Palestinians now claim only that part of Palestine where Arabs now live and for which they do indeed hunger, and rightly so.

It has been reported recently (by Dan Margalit of *Ha'aretz*) that Arafat himself finally made a gesture toward Israel, trying to arrange a meeting between PLO leader Abu Iad and Deputy Prime Minister Yigal Allon. The contact was apparently rebuffed by the Meir government.

The Qiryat Shemona massacre was explicitly undertaken by Ahmed Jebreel's fanatic thugs to subvert rapprochement between "Zionists" and "Palestinian defeatists." By "defeatists," Jebreel's group was presumably referring to both Arafat and Naif Hawatmeh of the PLO, both of whom have been reported as favoring a separate Palestinian state. Jebreel has connections with Saika, the Syrian terrorist group, and George Habash's PFLP, both of which have fanatically opposed any accommodation whatever with Israel. In view of this background, the massacre should not preclude contacts with the PLO but should emphasize all the more their urgency.

The Likud's approach to such vital security matters seems dramatically out of step with the Israeli public's decidedly "dovish" turn since October, yet its strength appears to be growing significantly. It is not clear how unconditional this support will be, for Likud seems quite content to try to slide into power on the slippery slope that could be created for it by further Alignment scandals and domestic failures. It is uncanny and troubling how eager to accommodate this opportunism the Alignment has seemed to be since last October.

## POSTSCRIPT: TEL AVIV, APRIL 23

A combination of public pressure and renewed political deadlock has finally forced the Gush to be more realistic. After concluding that his own standing with the public was too low for him to attempt to lead the government himself, Sapir spent over a week coyly trying to find a "new" face from the veterans of the ex-Mapai bloc to replace Golda Meir. He failed. Like Sapir himself, none of the other possible candidates relished the prospect of becoming the new target for public bitterness.

When the Alignment's coalition partners declared that they would now not join any new government, making inevitable new elections in the near future, Sapir shrewdly decided that he had better begin to share power with the party's young Turks, and he then threw his support to the most popular figure of this group, Yitzchak Rabin — the unofficial new leader of the party's doves and moderate left.

Sapir's decision to back the party's left wing and thereby oppose a national coalition with the Likud had broader consequences. The right-wing leaders of the Rafi faction, though smarting over Dayan's now likely departure from government, reckoned that they had better start pushing through some open doors on their own. Doing an about-face on Rafi's threat to bolt to the Likud and emphasizing the need for party unity, Dayan's heir apparent, Shimon Peres, declared that he would himself be a candidate for the party leadership unconditionally. To his credit, Peres then set the tone for an open and courteous contest with Rabin; in losing, he went to great lengths to calm factional bitterness, and he has, for the moment at least, earned for himself a reputation as a moderate and the esteem of an apparently united party.

However, the climax of this drama came in a seedy Tel Aviv meeting hall where the 600-member central committee of the Labor Party (composed of Mapai, Achdut Ha'avoda, and Rafi; Mapam is a partner in the Alignment, not in the Labor Party) met to elect Yitzchak Rabin to lead the party and the government. The vote was surprisingly close and tempers were still raw from the meeting of the previous night; but the political intrigues that led up to this vote seemed genuinely dwarfed by the slowly emerging recognition that this was nevertheless a historic moment. Without quite letting go, Israel's founders were passing on their power to a new generation.

Nor does the fact that Sapir "swung" the election to Rabin contradict what seem good prospects for internal party reform and reorganization. No one knows how well Rabin would have done on his own had Sapir kept out of it, and both Rabin and Peres have plainly implied that they regard themselves as allies in what should now be an easier struggle to open up the party, eliminate factions, and, ultimately, break the power of the Gush. Equally important, Rabin's election appears to mark the beginning of the end of Israel's parliamentary crisis, although probably not the end of Mrs. Meir's caretaker government. For it seems unlikely that Rabin will succeed in forming a durable government where Sapir expected to fail. Most politicians here are agreed that new elections should await the final Agranat Commission report expected this summer. (Meanwhile, this caretaker government should be able to manage the Syrian disengagement.) Rabin's victory therefore won't be fully achieved until he faces a general election in the fall, presumably as the leader of a more democratic party. And this only if he can get by Likud's challenge.

But in spite of a reckless last-minute attempt by Ezer Weizman to discredit him (as "incapable of withstanding stress"), Rabin now seems to have every hope of becoming a strong and popular leader, perhaps the only public figure in the country now capable of unifying a strong majority of Israelis for the difficulties ahead. One hopes that he will have the courage to persist with pragmatism and open-mindedness when confronting the narrowing options for a diplomatic settlement with the Arab states and the Palestinians, and that he would earn an equally pragmatic response from the other side. Both the Israelis and Arabs deserve no less.

# Israel Letter:
# The New Trap

I

*Jerusalem, early October 1975*

The recent Sinai agreement was negotiated in an atmosphere of growing confusion that is new and disturbing for Israelis. Although the economic recession has led to a sharp rise in emigration — some estimates range as high as 20,000 a year during 1974 and 1975 — there is no feeling of pessimism about Israel's being destroyed. Most Israelis still accept the endless rounds of reserve duty, the tedious vigilance against terror, and their bitter isolation from other countries as the price of survival, which they take for granted.

What is more deeply worrying are the visible signs of uncertainty among the Israelis about the goals of their extraordinary staying power. The reassuring conviction of the last eight years that there was a broad consensus about national purposes has been put in doubt.* So long as there seemed nothing more to contend with than unyielding Arab enmity, typified by the Khartoum Resolution of 1967, the popular slogan *ein breira* ("there is no choice") was comforting, if macabre. Now that Israelis face some real choices, they must also face up to their internal divisions.

*See Nahum Goldmann's "The Psychology of Middle East Peace," *Foreign Affairs*, October 1975

Writing in the daily *Ma'ariv* just before Kissinger's arrival, the Hebrew University philosopher Shlomo Avineri revealed some of the ideological turmoil lurking behind what often appear to be merely tactical issues. Zionism, he argued, was intended to liberate and revive not Jewish lands but Jewish people. What was significant was Avineri's evident sense of urgency that this elementary principle must now be reasserted and defended. For the prospect of withdrawal from the occupied territories is bringing to the surface a central but long-neglected question: Is merely producing more Jewish power an end in itself?

Particularly since the war of 1967, Israeli leaders have assumed with moral certainty that the efficient use of force is the key to survival—not only strategically but culturally. The military became glamorous, its leaders uncritically revered, and some of the more fanatical right-wing commanders of pre-1948 Zionism became approved folk heroes.* More important, the occupation of the Golan Heights, the West Bank, and especially the Old City of Jerusalem seemed to provide not only the tangible guarantee but also the symbolic vindication of the Zionist project. Even Israel's paper currency has begun to depict different views of the Old City's walls; the portraits of workers, scientists, and poets are being discarded.

This policy of encouraging, or tolerating, various kinds of Jewish settlement in these conquered territories has engendered a cult of the land, a spiritual élan heavily laden with vulgarized religious mysticism and messianic righteousness. And such sentiments have become much more decisive in Israel's politics than any strategic value the settlements may have. Many young Israelis have been schooled in continual war and lack the political sophistication of older generations: as one talks to them, and observes their vehement demonstrations, one realizes that withdrawal from these territories would now mean repudiating the heroic destiny that they see as justifying all their sacrifices.

*This "rehabilitation" of the terrorist underground still continues. Israeli television has recently featured an admiring special program on Ya'ir Stern, founder of "The Freedom Fighters of Israel," without so much as subjecting his nationalist views to debate.

In its most strident form, this political feeling has now found a political voice in Gush Emunim—literally, the Front of the Faithful—a nonparty movement composed of "religious" radicals, young members or sympathizers of the right-wing Likud, as well as a mixed bag of war heroes, cultural figures (e.g., the songwriter Naomi Shemer), and West Bank and Golan settlers.* Boastful about the IDF's military prowess, arrogant and narrow-minded in their interpretation of Jewish "self-determination," they lately have become the hard core of opposition to compromise on the occupied territories and to diplomatic initiatives. When Henry Kissinger came to Jerusalem, Gush Emunim sent thousands of young men wearing knitted yarmulkes into the streets, its demonstrations leading to violent clashes with the police. It showed it could muster over 25,000 people in protest against the Sinai accord.

However, these impressive demonstrations were not necessarily an accurate measure of Gush Emunim's political strength. According to the polls, perhaps 70 percent of Israelis—some of whom took to the streets themselves in less impressive marches—were willing to approve of September's interim settlement, although they did so equivocally and tensely. But Gush Emunim's influence is potentially much greater than even its present numbers might suggest, for it has succeeded in boldly expressing ideas that more conventional Israeli leaders have been unwilling to challenge openly for a decade. It proclaims, for example, that occupying and settling the West Bank are not merely tactically necessary but must be celebrated as unifying Eretz Yisrael. Gush Emunim has grabbed the center of the stage in a drama in which Rabin's still tottering government has been unwilling to take part.

Indeed, since the job of Prime Minister fell into his lap over a year ago, Rabin has been reluctant to embroil himself in any controversy about the shape of Israel's future. He has instead been cautiously and persistently committing himself to the path of least resistance. He replaced Shulamit Aloni's dovish group in his coalition with the National Religious Party, which insists that the entire West Bank must stay in Israel's hands for religious and "historic" reasons. He then pandered to rightist agitation in

*See Judith Miller, "Israel: The Politics of Fear," *The Progressive*, July 1975.

the Labor Alignment and in the NRP by acquiescing in the accelerated pace of surreptitious Jewish settlement of the West Bank. Attempting to silence attacks from the Likud, he took its flashiest and most popular leader, General Arik Sharon, onto his personal staff—Sharon advocates holding on to the West Bank and the Golan forever—secretly promising that he would be chief of staff in 1977. And during the Sinai negotiations of last March, Rabin made his demand that Sadat agree to "nonbelligerency"—a demand that his foreign minister, Yigal Allon, was willing to forgo, and that was a principal cause of the collapse of Kissinger's mission.

Since then, Kissinger has obviously been determined to provide Rabin with a very different path of least resistance. During his brief visit to Washington in June, Rabin was made to feel that Israel's relations with the Ford administration had nearly been wrecked in March and had to be salvaged. Ford and Kissinger told him that American interests in the Middle East—both economic and strategic—would be compromised if Sadat's "step-by-step" progress toward Washington were impeded by Israeli "inflexibility"; and in case Rabin had difficulty persuading the people back home of this, they dramatically announced that they were "reassessing" the entire Mideast situation, including military aid to Israel.

The October war was bound to convince Kissinger and both presidents he served of what the State Department has been asserting for many years, namely, that the Persian Gulf is not a place where Israel can be counted on to act as a U.S. police agent, even with the Shah's implicit cooperation. Pax Americana would be better served, no doubt, by enlisting the support of Cairo and the more active cooperation of Riyadh, both of them eager to outfit themselves with American arms and logistical equipment. The prospect of petrodollars seems to be effectively silencing pro-Israel hawks in the Pentagon; and although the traditional solidarity with Israel of the U.S. Congress is steady, this support could prove ephemeral.* Since the Sinai accord, the

---

*Recent polls have shown Americans opposed to stationing U.S. technicians in Sinai by a sobering two-to-one margin while claiming overwhelmingly to be supporters of Israel. Clearly also there is little popular enthusiasm for supplying Israel with billions of dollars of aid during a time of recession.

Congress has been slower than ever before to come across with
money and arms for Israel.\* Kissinger's threat of a reassessment
produced a strong, majority show of support for Israel in the
Senate. But if the McGovern Report is any indication, a sizable
number in Congress are committed only to the "little Israel" of
before the 1967 war—not to American support for an indefinite
Israeli occupation.

The last few months may not have vindicated Kissinger's statements that what is good for America is good for Israel. But they
have convinced Israel's political leaders that what Kissinger sees
as bad for the United States can be made to be disastrous for
Israel. Consider, for example, the recent behavior of Yitzchak
Navon, the highly respected chairman of the Knesset Foreign
Affairs and Security Committee. He is a member of the tough-
minded Rafi faction of the Labor Alignment, a crony of Defense
Minister Shimon Peres—the leader of those who pressed Rabin
to take a hard line during the March negotiations. Beginning in
early August, Navon campaigned hard in favor of a new agreement without so much as mentioning Egypt; an open breach
with America had become unthinkable.

In forcing Israel to agree to the September bargain, Kissinger
showed some grasp of Israeli politics and particularly of their
current breaking point. He offered the Israelis relief from their
fantasies that they would be "sold out" while allowing them to
avoid facing any of the large questions about the future of the
occupied territories.

So far as the Sinai was concerned, the Chief of Staff Mordechai
Gur had already abandoned the static defense strategy that dominated Israeli planning since the War of Attrition of the late
1960s. He openly approved of the new line of defense and expressed satisfaction at getting the highly fatal military hardware,
including the Lance missile, which had been held up since March.
Even the Likud hard-liners had to agree that a surprise attack
across the new buffer zone—with its UN soldiers, its electronic
warning devices, and promised U.S. technicians—would be next

---

\*See Leslie Gelb's analysis of Senator Eagleton's speech, *New York Times*, October
1, 1975.

to impossible. The loss of the Abu Rodeis oil fields will be more than regained if Israel receives the $2.3 billion Kissinger promised for its arsenals and its limping economy.*

As for Sadat, he renounced the use of force, agreed to let Israeli cargoes through the Suez Canal, and closed down the independent PLO radio in Cairo. Yet Kissinger provided him with a clear victory. The unilateral pullback of Israeli troops from the Canal Zone and the oil fields allows the Egyptian leaders to claim that, unlike Nasser's, their 1973 attack won a political battle. As Shimon Shamir, the leading Israeli Mideast expert, has argued, Sadat might now be expected to devote more attention to the staggering problems of Egyptian poverty with the help of Western aid and technology. He can count on $250 million in U.S. funds, $300 million a year in new oil revenues (above domestic consumption), as well as substantial savings on Lloyd's insurance rates for canal shipping.

## II

The Sinai agreement thus satisfied some real interests, pulled Egypt further away from the USSR, and allowed Kissinger to show he could put on yet another extravaganza—all of which obscured its reality, which is that it is no more than an elaborate cease-fire between two parties to a many-sided conflict.

Rabin himself admits that the pact offers no more than a chance to "buy time"—but he cannot acknowledge openly that several time bombs at once are meanwhile ticking away. If the pact is providing "momentum," as Kissinger insists, it is as much toward collision as toward conciliation. For it remains a Mad Hatter's affair, each side refusing to say what it means by "peace."

Most conspicuously, the agreement takes no account whatever of the Palestinian question—a deliberate omission because neither side could make a single concession about Palestinian rights

---

*London's Institute for Strategic Studies reported recently that Israel spends $1,043 per person yearly on defense. This is two and a half times what the superpowers spend. Without U.S. aid, the inflationary pressures would be unbearable.

that would not have caused an uproar of protest at home: if Rabin had vaguely agreed to "Palestinian self-determination," he would have risked his government's fall. The tacit solution was therefore to put the future of the Palestinians at the bottom of the list of Mideast problems. But the Palestinian issue is the crux of the conflict, and the longer it is evaded, the more repellent any of the conceivable solutions become for one side or the other.

In Israel, hatred for the PLO is running high, incited in large measure by the relentless terrorism and slanders of the Palestinian leaders. Israel meanwhile frequently bombs the Lebanese villages where PLO forces are known to hide out but where civilians are inevitably killed. One hears rumors of "moderate" factions in Beirut, of Arafat's dwindling power. But, with only a few exceptions, such as Said Hammami, the London representative of the PLO,* the PLO leaders go on flatly denying Israel's right to exist. Nor has any alternative to the PLO even begun to show itself in the political vacuum the Israelis have foolishly created on the West Bank.

More immediately threatening are the new dangers on Israel's frontiers with Syria and Jordan. Few people in Israel expected that Hussein, America's old protégé, would engineer an alliance with Syria, the leader of the so-called Refusal Front of pro-Soviet countries (including Iraq and Libya). Since he was dealt out of the Rabat conference a year ago, Hussein has continued to collaborate with Israel on civil services on the West Bank. But during the last six months he has agreed to coordinate his military policy with that of Syria, stopping just short of a joint military command. He threatens openly to turn to the USSR if he doesn't get the elaborate air defenses he wants from the United States. Although Hussein has been trying to mediate between Egypt and Syria,† Jordan would now be a serious threat to Israel in any future war.

What is so troubling for those Israelis who still hope to return

---

*See his views favoring a Palestinian state that could coexist with Israel in *New Outlook*, March–April 1975, as well as the interview with Sabri Jiryis in the September issue.

†See Terence Smith, *New York Times*, October 1, 1975.

the West Bank to Hussein—and that hope is still the government's official position—is Hussein's apparent feeling that he now has nothing to lose. He seems to have given up any hope of undoing the PLO's support, whether in the UN, the Arab capitals, or among the West Bank Palestinians. He has to swim rather than sink, and the current has swept him toward Damascus. Defense Minister Shimon Peres has had to take this new alliance seriously; and he has ordered a hardening of Israel's positions all along the Jordanian front.

As for Syria, the dangers of war on the Golan Heights, instead of quieting down, as Kissinger implied they might, have now become seriously menacing. Claiming to fear that Sadat will make a separate peace, Assad, encouraged by the Russians, has been threatening to play a dangerous game of brinkmanship with regard to the UN forces on the Golan, whose mandate runs out in November. At the UN, his foreign minister, Abdul Khaddam, denounced the Egyptians and the United States for breaking up Arab unity and called Israel's treatment of the Palestinians far worse than anything done by the Nazis. If he did not absolutely reject any new negotiations, he came very close to doing so.

If this blustering continues, the elimination of the UN buffer zone, narrow as it is, would be terribly dangerous. Both the Israelis and the Syrians are capable of preemptive strikes. Assad could well try to improve his bargaining position and to undermine the Egyptian accord by a new war of attrition—something that paid off earlier, during the disengagement negotiations in 1974. And should fighting with Syria break out, all of Kissinger's schemes would quickly unravel. No doubt with this in mind, Kissinger told Israeli journalists that he expects to be back here in the fall and that he does not believe that the obstacles to an interim settlement on the Golan are insurmountable.

Here we can see clearly the trap in which Rabin finds himself. While the Syrians seem nearly to have shut the door on talking with Israel, and while the Israelis insist at the UN that they are eager to talk, Rabin himself has told the Israelis that, so far as an interim agreement is concerned, the "room for maneuver" on the Golan is "next to nothing."* But as long as he refuses to

---

*Yediot Acharonot,* September 14, 1975.

discuss the Palestinians, only interim agreements can be placed on the agenda. Rabin, moreover, did not simply mean that the Golan, in contrast to the Sinai, is only forty to sixty kilometers deep. He was begging a far more volatile question.

The effect of last year's disengagement pact with the Syrians was to leave Israel's Golan border running along the ridges that overlook the string of new settlements that Mrs. Meir's government impetuously constructed on the territory conquered in 1967. First conceived as a security measure, these settlements quickly became a pretext for outright annexation. Any interim pact with Syria—no matter how "cosmetic," as Rabin likes to put it—will either place these settlements in jeopardy or mean that some will have to be abandoned. Sources close to the government are whispering about a so-called octopus formula, by which the relatively narrow spaces lying between the settlements would be ceded back to Syria, thus leaving the settlements themselves "intact." But you cannot weave a border in and out of a settlement and expect the men and women who live there to have much faith in their future.

It seems far more probable that the fight will be waged over the *present* line—and any wavering over that line could bring down Rabin. In late September, Gush Emunim organized a march of 5,000 demonstrators to the Golan. The marchers, moreover, included a good many members of the left-wing and usually dovish Shomer Hatzair kibbutzim—which shows how powerfully attached to the Golan Israelis have become. Indeed, Rabin recently has been aggravating his own problems by approving more settlements on the Golan.

No doubt Kissinger could try to force another interim pact through the Knesset. But this time it would likely mean that those Labor politicians who have proclaimed that "settlements are not erected only to be withdrawn" would have to eat their words, and some will gag. And although Rabin appears to have gained control of the Mapai Party, the pliable and largely dovish core of the Labor Alignment, his own party and government risk being pulled apart by powerful politicians who won't compromise on the Golan settlements. For example, Israel Galili, Golda Meir's old political fixer, was the minister who originally presided over the Golan annexation after the 1967 war. He will likely oppose any move from the present line, carrying with him some of those in the Achdut Ha'avoda faction in the Alignment. The mainly hard-line Rafi faction, whose position is advanced by key ministers such as Shimon Peres and Gad Yaacobi, may find an American-dictated Golan agreement sufficient pretext to bolt to the Likud. (Three Rafi backbenchers, including Dayan, already voted against ratification of the Sinai pact.)

Reserve General Mati Peled, who served under Rabin for many years, suspects that Rabin, more concerned with staying in power than anything else, fully expects to be "forced" back to the 1967 borders by the Americans. But Rabin's political gains have been dramatic mainly in an opportunistic sense. Rather than confronting his opposition, he has been making concessions to it. He is still not powerful enough to impose Kissinger's will upon Rafi, nor, when it comes to a showdown, can he expect to claim more than approximately fifty-five seats in the Knesset—i.e., six short of a majority.

For Rabin's coalition with parties outside the Labor Alignment is already under heavy strain. The politically devout old guard of the National Religious Party has been hard pressed by its young and mystically inclined fanatics, who are closely connected with Begin's Herut faction of the Likud and more so with the crusaders of Gush Emunim. These old Religious Party leaders will not sit in a "defeatist" government unless it is made clear to them that this is the only kind of government in which they can sit, i.e., should Rabin exploit his new and perhaps temporary popularity by calling a quick election and winning a personal mandate. Even the usually tame leaders of the Independent Liberal Party have been making perfunctory threats to abandon the government over a Golan withdrawal.

Nor can Rabin derive much consolation from the dovish left. Mapam leaders have been threatening to quit if Rabin refrains from proposing an overall settlement; and these noises must be taken more seriously now that the declining Mapam Party will have to compete with a serious new dovish coalition for the votes of the leftist kibbutz members. In late March, Lova Eliav finally left the Labor Party, joining with Shulamit Aloni, Mati Peled, and others to form the Yaad (Target) group. Together with the

"New Left" Moked Party, they control five Knesset seats and have a good chance of gaining more in the next election.

But although Yaad's leaders are skeptically determined to support Rabin on the Sinai withdrawal, Lova Eliav himself told me that he regards the "step-by-step" strategy as doomed unless it can be linked to progress toward a settlement of larger questions. He and most of the Israeli left are pressing for a direct confrontation with the Palestinian problem: they want Rabin to make it clear that Israel will negotiate with those Palestinians who recognize that Israel exists. They contend, persuasively, that this will convert the Golan and Sinai questions into a haggle over real estate and security guarantees instead of a bitter dispute over a principle on which Israel must anyway compromise. Indeed, they have declared themselves prepared to join in bringing Rabin's government down over the Palestinian issue.

Even a token withdrawal on the Golan promises to become a bitter struggle over the basic principles of Zionism. Since 1967, most streams in political Zionism have taken a decisively rightward course, associating the practice of Jewish social and national reconstruction not with the painful tasks of developing a modern and pluralist Jewish civilization, but rather with "Jewish" sovereignty over lands and the fulfillment of "historic rights." The Golan has become a symbol of choice between the Israel that offers Jews realistic political autonomy and the one that promotes a Jewish *risorgimento*.

As the focus shifts to the Golan, Rabin will be facing the first really serious test of his leadership. Political manipulating, which he has executed so successfully, will no longer do. Moreover, Rabin will have to be tactful, for the government coalition he has inherited has been largely responsible for the frenetic and romantic nationalism he will have to confront and discourage if he is to bring off future diplomatic accords. He cannot begin merely by cracking the heads of the Gush Emunim. Its intense young members are seen as zealous patriots, and they are after all fighting to save the homes of settlers who, at much personal cost, settled in occupied territory with the government's backing. Rabin's difficulty will be compounded further by the persistence of open Arab hostility, which has always led Israelis to make seductive conclusions about the saving value of military power.

But this is a test Rabin can simply no longer avoid. Events have made him Prime Minister, and events now require him to be a leader. He is clearly not, as Lova Eliav wittily says, a "sphinx with no secrets." But Rabin has been a highly timid politician with a constituency far too small to support the prospect of withdrawal he now seems to accept tacitly but cannot forthrightly defend. Unless he can quickly capitalize on the esteem with which he is for the moment regarded by a majority of Israelis* — i.e., unless he wins a mandate to pursue with Kissinger a policy of compromise on the occupied territories before the situation deteriorates on the Golan Heights — it is difficult to see how the new agreement can be a prelude to anything but more bitter tension and, ultimately, to conflagration.

---

*Polls *prior* to the settlement gave him a rating of between 53 and 60 percent.

# A New Israel

I

*Jerusalem and New York, June 1, 1977*
Political revolutions can be compared to kicking through rotting doors, and Israel's Labor Alignment provided just such a barrier to Likud's* stunning victory on May 17. It is now well known that the Labor Party was broadly perceived to be corrupt, suspected of hoarding illegal slush funds. Quite aside from Prime Minister Rabin's currency violation, the party was implicated in kickback schemes, and as a result some of its key officials— Asher Yadlin and Michael Tzur—were jailed. Avraham Ofer, the former Housing Minister and a leader of what is left of Mapai, committed suicide before he could be thoroughly investigated. Furthermore, Labor's campaign was uninspired—more or less a reflection of its remaining leadership—and pursued without genuine enthusiasm. The Friday before election day, the party took a full-page advertisement in *Ha'aretz* in which a number of prominent academics grudgingly and circuitously

---

*By Likud, I mean to denote also splinter factions aligned with Likud, most prominently Ariel Sharon's Shlomzion movement, which won two seats. In all, Likud's strength stands at forty-five members of the Knesset to the Alignment's thirty-two. Likud can also count on the parliamentary support of Moshe Dayan, who resigned from Labor but kept his seat when he was named foreign minister by Begin. Dayan's friend Gad Yaacobi may vote for Likud as well.

Likud will also get the vote of Flatto-Sharon, a big-time French swindler who figured that parliamentary immunity was the best way to beat extradition and admitted spending five million Israeli pounds to buy the required votes.

explained why voting for the Labor Alignment was the least depressing of available choices. Less highly educated people were apparently not impressed.

But the Alignment was perceived by many people as also compromised and corrupt by the way it distributed political favors and economic patronage, doing so with the arrogant confidence of a traditional aristocracy. When times were better, such highhandedness could be overlooked; but times are not good in Israel today. For the last three years inflation has been running at 40 to 50 percent. As a result, real wages have been falling sharply while labor unrest (including wildcat strikes) and white-collar crime have increased dramatically. Much of this inflation can be attributed to a rise in the world price of oil and food staples and, more significant, to Israel's huge defense budget, now making up about 40 percent of total expenditures and 35 percent of GNP. This, however, is by no means the whole story.

A good part of Israel's ruinous inflation derives from the economic policy blunders of Labor's former finance minister and political boss, the late Pinhas Sapir. From 1967 on, Sapir deliberately set out to industrialize and develop Israel's economy by subsidizing private investments, claiming that Israel must rationalize production by encouraging "market forces." At first this was intended to lure foreign Jewish investors—but Sapir also felt he had to attract capital with matching, low-interest government loans to assure a profitable return. He soon extended this practice to domestic investors. The policy rapidly degenerated into the "system"—ha'shitah—in which Sapir (acting in the name of a workers' state) had unprecedented economic power, bestowing bundles of money and wry Yiddish wit on the big-shot entrepreneurs of Tel Aviv, London, and New York and on the Histadrut enterprises as well.

Instead of creating a streamlined mixed economy, Sapir's "market" approach only created an oligarchy of people with connections in both the public and private sectors. It also generated sporadic growth and the obvious enrichment of Israel's bourgeoisie—all behind the mask of the traditional Labor "movement." Sapir, moreover, created a fiscal monster that became apparent after the 1973 war, which dampened Israel's post-

1970 boom. His resignation and subsequent death left the program in a shambles; without him there was nobody left to manage the flow of money from abroad and to coax investors into some of the government's economically important but less profitable projects (e.g., textile mills in the new "development towns").

Sapir's undistinguished heir, Yehoshua Rabinowitz (who was rewarded with the Finance Ministry after being defeated for re-election as mayor of Tel Aviv), did little to salvage the situation. The Israeli government is still stuck with outstanding low-interest loans amounting to billions of Israeli pounds, and today has to borrow at interest rates fully 25 percent higher than those at which it had been lending. Almost 26 percent of Israel's budget is now gobbled up by new subsidies for capital investment and by servicing the debts on old ones; literally, socialism for the rich. To make matters worse, state welfare programs have had to be cut correspondingly. They now account for only about 18 percent of the national budget.

Furthermore, Rabinowitz has failed to enforce the new tax regulations, which the Ben-Shachar Commission drew up over three years ago. Tax evasion is still a way of life among Israel's bourgeoisie. Conservative estimates have put the amount of un-reported or "black" money in Israel's economy at around fifteen billion Israeli pounds. This money is spent quickly, mainly on luxury housing or imported commodities, and traded on the black market for export to Switzerland. It is little wonder that merchants are accustomed to 50 percent profit margins on durable consumer goods.

The Labor Party has thus created a crippled, incompetent, highly inflationary capitalism, which is hardest on the workers and middle-class wage earners who are Labor's natural constituency outside the workers' agricultural settlements. But this kind of capitalism also offends the sensibilities of the same *nouveaux arrivés* who have benefited from it. The real source of the anomie that seized so many voters in the weeks before the election was in the feeling that the machinery of daily life was out of control and that the very survival of the country was at stake. Much of this feeling was sublimated into the language of pessimism about "Zionism" and national defense: "How can we survive the Arabs if American Jews won't want to live here?"

In part, then, the vote for the Likud, as well as for Yigael Yadin's Democratic Movement for Change (DMC), was a vote to turn the government over to men who want to see the ethics of a market society honestly declared and enforced. It reflects the view of a good part of Israel's upper middle class that the country has become a market society of profit-seeking enterprises and that it ought to be administered by those who recognize this fact and are not cynical about it. The vote promises the arrival in political power of Israel's corporate elite—men such as Mark Moshevitz, the past president of the Israeli Association of Manufacturers, Buma Shavit, the current president, both prominent in the Liberal Party wing of the Likud, and Step Wertheimer, the prominent industrialist who has associated himself with the DMC. It also invites some radical economic reforms congenial to them.

Not coincidentally, Likud's Finance Minister–designate, Simcha Ehrlich (a former leader of the Liberal Party—once the General Zionists), has already promised sweeping relaxations of government interventions in the economy. There will be, he says, an end to food subsidies; a reduction in government spending; an end to bonds linked to the cost of living, the favorite of workers' pension funds. Government lands will be sold off. There will be a greater "tolerance" for unemployment and compulsory arbitration of wage disputes in "essential" services. Ehrlich has also promised an amnesty for those who reveal their black money and pay a tax on it (I wonder if he thought of just changing the currency). The inflationary capital subsidies will be phased out except for housing. He has also announced that he would appoint Milton Friedman, the University of Chicago economist (and the author of *Capitalism and Freedom*), to the post of chief economic adviser. The latter has already speculated that the Histadrut and the state should be made to sell their corporations to private concerns (*Ha'aretz*, May 24), a policy that would fundamentally change Israel's political economy. Histadrut, the vast labor organization, for example, runs enterprises of all kinds throughout Israel.

Friedman's blind faith in the "hidden hand" of the market

may prove too dogmatic even for the Likud. Nevertheless, that Ehrlich's Draconian measures can be generally hailed as "progressive" suggests how completely Sapir and Rabinowitz have prostituted the Israeli economy in the name of social planning.

Had Labor failed only to manage the economy, that might have been enough to defeat it. Beyond this, as I have noted before, the Labor Alignment has been consumed by factional dissent and ideological atrophy for many years. Labor never really recovered from the Lavon affair (1960 to 1963), which split the party into two rival groups. On the one hand stood the so-called old guard of Mapai and Achdut Ha'avoda (Pinhas Sapir, Golda Meir, Avraham Ofer, and Yigal Allon). They tended to be dovish on foreign policy, concerned to maintain the Histadrut as the manager of many welfare programs, and careless in using socialist rhetoric as a cover to protect their entrenched privileges.

The other faction, the young technocrats of Rafi who followed Ben-Gurion out of Mapai (Shimon Peres, Moshe Dayan, Gad Yaacobi), wanted the state bureaucracy, rather than Histadrut, to run welfare programs and cultural affairs (*mamlachtiyut*). They favored the army rather than the Labor movement as the chief vehicle of social integration; in their view, the immigrants from North Africa would most successfully absorb Israeli ways in military service. They were also inclined to disengage the state from direct economic activity. And since Ben-Gurion recruited them mainly from the army, they tended to be hawkish in foreign policy, supporting a policy of heavy retaliation against the bases of Arab infiltration before the 1967 war, and resisting the principle of territorial compromise on the West Bank thereafter.

This conflict was never fundamentally resolved. The apparent unity of the Labor Party, reconstituted in 1968 during the upbeat months following the Six-Day War, was merely a facade that crumbled after 1973. These strains also exacerbated personal rivalries, as evidenced in recent months by the steady subversion and near defeat of Yitzchak Rabin by his Defense Minister, Shimon Peres. Such spectacles caused many Israelis to hunger for strong leadership. Peres (and Rafi) finally — and, it now appears, temporarily*—won control. But it was an empty victory; by then, many had had enough of the Labor Party itself.

More important, this squabbling prevented Labor from taking an articulate and decisive stand on the status of the occupied territory. Especially after Prime Minister Levi Eshkol died in 1969, Labor's moderates were helpless to force the withdrawal of the illegal squatters' settlements on the West Bank erected by right-wing and religious groups under the leadership of Rabbi Levinger. The first of these settlements was Qiryat Arba, founded on the outskirts of Hebron in 1968. Such settlements achieved precisely what their founders intended: they became the "facts" that have changed the priorities and compromised the flexibility of Israeli diplomacy. But they also became the tangible vindication of a new "Zionist" vocabulary and "pioneering" élan—strident, mystical, atavistic—with which a new generation of Israelis has been growing up and which find their purest expression in the intensely chauvinistic movement called Gush Emunim.

During this election young voters from all backgrounds turned to the Likud and to the National Religious Party (NRP) in overwhelming numbers. These parties consistently promoted a rhetoric that frankly justified the West Bank settlements, while the government was often equivocal about them in principle and helpful to them in practice. Unfortunately for Labor, young Israelis—especially those in the army—tended to vote this time to get their parents to live up to what they perceived are the latter's ideological pretensions. The Labor Party's moderates, who believed in a more open policy toward the occupied territories, were cowed for six crucial years by Golda Meir's punitive discipline. They were thus as responsible as Begin and Gush Emunim for a political language that takes the annexation of the West Bank virtually for granted. Rabin's lack of ideological initiative on these questions, by the way, also made his own government's more moderate actions appear cowardly, especially

---

*Peres's hold on the party is by no means secure. Rabin has already come out of his self-imposed exile and announced that he will resume the prime ministership until a new government can be sworn in. Clearly, he is ready for another duel with Peres.

when later endorsed by Shimon Peres, who, as Begin delighted in reminding everyone, was himself a leading advocate of annexation before assuming control of his divided party.

Labor has made itself anathema or superfluous to so many sectors of Israeli society that its chances for recovery would be bleak under the best of circumstances. But because of Israel's proportional representational system—likely to be retained unless the DMC is seduced into Likud's government with the promise of electoral reform—none of Labor's current and much-disliked leadership has been turned out of the Knesset. Its disingenuous talk after the elections about "revitalizing" the Labor movement convinces nobody. Indeed, the Israeli labor movement—which formerly organized industries, welfare services, and trade unions under the umbrella of a party that traditionally controlled the state—has been strained by inherent conflicts of interest (e.g., between managers and workers) and has become something of an anachronism in modern Israel. It would have difficulty in reorganizing even if it were presided over by Berl Katznelson, the austere founder of the Histadrut in the 1920s, and not by the spoiled politicians who now seem anxious to scramble for the remaining crumbs.

Nor does Labor have many bright faces coming up through the ranks. Younger leaders such as Yossi Sarid, Micah Harish, and Uzi Baram are shrewd men, but they have no national stature, and they could be equally at home in Yadin's DMC; they may be inclined to join Yadin, especially if he remains in the opposition. Some leftist academics who would want to agitate within the Labor Party for a Western European social democratic approach—Shlomo Avineri and Yeri Yovel—offer some hope; but, like most Israeli intellectuals, they have so far not been persistent or bold enough to struggle openly for political power.

Labor's leadership is thus a dwindling political force. It is now staking everything on a good showing in the coming Histadrut elections scheduled for June 21. But Labor's candidate for secretary-general, Yerucham Meshel, has already angered the workers with his indifferent attitude to their wage claims while he and his cronies were in power. More activist and popular Labor leaders such as Yitzchak Ben-Aharon were pushed out of power by Golda Meir after the 1973 war for opposing her foreign

policy. So even if his (i.e., Labor's) list in the Histadrut is re-
elected, Meshel will not be able to lead a cohesive, disciplined
work force in defiance of Likud policies. On the contrary, Labor
has thrown away this kind of working-class loyalty.

II

Yet it would be wrong to surmise from these observations that
Labor's defeat was merely the result of a fickle protest vote. One
should not underestimate the force of the kick that finally broke
down the door. Anyone in fundamental agreement with Labor
on diplomatic, social, and "Zionist" issues, but desiring a change
in economic and moral leadership, had an attractive alternative
in Yadin's DMC. But Yadin's party won only fifteen seats. Its
vote, moreover, came mainly from affluent Ashkenazi suburbs,
from the moshavim (the prosperous cooperatives), and from a
part of the intelligentsia. While Yadin split the Labor vote, the
two parties still make up only a parliamentary minority. Likud,
on the other hand, won by itself a solid forty-five seats, and it
has also put together an impressive political coalition which, if
present demographic trends persist, is likely to endure and even
expand considerably.

I have already mentioned the war-hardened and ideologically
strident young people who have swung their influence to the
Likud. We should also remember that three times the number
of Israeli-born voters participated in this election than did so in
1973. Moreover, Israel's bourgeoisie of corporate executives,
bankers, entrepreneurs, and the much larger constituency of
merchants and petit-bourgeois tradesmen who want to emulate
their success are steadfastly behind the old Liberal Party wing
of the Likud. This constituency, like that of the young people,
is likely to grow in the future, particularly within the market
climate created by a Likud government. Its members are also
likely to go along, at least in principle, with Begin's desire to
keep the West Bank under Israeli control. Many of the least
desirable construction and industrial jobs within Israel—jobs
for some 100,000 workers—are now filled by Arabs from this

territory and from Gaza. It would be extremely difficult to replace them with Israelis.

Labor has lost the prestige of incumbency. It has already lost to the Likud the support of Israel's two largest dailies, *Ma'ariv* and *Yediot Acharonot*. Likud can now assume the glamorous trappings of government while continuing to ascribe its problems to Labor's legacy.

A fourth pillar of the Likud are the followers of the old Herut Party, who have stubbornly viewed Begin and his Irgun underground as the crucial instrument of British defeat in Palestine and consequently of the securing of the state. Ultranationalist in the tradition of Jabotinsky, closely knit by common political, recreational, and youth organizations and by their own competing version of Zionist history—especially regarding the alleged indifference of Labor Zionism to the fate of European Jews before the Holocaust—Herut will remain a hard core (fifteen seats) of Likud's support. Moreover, Herut's followers regard Likud's victory as the consummation of a forty-year struggle. Some of Herut's older leaders, such as Shmuel Katz and Geula Cohen, can be counted on to proselytize among the very young with zeal and with the weight of the state apparatus behind them.

But aside from Herut, the young, and the bourgeoisie, the key to Likud's victory, and its future, is the so-called second Israel (*Yisrael Ha'shniyah*): those Sephardic Jewish refugees from Arab countries who have never really been absorbed into Labor's scheme of things. The citizens of the second Israel are fiercely resentful of the Labor movement for having turned the whole country into what they perceive as a European closed shop. Three years ago I noted that we can understand nothing about Israeli politics unless we appreciate how widely Labor has been seen as the party of privilege and cultural snobbery, especially among residents of and escapees from the poorer Sephardic neighborhoods. The latter probably accounted for about twenty Likud seats. If political analysts like Dan Horowitz of Hebrew University are correct, their vote will be even more significant next time. Sephardic Jews accounted for only 43 percent of voters in this election. Next time they will likely constitute a majority.

Members of the second Israel have adopted the Likud as their instrument for achieving a national identity, and they are beginning to know their own strength. They admire Begin and his likely successor,* Ezer Weizman, the former air force chief now expected to be Minister of Defense, mainly because they and the Likud have made all the right enemies.

Most members of the second Israel fled Islamic states in several waves between 1948 and 1957. Primarily in the later years, they came from Morocco and Algeria, where they had been, for the most part, small merchants, traders, hustlers, who tried to survive the urban jungles of such cities as Casablanca and Algiers. Most came to Israel with little education; the more educated or prosperous either stayed put or wound up in Paris or Montreal or New York. Moreover, they arrived as intransigent individualists, convinced of the values of the market, family centered, and suspicious of Labor Zionism's collectivist social theories.

They were also wholly unaccustomed to democratic politics, a weakness that Labor *apparatchiks* quickly exploited in ways that would have made Richard Daley blush.† These immigrants were even more estranged from the Zionist vision that understood Jewish nationalism and territorialism as methods to create a modern Jewish secular state, one combining cooperative ethics with an openness to European culture. They were certainly apathetic to Zionist principles, which derived from resisting European persecution. Rather, they arrived in Israel with a deep hatred for Arabs, which better reflected their own collective tragedy.

Coming from premodern Arab societies, these Sephardic immigrants tended to see Jewish life as based on religious unity. Although most of their Israeli-born children quickly shook off a rigorous devotion to the liturgy and the Laws, they nevertheless persisted in seeing Jewish life according to messianic religious categories. This tendency was abetted by the heroic rhetoric of Ben-Gurion and his young protégés — Yadin and Dayan — who,

---

*Succession, of course, is no minor issue for the Likud in view of Begin's poor health. However, Weizman has proven his political acumen and personal popularity by orchestrating Likud's victory while Begin was in a hospital.

†The managers of Flatto-Sharon's obnoxious campaign, in which he paid organizers large sums to deliver votes, insisted that they did nothing that Mapai did not do for years.

from the 1950s on, devoted much energy to a cult of the state. (Yadin's Masada excavations, which recovered so graphically the images of the ancient Jewish commonwealth, were this cult's most striking fixtures.)

The second Israel needed little prodding to develop resentment for Labor Zionism's administrative practices. Their daily life required an endless round of encounters with the well-connected bureaucrats of the Histadrut and the state, whom they saw as condescending Europeans; the latter channeled them into relatively low-paying jobs and ersatz neighborhoods on the fringes of Tel Aviv and Jerusalem and into development towns like Dimona and Yokneam. They were, moreover, made to feel inferior within Israel's revolutionary Hebrew culture, lacking in the ideological sophistication and moral charm of the socialist pioneers. They particularly resented the kibbutzim, into which they were unable to integrate and which, after several years of bitter friction, began to employ them as wage laborers in violation of their own historic principles.

During the sixties and seventies, most of the second Israel gravitated to Israel's larger cities,* becoming the *sans-culottes* of Israel's increasingly capitalist and industrial economy. Excluded from the often large grants of foreign currency which thousands of European refugees secured in the program of German reparations, and without the training or social pedigree needed to rise in the social scale, the most fortunate turned to small enterprises, low bureaucratic jobs. Culturally they turned back on themselves, became introverted. Most became part of an anti-socialist (i.e., anti-establishment) proletariat, raising their children in conditions of poverty and turning to political leaders like Menachem Begin, whose rightist diatribes seemed persuasive. They were joined in this election by a good many of the recent immigrants from the USSR.

*

---

*There were some notable exceptions. Lova Eliav, former secretary of the Labor Party, arranged for thousands of Sephardic immigrants to settle on moshavim in the Lachish region of the northern Negev. Eliav, by the way, who abandoned Labor in 1975, led a socialist and dovish slate (Sheli) in this election but secured barely two seats.

Begin, of course, is a descendant of Zionist Revisionism, not of the second Israel; but under his leadership the Likud and its precursors effectively, some might say demogogically, built on the pent-up contempt of the new immigrants for Israel's traditional elites. The Likud, therefore, is now regarded by the second Israel as its own vehicle for social leveling and, more important, social respectability. Likud's economic policies can be expected to do little for their economic distress. But it would be a mistake to suppose that they will quickly abandon this party as a result. When bread runs short, there are always circuses.

The final element of Likud's coalition is the National Religious Party (twelve seats), now taken over by its own fanatical young guard, led by Zevulun Hammer. The NRP has in fact become the Likud's ideological mentor, supplying the promises for Herut's promised land rhetoric. The party also provides a home for the principal leaders of Gush Emunim, who now feel that they will have a free hand to settle the West Bank. Begin recklessly promised them this much the day after his party's election.

More immediately ominous for Israeli secularists is the likely appointment of Zevulun Hammer to the Education Ministry. Begin has indicated that he would give Hammer the authority to upgrade the status of religious education in the schools. It also seems likely that Likud will permit the NRP-controlled Interior Ministry to define as Jewish only those converts who have been put through the Orthodox rabbinical mill. (Remember the debate over "Who is a Jew?") Achad Ha'am, the ideologue of secular "cultural" Zionism, must be turning in his grave; Reform and Conservative Jewish leaders in America must be equally dizzy.

In order to broaden this religious base (and thus earn a simple majority of Knesset seats), Likud even seems willing to bring in the ultra-orthodox Agudat Yisrael Party. The latter represents the intensely pious Jews of the Meah Sha'arim quarter of Jerusalem, of the town of Safed, and of other picturesque throwbacks to pre-Enlightenment Judaism. In addition to its fundamentalist demands regarding the legal definition of Jew, Agudah seems likely to demand tighter laws against work on the Sabbath, autopsy, abortion, and Christian proselytes. One can imagine what they intend to do with even mildly erotic films.

III

Still, it is the question of war and peace that is on the mind of
anyone trying to assess the significance of Likud's victory. After
more than six months of preparatory talks, the Carter administration appears to have had a severe blow dealt to its Middle
East plans, which generally followed the scheme of the Brookings
Institution. The key elements of Carter's package were to emerge
during staged negotiations leading to the Arab recognition of
Israel. They were to include an agenda that would specify the
consequences of a peace (diplomatic exchanges, commercial freedom, etc.) and would assume, in principle, Israel's agreement to
withdraw from virtually all the territories occupied since 1967.

It is most unlikely that this plan would be acceptable to Menachem Begin. He is entirely committed to keeping the whole of
ancient Eretz Yisrael under Israeli rule. He will probably not
annex the West Bank outright, although he has Likud's sanction
to do so; why risk adding 700,000 more Arabs to Israel's voting population? But Begin has already given encouragement to
widespread Jewish settlement of the West Bank and may be
tempted to extend Israeli law to the territories that, for the most
part, are still governed according to Jordanian laws.

These developments are every bit as frightening as they appear. However, they do not necessarily promise war in the immediate future. Egypt, still the most important military power
in the Arab world, has not yet absorbed its newly acquired French
and British weapons into its military forces. Moreover, the Egyptian government would probably not now wish to disrupt its
Canal Zone reconstruction plans. The cities along the Canal represent Egypt's best, perhaps only, hope to resettle the estimated
thirty million Egyptians who will likely be born in the next two
decades. Should these masses remain in the Nile Valley — laying
concrete over rapidly diminishing farmland — Egypt, as demographic experts predict, risks an unspeakable human tragedy.
Sadat's regime is well aware of such disastrous possibilities.

Nor do the Saudis, the currently unchallenged diplomatic and
economic Arab power brokers, appear to want renewed fighting.
They know Israel's army has never been stronger. To challenge
it would only invite the re-emergence of radical, pro-Soviet sentiments in Syria and other Arab countries near Saudi Arabia's

borders, and strain their own close relations with the United States. Rather, they seem eager for a Pax Americana and seem reconciled to Israel's presence in the Middle East as the price they must pay.

Even the Syrians have recently seemed willing to go along with some American initiative. Soviet experts, according to one unconfirmed report, have warned Assad not to attempt large-scale actions against Israel.* And Carter's meeting with the Syrian President a few days before Israel's election produced at least some equivocation on Assad's part regarding the PLO's maximum demands. Indeed, Syria has now consolidated its hold on northern Lebanon and will not wish to give the PLO a chance to rekindle its independent ambitions so soon after the Syrian army had itself doused them. It is true that nearly all Arab states are now talking of war, but this kind of talk is cheap in the Middle East. The region, after all, is at war. Still, one should not minimize the dangers; it will take a high degree of Soviet-American cooperation to prevent fighting from breaking out as the military buildup continues on all sides.

The more immediate problem for Israel will be the West Bank itself. Militarily and diplomatically, the new Israeli government faces great danger if it tries to go ahead with Begin's dreams of unleashing Gush Emunim settlers there. The apparent quiet in the territory is deceiving. West Bankers are strongly opposed to the occupation; they voted overwhelmingly in last year's municipal elections for candidates who defiantly claimed they were pro-PLO. They will remain pliable so long as peace talks appear imminent; there is cause to dread their reactions should a Likud government frustrate these talks or step up Jewish settlement near their cities.

Nor has the Israeli occupation been as benevolent as American Jews have been told. Informed sources in Israel told me that about 60 percent of West Bank and Gaza males between the ages of eighteen and fifty have had to be detained at least one night in jail during the last ten years. And these arrests took place during a time of relative political calm. In addition, Arab resi-

*Foreign Report*; published by the Economist Newspaper Limited (London, No. 1485, April 27, 1977).

dents of the territories have already proven that they are capable of bombing Jewish areas, or of strikes and student riots that the Israeli army has quelled with the kind of brutality that stiffens Arab resistance.*

Such actions by the army, it should be noted, also erode support for Israel among American and Western European opinion makers. Likud's policy could therefore become a pretext for attempts to expel Israel from the UN and would cause serious embarrassment among Israel's remaining friends.

The picture is not unrelievedly gloomy. Although Begin himself should not be expected to "grow in office"—the man has been single-minded for forty years—a Likud government will be only slightly more united on these diplomatic strategies than was the Labor Alignment. The Liberal faction—Arye Dulzin, Simcha Ehrlich, Elimelech Rimalt, and others—are not so much opposed to West Bank annexation as they are anxious to remain on firm ground with the American government. Under pressure from Carter—and he is already exerting it—the Liberals are unlikely to allow Begin to squander American military and, more urgent, economic support. This is why they have been opposing Begin's attempts to name Moshe Dayan to the Foreign Ministry—an appointment that could keep Yadin's DMC from joining the government. The Liberals, understandably, are eager to add more moderate forces to Begin's coalition.

But if Dayan does become foreign minister—the Liberals probably do not have the power to thwart Begin short of dissolving the Likud even before the party assumes control of the government—the former Labor hawk may also try to blunt Begin's annexationist demands. While on his shuttles, Kissinger used to remark that Dayan was Israel's most realistic negotiator regarding American interests in the region. Dayan was also the author of the "open-bridges" policy, which transformed the West Bank into a kind of Israeli-Jordanian condominium. He stated

---

*Although not directly connected to West Bank resistance, Israeli Arabs are also growing more militant. They voted decisively for a combined slate of Arab nationalists and Israeli communists (Rakah) this time, increasing their Knesset representation from four to five.

flatly in a television interview that he would oppose annexation so long as American peace initiatives had some prospect of succeeding.

But Dayan remains a mysterious figure, curiously timid and fatalistic at the same time. Since 1973, he has been inclined toward moodily supporting the zealots of Gush Emunim. He has also been deeply offended by the widespread allegations that he was most responsible for Israel's lack of vigilance before the war. It is difficult to gauge how he will respond to the strains of peacemaking. Even under Golda Meir, Dayan often seemed eager to avoid political conflicts in favor of going on some archaeological dig.

Begin may also find it difficult to impose his will on his own general staff. Although we should welcome such resistance with caution — Israeli democracy is fragile enough — it is important to remember that most of the really important posts in the army are now held by men congenial to Labor. Many come from kibbutzim. Quite apart from the fact that they have been brought up to think of Begin as a scoundrel, they will not relish turning the army into an occupation police. Nor will many thousands of reservists welcome service as the instruments of law and order in Nablus or Jenin. The same holds true for much of Israel's government bureaucracy. Since almost all junior and intermediate civil service appointments for the last thirty years are people who were acceptable to Labor, Begin and his ministers may find some of their more strident policies surreptitiously sabotaged.

Some will also find consolation in the state of Menachem Begin's health. He will not, I think, forgo the Prime Minister's office if he can avoid doing so, but it is by no means certain that he will be able to carry out his duties very long. Ezer Weizman, who I already suggested is Begin's likely successor, seems now to have acquired some of the political maturity of his uncle, Chaim Weizmann, who towered over the Zionist movement during the 1920s and 1930s. Despite his daredevil past,* he can certainly be

---

*As a flyer, Weizman is reported to have bet a friend that he could fly a Piper between the towers of the Haifa oil refineries. He apparently made it. As Minister of Transport in the National Unity coalition under Golda Meir, Weizman is said to have shot out the tires of a speeding driver who had gone through a red light.

counted on to deal more pragmatically with the Americans than would Begin.

The most optimistic prospect just after the election was that Yadin's DMC would eventually agree to join the Likud's new government. The DMC has set rigid terms regarding electoral reform — perhaps too stringent for the Likud. Moreover, if Dayan's appointment is finally confirmed over the Liberals' objections, it seems most unlikely that Yadin could be offered a post satisfactory to him. Nevertheless, should his party work out a formula for joining the government, Yadin and other DMC ministers such as Amnon Rubinstein or Meir Amit would be strong voices against annexationist policies. Yadin has insisted that West Bank settlements can be justified only for security reasons — he seems drawn to the Allon plan for defensive paramilitary settlements on the Jordan River. Together with the Liberals and the Aguda (whose rabbis prefer to leave the uniting of Eretz Yisrael to the Messiah), the DMC could help to tame the more strident wing of the Likud and NRP.

Ironically, even a Likud government constituted without the DMC might conceivably be more successful than Rabin in holding the line on settlements and working seriously for peace through an American initiative. Likud's hawkish ministers will be more trusted by their nervous followers to recognize an American ultimatum when they see one. However, without the DMC, far fewer voices in Begin's cabinet will be insisting on territorial compromise.

Likud will not be defying the Israeli public if it chooses a more moderate course. Polls show time after time that only 30 percent of Israelis want to annex the West Bank as a matter of principle; some two thirds are willing to give up territory as part of a negotiated peace settlement — if they can be reassured that the settlement will not become a Trojan horse. Similar polls reveal that even more Israelis — 75 to 80 percent — have faith in American designs and goodwill.* They have been bewildered and badly led by former governments, but they are not warmongers.

---

*These are the findings of Israel's respected Institute for Applied Social Research. The head of the institute, Professor Louis Guttman, summarized them to me in an interview.

In voting for the Likud, Israelis have changed their political direction on many fundamental issues of Israeli life: a quite different Israel has pushed through the accumulated layers of the old Labor Zionist establishment, and neither Israel nor "Zionism" can be the same. Should Begin survive to attempt his annexationist crusades, however, Israelis may find that, by voting him in, they have embarked on a course even more perilous than they had imagined.

# Israeli Nerves After
# Camp David

*Jerusalem, November 15, 1978*
Israeli Jews assume diplomacy to be less the art of the possible than the ritual forestalling of disaster. This is, I suppose, a subtle distinction. Still, it helps to account for Israelis' earnest celebration of the Camp David agreement despite their skeptical attitude toward its provisions.

Consider the polls. Almost four fifths of Israelis polled in September endorsed the two framework documents, and an even larger number approved the performance of the political leadership that engineered the compromise. Ninety-two percent approved the comportment of Defense Minister Weizman, who is most identified with the American-backed land-for-peace strategy in the Sinai.

Such endorsements should, however, not be construed as support only for the obviously seductive peace with Egypt: Camp David's autonomy plan for the Palestinians (i.e., the recognition of their "legitimate rights," the termination of the military government and corresponding dependence on Jordanian police to keep the peace on the West Bank, the contraction of the IDF to 6,000 troops in specified enclaves, the plan's "transitional character," the seeming discouragement of new Jewish settlements) was contrived to accommodate the goals of the Brookings report, not Likud's platform, and most Israelis seem to know it. In fact, over 50 percent expect that the plan will lead to an independent Palestinian state in spite of Begin's assurances to the contrary.

They have learned (what better teacher could they have had than Begin himself?) that they cannot, and should not, defy American interests in Egypt and the Gulf, nor foil American designs on Syria. Nor do they now doubt—particularly after Undersecretary Saunders's explicit clarifications for Hussein and some Palestinians—that the Carter administration views an effectively instituted autonomy plan as the hinge on its own long-term policy in the area. So Israelis cannot but consider Camp David to be a comprehensive diplomatic agenda that might eventually establish Israel's status in the Middle East and in global affairs.

Yet it is precisely when Israelis are pressed to speculate on developments entailed by their own broader views that they are most troubled. Over 60 percent expressed doubt that a comprehensive peace would finally be concluded. Tens of thousands demonstrated their apprehensions still more graphically by jamming the beaches of Sinai over the Succot holidays, as if to prepare for another prolonged struggle with claustrophobia. Even the promise of peace with Egypt—Israelis have compulsively recited the good arguments for it to themselves since the first disengagement agreement in 1974—seems no less fragile and fantastic today, for all of Sadat's reassuring consistency and Begin's reassuring inconsistency. These common suspicions are not groundless. Israel's signing of a peace treaty with Egypt will do little more than consolidate and extend the reciprocal interests that had evolved since Kissinger's shuttles (Israeli intelligence, remember, has served more than once both Egypt and the Saudi royal family against the conspiracies of Soviet clients, e.g., Libya). These reciprocal interests of Israel and Egypt are complemented by extensive political and journalistic contact between citizens of the two countries since President Sadat's visit to Jerusalem. Such a peace treaty is not a small achievement. But progress toward full normal relations, Israelis instinctively know, will continue to be impeded by the Palestinian issue, about which Begin and Sadat remain ideologically incompatible and to which each leader seems more vulnerable at home.

Begin will not want to negotiate away Jewish claims, however tendentious, to the West Bank and Gaza. He has been promoting Camp David among his hard-line allies in Israel as a separate peace, which will permit him to avoid doing so. He has not prepared the Israeli public for further concessions. Sadat can, in practice, remain aloof from Palestinian demands for an independent state, but he cannot repudiate such demands nor be openly reconciled to an Israel that does. He has, with Carter's encouragement, been promoting Camp David as the foundation of a comprehensive peace: both leaders are eager to entice Hussein and West Bank Palestinians to participate in the autonomy plan and thus ensure that this plan will yield the alternative Palestinian leadership it was conceived to evolve; both are eager to secure Saudi patience. Sadat is also expecting American pressure on Israel to continue to serve as the operative link between the Israeli-Egyptian peace and Palestinian autonomy and to prevent any further Jewish encroachments on Arab areas of historic Palestine. The framework agreements thus provide the makings of an intense test of strength between the Israeli Prime Minister and American leaders with, Israelis readily understand, the issue of Jewish settlements in "Judea and Samaria" dominating and subverting bilateral relations between Israel and Egypt.

Begin would have the support of his current coalition to reject any suspension of settlement activity; otherwise he will face a crisis within the coalition. He had to order the "thickening" of existing settlements during the negotiations with Egypt in order to preempt the impending revolt of seven Herut and National Religious Party ministers. Begin could probably overcome such future difficulties by calling an election soon after the pact with Egypt is signed. His support from the majority of the Likud — i.e., from the more sycophantic members of Herut, the dovish Liberal faction, etc. — is firm, and he could increase his hold on the growing Israeli center by digesting Yigael Yadin's weakened "Democratic Movement" and purging the Likud of frenetic and chauvinist hawks such as Geula Cohen and Moshe Shamir. There is little doubt that Begin would win a substantial parliamentary majority were he to adopt this strategy and, along with Dayan and Weizman, commit the country to the peace process he helped to initiate. He would not get much of a fight from the Labor Party, which is still hopelessly divided under the unlikely leadership of Shimon Peres, Dayan's old political fixer.

Besides, Labor never delivered a peace treaty during the "ancien régime" and it is not clear that moderates within the party would ever have been able to do so if Begin remained in command of the opposition. Even now, Labor-affiliated agrarian movements are agitating for the protection of their settlements in north Sinai, the Golan, and the West Bank.

But Begin's unprecedented political independence may be beside the point: his potentially decisive contribution to peace may be confounded, not by the opposition of others, but by his own conscience. He is a man whose pragmatic conclusions with regard to the north Sinai settlements, Palestinian rights, etc., are still inconsistent with his transcendental premises. The Nobel-anointed prestige of the peacemaker, in which he seems to genuinely delight, may not finally attract him as much as the birthright—which, he thinks, the Americans would induce him to sell for a mess of pottage.

These problems considered—and Israelis consider them—it is still an open question whether Palestinian autonomy can be put into practice at all or whether Israeli-Egyptian peace can thrive in its absence. Palestinian leaders in the West Bank and Gaza (Kawasmeh, a-Shawa, and even pro-Jordanians such as Freij) have already declared that they will not participate unless they receive assurances in advance that autonomy will ultimately produce a Palestinian state. Begin may never agree to such a prospect, but he will certainly not do so now, that is, while the PLO, to which virtually all West Bank leaders defer, refuses to renounce terror against Israeli civilians, let alone accept the terms of the Camp David agenda. One may argue that West Bank leaders are impeachably shortsighted. Were they to accept autonomy, they would quickly preside over a political faction greater than any combination of Jewish settlements and would be in an excellent position to press for full independence, achieve international recognition, and, given a manifest demonstration of peaceful intentions toward Israel and Jordan, earn the goodwill of the Carter administration. They might, like Sadat, even earn the goodwill of the Israeli public. One might also argue that Begin and Dayan encourage Palestinian rejectionism—perhaps deliberately—by dismissing even the principle of Palestinian self-determination and promising new West Bank settlements to boot. That such displays of bad faith are equivalent is of little consolation to those in Israel for whom peace has become a tangible hope and Camp David, they fear, an elaborate trap.

Israelis do not fear renewed Egyptian involvement in a pan-Arab, pro-Palestinian Jihad. But this was not their fear before Camp David in light of Egypt's permanent interests. Israelis are concerned, rather, that they have exchanged "no war" for a peace that can be reversed, particularly if the apparent rapprochement between Syria and Iraq leads to renewed fighting on the Golan and in Lebanon.

After all, an Egyptian embassy in Jerusalem may be instructed to galvanize the Palestinians and to transmit ultimatums. And this is an expensive, reversible peace. The strategic concessions that Israel made at Camp David were insignificant: settlements are worthless in the face of modern weaponry, and a demilitarized Sinai is as good as one controlled by the Israeli army, maybe better. But the down payment on peace that was extracted from Israel at the summit—i.e., the net cost of rebuilding the army and air bases in the Negev, the loss of Sinai oil revenues, the compensation to settler families, etc.—constitutes a huge projected drain on Israel's budget (more than $4 billion). Such expenditures hit hardest the already hard-pressed, inflation-cursed wage earners, who seem to be the only ones paying taxes nowadays. These are expenditures that would seem justified only if they were a prelude to the opening of the Egyptian market to Israeli manufactured goods, professional services, and technology and if defense costs could be substantially reduced. This is just what Camp David seems *not* to promise. The Palestinian issue appears to keep the whole deal in jeopardy while Israel's economic hardships, and nerve-racking dependence on American aid, continue to grow.

Nevertheless, I think there is a danger of underestimating the progress that was made at Camp David on this most abrasive question, particularly if we ignore the summit's less perceptible but substantial effect on each side's political discourse. Prior to the accords, there existed no definite political program to which moderate Palestinians—i.e., those angling for a Palestinian state at peace alongside Israel—could honorably subscribe without laying themselves open to charges of defeatism and treachery. This is no longer the case: the letter of the framework agreement provides for the creation of an evolving Palestinian self-determination, which even those close to the PLO may help to fashion.

Correspondingly, Israeli moderates—and, it turns out, there are many when events engender optimism—are now in a position to argue for the preservation of an established peace, for which the terms were negotiated by muscular nationalists. The moderates no longer need hesitate to attack the "realistic" image of monolithic Arab enmity and perpetual war.

More to the point—and this may be Camp David's most significant result—the special annexationist logic of Gush Emunim and the Land of Israel movement (settlements equal land equals security equals Zionism equals Redemption) has been ruptured by a stroke of Begin's pen. No doubt, intense resistance to further withdrawals of settlements or to the suspension of plans for new ones will persist: the West Bank elicits much more passion than the Sinai, not only from scripture hawks, but also from the more reactionary wings of the old labor movement (Tnuat Hamoshavim, Kibbutz Hameuchad, etc.). These people view the prospect of retarded settlement as further evidence of their having been swamped by the urban, bourgeois, and largely Sephardic "other Israel" that swept the Likud into power in the last election, and who are further demoralized by the collapse of their own self-congratulatory equation of national security with collective pioneering in the West Bank and the Golan.

Nevertheless, the animus driving annexationist sentiment has been quelled. Israelis have shown that they can be pushed in for a penny and they will be pushed in also for a pound. Such, at least, is the hope of the urbane and cerebral young officers of Peace Now, who are broadly seen to have been vindicated by the actions of Israeli leaders at Camp David and who now personify the "national consensus" in Israeli editorials more readily than the messianic settlers of Gush Emunim.

Golda Meir, who greeted the news from Camp David with thoughtless indignation, complained that she could have made "a peace like that" long ago. Not the least important consequence of the summit is that most Israelis are asking themselves why she did not. These accords have produced, not a revolution in

Israel, but something like a gestalt switch: Judea and Samaria, Begin's disclaimers notwithstanding, have again become the West Bank, the Arabs of Eretz Yisrael have become Palestinians, and the oil-thirsty gentiles in Washington have become the pillars of the Free World. It remains to be seen if responsible Palestinian leaders have the courage and guile to reinforce such images before they are blown apart by some terrorist's bomb.

# Begin vs. Begin

I

When President Sadat came to Jerusalem in November 1977, he stole the initiative from Arab "rejectionists"—not only Syria, Iraq, Libya, but all the important factions of the PLO. Among these are Yasir Arafat's Fatah, the Syrian-backed Saika, the Iraqi-backed ALF, Naif Hawatmeh's PDFLP, and George Habash's PFLP. What seems forgotten now is how bitterly most of these countries and factions were feuding with one another then. The Syrian and Iraqi Ba'athists were competing to dominate the region north of the Persian Gulf. Fatah and Syria (and Saika) were at odds over President Assad's strong-armed intervention in Lebanon, particularly the Syrian army's acquiescence in the murderous crushing of Fatah by Maronite forces at the Tel-a-Zaatar refugee camp in early 1977. Fatah was also feuding both with the Libyan-financed PFLP over Arafat's apparent readiness to negotiate with the United States and with the Iraqi ALF, which had long resented Arafat's prior involvements with the Syrians. The Syrians had, after all, accepted UN Resolution 242 and had negotiated a disengagement agreement with Israel; like Fatah, they were eager to go to Geneva.

Surrounded by such ideological antagonism and ambition, Arafat's position was diminished. His only patron was King Khalid of Saudi Arabia, who cautiously preferred Fatah's "non-Marxist," pan-Islamic line to that of the "radicals" and was hedging against Syria's growing power. After he went to Israel, however,

Sadat soon had the tacit support both of Khalid (whom the Egyptian army implicitly protected) and also of Hussein. His initiative seemed superbly pragmatic. It offered a chance to secure the return of Arab lands captured in 1967, to pressure the Americans into forcing Israel to change its position on Jerusalem and the Palestinian question—and to do so without a risky Geneva conference and without giving the Soviets a part in the negotiations. Hussein in 1977 still had substantial allies in the West Bank and Gaza—the mayors of Bethlehem and Gaza, Freij and a-Shawa, the former mayor of Hebron, Ja'abri, the Ramallah lawyer Aziz Shekhadeh, and Anwar Nusseibeh, Hussein's former Minister of Defense, among many others. He was still anxious to rule the mosques of Jerusalem, still seemed open to some kind of deal.

Sadat, in short, could not have chosen a better time to break the old taboos and change the rules. The Palestinian Arabs in the West Bank and Gaza were, then as now, mainly supporters of the PLO—the only visible symbol of Palestinian self-determination—but this was vague support since the PLO's leadership was obviously disorganized and exhausted. Sadat (and, it was assumed, Hussein) seemed to promise a more plausible first step to political independence from Israel. The Palestinians could not be immune to the huge popular success of Sadat's trip in Jerusalem and Cairo. A delegation, mainly from Gaza, went to Cairo to greet the "hero of peace" three weeks later. That peace seemed a real alternative to the occupation was dramatized by the way Arafat sat shocked and helpless in the Egyptian parliament as Sadat announced his determination to address the Knesset.*

Had the Israeli and Egyptian governments worked out some peace settlement soon after Sadat's visit to Jerusalem, the PLO leaders, like the rest of the Arab world, would have had to continue to respond to events that outflanked their policies and exacerbated their old divisions. And the settlement would have been reinforced by the enthusiasm of tens of millions of Egyp-

---

*Eric Rouleau recalls in *Le Monde*, March 27, 1979, how close Sadat had come to eclipsing the PLO in November 1977.

tians (many more than the combined population of all rejectionist Arab states), who had been prepared by Sadat's regime to view peace as the beginning of domestic development: population would move from the Nile Valley to the Canal Zone, conditions for foreign investment would improve, funds would shift from the army to public utilities, to economic integration with Sudan, and so on. There was little cynicism evident in Egypt during those days; and Sadat's growing prestige might have been a decisive American and Israeli asset in the search for a comprehensive settlement with the other Arab nations.

Peace would have been concluded at the Ismailia summit in December 1977 had Israel agreed to evacuate the whole of the Sinai—including the Rafiah settlements—and to endorse the principle that "Palestinians be given the right to participate in the determination of their future." This was the Aswan formula announced by Sadat and President Carter after the summit meeting failed to produce an agreement on principles. For Begin to endorse this formula would also have meant suspending Jewish settlements on the West Bank and keeping silent about the future status of Arab Jerusalem. Political organizing on the West Bank would have to be permitted as well, along with an increase, by surreptitious stages, in the presence of Jordanian administrators and police.

Shimon Shamir of the Shiloah Institute, one of Israel's best-informed experts on Arab politics, believes such actions by Begin could have then served as the basis for a treaty. So do Egypt's acting foreign minister, Butros Ghali, and the American ambassador to Israel, Samuel Lewis. But in late 1977 and early 1978 Begin balked, suggesting an autonomy plan a little like the one Tito granted Croatia. He denied that UN Resolution 242 would apply to the West Bank—still, to him, Eretz Yisrael. He acquiesced in Ariel Sharon's bulldozer diplomacy by which he kept extending settlements in north Sinai.

Now (as he did at Camp David) Begin has openly capitulated on most major points, including complete withdrawal from the Sinai—but not on suspending settlements. He has also withdrawn most of the objections he posed after Camp David to Egypt's treaty obligations with other Arab nations in case of war. Not that these objections were ever decisive: if war comes, each country's interests will prevail over its signatures. In any case, Egyptian Prime Minister Mustafa Hallil announced to the Egyptian Parliament on April 9 that Egypt will side with Syria in a "defensive war" to retake the Golan Heights if its negotiations with Israel fail. He also said that "normalization" with Israel can only proceed at a pace that corresponds to progress in achieving full Palestinian autonomy, at least in the Gaza Strip as a first step. Israel for months sought to avoid this "linking," but none of Hallil's statement is contradicted by the text of the treaty Begin signed.

Few observers have noticed that, according to the treaty, negotiations on normalizing trade and tourism are to begin only after six months, i.e., after negotiations on autonomy are already supposed to be fully under way. General Mati Peled, who is closely acquainted with Egyptian leaders, told me if these collateral negotiations bog down, he doubts Egypt would send an ambassador to Israel after nine months — as the treaty specifies. Then we shall have not peace but some nervous and de facto "interim agreement," with the Israeli army withdrawing to a line running from El Arish to a point west of Sharm al Shaykh. There will be no optimistic momentum, no progress on commercial and diplomatic relations, and no American military and diplomatic presence between the Israeli army and the Egyptians.

Former Prime Minister Yitzchak Rabin has already predicted this kind of deadlock. Naphtalie Lavie, Foreign Minister Dayan's closest aide, hinted to me that this would be considered a "tolerable" outcome. But there can be no doubt that it could degenerate into a situation far more precarious for Israel than any since the 1967 war. And the Carter administration, which openly supports Egypt on the Palestinians, will not be sympathetic to Israeli claims for support under the separate agreement Secretary Vance negotiated with Dayan.

Begin cannot avoid this dangerous deadlock unless he makes good on an autonomy plan he really abhors. Unlike the one he presented Sadat at Ismailia, the one he suddenly endorsed at Camp David promises "full" Palestinian autonomy: an elected council, an end to the military government, a "strong" indigenous police force, the retreat of the Israel Defense Forces to specified enclaves. Furthermore, this autonomy was and is to be "transitional," leading to Palestinians enjoying their "legitimate rights"—a clear strengthening of the Aswan formula. Israel's withdrawal of north Sinai settlements will be a clear precedent for the Golan and West Bank (Begin's demurrers notwithstanding).* Dr. Moshe Sharon, Begin's own former adviser on Arab affairs, called this autonomy plan a certain step to an independent Palestinian state and a precarious one at that, because tensions between "autonomous Palestinians" and Israeli settlers are, in his view, bound to stir up nationalist and secessionist sentiments among Israeli Arabs as well. Israeli hawks such as Ariel Sharon and Mier Har-Zion have already issued dark warnings to the Arab citizens of Israel that they not "repeat the tragedy of 1948."†

Yet all these Israeli concessions already seem stale, deceptive, possibly futile. Begin has himself cut down the possibilities for peace by stalling so many months. According to the reports of many journalists,‡ the Egyptian public is solidly in favor of peace, a sentiment confirmed by the huge vote for Sadat in his referendum of April 19. But as the more skeptical students who were interviewed pointed out, the word "peace" has now become a euphemism for inflated economic hopes. Most Egyptians resent the feeling of being cut off from an "Arab world" of which they consider themselves the center. And although tens of thousands of Egyptians continue to work in the Persian Gulf, the rest of the Arab world is now diplomatically lined up against Egypt, committed to the sanctions voted at the second Baghdad conference in late March. Egypt has even been expelled from OPEC.

---

*Israeli withdrawal from North Sinai is taken as a precedent not only by Arab parties but also by President Carter. In his carefully worded response to King Hussein's "14 Queries," Carter reiterated that Jewish civilian settlements in the West Bank are a violation of the Geneva Convention (*Ma'ariv*, April 17, 1979).

†Israeli settlement of the West Bank has contributed to nationalist feelings among Israeli Arabs by implying that the 1949 borders are not final: irredentist claims cut both ways. Moreover, the resources (approximately $3 billion) spent settling occupied territory were not spent on settling northern Galilee, where Arabs are now a strong majority.

‡For example, Israeli television journalists Rafik Halabi and Ehud Yaari conducted an extensive series of interviews during Begin's visit. See also Amos Elon's report, *Ha'aretz*, April 11, 1979.

The Saudis have broken diplomatic relations with Egypt but are unlikely to cut off covert aid to Egypt or, more important, to withdraw an estimated $2 billion in deposits from Egyptian banks. The Saudi royal family's political and economic connections to American oil concerns and Western banks have become stronger with the growth of its oil revenues,* and it will not— in spite of the tendency of the national guard's Prince Abdullah to flirt with the Soviets—bring the Western economies down on its head. It is doubtful that the Saudi leaders will want to antagonize Senator Church further and thus risk losing the expected delivery of seventy-five F-15s. But the Saudis also have a stake in "Arab unity": they think, and with some reason, they are vulnerable to pro-Soviet radicals in south Yemen and Iraqis in the north and they cannot afford to live under the kind of military threat posed by Nasser during the 1950s and 1960s. They can punish Sadat by remaining aloof and punish the rest of us, including President Carter, by yielding a few more percentage points to the demands of the OPEC price hawks. The recent 9 percent rise in the price of crude oil was a signal that they resent Sadat's "independent" course (quite aside from their desire to show they have a heavy interest in Jerusalem).

A year ago the Saudis would not have had to worry about pressures on them to close ranks against Sadat. But as the negotiations dragged on, Syria and Iraq have had time to make a spectacular reconciliation—a Ba'athist *sulkh* motivated by Sadat's threat to deny them the advantages of joint warmaking. In these circumstances, King Hussein could not remain neutral. He has decisively joined with Syria in opposing the Camp David agreements—from which, as Begin's statements have implied, he would get nothing but the honor of policing the Palestinians for five years.† Hussein has even been mending his fences with Arafat and has promised joint action with the PLO in organizing West Bank resistance. Moreover, it seems unlikely that Jordanian security officials could have been unaware that Fatah was at-

---

*See Fred Gottheil's "The Manufacture of Saudi Power," *Middle East Review*, Fall 1978.

† Anthony Lewis's report on Crown Prince Hassan's criticism of the agreements appeared in *Ha'aretz*, April 23, 1979.

tacking across the Jordanian border near Kibbutz Tirat Tzevi in mid-April. (The attackers were killed by Israeli soldiers.)

For Israelis, the most ominous result of their government's faltering has been the recovery of the PLO. With Syria and Iraq working together, their clients in the PLO are much more unified than before. Arafat's Fatah seems, paradoxically, much weaker in the face of the power which can now be arrayed against it — hence the failure of Fatah to organize a national government-in-exile under its own leadership at Damascus this winter. But Arafat presides over a much stronger PLO organization, and his personal prestige was sharply increased this winter by his connection with Iran's Khomeini. For the first time since the Lebanon debacle, Arafat now has some leverage independent of Syria: by leading the fight against Sadat he can appear as the unifier of pan-Arab, pan-Islamic, and Palestinian interests.

As for the Palestinians in the West Bank and Gaza, they have responded enthusiastically to the PLO's apparent rehabilitation. Mayors, professional associations, professors and students, labor unions, bureaucrats — they are all more organized and united than at any time since 1967 under the exclusive influence of pro-PLO politicians such as Mayor Faid Kawasmeh of Hebron and Karim Khalaf of Ramallah. The West Bank and Gaza were shut down tight in protest on the day the treaty was signed, and there has been a marked rise in terrorist activity around Jerusalem and elsewhere in Israel. Even the old supporters of Hussein, e.g., Mayor Freij of Bethlehem and Anwar Nusseibeh of Jerusalem, have been sharply critical of plans for autonomy, notwithstanding the large offers made to them by such American diplomats as Harold Saunders. The prestigious, hitherto independent mayor of Gaza city, Rashad a-Shawa, is planning to visit Arafat in Beirut presumably to coordinate plans in view of Sadat's intention to establish autonomy in the Gaza strip.

A-Shawa, apparently with the PLO's blessing, has nevertheless suggested that autonomy might be acceptable to him if it could become a demonstrated step to a Palestinian state, as the Egyptians adamantly claim. Farouk Kadoumi, head of the PLO's political department, has publicly taken the same line since November, when, at the first Baghdad Conference, even the most strident Arab rejectionists joined for the first time with Saudis and the Jordanians in calling for a negotiated settlement under UN auspices. General Peled, who regularly takes part in exchanges of views with Fatah leaders, now believes that if negotiations between Israel and Egypt produce autonomy proposals consistent with those of Peled's Sheli Party, Fatah will join these negotiations. The Sheli Party resolution to the Knesset called for a suspension of Jewish settlements and "full" Palestinian control over internal affairs, land, and other resources, leading to an independent Palestinian state after five years.

General Peled's speculations may be optimistic. PLO terror continues unabated; and it is hard to forget that the PLO, when it had Sadat's invitation to negotiate with Israelis at Cairo in January 1978, refused to accept it. But every Palestinian sees the suspension of Jewish settlement as the real test of Israeli and American intentions. Without it, they will oppose "autonomy" as if it were a prelude not to Palestinian independence but to Israeli annexation.

## II

It is precisely on the crucial question of Israelis settling the West Bank that Begin's ideology and record are most vulnerable. While he procrastinated diplomatically, producing no concrete diplomatic advantages and many disadvantages, Begin's government has been fencing off thousands of dunams of Arab land and tripling the number of Jewish settlers: from 2,000 in the summer of 1977 to 6,000 today. These are not large amounts of land, but the settlers are fanatic and well armed. They think they are "Zionist" pioneers and have begun to treat Begin as if he were a representative of the British mandatory government. Not that Begin has ever even hinted that he personally would want to give up claims to sovereignty over the West Bank or allow the status of these Jewish settlements to be compromised. Last November I heard him tell a meeting of his hard-line Herut faction of the Likud that he would bring the negotiations on autonomy to a standstill if Herut's positions were to be chal-

lenged. On April 22, his government approved two new settlements between Ramallah and Nablus.

Moreover, the military government has now established civilian regional councils for the Jewish settlements, an evident prelude to some Israeli claim of sovereignty over at least part of the
territory. Most provocative and discouraging of all, the director-
general of the Prime Minister's office, Eliyahu Ben-Elissar, has
prepared plans for autonomy under which Israel would keep
exclusive control of (1) the West Bank's water table, (2) its "state"
lands—i.e., common lands farmed by Arab peasants which, before 1967, had been registered in the name of the King, (3) its
communications and roads, and (4) public order. Finally, Israel
will control immigration into the West Bank and Gaza. Palestinian Arab residents, according to this plan, will have autonomy
over their persons but not over their resources. According to
*Davar*'s thoughtful West Bank correspondent Daniel Rubenstein,
this much autonomy would be substantially less than that currently enjoyed under the military government.

Still, the settlers denouncing Begin could be right in suspecting
that he may now be much closer to serious peacemaking on the
Palestinian question than ever before. He may be closer as well
to suspending Jewish settlements as a first step as negotiations
approach with Egypt over autonomy. As the dovish journalist
and Sheli Party Knesset member Uri Avnery put it recently, the
really important fight is now between Begin and himself. All the
reasons Begin had had for coming this far—who could imagine
his agreeing to return the whole Sinai and dismantle settlements
if he were still in opposition?—are stronger now that the treaty
is signed.

It is true that some of Begin's faltering over the past sixteen
months may be attributed to his need to placate the outspoken
hawks in the Likud who are outside his own Herut faction—
Ariel Sharon and Yigal Hurwitz—and what might be called
scripture hawks in the National Religious Party—particularly
Zevulun Hammer and Yehuda Ben-Meir. But Begin's internal
difficulties with the allies in his coalition have been greatly exaggerated in the Western press. Begin is the first among unequals
in his cabinet. His reputation as a hard-liner ever since he com-

manded the Irgun, combined with the similar reputations of
Foreign Minister Dayan and Defense Minister Ezer Weizman,
has been more than adequate to isolate and discredit his hawkish
critics in the Knesset and outside. The physicist Yuval Ne'eman,
who implacably opposes any compromise with Arabs, is now
trying to organize an "anti-defeatist" political party against Begin
and has met with little success. As I wrote after Begin's election
(see page 82), the public would tend to trust any government
he heads to recognize an American ultimatum when it sees one,
and he would be in a far stronger position to compromise than
was Rabin's government.

Furthermore, Begin's electoral backing for signing the treaty
with Egypt and for continuing to go along with Carter is at least
double his potential opposition. Polls show consistently that at
least 65 to 70 percent of Israelis generally trust the United States,
consider its support indispensable, and think Sadat sincerely
wants peace.* More significant, the same number say the occupied lands are invaluable only for strategic—not for religious
and "Zionist"—reasons. They oppose settlements that seem an
obstacle to peacemaking, oppose transferring Israeli government offices to Arab East Jerusalem. In view of these opinions,
their overwhelming opposition to a Palestinian state seems to me
largely a reflex reaction to PLO terror and what they see as the
danger of its being installed officially next door, and not a matter
of principle.

By contrast, only 15 to 20 percent declare that they support
annexationist policies—more civilian settlements, more "territorial depth." Most of these voters support the NRP, which, for
all its bluster, has no alternative to Begin since it stands to lose
so much in opposition, e.g., the rabbinical prerogatives in ad-
ministering marriage, divorce, dietary laws. Moreover, the NRP
is itself divided. Four of its twelve members of the Knesset
are doves and a small but increasing number of the rank and
file subscribe to the "Power and Peace" (Oz V'Shalom) faction
headed by David Glass. Glass told me that this group would leave
the NRP if the latter chose settlements over peace. On the other
hand, the NRP's youth organization, the Bni Akiva, has threat-

*See, for example, *Yediot Acharonot*, November 10, 1978, and April 13, 1979.

ened to leave the party in the event of an opposite decision. The Machiavellian old guard, headed by Interior Minister Joseph Burg, is anxious about such a split but more anxious to control the ambitions of religious hawks like Zevulun Hammer and Yehuda Ben-Meir. That is why the recent appointment of such a fixer as Burg to handle the West Bank and Gaza autonomy negotiations is not quite as dismal as it seems, but points to Begin's determination to avoid clear-cut commitments on autonomy at this stage.

Other sources of political opposition to further concessions came from the old right-wing Labor pioneers in the moshav movement and the Achdut Ha'avoda Party. They persist in the once plausible and now obsolete identification of settlements with security. These are a rather small group of highly political men and women (e.g., Amos Hadar, Shoshana Arbel-Elmosnino, Israel Galili) whose sons and daughters settled on the Golan, in north Sinai, and in the Jordan Valley under the regime of Golda Meir and Dayan. They believed that, like their grandparents under the Turks, they were securing the frontiers of Jewish society. Now Dayan has himself renounced such anachronistic reasoning, as he had to when he voted along with the ninety-four others to withdraw from the so-called Rafiah settlements in the Sinai. But the forces of Israel's "agrarian reaction," as Amos Elon put it, have refused to accept Dayan's about-face. They fear that as agricultural "pioneering" is further discredited, they will be engulfed in what they see as the hedonist, materialist, urbanizing trends of modern Israeli society. Begin, it must be said, is not at all beholden to these Laborites who now accuse him of abandoning settlements "*he* never built"; he has had a cultivated revisionist contempt for them most of his life.

By far the most serious political problem for Begin comes from his own Herut faction, from his old Irgun cronies such as Ya'acov Meridor, Haim Landau, and Knesset Speaker Yitzchak Shamir or from younger intransigents — Begin's own bright young men — such as Moshe Arens, the Knesset Foreign Affairs and Security Committee chairman, and M. K. Yigal Cohen-Orgad. These men cannot challenge Begin's control of Herut, but they can nudge him toward making guilty proclamations of loyalty to Eretz Yisrael and to "Jabotinsky's thought." They are currently trying to get him to fire Dayan, whom they view as the engineer of Begin's concessions. Worse, they can embarrass him into "standing up" to the Americans and going easy on the hysterical young Israelis who are insisting on settling on the West Bank. This dogmatic group of Herut leaders could ruin Begin's confidence in the process to which he has made himself hostage. They could provoke that cynical, petulant sense of impotence with which he defies—and helps to create—a world turned against the Jews.

Indeed, the tightly organized groups around Gush Emunim (Bloc of the Faithful) have become the most formidable challenge to Begin partly because they have so much backing in his own party. These "faithful" groups have been pressing Begin to let them settle further in "Judea and Samaria." Their allies in the government, in violation of official decisions, have funneled both money and supplies to them in the field. As the Minister for Agriculture in charge of settlement, Ariel Sharon has been particularly irresponsible in encouraging this irregular financing. And Sharon has grandly promised Gush Emunim that Begin's government will approve a huge expansion of West Bank settlements, housing over 60,000 new settlers, over the next five years, at a cost of 600 million pounds, or about $27 million.

Even more ominous, the Gush Emunim settlers have now committed themselves to armed resistance. Led by a vigilante lawyer, Eliakim Ha'etzni, Gush settlements are organizing "patrols" to "keep order" in Arab towns. When they decide that the army is not acting quickly enough, they intend to use force to stop Arab demonstrations, clear roads, etc. Armed settlers from Ofra near Ramallah are generally suspected of firing the shots that killed two Palestinian high school students in Halhul—in self-defense, so it is claimed. But such actions—if they are not stopped now—could develop into a kind of vigilante terror sure to sour Israeli-Palestinian relations even further. This, the settlers feel, would be to their advantage.

If peacemaking is to move to some more constructive stage, Begin's government must act decisively against these groups and suspend Jewish settlements in the West Bank. Even if "autonomy" is never instituted, the Israeli government could only hope to keep the Egyptians and Palestinians open to some other more realistic plan—assuming one could be found—if it curbed the proponents of this absurd expansionism. It will certainly not be easy for Begin to do so given his own views of Judea and Samaria. His old revisionist strategy for rehabilitating the Jews always aimed to retrieve the culture of those presumably more elegant and martial biblical Jews who lived in this "promised land" until the first century. He has already made a secret promise to the NRP and Sharon that he will permit new settlements in the near future. Insiders in the Herut Party have told me that he signed a commitment to them to resign if he departs from Ben-Elissar's principles on Palestinian autonomy.

But Begin's coalition now has a much strengthened peace faction as well. He knows he will defy it at his peril. The Camp David agreements have sharply focused the available diplomatic choices. There is now one and only one peace agenda to which the Americans and Egyptians can practically agree. Israeli leaders can choose only to go along with it—with all its implications for the Palestinian question—or not; and Begin's four senior ministers have chosen to go along.

Moshe Dayan believes that he has rehabilitated his name with this treaty; he has given notice to Begin that he will not tolerate actions that jeopardize it. It is generally acknowledged that Dayan exerted subtle but decisive pressure on Begin to come to terms with Sadat at Camp David and after. Begin has maneuvered the autonomy negotiations out of Dayan's hands, but he cannot hope to keep Dayan in the cabinet indefinitely under such conditions. Dayan is now publicly warning Gush Emunim not to play "catch as catch can" in the occupied territories.* What is more, he has been saying that the precedent of Sinai can apply in the Golan.

Ezer Weizman, who threatened to resign if President Carter should leave Jerusalem empty-handed, seems even more committed to this peacemaking than Dayan. He has unambiguously emerged as its most forward-looking and eloquent proponent. As Minister of Defense, he runs the occupation. He has, like

*Yediot Acharonot*, March 31, 1979.

Dayan, pointedly cautioned West Bank settlers against further squatting and vigilantism and, unlike any Labor Defense Minister, has been willing to use the army against them in the past to enforce government decisions.

Begin's third senior minister to back Camp David is Yigael Yadin, the Deputy Prime Minister. He had Begin sign a coalition agreement in late 1978 to the effect that every new settlement proposed by the government would have to be endorsed by the Knesset Foreign Affairs and Security Committee. There, in spite of its chairman, the hard-liners are outnumbered. Gush Emunim will not have its way in the face of the combined objections of these ministers. Its proposed "cornerstone-laying ceremonies" at ten new sites on the West Bank during Passover were canceled by order of the military government. Weizman is generally believed to have given this order.

Not that these ministers have as much electoral weight as the NRP and Herut. Dayan has no party. Weizman is still widely considered within the Likud to be rather shallow and reckless. Yadin leads only the hollowed-out remains of the Democratic Movement for Change—the half in which the old Herut maverick, Justice Minister Shmuel Tamir, has emerged as the strong man. The other half, led by the liberal lawyer Amnon Rubinstein, has gone into opposition. Nevertheless, Begin knows that unlike the NRP, these ministers, especially Weizman, are popular among the large, educated middle class in Israel. He can reshuffle his cabinet, but the three ministers could make common cause with the Labor opposition and those to its left.

The Labor Party was unable or unwilling to withdraw from the northern Sinai settlements. It would probably not have been able to bring Israel to a peace treaty with Egypt. But, unlike Begin, most of the Labor leaders have conceded that Israel's cultural borders should correspond to its political ones: they are very wary of Jewish settlement in the heart of Arab populations and are currently calling for some "territorial compromise" on the West Bank which does not compromise the security of Israel's own urban heartlands.

Shimon Peres, Dayan's old ally, now presides over a party that, he knows, is much more sympathetic to Palestinian nationalism than in the past—two of Labor's chief organizers, Uzi Baram and Yossi Sarid, have become enthusiastic supporters of Peace Now (Shalom Achshav)—and certainly more so than the Likud. He has himself revived the Yariv-Shemtov Formula, which supports negotiations with *any* authoritative Palestinian group prepared to employ peaceful methods and recognize Israel. Moreover, since Hussein and Arafat have had an apparent rapprochement, the traditional Labor policy of solving the Palestinian problem through a "Palestinian-Jordanian state" may now be less wistful than in the past. Of course, a Fatah-Jordan negotiating partner is not what Labor leaders had in mind, but just such a partnership—i.e., between PLO moderates and Hussein—might enhance the prospects for a largely demilitarized West Bank in the event of Israeli withdrawal from it. In any event, Begin has broken some taboos of his own. It may have occurred to him that Labor's traditionally more dovish policies are consistent with the peace expectations he has himself encouraged.

The polls would confirm such speculations. It is possible that the Likud would now win re-election as the Nobel Prize–winning party of peace. Mina Zemach, the only pollster to predict Begin's victory in 1977, now shows Likud's winning forty-four seats to Labor's forty-one. But whenever Begin's ability to continue making peace is in doubt, especially if he is suspected of sacrificing peace to "ideological" considerations, the party's popularity plunges. The Zemach poll showed Labor with forty-five seats to Likud's thirty-five during Begin's make-or-break trip to Washington this March. At any rate, the Labor Secretary Chaim Bar-Lev is now confident enough to announce that Labor is eager for an early election.

But Likud's "annexationism" aside, Begin's greatest weakness is in Israel's economy. Likud came to power mainly because Labor had been viewed as high-handed and corrupt by Israel's largely Sephardic wage earners and its largely Ashkenazi intelligentsia. Since then Likud's Finance Minister, Simcha Ehrlich, has brought in "liberalizing" measures, which have only strengthened Israel's "black money" underground economy. Tax evasion, once a problem, now is felt to be a plague. Some 80 billion Israeli pounds are, according to Begin's own Energy Minister,

in circulation among Israel's 100,000 or so independent businessmen. Of these, 34,000 are not even keeping books. Perhaps
half of Israel's inflation, now running between 60 and 70 percent,
is caused by the huge amounts of undeclared money in comparatively few hands, pulling up prices of consumer goods, furniture, clothes, and especially apartments.

A two-bedroom flat in Jerusalem now costs about a million
and a quarter pounds, while the average wage is about 6,000
pounds a month. Middle-class life has already become an advantage that wage-earning parents cannot hope to pass on to
their children. This is the reason for the high rates of emigration
and also, alas, for the enthusiasm among young Jerusalem cou-
ples for subsidized housing in occupied territory around the city.
Instead of getting the state to act against tax evasion, Ehrlich
has relaxed controls on foreign currency. The result is a heavy
influx of dollars that keep the Israeli pound much too high with
respect to world currencies. This has put enormous pressure on
Israel's exporters and may lead to a recession in the country's
most productive industries.

Ehrlich has also cut the budget, mainly by cutting subsidies
for essential foods. But since so much black money is, like government capital subsidies to banks and bureaucracies, invested,
sometimes anonymously, in government bonds linked to the
cost-of-living index, these painful cuts in workers' living standards have done little to curb inflation but have redistributed
income to groups whose problem is, literally, too much money.
Nor are Israel's million or so often striking workers impressed
by Ehrlich's offer to convert black money into white with a puny
35 percent tax. The polls reveal that many salaried workers are
now more impressed with Labor's social-democratic promises in
spite of their lingering suspicions about Labor's ability to deliver
on them. The Histadrut managed to organize an impressive
demonstration — 150,000 workers — against Ehrlich's policies in
Tel Aviv and Haifa.

Ehrlich has understandably also made himself a champion of
the "peace process." He has been making up part of the deficits
in the government's budget, burdened also by huge outlays on
defense, with American money. He is afraid to lose the small
capitalist constituency of his Liberal faction by fighting tax eva-

sion seriously, and is even more afraid of losing up to $2 billion a year in American aid and preferred loans in a squabble over West Bank settlements. Ehrlich is anticipating, not without justification, some economic gains if a stable peace with Egypt can be achieved: revenues for Israeli technical experts, new markets, etc. On the other hand, he knows Israel is economically unprepared for a new state of siege without help from the American dole.

Nor can Begin presume that Washington's Israel lobby will successfully bring pressure on Carter and Congress to be openhanded if Israel insists on an annexationist settlements policy. Polls show that only 30 percent of the U.S. electorate favors an increase in economic aid to Israel and 73 percent would oppose increased military aid. Carter knows the voters may wonder why the federal government will do for defiant Israel what it will not do for Cleveland. There is also substantial opposition in the Democratic Party to new West Bank settlements—from politicians as different and as powerful as George Ball and Senator Ribicoff—and American Jews have little influence outside the Democratic Party. Arthur Hertzberg, past president of the American Jewish Congress, told me in Jerusalem that American Jewish leaders, while publicly loyal to Begin, have been unusually circumspect about accepting permanent occupation.*

Finally, should Begin decide to suspend settlements, he will also enjoy the support of a much larger popular movement than the one that can be marshaled against him. Peace Now has grown beyond the protest led by 350 reserve officers. It can probably count on the more than 100,000 people who took to the streets before Camp David. Its platform opposing new settlements has been endorsed by scores of well-known professors, professionals, and pop stars, twenty-five members of the Knesset, and most political writers in the daily press. Moreover, the movement's nominal leader, Dedi Zucker, assured me that his movement will be particularly vigilant against Gush Emunim's squatter settlements in the coming months and may even attempt to block the new settlements in the West Bank physically.

*NBC poll, March 29, 1979. See Hertzberg's article in *Ha'aretz*, March 16, 1979.

It would be wrong to underestimate the influence of the Peace Now movement in the cabinet. Sources close to Defense Minister Weizman have revealed that he and Begin are greatly concerned about the army's morale. They are anxious not to risk forcing it into a battle that so many key officers will consider to have been avoidable. Nor does Weizman, an air force pilot by training and in spirit, relish the IDF's becoming an occupation police.

Israel's growing peace forces have been notably civil toward Begin now that he has signed the treaty, but their message to him is that they consider the Israel-Egypt treaty as a good deed with a future. Israelis are tired of their claustrophobic history and now have something very precious to lose. More than anyone else, Sadat seems to have understood this, agreeing to "open borders" immediately and giving free rein to Israeli journalists in Cairo. Begin, still trying to live down his terrorist past, is not eager to be the one to squander this much progress.

But Sadat will be undone if President Carter does not act quickly to dispel the appearance that this is a separate peace that gives Begin a free hand in the West Bank, while the Palestinian residents there are left with no choice except opposition under the PLO's direction. Of course, any long-term effort to reconcile Israeli security with Palestinian nationalism will not be easy: both peoples now share an integrated economy,* an ecology, a water supply, and a rather small territory with an interdependent system of roads and communications. They also share deep suspicions of each other's designs on Jerusalem. Moreover, the PLO and Israel — or Israel's client, Lebanese Major Said Haddad — clash daily in southern Lebanon. So it is difficult to take a first step toward peace without being able to see five steps beyond: e.g., Israelis ask if they should gamble with control of the common water resources under Israeli and West Bank hills while the abundant waters of the Nile and the Litani River in Lebanon seem out of reach to them without a comprehensive peace.

The answer can only be that, without such a gamble, comprehensive peace itself will be out of reach, and this, like a con-

---

*Just how far the West Bank economy has been integrated with Israel's is summarized by Brian Van Arkadie, *Benefits and Burdens*, a report of the Carnegie Foundation, 1977.

solidated peace with Egypt, is more crucial to Israel's future than anything else. Moreover, it is not much of a gamble to suspend settlements and challenge the Palestinians to renounce terror and accept UN Resolution 242, as the United States demands, in return for negotiations. But even if the PLO is not ready for peace, stopping settlements could clear the way for an attempt by Dayan to court the Syrians in the manner he used to court the Egyptians prior to November 1977. Dayan's public suggestion on April 17 that the Golan may be traded for peace would seem to hint at just this kind of initiative. A suspension of settlement will also keep West Bank settlers and their opponents off balance and more convinced that U.S. pressure on behalf of Palestinian "rights" cannot be disregarded by Begin. Presidential primaries or not, it is squarely up to President Carter to keep these possibilities alive.

Make no mistake. Menachem Begin is fanatically committed to a unified Eretz Yisrael. But realities, imposed with some skill by President Carter, have maneuvered him into being magnanimous in the recent past. Jabotinsky, Begin's mentor, for all his emphasis on aggressive militarism, also talked of the Jews attaining a state of mind, or comportment, he called *hadar* — suggesting control, conscious grace, noblesse oblige. If Begin is capable of this virtue, its time has come.

# The Victory of the New Israel

I

*July 8, 1981*

The Palestinian scholar Walid Khalidi said to me recently that Menachem Begin may yet succeed where Nasser failed in bringing unity to the Arab world. No doubt this is why Yasir Arafat expressed satisfaction in June at the good prospects for Begin's re-election. Yet the diplomatic and military pressures now mounting against Israel from Arab rejectionists, European leaders, and State Department officials have not united the Jewish state. The mean-spirited campaign that preceded the June 30 election has in fact revealed a country passionately divided by ideology, class, age, attitudes toward Orthodox faith and law—and, crucially, ethnic origin. The ingathering of the exiles, it seems, has been a simpler matter than consolidating the nation.

What this election has also made clear is that the pro-Likud constituencies of the "new Israel," composed mainly of Jews of North African origin, have proven even more convincingly to be a majority—albeit a slim one—in this turbulent society. It was these Jews whose support for Begin was decisive in the elections of 1977. They now may have superseded once and for all the institutions and values of historic Labor Zionism, which before 1977 had presided over the Jewish settlement and the state without interruption since 1933.

Their victory was more convincing this time because, by contrast to the campaign of 1977, they now supported a Likud government running on a record of economic mismanagement, civil corruption, and growing diplomatic isolation. Yet Begin's coalition has held its strength: Likud will have forty-eight seats in the tenth Knesset to Labor's forty-seven, and it seems the only party the president can call on to form the next government. By contrast, Labor and the Democratic Movement for Change shared forty-seven seats in 1977 to Likud's forty-five.

To understand just how disastrous Likud's policies have been to Israel's economy, consider that in 1977 about ten Israeli pounds traded for one American dollar, while today the rate of exchange is 115 to the dollar and is climbing daily. Of course, this figure by itself is misleading: Israel has an efficient system of cost-of-living escalators which the Finance Ministry under Yoram Aridor has recently instituted along with a larger package of reforms. Wages, bank accounts, marginal tax brackets, and so forth are now all 100 percent linked to the inflation, which is why, iron-ically, savings rates among Israelis are among the highest in the world in spite of the startling rate of inflation with which they must contend.

Still, as Uriel Linn, the Likud-appointed commissioner of state's revenue (and now a strong candidate to become governor of the Bank of Israel), conceded to me, the climate is foul for the long-term investments in industrial and high technology pro-duction that Israel needs to avoid economic collapse—including investments in aviation, computer software, and medical equip-ment, which now make up 9 percent of the GNP.

Much of Israel's most vigorous industry is, in fact, now fi-nanced by foreign credit, and Aridor's recent economic policies have greatly depleted reserves of foreign exchange—some fear by as much as a half-billion dollars—in an effort to reduce short-term inflation rates in time for the election. He did this by low-ering the purchase tax on a number of consumer goods—cars, televisions, refrigerators, and more—which Israelis from all classes rushed to import from European suppliers. The balance-of-payments deficit may reach $5.5 billion in 1981. Moreover, the Israeli treasury under Aridor's direction has maintained an artificially high value for Israeli currency during this period, which is informally pegged to the surging American dollar. This combination of soaring inflation at home and overvalued Israeli pounds in Europe has put Israel's crucial export industries, and agriculture, in such bad shape that Aridor had to pay exporters a 5 percent subsidy in June just to keep them solvent.

Aridor's depletion of foreign reserves to promote a pro-Likud mood—something his predecessors Simcha Ehrlich and Yigael Hurwitz have stubbornly resisted since 1977—may so adversely affect the solvency of Israel's government that its guarantees to foreign banks lending money to Israeli industry will become as worthless as those from "developing" countries. Hebrew University political economist Avishai Margalit fears that credit may dry up in the near future and create unemployment in just those sectors of the Israeli economy that are the keys to the country's future. In 1979, about $73 million in foreign investment was liquidated; in 1980, about $202 million. So Margalit may be right that foreign investors have already begun to withdraw credits.

Likud's most serious economic failure has been its laissez-faire —one might say, *après-moi-le-déluge*—approach to economic productivity, in which there has been virtually no rise for the last five years. Don Patinkin, an economist at Hebrew University, points out that actual growth under the Likud from 1977 to 1981 is running at about 19 percent, half of what it was on average during the two preceding Labor governments.* The main reason for this decline is the faith of Likud's finance ministers that Israel's entrepreneurs living in the suburbs of Tel Aviv will use their growing fortunes to invest in Israeli industry during this inflationary time instead of playing the market in bonds and stocks. Capital gains on both are, remarkably, tax-free in Israel. The government props up the market with indexed issues to secure short-term revenue. There may be a cautionary lesson here for Representative Jack Kemp, who was in Israel recently to study the Likud's economic record, which an economist friend of mine calls "supply sadism."

Israel's most respected economists, such as Patinkin and Pro-

*See *Yediot Acharonot,* June 26, 1981.

fessor Haim Ben-Shachar, who was slated to be Finance Minister in a Labor government, wants to see the government and the Histadrut — Israel's general federation of labor — again take the lead in organizing new industrial production. Labor Party experts also claim that he would have attempted to cut the swelling defense budget and certainly phase out the millions of dollars in expenditures on West Bank settlements. If these austerity measures are not soon enforced, the value of the Likud's shiny new shekel seems likely to decline twice as fast as that of the pound. Obviously, this economy is no place for poor people, or much of the middle class for that matter, which largely explains why some 100,000 Israelis have moved to the United States and Canada in the last four years. The inflation has barely touched real wages, but it has put housing — still the most lucrative speculative investment in Israel — out of reach for virtually all families who do not qualify for government flats in Jerusalem suburbs or development towns.

I wrote in 1977 that the Likud government could not be expected to do much for Israel's poor and that it might have to create circuses (such as altercations with Helmut Schmidt?) when the bread runs out. No one expected then that their Finance Minister would simply borrow money to subsidize bread — and poultry, milk, gasoline, and other essential commodities — for several months before an election to contrive an illusion of prosperity. This is just what Aridor has done. Since February he has announced subsidies that will cost 18 billion shekels — while the whole year's budget calls for 6 billion in subsidies. He has, in effect, spent 30 percent of the national budget during the months he was to have spent just 15 percent. He has even had the temerity to borrow almost 900 million shekels from some domestic private banks and not from the Bank of Israel in order to keep the impact of short-term inflation to a minimum. To his credit, Yaacov Levinson, president of the Workers' Bank, would not go along. But the subsidies will have to be reduced, and economists are predicting 250 percent inflation — or more: 35 percent of Israel's budget already goes to servicing the national debt, nearly a 9 percent rise since 1977, and little has been done about the widespread problem of tax evasion, which Uriel Linn considers a "serious spur to inflation."

II

Aridor's actions invite what seems to me the most intriguing question of this election campaign: To which of the 800,000 Israelis who make up the Likud electoral plurality, aside from the religious parties, can such an irresponsible economic regime possibly appeal? Also, what deeper loyalties has the Likud been drawing on to maintain its coalition in spite of its failures of social administration? The answers lie in some of the basic demographic facts of Israel's politics. Both Likud and Labor count on the support of specific groups of voters. In the case of the Likud, these include Tel Aviv industrialists and commercial promoters and hawkish veterans of the old Irgun and Sternist underground and the young. It has also counted on the Sephardic poor of the *shechunot*—the marginal, hastily constructed neighborhoods of Israel's cities—and development towns such as Dimona.

The latter group remains the core of the Likud's power, and Aridor's largesse was directed mainly to them—to the industrial workers, vegetable peddlers, taxi drivers, waitresses, and petty clerks of the second Israel, who are mainly of Moroccan origin. They, or their parents, arrived in Israel in the 1950s and came to view the movement and the Histadrut as a condescending network of high-handed Ashkenazi bureaucrats who maintained control over the property and industries of the emerging state. The Moroccan immigrants had little patience for agricultural communes—although a good number joined moshavim. They refused to shed their cultural traditions and warmhearted patriarchal families for the sake of Labor Zionist theories they could barely understand.

Few could speak Hebrew, most of the women were illiterate, and nearly all remained fixed in a universe of Jewish law and Oriental custom. They were shunted off for years to tent cities —*ma'abarot*. Superficial and reckless theories of "modernization" were inflicted upon them by European settlers who were inspired by their own revolutionary euphoria.*

---

*The Haifa University sociologist Shlomo Swirsky has acutely criticized the "modernization" doctrines used in Israel.

The new immigrants and their children were then housed in slapdash housing developments that quickly became slums where schools were inadequate. Their previously strict Orthodox religious practices gave way to a mood of religiosity tempered by Israel's urban street culture. They were hired by the Histadrut and various corporations but could not gain power in unions dominated by old Labor officials. Some wound up in prefabricated towns and abandoned Arab villages in rural areas, such as Beit She'an, where, once they proved allergic to socialism, they were shunned by the residents of nearby kibbutzim and established moshavim such as Degania, Mesilot, and Beit Alfa. The Labor aristocracy on their collectives used to consider it bad form to allow their children to marry the Moroccan immigrants. Most of the intelligentsia of the Moroccan Jews went to live in France or Quebec. Today, only about 20 percent of Israel's university students come from the second Israel.

Of course, much of the second Israel suffered from the good intentions of what Eli Vazana, a young Moroccan Jew I talked to, calls the establishment. Vazana is a resident of Katamon Tet, Jerusalem's Moroccan quarter, which overwhelmingly backs the Likud. He was one of the founders of the reformist Ohalim movement, which the Begin government, to Vazana's regret, absorbed during the last two years. Vazana and other Moroccan Jews I talked to acknowledged that a substantial Sephardic middle class has emerged since 1967; but the success of these owners of small retail stores, car repair garages, and other small businesses has only confirmed the rest of the Moroccan community in its suspicions of socialist planning and ideology. The Sephardic middle class has been joined, in recent years, by the overwhelming majority of immigrants from the Soviet Union, who now number about 200,000 and seem even more contemptuous of democratic socialism.

Although there has been little integration of neighborhood schools in the last decade, the rate of intermarriage between Ashkenazi and Sephardic Jews in the new Israel is nevertheless very high—perhaps 30 percent—and might eventually solve the problem of social integration more effectively than any social policy. But Israelis, especially those whose history in the country is short, have little patience for the long view. The Oriental Jews from the *shechunot* neighborhoods, Eli Vazana told me, remain impressed by Begin's Manichaean view of the world and his displays of piety.* He has always touched a responsive chord among these refugees from Arab countries who have inevitably been made to feel impotent by Labor intellectuals and political bosses and who relish the feelings of superiority evoked by Begin's martial rhetoric.

Most respond to Likud diatribes against Jewish fecklessness precisely because they see old Labor patronage as a domestic form of it—this in spite of the fact that it is the sons of the Labor aristocracy who still serve in elite army units in disproportionately large numbers. So aside from Aridor's gifts, Begin's tough talk against the Syrians in south Lebanon—as well as his bombing of the Iraqi nuclear reactor—have caused the *shechunot* to come back to Likud in a rush. Jews of Sephardic origin make up about 60 percent of the voting population—50 percent of those who actually vote—and consistently choose Likud over Labor by three to one. But numbers alone do not reflect their impact on Israeli politics. This time, little gangs of toughs from the *shechunot* began breaking up Labor Party rallies. They also threatened passersby who wore Labor Party pins and broke car windows with Labor stickers. When Dan Margalit, a writer for *Ha'aretz*, tried to organize a "Hyde Park" debate in the Macheneh Yehudah market of Jerusalem, some young thugs beat him up.

The common perception within the second Israel that the Likud is its instrument for exerting national power is by no means fatuous. In spite of the fact that Labor's Knesset list included twice as many Sephardic Jews (eighteen) as that of the Likud, none of Labor's leadership is from the second Israel. By contrast, David Levy, a self-taught Moroccan Jew from Beit She'an, is a powerful force in the Likud today. He is second after Begin on the Likud list, the czar of housing and social policy, and head

---

*It should be said that many other European Jews in Israel will not draw such facile political conclusions from recent Jewish catastrophes. The most described play this season is *Purim Party of the Son of a Dog*, adapted from Yoram Kaniuk's novel, which attempts to deal forthrightly with the madness that the Holocaust experience has induced in some survivors.

of the Likud faction in the Histadrut central committee. On the other hand, the indifference of so many Moroccan immigrants to the voices of respectable economists—such as Arnon Gafni, president of the Bank of Israel, who views Aridor's policies as a violation of public trust—demonstrates just how estranged the residents of the second Israel are from the elites who have been trying to run Israel as a modern democratic society.

Nevertheless, should another Likud government finally be formed, it will have some internal divisions. Likud's bourgeois, "liberal" wing is now led by Yitzchak Modai, the Energy Minister, an ex-army colonel who is more hawkish than his predecessors on diplomatic questions but clearly opposed to maintaining policies that will bring financial ruin to a part of the old Liberal Party constituents. Begin's own likely successor in the Herut Party is Ya'acov Meridor, an old crony from the Irgun underground, a businesslike and colorless man who has spent his life developing international maritime ventures and filling Herut's coffers.

Both Meridor and Modai can be expected to demand budget cuts that will adversely affect the full employment currently enjoyed by the *shechunot*. As of this writing, Aridor has already told the professionals at the Treasury to raise the value-added tax to 15 percent and gradually lift subsidies on consumer staples. Tougher medicine is forthcoming, and it is worth remembering that the same poor people who put Begin in office in 1977 were a few months before demonstrating in the streets to protest rising prices.

Yet, as in 1977, there is no reason to assume that disaffection in the second Israel from the Likud's fitful commitment to "fiscal responsibility" will translate into support for Labor. Rather, a new populist and radically chauvinist party called Tehiya (Revival) is waiting in the wings. Tehiya has brought together the leaders of Gush Emunim, firebrand Herut dissidents such as Geula Cohen, and Tel Aviv University's Yuval Neeman, a physicist and defense technocrat known as "Dr. Strangelove." They have as yet put forward no new social policies and claim to be campaigning to undo the provisions of the Camp David accords, but they have emerged from the election as a fresh and concentrated version of the old Herut. They gained only three seats this time, mainly from the young and from settlers in the West Bank, but were doing much better in the opinion polls before the race appeared to be neck-and-neck. Geula Cohen's son is now national president of the Association of University Students.

A word about the young seems appropriate here, since more than a third of the voters this time were under thirty and their numbers have been growing steadily. Dr. Ziona Peled, of Israel's prestigious Institute for Applied Social Research, reported to me that during a survey in mid-June among Israel's young—those between eighteen and twenty-nine—at least 55 percent indicated a preference for the Likud and other right-wing parties. Only 20 percent, mainly young people with higher education, chose Labor, which means that there is a majority for the right even among youths of Western Ashkenazi origin.

Of all the recent data, this seems to me the most ominous. The occupation of the West Bank has, after all, gone on for over fourteen years, and every voter under thirty will not remember what Israel was like within the old borders of the Green Line. For them "Judea and Samaria" are places where most of them did their army training and where settlers, who may be among their friends, prove their "pioneering spirit," presumably in the manner of the *chalutzim* who settled the Jezreel Valley during the 1920s and 1930s. The latter, of course, were part of a Labor Zionist effort to consolidate a Hebrew-speaking Jewish homeland during a desperate time. They did not settle with bulldozers, low-interest mortgages, jobs in the city, and the power of the Israeli state and army behind them. The *chalutzim* certainly did not expect to be a vanguard of occupation of a million Arabs.

But Israeli young people, much like the young everywhere, have now grown up with television journalism, in a simpler political universe explained by two-minute news stories featuring vivid images of Israeli and Arab leaders and American politicians who appear to think politics some dramatic test of strength.

Unlike young people almost everywhere else, young Israelis spend their days in grueling military service, learning how to take part in Israel's cybernetic and disciplined army. Some are already hardened by the last war, and all must prepare themselves psychologically for the next. This is not to say that Israel's young betray no political pluralism: six of the pilots who bombed the Iraqi reactor greeted Begin at their base with their family cars plastered with pro-Labor stickers—which some of the army garage mechanics tried to remove. But one cannot ignore the growth of hard-line sentiment among young people in Israel, and the Likud has not failed to exploit it now, as in 1977.

Begin's coalition, finally, will have to rest again on the support of the two major religious parties, the National Religious Party and the Agudat Yisrael. The NRP, now led by its young guard—Education Minister Zevulun Hammer and Yehuda Ben-Meir, who have been close to Gush Emunim and the West Bank settlers—won only six seats this time. They apparently lost support to Geula Cohen's Tehiya but also to Tami, a small self-proclaimed party of Moroccan Orthodox led by former NRP stalwart and Minister of Religious Affairs Aharon Abu Hatzeira. Hammer and Ben-Meir are the products of messianic Zionist yeshivas, but they are now smooth politicians. They coldly dropped Abu Hatzeira when he was indicted—though not yet convicted—for graft, which further exacerbated ethnic tensions throughout the country, particularly after he was cleared of the initial charges against him. NRP ministers, including the old party boss Dr. Joseph Burg, have declared that they will not sit in the same government with Abu Hatzeira. But Tami's two seats are now necessary for a Begin majority and the NRP will ultimately be willing to accept them.

The NRP's chief concern still is to maintain the prerogatives of the Orthodox rabbinate over civil law—the so-called status quo in marriage, divorce, burial, and so forth—and also to preserve what they delicately call the "unity of the land of Israel." In addition to their contempt for Tami—Abu Hatzeira remains under indictment for other offenses—NRP leaders seem genuinely worried about serving in a government that would have so slim a majority and yet have to take the consequences of its former economic recklessness. It has been pressing in vain for a national unity coalition that will include Labor and perhaps demand new elections thereafter. The NRP fixers have made such protests in the past and will now be more content to serve Begin than to try to heal their breach with Labor and then also have to contend with the secularist radicals in Labor's camp, including the followers of the leftist Mapam faction and Shulamit Aloni's Civil Rights Party.

The Agudah Party, whose four seats represent the Charedim, the zealots of the Meah Sha'arim quarter and other strongholds of anti-Zionist sentiment, is less likely to be satisfied with maintaining the status quo in civil life. Since 1977, the Agudah has managed to squeeze out of Begin's government some preliminary concessions to the traditional halachic law. All new laws not based on existing precedents in Israel must now be legislated in "the spirit of the tradition of Israel," i.e., in the spirit of Talmudic law and not British common law. The Agudah leaders have also succeeded in making it far more difficult for women to obtain abortions, while making it easier for daughters of Orthodox families to escape military service.

Charedim living in newer neighborhoods of Jerusalem have also been fighting pitched battles with municipal authorities for three years to prevent drivers from using roads near their apartments during the Sabbath. They are likely to want tougher laws against public transportation during the Sabbath as a price for rejoining Begin. More important, they are sure to demand that the Law of Return be amended to specify as Jews only those converts who have been certified by the Orthodox rabbinate. This amendment would enrage not only secular Jews in Israel but also Conservative and Reform Jews in America. Secular protests can turn ugly. Kibbutzim members have in the past driven cars and tractors into the city on the Sabbath to demonstrate against Orthodox control. Nevertheless, Begin will almost certainly respond positively to Agudah's demands.

Begin will carry the day in any such decision because he rules the Likud more strictly than before. Former Defense Minister Ezer Weizman, once Begin's chief rival in the Likud, has sat out this election, predicting that new elections would be forthcoming. So Begin's Likud is now packed with loyalists, and a new Likud government will not have to include Yigael Yadin's Democratic Movement, now defunct. Yadin was thought a moderate and secularist force in 1977, though in fact he sat as Begin's vice premier in the manner of a captive and it is thought he well deserves the political oblivion he now faces.

Nor will Begin have to include Moshe Dayan this time. Dayan broke with the Likud government in bitterness last year and barely won two seats as the head of an independent list called Telem. He wanted to be Begin's negotiator at the Palestinian autonomy talks. But Begin is still smarting over the charge from his right-wing allies that Dayan had manipulated him into the agreements at Camp David. Besides, Begin knows that the rest of Dayan's list—including Mordechai Ben-Porat and Yigael Hurwitz—are friendly to the Likud and would join it should Dayan resign because he does not want a back-bencher's seat. So Weizman may have been wrong to suppose that a new Begin government will soon fall merely because it will be reaping an economic whirlwind. Indeed, any government Begin forms will likely try to hold together at all costs for four years more: the NRP and Agudat Yisrael do not view themselves as opposition parties.

## III

Although it now seems evident that the Likud alone may be able to organize a parliamentary majority as a result of the June election, Labor's better showing this time raises the question of its own long-term prospects. Begin cannot remain active in political life indefinitely—his heart is widely viewed here as a medical miracle—and no successor in the Likud can command the kind of support he takes for granted. Meridor is not popular in the second Israel. David Levy and General Ariel Sharon have a strong following there, but they do not get on and do not have Begin's rabble-rousing skills. Neither would appeal, moreover, to the Likud's new Tel Aviv bourgeoisie, typified by Gideon Patt, the Minister of Commerce and Industry, who thinks Sharon is insane.

Still, what must first be said about Labor's current leadership—Shimon Peres, Yitzchak Rabin, Chaim Bar-Lev, Abba Eban—is that they should have retired from political life four years ago. Imagine the consternation of Americans if, after Watergate, the Democrats were still being led by Lyndon Johnson. The last-minute reconciliation of Peres with Yitzchak Rabin—

urgent as it was for Labor's campaign—will only hold the party back. Yossi Sarid, a well-connected Labor member of the Knesset, told me during the night of the election that the party apparatus is currently strong, but it may not remain so if it stays out of power; that it cannot hope to regain power unless it can make inroads into the second Israel. He left me to surmise that neither Peres nor Rabin seems likely to do this, although Rabin remains far more popular in the *shechunot* owing to his record as Chief of Staff during the Six-Day War, and, ironically, the reputation for honesty he acquired by resigning the premiership in 1977 after his illegal bank account was discovered by an Israeli reporter.

Peres—who gained in prestige by acquitting himself well in his TV debate with Begin—was singularly unpopular throughout the campaign and could not reach out beyond the traditional Labor constituencies: the comparatively affluent middle class, the older and well-fixed workers within the Histadrut, the intelligentsia, older voters of European origin, and, most important, the residents of the Hityashvut Haovedet—the agrarian collectives. A fresher face might have also failed to form a new Labor government, but the results were close enough to increase speculation about Peres's future. One indication that new leadership might have made a difference is that the return en masse of so many "undecided voters" to the Likud began to be reflected in the polls immediately after Workers' Bank president Yaacov Levinson announced he would not serve in the Peres government. Of course, most of the undecided were from the second Israel and thus largely headed back to the parties of the right anyway—which is why those Western reporters who were announcing a likely majority for Peres in February (when 35 percent were undecided) seem irresponsible. Still, just three or four seats from the young or the *shechunot* would have swung the election in Labor's favor. Peres and the rest were—and are— clearly identified with former Labor regimes and are not the leaders to win them.

Moreover, Peres ran a shoddy campaign, one unworthy of his talents. First, he tried to outperform Begin as a devotee of West Bank settlement—in private, he would concede much more flexible views — and then he attempted to rally an "Ashkenazi back-lash" to the hooliganism of the pro-Likud punks who disrupted his rallies. He did not, as the historian Yehoshua Arieli observed, present a social democratic, peace-loving vision to the substantial part of Israeli society that might still be moved by it; this is not yet a country that is sufficiently urbane to do without social vision. Since 1967, Labor has consistently allowed right-wing groups to preempt questions on which Labor could have encouraged a national debate: e.g., whether or not to settle the West Bank. Peres's campaign reflected this failure of nerve by harping on Likud's failures and stressing how much "stronger" the country would be under Labor leadership.

Peres also held out the clearly anachronistic prospect of a territorial compromise with Jordan — something that both King Hussein and Moshe Dayan have insisted is impossible* — instead of forthrightly taking up the challenge of settling the Palestinian question in the ways envisioned by the Camp David accords. Also, political commercials on television had a significant part in galvanizing party loyalties this year, and my impression was that Likud won the battle of the jingles hands down.

Still, the best augury for the Labor Party this time was the extreme devotion of the kibbutz movement to it after Begin's re-election appeared imminent. The Hityashvut Haovedet found its voice after years of growing indifference to Labor Party interests, and three weeks before the end of the campaign it was able to contribute much by way of manpower, organization, and spirit. Along with the writers and intellectuals — including Amos Oz, A. B. Yehoshua, Don Patinkin — who quickly came back to Labor, the Hityashvut raised the level of Labor's propaganda. Its workers helped to revitalize the party's image and spread an infectious "stop Begin" sense of urgency among the Likud's traditional opponents. Tens of thousands of young people from the kibbutzim came to a last-minute rally in Tel Aviv and sent election day workers to polling areas as far away as Jerusalem.

By contrast, the splinter parties of the left, led, respectively, by Shulamit Aloni, Amnon Rubinstein, and Meir Pa'il, continued to carp at Labor until the day of the election. Much of their

*See Dayan's new book, *Breakthrough* (New York: Knopf, 1981), chapter 5.

criticism was justified. Labor's list is no doubt less dovish and liberal than what, say, Oz, Yehoshua, Patinkin, and Arieli would have wished, and certainly less talented than the lists put together by Labor's left-wing detractors. But I cannot believe that the small leftist parties did themselves credit in pointing out Labor's weaknesses so relentlessly since they could not hope to replace it themselves. The lists of Aloni and Rubinstein barely won three seats between them, and Pa'il did not even make it to the Knesset; but they nevertheless withheld their endorsement of the Labor Party just when it was most needed. Much more irresponsible were the Israelis who planned trips abroad for the day of the election in order to beat the fare hikes on July 1. Polls showed months ago that these trips would seriously influence the results of the election, since probable Labor voters going abroad outnumbered probable Likud voters by two to one. Yet 250,000 — fully 10 percent of the electorate — were absent from Israel on election day.

One surprising feature of Labor's comeback was its substantial number of votes from Israeli Arabs, accounting for between two and three seats. The communist Rakah Party lost an equal number of seats, which means that about a quarter of the Arab voters switched to Labor this time. Some may be tempted to believe that this shift in Arab votes to Labor reflects the increasing faith of Arab citizens in the conventional politics of the state. In fact, the rate of Arab participation dropped from 83 to 65 percent this time, and the swing away from Rakah reflects the radical estrangement of more and more Arabs from Israel's future. Jellal Abu-Tuami, head of an exceptionally active Citizens for Peres committee in the Arab sector, told me that the Arab vote for Labor was, in his view, a desperate act of revulsion against the growing power of the Israeli right. Several weeks into the campaign, Meir Kahane, leader of the fascist Kach Party, presented a platform that called for jailing Jews who have Arab lovers. This shook the Arab community. Kahane got a few thousand scattered votes and will not sit in the Knesset, but Arabs could not help taking a dim view of the political forces that produced his candidacy.

Israeli democrats and civil libertarians, such as the writer

Yoella Har-Shefi, have been making efforts to work with the Arab community, and for the first time an Arab politician will sit for Labor in the Knesset. But as of this writing, Abu-Tuami has yet to receive a phone call from Peres or anyone else in the Labor establishment to express appreciation for his efforts. Instead, Ra'anan Cohen, head of the largely inactive "Arab section" of Labor, which Abu-Tuami wants to see disbanded, is taking credit for the Arab vote and praising Arab voters for their "political maturity." Abu-Tuami feels there might be even more votes for Labor among Arabs if the party could change this patronizing attitude, but he fears that time may be running out.

As to the other changes that Labor needs to make, the party cannot expect to win a majority in the country without taking serious steps to win back some of the voters in the second Israel. The most optimistic Israeli commentators predict that Yitzchak Navon, the popular president of the state and himself a descendant of one of Jerusalem's respected Sephardic families, may resign the presidency to fight for the party leadership. He would certainly do better than Peres among voters not drawn to Labor—he was always thought the most affable of Ben-Gurion's protégés—but Navon has never been tested as a national political leader. He cannot legally re-enter politics for a full year after resigning, and so seems unlikely to affect the immediate political confusion that would ensue if the NRP finally stayed out of Begin's government or succeeded in bringing about new elections.

Ezer Weizman, a charismatic figure who has always been admired in the *shechunot,* might hope to lead a third force in new elections. This could then be joined to a Labor plurality should Begin's government, which would remain in office as a transitional government, be discredited by the impending economic crisis. But Labor will have to take more fundamental action to build bridges to the second Israel than simply putting forward, or joining with, a more acceptable candidate.

One reform that could improve relations between ethnic groups concerns the Histadrut. Sephardic workers make up about 80 percent of the industrial proletariat, but under the current rules workers' councils, in which these Sephardic laborers predominate, have no direct control over the Histadrut's central committee. The latter is elected in a separate poll for which party lists are manipulated by Labor Alignment higher-ups. Not surprisingly, Labor's slates have always been heavily weighted in favor of old guard, European leaders like the secretary-general, Yerucham Meshel, who is now anathema to much of the rank and file. Yair Zaban, a new Labor member of the Knesset (Mapam) and for years a radical member of the Histadrut's central committee, expressed to me his concern that a portion of the workers' councils will put up their own lists for the next Histadrut elections if the double form of representation that disenfranchises them is not eliminated. Should such independent lists spring up, the Likud's ubiquitous David Levy may take control of the Labor unions as well.

Labor will also have to move to end the estrangement of residents of development towns from the old Labor settlements among which they live. Zaban is pressing for new institutions that would plan industry and social policy on a regional basis, something that would force kibbutz business enterprises to cooperate, and in some cases integrate, with enterprises in development towns. Such cooperation, he holds, would greatly increase opportunities for social reciprocity in Israel's hinterland and, finally, provide the basis for the integration of school systems that are now considerably better in the kibbutzim and established moshavim. Just such a strategy for reorganizing the public economy and educational system along regional lines was put forward to me by Jellal Abu-Tuami as the most plausible way to integrate Israeli Arabs into the national life. It seems an idea whose time has come, but Shimon Peres does not seem bold enough to carry it through.

IV

Diplomatic problems, however, continue to put questions of social reform in eclipse. Begin will now remain in office for at least a while longer and likely beyond April 1982, when the Camp David timetable calls for Israel to return the remainder of the Sinai to Egypt. This will mean dismantling some strategic air bases and well-established settlements. But Begin's top ministers and advisers on foreign policy matters — Yitzchak Shamir, the foreign minister, Ariel Sharon, and Moshe Arens, chairman of the Knesset Committee on Foreign Affairs and Security — were all opponents of the Camp David accords and wary of having these final parts of the Sinai revert to Egyptian control. The Palestinian autonomy talks always seemed to them doomed precisely because they can imagine no West Bank concessions.

To this group, which Begin has certainly joined in spirit since Weizman and Dayan resigned, the Jewish settling of the West Bank remains essential not only in order to preempt the evolution of a Palestinian state — which most Israelis now regard as a Trojan horse for terrorism — but also as fulfulling some Revisionist Zionist mission to unite Eretz Yisrael. Since Tehiya's three representatives in the Knesset share these views — and are even more fanatical about them — and since Tehiya is one of several groups who might hold the key to a Likud majority, Begin may harden his line on the Palestinians still further. He may accelerate settlement, reclaim exclusive water and residual land rights — which he was reputed to have conceded in conversations with Sol Linowitz, President Carter's negotiator — in the hope that President Sadat will scuttle the Camp David process before the Sinai withdrawal is complete.

Begin's group certainly would want to avoid having the Israeli-Egyptian peace break down, as they believe it may, after the Sinai has been evacuated; they would rather have Sadat — not Begin — be the first to flinch. One can only imagine that such calculations crossed Begin's mind when he arranged to be photographed bear-hugging Sadat for the world press just two days before Iraq's reactor was bombed.

That raid may have nevertheless done more for peace than for war, at least for a while. Harvard's Nadav Safran, who was one of the first to promote contacts between Israeli and Egyptian leaders and who is certainly no friend of Begin, told me that he thinks the raid may have been a benefit to current American peace initiatives insofar as it has deflated the illusions among some Arab nations that they could plausibly make war on Israel as long as they had a bomb of their own. Of course, the bombing of the reactor was a diplomatic disaster for Israel in the UN; and State Department officials cannot view with favor the announcement of Sadam Hussein of Iraq that he intends to improve relations with Moscow. But, so long as Israel maintains a monopoly on the threat to use nuclear weapons, it can match the worst threats directed against it by such bloody-minded regimes as Hussein's or Qaddafi's. A nuclear race in the Middle East, one in which each side will be sprinting for a "second strike deterrent," could turn the area into the fuse for nuclear holocaust: the Syrian missile crisis graphically shows how easily, and how often, military threats in the area can escalate, and neither the military leaders of Israel nor, say, Iraq would want to risk the other side's striking first.

Yet, even if this raid could be viewed as one more detail in a long and brutal conflict, it has left this question: What will Israel's government do with the five or ten years of clear military preeminence the raid seems to have reconfirmed? So far as the West Bank is concerned, the Begin government has been providing a chilling answer. In just four years, General Sharon, acting less like Minister of Agriculture and more like Colonial Secretary, has orchestrated the quadrupling of the West Bank's Jewish settler population, which now stands at about 21,000. He has funneled millions of dollars to build facilities for Jewish settlement—roads, housing, water supply, and so forth—and has recently spent about $10 million more without securing authorization from government budget committees. Meanwhile, the settlers have been allowed to organize their own military units and are heavily armed in their new collectives—i.e., Karnei, Shomron, Ofra, and others that have been placed close to the most heavily populated Arab cities of Hebron, Nablus, and Jenin.

The Ramallah lawyer Aziz Shekhadeh, a man of great courage and moderation who supported the Sadat initiative in the face of PLO opposition, told me recently that he fears the Israeli Power Corporation will soon take over the old Jordanian Jerusalem Electric Company and merge it with Israel's grid. His son, Raja, also a lawyer, has prepared a brief in which he charges that it is now possible, according to the ordinances of the military government, for "Israeli settlements and any other body of which the military Government approves to expropriate land quietly without having to go through the requirements of announcing their intentions or obtaining the permission of non-military bodies."* Raja Shekhadeh's fears may be exaggerated in view of earlier Israeli Supreme Court decisions that have impeded some land expropriation, but thousands of dunams of what the Israeli authorities call state land—really *miri* lands that were not considered in the public domain under Jordanian law—have been confiscated. Such actions have depressed the West Bank economy; about 260,000 Arabs have left between 1968 and 1980.†

Moreover, the integration of the West Bank into Israel's political economy is proceeding swiftly. The West Bank imports more from Israel than anywhere else and in 1979 ran a trade deficit of approximately $49 million. Seventy thousand West Bank workers earn their livings in the Jewish state without trade union protection. Meron Benvenisti, a former vice mayor of Jerusalem, has recently issued a report which charges that the economic integration of the area into Israel is approaching what it might be if the West Bank were annexed politically.

The new mayor of Hebron, Mustafa Abdul Nabi Natshe, shares Benvenisti's apprehensions; he told me that only about 10 percent of the teachers and civil servants in the West Bank still remain on the Jordanian payroll. But the process of political repression has, in Natshe's view, gone "from bad to worse," and this seems to him a much more serious obstacle to future relations between Israelis and resident Palestinians, who, Natshe insists, would otherwise want to push the PLO toward a political settlement. His predecessor, Faid Kawasmeh, was widely viewed as a moderate with good connections in Jordan and Saudi Arabia. He secured a $10 million grant from the Saudis to improve Hebron's municipal facilities, but he was summarily deported after some terrorists attacked and killed

---

*The West Bank and the Rule of Law, a study commissioned by the International Commission of Jurists, 1980, p. 108.

†See Adnan Abu Odeh, "Jordan and the Middle East Crises," *Foreign Policy & Defense Review*, American Enterprise Institute, Washington, D.C., vol. III, No. 1, 1981, p. 11.

a group of Jewish settlers in Hebron last year. Since then, all
political meetings have been banned, a far cry from the atmosphere immediately after the announcement of the Camp David
agreements.

Even throwing rocks is now met with harsh police action. A
young boy was shot and killed in a melee after he threw rocks
in a refugee camp north of Hebron just three weeks ago. This
is not to say the military government is without sensible fears of
its own but to stress that the political tension is reaching a critical
point and that the leaders of the West Bank — mayors, university
teachers, lawyers, and so on — are now more committed than
ever before to PLO leadership. Several of them told me that
Begin's re-election will precipitate an eventual uprising. Some
of this may be bluster; but Rafik Halabi, Israeli television's West
Bank correspondent whom Sharon has tried to have fired repeatedly for reporting West Bank events in an even-handed
manner,* told me that he now meets with hostility in many places
that formerly welcomed him warmly. He does not dare to enter
any of the Jewish settlements.

Gush Emunim settlers meanwhile continue to expand their
footholds in the West Bank, the latest in the ruin of the Avram
Avinu synagogue within the Hebron casbah and in the Beit
Hadassah Hospital, where a naive twenty-year-old woman from
Brooklyn explained to me and other reporters† how she and
her fellows were "touched by the hand of God." To build a Jewish
quarter in Hebron is, true enough, no offense against civil liberty
so long as the settlers are prepared to abide by the laws of the
majority. But, as she quickly told me, this is not the point: "The
Arabs must learn that we rule here." And, although she claims
her comrades would never fire at other Jews, one cannot help
wondering if Sharon has already set the stage for civil war or
for rampant vigilantism against the Arab community.

*

* Halabi, by the way, fears that there will be a "house cleaning" in the television
news department if Begin forms a new government. The Israeli press has already
charged that Begin intends to put Israeli television under the supervision of the
Prime Minister's office.
† See Anthony Lewis's column in the *New York Times*, July 5, 1981.

Should Sharon become Begin's Defense Minister, the Arabs of the West Bank would have that young woman's point driven home even more clearly than during the last four years. The budget and other means of Sharon's Agriculture Ministry pale next to those at the disposal of the Ministry of Defense. Granted, many old liberals in the Likud and most of the army's senior staff officers despise Sharon for his megalomania and also for his attempts to squeeze more money out of the defense budget by charging the General Staff with wastefulness. Begin, no doubt, would like to retain the ministry for himself or hand it to Moshe Arens. But Sharon's vote may now be enough to bring any new Likud coalition down, and no one doubts that he would threaten to do this in order to take over the Defense Ministry. Tehiya might well make Sharon's appointment a condition for allowing Begin an initial vote of confidence.

The rejectionism of the PLO is no better than Sharon's, but it may become beside the point if the Israeli government continues to try to solve its problems by annexation when it should be facing the possibilities of partition. In five years there may be nothing more to talk about, no way to draw national boundaries between Israeli and Palestinian populations. And it would be vain to assume that Palestinian young people will meanwhile sit on their hands. Caches of arms are regularly discovered on the West Bank. Who knows how much is not detected, or how many thousands of Israeli troops it would take to put down Palestinian rioting should this become more widespread? Shimon Peres would, at least, quickly halt settlement in the heart of Arab concentrations of population and has indicated a willingness to negotiate genuine autonomy arrangements on the Gaza Strip as a first step.

Still, Begin's misguided policies may put him on a collision course with the Reagan administration regardless of the President's campaign denial that the West Bank settlements are illegal. Members of Reagan's inner circle—e.g., Edwin Meese and Caspar Weinberger—are strongly committed to the defense and interests of the Arab regimes in the Gulf—particularly to Saudi Arabia, Incorporated. They are also keen to develop a network of anti-Soviet alliances in the Middle East led by Egypt, where the United States already has about 4,000 military personnel and over a billion dollars in new investments. But Weinberger and George Shultz, who is also said to be respected by Reagan, have, by the way, long been involved with the Bechtel Corporation, a contracting firm that has built military bases and other facilities for the Saudis, and Weinberger is known to be intent particularly on beefing up America's rapid deployment force, which will need even more Gulf bases.

The California corporate executives who have strongly backed Reagan are well aware of the extent to which the Sun Belt economy depends on further sales of high technology military and aviation hardware to Arab states. Will a Republican president risk ruining relations with such good clients in order to appease the family of the young woman from Brooklyn? These are, of course, bad reasons to stop Begin from continuing a policy of West Bank annexation. But most Israeli moderates I have talked to here seem in despair about the Begin government and look to the United States to get tough with it. They are deeply worried that if, following this election, the West Bank were absorbed into Israel, their country's claims to be a democratic society would be extremely difficult to defend. They are more worried that their children will die in a futile war.

Amos Elon, Israel's leading political columnist, and many other moderate Israelis bluntly expressed the hope that American Jews will hold their peace if Reagan puts pressure on Begin to stop West Bank settlements and negotiate seriously on the Palestinian issue. Elon believes that "on the whole, the impact of American Jews on Israel has been destructive." He might have added that, in attempting to shield Begin from American government reservations regarding annexationist policies, American Jewish leaders have only weakened their ability to join other American liberals in preventing sales of murderous arms to Arab countries: according to Leonard Fein, the editor of the liberal American Jewish magazine *Moment*, Max Fisher—a former chairman of the American Governors of the Jewish Agency and, "arguably, the most powerful Jew in America"*—softened his opposition to the sale of AWACs to Saudi Arabia in order not to allow an

*Moment, June 1981.

open split to develop between the Jewish community and the Reagan administration over Middle East policy. Fisher, it seems, was reassured by Reagan's promise to impose a "military balance" between Israel and its neighbors. Elon would rather have Reagan impose peace by stopping the integration of the West Bank into Israel before it is too late.

# Can Begin Be Stopped?

*June 1983*

Is the Reagan plan dead? On April 10, King Hussein announced that Jordan would neither act "separately nor in lieu of anybody else in Middle East peace negotiations." This has seriously undermined hopes that President Reagan's call on September 1 for Palestinian self-rule in association with Jordan would revive the "peace process." The King's statement also releases Reagan from the promise he made to Hussein in December that if Jordan were willing to enter talks, he would confront the Israeli government over its settlement policies before any negotiations. As if to underscore the threat of that promise being made again, the World Zionist Organization (which does what the Israeli cabinet wants) revealed in early April a plan for fifty-seven new settlements in the West Bank to be completed by 1987. Some would be added to those in the heart of Arab-populated areas, between Nablus and Jenin. Also planned are 250 miles of new roads and up to 125 acres a year for industrial projects "to encourage private initiative."*

This looks like a formula for settler colonialism, and also for expelling those Arabs who actively oppose it. Yet a senior State Department official told me a week after Hussein's announcement what had, he said, always been made clear to Jordan. "America cannot force any issue on Israel in the absence of an

*\*Jerusalem Post*, April 10, 1983.

Arab peace partner." He denied that Hussein's statement fore-closed further action in support of the Reagan proposals, but he conceded that there was nothing left for the administration to do except "more of the same." Can that be enough? Or, having outlasted this last show of Arab disharmony, does Prime Minister Begin now have a free hand to annex the West Bank?

The State Department's insistence that such a question is pre-mature may be more than a brave front. If the alternative to the Reagan proposals is oppressive Israeli rule of a million Palestin-ians, then Jordan still has strong reasons to negotiate. There has been some confusion in the press about this because few com-mentators have been willing to distinguish between the Reagan plan in principle and the "initiative" regarding possible talks with Israel, which Reagan and Hussein seemed to agree on last De-cember in Washington. Hussein has announced that he is unable to participate in the initiative. But he cannot repudiate the Rea-gan plan.

In fact, careful readers of his statement will see that Hussein not only did not "reject" the Reagan plan — as the *New York Times* headline put it — but strongly endorsed it: "We believe and con-tinue to believe," the King said, "in the establishment of a con-federal relationship that would govern and regulate the future of the Jordanian and Palestinian peoples." Jordan and the PLO, he said, should come to an agreement about confederation in advance — a clear contradiction of the resolution of the Palestine National Council at Algiers, which called for an independent Palestinian state before confederation. "A confederal relation-ship would be sought if only . . . in recognition of the bonds which have linked the people of Jordan and Palestine through-out history."

In the current situation, which Hussein characterized in his statement as "no war–no peace," the Jordanians are potentially the most vulnerable side. Hussein as much as conceded this: "Israel forges ahead . . . with a systematic policy of evacuating the West Bank to change the demographic composition of the occupied Arab territories. . . . We strive to confront this pro-gram, which stands to affect Jordan more than any other country and which threatens Jordan's identity and national security."

Palestinians make up a majority on the East Bank, and some 300,000 have come from the West Bank in the last ten years. An independent Palestinian state on the West Bank and the Gaza Strip — such as the one demanded by the Palestine National Council at Algiers — would undermine the legitimacy of Hashemites in Amman more directly than it would threaten Israelis in Tel Aviv.

So the administration intends to redouble its effort to reassure Hussein that he alone is America's choice to make a settlement for the Palestinians, and that Arafat can have a part only if he will lead Fatah to a Jordanian confederation. The administration might have been clearer about this all along. A State Department official told me that Hussein decided not to "make his move" now partly because of the mixed message Arafat kept getting from President Reagan, via the Saudis, that Hussein's failure to achieve an agreement with Arafat might lead to de facto American recognition of the PLO.*

The King, it must be said, showed none of this ambiguity in his statement. Rather, he openly mocked Arafat's political pretensions: "We leave it to the PLO and the Palestinian people to choose the ways and means for the salvation of themselves and their land, and for the realization of their declared aims in the manner they see fit." He ended with a warning: "As for us in Jordan, we find ourselves more concerned than anybody else to confront the de facto annexation of the West Bank and Gaza Strip, which forces us to take all measures to secure our national security in all its dimensions."

Hussein may yet try some dramatic move, such as a plebiscite on the East Bank, to demonstrate the support of Jordan's Palestinians and gain more support on the West. ("I can't talk about that," the senior State Department official told me.) But Hussein cannot go ahead with much of anything without Saudi backing. And the Saudis let him down. They became anxious about the pace of Syrian rearmament — there are more than four thousand Soviet advisers in Syria — and about the power of pro-Syrian Palestinian radicals to commit acts of violence in the Gulf.

*Karen Elliot House confirms this point from the King's side; *Wall Street Journal*, April 14, 1983.

The Abu Nidal group's assassination of Isam Sartawi in Portugal was a clear enough sign of that power. Harvard professor Nadav Safran put it this way: "The Americans did not move fast enough. Now the Saudis fear Syrian threats more than they are encouraged by American blandishments. Hussein — whom the Saudis have long viewed as an ally — now feels that he cannot depend on their support even for a first step."

Hussein has an obvious stake in the administration's promise to get a moratorium on Israeli settlements. The Saudis seem to feel they have a greater stake in maintaining a show of Arab unity that will obscure their weakness. In spite of the administration's controversial campaign to sell them AWACs and other advanced weapons — perhaps because of it — the Saudis are skeptical about U.S. promises to apply economic sanctions to Israel. Moreover, Saudi oil revenues are declining and the Saudi budget has a deficit of $10 billion. King Fahd is in a cautious mood. While the administration has suspended deliveries of F-16s to Israel until Begin comes to terms on the Lebanon negotiations, Israel continues to command the skies without the new planes. And the Egyptian government is contributing to the Saudis' paralyzing show of solidarity with the PLO. President Mubarak, though he has encouraged Arafat to join the "initiative," has openly disagreed with Secretary of State Shultz's view that the PLO should lose its mandate to represent the Palestinians. Egyptians were deeply embarrassed by their peace treaty with Israel during the Lebanese war. The Mubarak regime has something to prove. So does Shultz, whose intervention in the Lebanon negotiations may be the prelude to an effort to rid the Saudi regime of its doubts about U.S. "resolve" to freeze Israeli settlements.

II

That resolve is certainly in question. Some of the administration officials I talked to openly confessed their doubts about the power of the United States to prevent Begin from annexing the West Bank. An American diplomat in Tel Aviv assured me that overt American pressure on Israel would only reinforce Begin's proven electoral majority. More recently, a White House official told me he was concerned about President Reagan's standing among American Jews as the presidential election draws closer. And one can never be sure how Congress will react, even if Reagan should want to get tougher with Begin. A State Department official complained: "In September Begin rejected the Reagan plan outright, and then, in December, the lame duck Congress turned around and increased the appropriation for Israel by $475 million." As if to rub that in, the American Jewish Committee sent to American newspaper editors the results of a new Gallup poll in February, claiming that "pro-Israel sympathies of Americans have returned to levels comparable to the period before the 'Lebanese crisis.' . . . Half of all Americans (49 percent) now continue to support Israel as against 12 percent supporting Arab nations." Is there nothing the American government can do but make its case to the Israeli public and hope for the best?

Just how much leverage on Israel, in any case, does the United States now have? Do the actions of Begin's government imply that it is less now than, say, during the Camp David negotiations, when President Carter's warnings to Begin were decisive in getting Israel to withdraw the north Sinai settlements? It is true that Israel is now building more of its own aircraft, missiles, tanks, and small weapons. But, in fact, U.S. power over the Israeli economy is far greater than ever before and is growing every month. And Israel's unprecedented dependence on American aid partly derives, ironically, from the Begin government's extravagant investment in the West Bank. Israel is using about $200 million a year to build housing, shopping centers, and industry there — much of which would not otherwise have been spent within the old borders. But the government is spending many times that sum to produce an illusion of social prosperity so that the Likud's major electoral constituencies — the young, the least educated, and North African Jews resentful of the old Labor aristocracy — will continue to go along with Begin's paternalist style and triumphalist ideology. Begin, to be blunt, is using American money to create a fait accompli that will make it impossible to carry out the American government's policy.

This manipulation of American aid has its origins in Israel's electoral politics. During the first three years of the Likud government—from 1977 to 1980—Israel suffered badly from a combination of the government's more liberal investment policy, rampant tax evasion, enormous military expenditure, and inflationary trends in the Western nations. The austerity budgets of the first two Likud Finance Ministers, Simcha Ehrlich and Yigael Hurwitz, provoked labor unrest and social resentment but still did not bring down the inflation rate below 100 percent. What was worse for the Likud as the election year approached was that this hyperinflation produced a fall in industrial production, though the worst effects of this were mitigated by the new American aid grants linked to the Camp David accords. Likud governments set up wage controls and cut subsidies of essential commodities such as food and gasoline, but these policies did little to reverse the decline in real income that soon began to alienate poorer voters from among the young and the Sephardic communities.

In fact, at the beginning of 1981, Labor was leading the polls by a wide margin. Some 35 percent of the electorate—mainly potential Likud voters—were declaring themselves undecided. This came as a shock to Likud leaders, who demanded that something be done about the economic situation. Of course, Begin's populist and revisionist Zionist rhetoric appealed to more than consumer anxieties. But Likud's leaders knew that their party's majority was largely owing to its promise to run the country more efficiently and fairly than the Labor Alignment had done.

Begin's much-discussed popularity among Sephardic Jews particularly depended on that promise. Even in 1981, only about a quarter of managers and administrators, and about 15 percent of scientific and academic workers, were Sephardic Jews—though such Jews accounted for well over half of the population.* And most of these highly placed Sephardim were immigrants from Iraq and Egypt, people who often voted for Labor;

---

*This information was compiled by Arie Ben-Shachar of the University of Toronto from the data on Sephardic and Ashkenazi Jews in *The Israeli Government Yearbook* for 1981 and 1982.

they were better off than the more numerous Moroccans, whose families came in the late fifties and now lived in the dense slums of Tel Aviv and Jerusalem or in dreary development towns. Most voters from Moroccan families were born in Israel but were not yet of it; they had religious fathers and illiterate mothers. They were not the children of the Zionist revolution, and they looked to the Likud to give them a share in the national identity.

The Likud, like the American Democratic Party earlier in this century, organized the interests of less well educated immigrants, the victims of prejudice, the poor, and the young and ambitious against entrenched elites. When, during the twenties and thirties, Republicans spoke of "free enterprise," many Democrats took this to mean "freedom for the bankers, the trusts, the WASPs." Similarly, when Israeli WASPs (White Ashkenazi Sabras with *Proteksia*) spoke of socialist Zionism, Likud voters thought of established Histadrut corporations, patronage jobs for the nephews of European Zionists, snobbish agricultural collectives that claimed to be models of national virtue yet would not share classrooms with the newcomers. In 1981, moreover, 87 percent of those in the top tenth income group were Israeli Jews of European origin, while Sephardic Jews and Arabs together made up some 70 percent of the lowest tenth. There was a considerable movement toward equality in the middle-income groups, but it was just this that was being put at risk by industrial stagnation.

Begin's third Finance Minister, Yoram Aridor, decided on a new policy that would disguise that risk. Before the 1981 election, he cut tariffs on cars and other much-sought-after goods, linked salaries to 100 percent of the cost-of-living index, and raised subsidies. These measures set off a buying spree such as the country had never seen. Since most people were buying goods that were actually falling in price—e.g., cars with a reduced tariff—the rate of inflation dropped for a few months. Government revenues also increased as a result of consumer buying, and salaries of government workers, now 35 percent of the labor force, did not rise as quickly as before.

Aridor claimed success, though his policies greatly increased the balance-of-payments deficit for 1981 and exacerbated the decline in Israel's industrial production. Still, he reassured voters, who quickly returned to the Likud. Of some 830,000 people who were added to the electorate between 1973 and 1981, some 650,000 voted for the Likud and the other parties of the right in 1981. They included not only young and Sephardic voters but also Russian immigrants and religious zealots impressed by the Likud's ability to unify its constituency around what they perceived as prosperity and by the hard-line policy calling for "unity of the land." The Begin government, moreover, has not much changed its ways since the narrow victory of 1981. While rates of inflation in other Western democracies have fallen substantially with the fall in oil prices and the general recession, Israel still suffers from 150 percent inflation, even with substantial cuts in the defense budget. Moreover, by the government's own projections, the Israeli economy will show no growth at all in 1983, for the first time since 1966.

There is a frenetic side to the new economic atmosphere. Salaries are linked to the cost of living, but one must scramble incessantly to protect one's savings; consumer credit is difficult to get, and ordinary mortgages are impossible. Some 700,000 investors—including high school students and kibbutz secretaries—were speculating in the shaky Israeli stock market when it crashed last January. Yet few in the country are feeling the pinch just now. Real incomes have risen about 15 percent under Aridor (although the number of Israeli Jews who live below the official poverty line has doubled). Subsidies for essential commodities, never more than 3 percent of the GNP under Labor, now run at 5 to 6 percent. Aridor has made the Bank of Israel sell off foreign exchange reserves to keep the Israeli shekel about 20 percent above its value so that consumers can continue to import durable goods from Europe.

One Treasury official, a professional economist who is appalled—like most of Israel's economists—by what Aridor is doing, told me that, by the Treasury's own estimates, Israelis imported 17 percent more consumer goods in 1982 than in 1981. Civilian imports for 1983 are expected to rise to $8.5 billion from $7.8 billion in 1982.* (A friend of mine, an importer, told me that Israelis imported some 100,000 video recorders in 1982.) Such artificial support for Israeli currency put Israeli exporters

*This was confirmed in *The National Budget: 1983* (Jerusalem: Bank of Israel Publications, January 1983).

at a serious disadvantage, which the Treasury is trying to make
up for with costly export subsidies, though not enough to reverse
the decline in Israeli agriculture. Nor are the actual costs of West
Bank settlement small ones. Loans to settlers, the cost of roads,
utilities, and military encampments, and other expenditures—
all amounting to more than $200 million—are hidden within
the overall development budget of the government and the Jewish Agency.

Where does all this money come from? The simple fact is that
Aridor covers the government's expenses with American aid or
else sells off accumulated foreign currency reserves that are essential for future economic development. Israel's balance-of-
payments deficit in 1982 was an astonishing $4.9 billion—only
$2 billion of which was for military procurement—and the pay-
ments deficit promises to be about the same in 1983. The American government covers about 45 percent of this deficit by grants
in aid amounting to about $2.3 billion. Approximately 25 percent
comes from American Jewish organizations, German reparations, and other sources. The remaining balance-of-payments
deficit is covered by gold and other hard reserves, of which,
according to the Treasury official I spoke to, perhaps $3 billion
to $4 billion remain. "Israel today is operating as if it can expect
optimal conditions of aid from the United States, without any
cuts or interruptions," he told me. "But any serious cut, even a
few hundred million dollars, would come as a great blow." In
fact, nearly all of the American aid not spent for military pro-
curement, about $900 million, is used to service Israel's accu-
mulated debt to the United States.

Some Israelis are doing very well in the new economy. The
banks—which act as brokers, agents, and major investors in the
stock exchange—have record profits. Contractors who build
new West Bank settlements or military installations—many from
the second Israel—are making fortunes. Israel's rising industries, the high tech corporations of Tel Aviv and Haifa, continue
to prosper and raise capital from as far away as the New York
capital markets. But the government's fiscal policies have made
credit for older industries difficult to come by, and these are
where a great many Israelis, especially Sephardim, earn their

livings. Today Israel's agricultural exporters, and many of its electronics and textile firms, borrow some $650 million from U.S. banks. The banks are willing to extend short-term credit at excellent rates so long as they see the American government guaranteeing the solvency of the Israeli Treasury—as Congress did in December.

Even a small diminution of government aid, however, would affect Israel's credit rating for the worse. The Hebrew University economist Eitan Sheshinsky told me: "If Washington sends signals to the American business community that the United States will not underwrite short-term credit with aid, it could have an immediate impact." Unemployment would rise dramatically, and not only among the Arab workers, who tend to be employed in construction.

### III

Begin and his top ministers understand the nature of Israel's economic dependence as well as do the economists who criticize them for it. So does Shultz, an economist who was once a colleague of Sheshinsky's at the University of Chicago. No serious discussion of prospects for the Reagan peace initiative should ignore how much damage the Reagan administration can do to Begin's standing by even a small shift in economic policy, a shift in its signals to American banks, for example, that would not affect military aid at all. Again, Begin's popularity runs deeper than his ability to make consumer goods available. But it is also less than meets the eye of the many journalists, who—like the American diplomat I talked to in Tel Aviv—suppose Begin's majority to be permanent whatever happens. The Sephardic middle class and the young voters who have thrown their support to the Likud have been impressed by Begin's ability to deliver what he promises. But these are swing voters who, while inclining toward the Likud, would have once voted for David Ben-Gurion. They now give Begin credit for intimidating the Arabs, "standing up to the Americans," and making them feel better off.

Political memories are shorter in Israel than they used to be. That is why so many are susceptible to demagoguery. It is true that the most susceptible, the hard core of Begin's young Moroccan supporters, revere him and still have hopes for Sharon. Many express the fear of being relegated to menial jobs now held by Arabs should Israel leave the West Bank—a concern that is widespread even if it is groundless. But there are equivocal feelings among them too, especially about the great expense of settling the West Bank while the housing density among Sephardic families is double that among Ashkenazi families. The polls continue to show that a majority of Israelis—if only a narrow one—favor trading large parts of the West Bank for peace.

Not that the polls show declining support for Begin among the young—whether Sephardic or European. The war in Lebanon has coarsened political debate, and one hears more and more talk of expelling Palestinians to Jordan and worse. There is, after all, satisfaction in using force to get one's way, in dominating people after living in fear of being dominated. The Jewish settlers in the West Bank have set the tone: some have complained in their newspapers that Arabs have been sitting on buses while Jews stand. The young soldiers who spend a month or two a year patrolling the sullen Arab towns become hardened, sometimes brutal; indeed, they have been ordered to act brutally.* And there is disdain for Jews as well. Some of Begin's supporters showed an ugly and threatening contempt for Peace Now demonstrators who were demanding Sharon's resignation from the cabinet after the Kahan Commission report held him indirectly responsible for the Beirut massacres. Not many of Begin's supporters, it is true, would have thrown the grenade that killed the Peace Now activist Emile Greensweig—whose last graduate paper was devoted to the need for political tolerance. But many people turned out to shout curses and warnings at his mourners. General Sharon did much to encourage such bullying chauvinism to flourish in Israel, as did General Rafael Eitan, the outgoing Chief of Staff, who suggested before retiring that West Bank Palestinians should be made to feel like "drugged bugs in a bottle." If only for their influence on the young, it is a relief that both are now out of the limelight.

The new Defense Minister, Moshe Arens, has shown himself

*See Leonard Fein's report in *Moment*, April 1983.

more pragmatic than Sharon as well as more restrained. He appointed a moderate professional, Moshe Levi, to replace Eitan. "Arens got something of a political education in Washington," a well-connected Likud member of the Knesset told me. "He is steely in his quiet way on the West Bank question, but he knows what a fight with America would mean, and that the American Jews could not prevent it or even be united behind Israel's policy." Arens is far more likely than Sharon to lead Israel to a settlement in Lebanon. Arens will not endorse the Reagan proposals, but would he favor a settlements freeze if Hussein were persuaded to come forward?

"It depends how this is done," the same Likud politician told me. "If Reagan threatens Begin openly, the Israeli government will announce a hundred new settlements the following morning. But if a strategy is coordinated in advance, if the policy is 'no settlements for the period of the negotiations,' as it was in Camp David, not only Arens but Begin too may have to accept it." (A veteran cabinet minister who joined us agreed with this.) Begin has said that he is willing to talk peace with Hussein with no conditions. Could he allow himself to be seen, at home and in the American Congress, as someone who would slam the door on the peace talks by refusing to halt settlements? Could a Likud government withstand the kind of economic retaliation that the Reagan administration could then undertake — without cutting military aid? The head of the Liberal Party faction of the Likud has already said that he "prefers a government crisis to a break with Washington." And there must be some in the National Religious Party — with six seats in Begin's coalition — who now share that sentiment. When the Knesset elected Labor's Chaim Herzog as President by secret ballot last March, most political observers believed that he had some NRP votes.

Even if the U.S. government managed to bring the Begin government down, however, this would not necessarily be a victory. As the Likud politician put it, "You would have Begin in opposition, nearly forty thousand settlers in Judea and Samaria, and a hundred thousand supporters of the Gush Emunim in the streets." Besides, he said, with most of the land under Israeli control, and scores of underpopulated settlements already under way, the "freeze" would be merely "symbolic."

He could be right, but it seems smug to suppose that an Israeli freeze on settlements would remain merely symbolic for the Israeli families who are now putting down roots in occupied territory a good distance away from Hebrew towns and cities. Few now go to "Judea and Samaria" to fulfill Gush Emunim's perverse idealism. Settlers go there because they see a bargain — for example, a five-room apartment for the price of two rooms in Jerusalem. Who would want to move their families under a cloud of negotiations — particularly when they remember what happened to the settlers in the Sinai two years ago? Besides, we saw after the Sadat initiative how leaders become hostages as much to the hopes they inspire as to the hatreds.

The Likud member of the Knesset was not wrong to suspect that once negotiations get started, Congress will not look with favor on Israeli actions that undermine them. Congressman Barney Frank of Massachusetts, one of the usually pro-Israel liberal Democrats, told me that if "Hussein comes in," this could transform congressional attitudes: "The Congress is committed to Israel's security," he said, "but it is more willing than ever before to differ with the Israeli government about how to keep Israel secure."

Nevertheless, it is the Israeli government, not the administration or Congress, that must negotiate the kind of compromise that will satisfy elementary Jordanian and Palestinian demands. Begin will not disclaim Jewish sovereignty in "Judea and Samaria." And when one looks for potential rivals to the Likud's power, the fact is that Israel's Labor Alignment remains a divided and feckless party and its leader, Shimon Peres, among the least respected politicians in the country.

Peres has been in the public eye for thirty years, and during that time — from his shady part in the infamous Lavon affair to his current feud with Yitzchak Rabin — he has gained an ineradicable reputation for opportunism. Nor does he command the respect of many in the party caucus. Peres defends the Reagan proposals to sympathetic audiences. But he would not do so in the Knesset last January when he sensed the tide was running against him. The moderates in the caucus begged him, a Knesset member told me, to endorse the Reagan proposals again. Instead he condemned the government for cutting the military budget. Peres has come out against new settlements. But when the Histadrut debated whether its construction firm should accept contracts to build in occupied territory, Peres endorsed a compromise that pleased nobody: no factories near Arab populations, but the company could build services and housing.

In fairness to Peres, his views are no less confusing than those of most of the Labor politicians for whom he speaks. Like him, most Labor leaders want to make a deal with Jordan and yet seem unwilling to defend proposals—especially regarding Jordanian rights in Jerusalem—that would attract Hussein. But it still seems possible that a Labor government would be more flexible than Begin's, that it would want Israel's borders to conform with the concentrations of the Hebrew population, and that it would, in the course of negotiations, settle for less land for more peace. A change of leadership in the Labor Party therefore would be important.

The only man who can now give that leadership is the former president, Yitzchak Navon, a man of liberal, some say dovish, views and a descendant of one of Jerusalem's distinguished Sephardic families—a promising combination of qualities. He has neither declared his intention to run nor proven his abilities as a political infighter. But an interview with him left me certain that he has at least come to be aware of himself as a unifying force. There is, he told me, no majority in the country for Begin's foreign policy. The Labor Party has not recovered from the October 1973 war. "People want a paycheck and they want their soldiers to defend them. We failed them on both counts in the seventies. Richard Crossman said: 'Oppositions don't win elections, governments lose them.' But the Labor Party is still divided along the old rifts. We have still not got over the Lavon affair. Thousands come through the President's residence every month looking for leaders to tell them what they want. The party needs strong new leadership that people can trust." He made no effort to discourage my conclusion that he hoped to provide it.

Navon is an affable man, proud of his writing (which includes plays for the musical theater). He has been close to power for a long time—he was Ben-Gurion's private secretary—but he has never been tainted by political corruption. He has also shown some strength. As chairman of the Knesset Foreign Affairs and

Security Committee, he was important in getting Israel to approve the interim agreement with Egypt in 1975. Like Ronald Reagan, moreover, he has a disarmingly common touch that works on television; he likes to think in aphorisms — "Jews came here to fight nature, not human beings" — and is able to reduce social problems to homely phrases. Navon's detractors call him inept, a softy, and point to his lack of executive experience. But he transformed the presidency into an active moral force, and he deserves much of the credit for bringing about the Kahan Commission. He has been able to bridge the ethnic divisions in Israel and, fluent in Arabic, is very popular with Israeli Arabs — who could be the key to a Labor majority. More important problems for him than his alleged softness are current rumors about his marriage breaking up and his lack of an obvious political base in the Labor Party.

Besides, would Peres and Rabin step aside? They may have no choice in view of Labor's miserable showing in recent polls — ten seats down from 1981. Navon's candidacy may seem irresistible to ordinary party members. One poll, in the new liberal Jerusalem weekly *Koteret Rashit*, shows Labor tied with the Likud if Navon were its leader. "There is a vacuum at the top," *Davar* political correspondent Danny Rubenstein told me. "What is left of the party machine would suck Navon into the leadership if he were ready to fight." If he fought, I asked the Israelis I talked to, and if he won, and if he proved strong and Labor won the election: would the new government deliver the country to the Reagan plan?

Nobody was very optimistic. The Reagan proposals assume that the West Bank is not yet lost to the Arab world. If we judge by demographic facts alone, this is true. There are still fewer than 40,000 settlers on the West Bank if one excludes the housing developments on the outskirts of Greater Jerusalem. It is not clear that any leader can reverse the political momentum that Begin has established. Even if, as a high official of the Jewish Agency admitted to me, Israel does not have the resources to heavily populate the West Bank with Jews, Begin can implant enough colonies to obstruct "any settlement that a Labor government might want to negotiate."

"The young people are impressed by facts," Rubenstein lamented. Like most other Israeli moderates, he believes that external pressure on Israel is weak because U.S. aid is part of the problem. "When are the Americans going to see what Begin is doing with their aid?" One hears this question from a remarkable number of people, including the country's most distinguished writers, journalists, and scholars, and even from members of the Knesset. It suggests how demoralized the country's democratic forces have become.

Begin, after all, is racing against them as well. True, 400,000 turned up for a demonstration to demand that the government conform to democratic standards. But most of those people today, as before, are counting heads, reading the papers, and losing heart. So Rubenstein may be right that it is no longer possible to advocate that aid to Israel continue as before, although, like many other Israeli liberals, he underestimates how bitter and divisive a fight over aid to Israel would become. Americans, and especially American Jews, should be thinking about how they support one Israeli future over another, support one group of Israelis over another. The Reagan plan presupposes democracy; its failure promises the colonial settler democracy that Zionist pioneers once tried so hard to avoid.

# The Divisions of Unity

*December 1984*
For Americans who have been disheartened listening to Menachem Begin and Yitzchak Shamir speak for Israel during the past seven years, the visit of Shimon Peres in October must have been something of a relief. In Washington, Peres talked of a plan for Israel's unilateral withdrawal from Lebanon. Instead of condemning the United Nations, Peres asked for an expanded peacekeeping force of UNIFIL troops "in order to provide security for Israel's frontiers."* When he spoke to the press about his country's requests for aid, he said little about Israel's virtues as an American strategic asset, but emphasized his government's plans to cut Israel's budget and imports and increase the productivity of Israeli industry.

When he met with Jewish writers and editors in New York, Peres explained how the new government would improve the "quality of life" on the West Bank and Gaza. Many of the Likud's former restrictions in the territories would be lifted: an Arab bank would be allowed; nearly all the books that had been banned would be permitted to circulate. The pro-PLO writer Raymonda Tawil would be permitted to publish a magazine.

Peres said that Arab mayors would be appointed for the five Arab towns now run by Israeli army officers—though the mayors who had been fired or deported would not get back their posts. Peres also spoke of accommodation with Jordan, of stra-

*See Peres's interview with Lally Weymouth, *Los Angeles Times*, October 14, 1984.

tegic cooperation with the Hashemite regime. Israel, he said, had "changed its settlements policy."

Though Peres speaks for a government half of which is composed of ministers from the Likud, he has not made a part of himself over in Begin's mold. Have the principles of Ben-Gurion's Labor movement outlasted the Likud? Just forming a "unity coalition" has given the Israeli government an ability to tackle problems that seemed beyond reach only three months ago. Does this mean that Israel can be expected to solve its deepest problem — its conflict with Palestinians and Arab states? The answers lie in the story of how the coalition came about and how it has been working.

I

Two weeks before the July 23 elections, when Shamir surprised Peres with an invitation to form a "national unity government," Peres dismissed the suggestion as a publicity stunt. Shamir was then trailing badly in the polls. The Likud government had started a questionable war and had obviously mismanaged the government's budget. Likud was running without any help from Begin himself. Shamir had been severely criticized by both major newspapers, *Ma'ariv* and *Yediot Acharonot*. Labor was united, well financed, and tightly organized; the long feud between Peres and Yitzchak Rabin was submerged.

Peres confidently replied to Shamir that a coalition of the major parties would undermine the parliamentary system. The very idea offended some Labor supporters. When Revisionist Zionist politicians from Jabotinsky to Begin have called for national unity, they usually meant their ideal of a militant corporate state.

The day after the elections, however, left-wing writers including A. B. Yehoshua and Amos Oz published a statement endorsing Shamir's offer. What liberal convictions could not justify, Yehoshua wrote, Israeli voters had made necessary. Of the 120 seats in the Knesset, Labor won forty-four, a plurality, but only three more than the Likud won. Two dovish, "civil rights" lists had six seats, while the ultranationalist Tehiya movement won

five. The rest of the seats, twenty-four, were divided among
thirteen other parties—religious factions, communists, annexationists, laissez-faire militants. That Labor did not win, Jerusalem's Mayor Teddy Kollek told me, came as a bigger shock
than the losses of 1977 and 1981. The alternative to a unity
government, Yehoshua insisted, would be growing cynicism
about democratic process—a "nation torn and split."

According to a poll in the daily *Ha'aretz*, 81 percent of Israeli
Jews agreed that a unity government should be formed, above
all to deal with the collapsing economy. The GNP had not grown
for two years. Inflation, already at 400 percent, began to climb
higher after the election; foreign exchange reserves, already
dangerously low, dropped by a third. There had been ninety-
three strikes in 1983, causing the loss of an estimated million
days of work. Investment of all kinds, even in real estate, had
largely ceased; volume on the Israeli stock exchange was down
to less than one sixth of what it had been the year before. Reckoned in dollars, tax collection had dropped by 15 percent.

By the end of July, fearing economic breakdown, Israelis converted some 300 billion more shekels into 900 million U.S. dollars. As soon as the vote was counted, economists at the Ministry
of Finance, now able to speak freely, warned that any further
drop in reserves of hard currency would put in jeopardy Israel's
ability to import grain and fuel. It would also threaten the government's ability to borrow short-term funds at favorable rates
on American capital markets. Larger interest payments would,
in turn, augment the foreign debt, which had already reached
some $22 billion, nearly 40 percent of the government budget
and a major cause of the inflation.

Shamir's cabinet, acting as a caretaker government, proposed
reductions in government spending. But the general secretary
of the Histadrut labor federation broke off negotiations with
Shamir's Finance Minister over a new wage contract for government workers. The Histadrut would consider a wage-price
freeze, the secretary announced, but he would not deal with a
government that had no authority. In private, he doubted that
a narrow Labor-led coalition would have any more authority
than the Likud. Could any narrow coalition restrain the unions

and reassure industrialists, shopkeepers, or farmers that Israeli money would be worth making?

There was also Lebanon. Contrary to the impression given in the American press, the war itself had not been unpopular. Israeli journalists had mainly turned against Ariel Sharon for the way he had fought it: nearly six hundred Israeli soldiers had been lost since 1982, and many more had joined peace groups in protest. But even after the Kahan Commission forced Sharon to leave the Defense Ministry for his part in the Beirut massacres, some 60 percent of Israelis supported the invasion.* If asked by the polls, they would say that the PLO was severely weakened.

The occupation of southern Lebanon was something else. Every week, several more Israeli soldiers, including reservists with wives and children, were killed or injured in routine patrols. Many fewer young Israelis than ever before were volunteering for career service or officer training.† The occupation was costing about $1 million a day. Israelis wondered if either party would have the courage to pull the Israel Defense Forces from advanced bases in areas dominated by Shiite militants. Wouldn't a narrow Likud government fear the charge of failure, a Labor government the charge of treachery? A few months before the election, some 32 percent of Israelis polled by a monthly magazine said they wanted a "government of strong leaders, not beholden to any of the political parties."‡

Liberal critics such as Yehoshua had opposed the war from the start and certainly wanted the IDF brought home. But they could take no comfort from that poll on leadership and still less from the elections themselves. Meir Kahane's movement, Kach, for example, drew some 26,000 votes from all segments of the population and double the national average from the army. Not only was Kahane to be a member of the Knesset, but a survey on August 3 revealed that some 15 percent of Jewish Israelis endorsed his idea that Palestinians should be deported to Arab countries and Israeli Arabs induced to emigrate.

---

*Data are taken from Dalia Shekhori's paper, "Public Attitudes in Israel toward the War in Lebanon," which she presented to the Kennedy School of Government at Harvard University, February 1984.
† Michael Grati, *Ha'aretz*, July 26, 1984.
‡*Monitin*, April 1984.

Kahane, it could be said, won only 1.2 percent of the vote. His election gave many other right-wing politicians, including Begin, the chance to criticize him for his racism. Yet many knowledgeable Israelis I talked to wondered whether the war against the PLO in Lebanon had irretrievably spoiled relations between Jews and the 600,000 Israeli Arabs. Labor and other moderate Jewish parties campaigned in the Arab sector as never before. But for the first time since the founding of the state, a majority of Arab citizens voted for lists endorsing the establishment of a separate Palestinian state under the PLO. The communists won four seats, and two were won by the Progressive List for Peace and Freedom, led jointly by Mohammed Mi'ari, a radical Arab lawyer, and Mati Peled, a reserve general who had met with Arafat.

Kahane's victory also raised doubts about the sympathies of the police. When his followers stormed through the Old City of Jerusalem after the election, smashing Arab shops, several border patrol officers were seen embracing them. At subsequent Kahane rallies, police kept order. When he went to open an "emigration office" in the Arab town of Umm-el-Fahm, the police surrounded him. But they arrested only rock-throwing Arabs who, along with hundreds of Jews, protested Kahane's mischief.

The day after Kahane's raid on the Old City, a well-known novelist who had been in the Warsaw ghetto told me that the time had come for democrats to take action. She supported Yehoshua's call for unity and wanted the police to be taken out of the hands of Interior Minister Joseph Burg, the leader of the National Religious Party. Still, she told me, it was time to "bash the heads" of Kahane's supporters. But who would be bashing whom? The only Jewish Israeli to die at a political rally in the past several years was from Peace Now, while West Bank settlers had organized and were supporting a terrorist underground.

Moreover, wasn't the hostility between the Sephardic second Israel — now the majority — and Israelis from European families such as her own as strong as ever? The campaign was more courteous than in 1981. Still, 70 percent of Sephardic voters supported the parties of the right. Only 60 percent had voted for Likud this time; the claim of the party's supporters that it could not be stopped from gathering more and more strength among Oriental Jews was shown to be wrong. But Likud's loss had not been Labor's gain. Many Sephardic voters now chose the more extreme right-wing parties.

Deteriorating relations between secular and Orthodox Jews only exacerbated ethnic tensions. The largely Sephardic Shas religious party—the "keepers of Torah"—had won four seats. Its leader, Rabbi Yitzchak Peretz, demanded the release from prison of members of the Jewish terrorist underground and the exclusion of women from the cabinet. Peretz even expressed warm words for Kahane, who had, meanwhile, dismissed democracy as inconsistent with Jewish law. There were violent protests in the town of Petah Tiqwa when the Labor mayor tried to allow theaters and restaurants to open on the Sabbath.

To Yehoshua, it seemed that fringe groups of all kinds were ready to drag more moderate people into street violence—and would succeed in doing so if hard times hardened intolerant attitudes. "After the first skirmish," he told me, "young people start fighting over the last one."

## II

By the beginning of August, public expressions of support for unity had become irresistible and Peres gave in to them. So did the Israeli President, Chaim Herzog, a former Labor politician, who asked Peres to work out a reciprocal coalition with Shamir. Although they started to negotiate, the party leaders, in fact, began to work to deny each other a parliamentary majority—not because they had changed their minds about joint rule, but because it was not clear to anyone, Herzog included, which party controlled the most seats from among the splinter parties, hence which man should become Prime Minister. By the end of August—after innumerable bargaining sessions and back-room deals—Peres and Shamir, remarkably, each controlled blocs of exactly sixty seats. The more closely one looked, the more irreconcilable those blocs seemed.

The Labor Alignment included Mapam, which represented mainly the left-wing socialist kibbutzim and consistently supported a policy of magnanimity toward the Palestinians. Peres also allied Labor with the two civil rights lists led by Amnon Rubenstein and Shulamit Aloni, both concerned to protect secular civil life from religious control. Peres got the support of former Likud Defense Minister Ezer Weizman, who claimed he had returned to politics to revive the "peace process" with Egypt and Jordan. Peres was even willing to rely on the tacit parliamentary support of the Communist Party and the new Progressive List for Peace and Freedom.

For his part, Shamir made an alliance with the five Tehiya deputies, who represented the neo-"Zionist" ideology of the West Bank settlers — the belief that military force should be used ruthlessly to consolidate Eretz Yisrael. He won the support of all religious deputies, including four from Shas and two even more strident messianists of the Morasha Party. Only the National Religious Party leadership negotiated seriously with Labor, though its younger leaders insisted on an alliance with Likud.

Along with most other politicians, Shamir condemned the election of Kahane; but the Likud leaders, especially Sharon, were willing to count on Kahane's vote. Indeed, Sharon kept his position in the Likud hierarchy by mobilizing the support of extreme Herut voters, though he is more committed to his own huge ambitions than to any biblical version of Israel. During the campaign Sharon crisscrossed the country, unaccompanied by any of Likud's managers, and drew enormous crowds, chanting "Arik! Arik!" Shamir invited Sharon to join Likud's negotiating team.

A new election seemed inevitable, yet neither Peres nor Shamir saw any advantage in having one. They began to meet privately. At the beginning of September they announced that they had finally agreed on a formula for sharing power. Labor and Likud would contribute ten ministers each to an inner cabinet of twenty, which would have final authority on all matters of diplomacy and defense — though the government's first concern would be to do something about the deteriorating economy.

Apart from the inner group, where there would be absolute parity, some thirty deputies would have ministerial rank, including three ministers from the religious parties. The government was to last fifty months; Peres would assume the Prime

Minister's job first, while Shamir would be deputy prime minister and foreign minister; after twenty-five months, the leaders would exchange positions.

The announcement surprised and excited Israelis. The deadlock had been frustrating, the negotiations distasteful, accompanied as they were by rumors that made the back-room dealings sound like a political auction. By this time it seemed fair, if oddly contradictory, that Labor and Likud would each retain a veto over the other's most intransigent policies. Labor could block Likud's demand for more West Bank settlements in places heavily populated by Palestinian Arabs, though Peres agreed to some five more settlements in places that would not, he said, impede Labor's strategy of "territorial compromise" with Jordan. Likud could stop Peres from making concessions to Jordan, though not from inviting Hussein to negotiate "without conditions."

Still, Labor had won greater authority in security matters, since Labor's Yitzchak Rabin was chosen for the Defense Ministry for the entire life of the government. Under Rabin would be a Likud deputy minister; but Labor's Chaim Bar-Lev would be Minister of Police. Correspondingly, Labor seemed preeminent in cultural affairs, since Yitzchak Navon got the Ministry of Education. What Likud acquired was greater control over economic policy, notwithstanding its disastrous inflation of the economy, often for its own political advantage. The Finance Ministry went to the liberal leader in the Likud, Yitzchak Modai, while Sharon —who criticized Shamir for conceding the position of Prime Minister to Peres—was appointed Minister of Trade and Commerce. Other Likud politicians were appointed Ministers of Science and Development and of Tourism. A new Ministry of Economic Planning, with vague jurisdiction, was created for Labor's shadow Finance Minister, Gad Yaacobi.

## III

In putting together the unity coalition, Peres and Shamir saved their political careers. Peres had been a less popular Labor politician than Rabin and Navon; now, according to the most recent polls, 40 percent of Israelis want him for Prime Minister, more than four times the number before the unity deal. On the other side, Sharon and Deputy Prime Minister David Levy, Likud's most powerful politician from the second Israel, have openly competed to replace Shamir. Even after the deal was announced, they demanded that further cabinet appointments be made not by Shamir, but by secret ballot in Herut; Shamir defeated them.

Yet aside from personal ambition and a fear of political deadlock, Shamir and Peres may have more in common than either has with any of the more extreme ideological parties that backed them — including the small parties that have come to seem the consciences of the bigger ones but were left out of the coalition. The zealots of Tehiya refused to enter a government with Labor. Peres, for his part, was willing to enter a coalition without Mapam, whose six members broke from the Alignment and went into opposition with Aloni and the leader of Labor's doves, Yossi Sarid.

Before the election, Peres told *Time* that he wanted Israel to be "socially, like a kibbutz." But since the 1950s, when he was Ben-Gurion's favorite technocrat in the Defense Ministry, Peres has stood for values that are opposed to the old kibbutz vision. With Moshe Dayan, Peres called for market efficiency, meritocracy, urban development, and an end to the domination of collectivist ideals in Israeli society.

In 1965, at Ben-Gurion's request, Peres and Dayan became leaders of the Rafi Party, which broke away from Labor for reasons that may seem remote today but reflect ways of thinking that are still pertinent. Like Herut and the Liberal Party — though not in alliance with them — the Rafi leaders wanted to challenge the deeply embedded power and state syndicalist ideology both of Histadrut and the Mapai, which had been taken over by Levi Eshkol, Pinhas Sapir, and Golda Meir. They had mounted an attack against Pinchas Lavon, the head of the Histadrut, until a scandal gave Ben-Gurion the opportunity to remove him — an action that caused a greater scandal. Rafi leaders saw in the Israel Defense Forces, and the defense bureaucracies and industries supporting them, the modernizing dynamism that was needed to assimilate hundreds of thousands of new immigrants from North Africa. They favored taking hard action toward the Arab world, along the lines of the Sinai campaign of 1956.

More recently, Peres has spoken of compromise with the Arabs. But his first goal, he has said, is maintaining the IDF's technological edge over the hostile Arab states. He has also written enthusiastically about the coming of postindustrial society, of robotics, automation, of Israel's potential role as a retailer of services to Europe, including software and medical care.* To counter Mapam's threat to leave the Alignment, Peres maintained Labor's arithmetical parity with Likud by absorbing Ezer Weizman's three Knesset members and Yigael Hurwitz, the former Likud Finance Minister who had opposed the Camp David accords. Hurwitz had been a close associate of Dayan, and like Peres—and Yitzchak Navon and Gad Yaacobi—he had been a supporter of Rafi.

Peres has had a longstanding feud with Rabin and has tried to cultivate such Israeli writers as Yehoshua. But Peres clearly seems drawn to men with Rabin's military background—such as Yaacobi, Chaim Bar-Lev, Mota Gur, the new Minister of Health, and "Abrasha" Tamir, a major general who left a high position as a strategic planner to join Ezer Weizman and who will now direct the Prime Minister's office.

Indeed, Peres's replacement of Mapam with Rafi people and former military men suggests that his coalition with Shamir may prove a resilient one. Peres, Rabin, and Weizman all worked with Shamir during the many years he commanded a branch of the Mosad, the Israeli intelligence apparatus. Peres collaborated with Shamir's former Defense Minister, Moshe Arens, to found the huge Israeli aircraft industry. Though it will cost the Israeli government another half-billion dollars, both Peres and Arens want to go ahead with development of the Lavi fighter. Correspondingly, Rabin and Weizman have been curiously close to Sharon, who served with them in the general staff. Modai, too, comes from the army, as does the popular Likud mayor of Tel Aviv, Shlomo Lahat. Shared backgrounds, of course, do not determine political moves. One can expect much backbiting, disagreement, and jockeying for position among all these men. But of the new government's principal ministers, only David Levy, who comes from a Sephardic development town and made a

---

*See Peres's contribution to *Israel Toward the 21st Century* (in Hebrew; Jerusalem: Van Leer Jerusalem Foundation, 1984).

success as a building contractor, seems the product of the Likud's grass-roots politics.

Israel's military-industrial bureaucracy currently employs about 25 percent of the country's industrial work force and accounts for some 16 percent of its exports.* Labor's top men have been at its center since the 1960s and have much experience in common with Likud's current leadership. Few of the latter have shared much with the Herut rank and file, who increasingly tend to be workers, foremen, small businessmen, usually of Sephardic origin. The key ministers from both parties may prove more pragmatically "statist," in the mold of Rafi, than deeply committed to any "Greater Israel" ideology.

If not for shared political and economic assumptions, how could they have come to terms so quickly on the tough monetarist policies that Modai unveiled the day after the government was sworn in? These included radical cuts of subsidies on essential commodities, the banning of luxury imports — cars, stereos, liquor — for six months, higher unemployment in the public sector, and a virtual end to government funding of new West Bank settlements.

On November 4, with the agreement of the Histadrut and the Association of Manufacturers, the government took further action to reduce the rate of inflation, currently 25 percent a month. For the next three months, wages and prices will be frozen and all prices will have to be fixed in shekels, not dollars. Because the government will continue to spend beyond its means — it now employs some 35 percent of Israeli workers — inflationary pressures will build at the rate of about 10 percent a month, although their effects will not be registered until February. The Histadrut has conceded that by then, workers will make up only about 80 percent of the erosion of their salaries caused by inflation.

Drastic as these measures would seem to Americans, they may not be harsh enough to shift workers from the government payroll to export industries that require more specialized skills. Such reputable economists as Meir Merhav of the *Jerusalem Post* have

---

*Yoram Peri and Amnon Neubach, "The Military-Industrial Complex in Israel," International Center for Middle East Peace (Tel Aviv).

called for adopting the dollar as the official Israeli currency. For his part, Modai has spoken of a further 25 percent reduction in government spending, which would lead to much higher unemployment—though not as high as what adopting the dollar would bring. The government's caution is understandable. General unemployment would lead to higher Jewish emigration and greater Arab restiveness. Nor would a more severe reduction in spending do much to balance the budget in view of the higher unemployment benefits that would have to be paid.

The unity government's cautiousness cannot be blamed on a disagreement between Labor and Likud. Since the government was formed, the ministers who have most openly criticized Modai's economic policy are David Levy and Moshe Katzav, Likud's young Minister of Labor and Social Affairs—himself from the second Israel. Levy and Katzav have accused Peres of indifference to the effects of austerity on the poor, who will now be unable to afford apartments or find jobs. The criticism, no doubt, strikes Labor leaders as hypocritical. But it may insulate the Likud from the consequences of the Begin government's recklessness and help preserve for the Likud its image as defender of the common man.

As the austerity measures become harsher, Levy and Katzav, as well as Sharon, could pose a deep threat to Peres. "The possibility remains," one close observer of Israeli politics told me, "that Peres will come to appear as a sort of Ramsay MacDonald. Some of the Labor politicians would have preferred to let the Likud form a narrow government and take the consequences of cleaning up the economic mess it created. Now Levy and Sharon and their followers, the hard core of the Herut Party, can attempt to dissociate themselves from the policies of Modai, a Liberal, and Shamir, whom they see as a has-been, and above all Peres, who will have to accept responsibility for unemployment. Peres has saved his position for the time being and he may get credit for taking charge at a difficult moment, but he may also have played into the hands of the Herut populists: no one should underestimate their ability to mobilize angry workers against Peres's leadership and discredit Labor."

It remains to be seen whether Shamir is indeed a has-been. The night of the election, using the old Herut rhetoric, he de-

nounced the Labor opposition as "defeatist." But that denun-
ciation might have been as mechanical as Peres's saying he
wanted Israel to be socially a kibbutz. For Shamir and Arens,
building the IDF has been the culmination of Jabotinsky's
dreams — not annexation of the West Bank. It was Shamir's government, after all, that uncovered and indicted the Jewish terrorist underground. One of Israel's leading military correspondents, Eitan Haber of *Yediot Acharonot,* told me that the army's
general staff under Arens had become far less mired in politics
than it was under Sharon and the former Chief of Staff — now
a leader of Tehiya — Rafael ("Raful") Eitan.

Immediately after Kahane's election, Arens's chief education
officer in the army announced an emergency program to teach
recruits about the "virtues of democracy." Raful, who has been
openly bigoted toward Palestinians, had ordered courses on
"Zionism" and the "love of Eretz Yisrael." Perhaps because of
such changes, Gush Emunim, the Jewish settlers' organization,
has concluded that even with Sharon in the government there
is a potential for genuine cooperation between Labor and Likud,
which would result in diminished government support for West
Bank settlements.

Sharon's ministry can, and likely will, authorize many private
development projects on the West Bank, where much of the
land is privately owned. Still, a leader of Gush Emunim, Eliakim
Ha'etzni, greeted the formation of the coalition with the announcement that his movement will revert to tactics for illegal
settlement that Zionist pioneers had used under the British
mandate — tactics the Gush Emunim actually used against Rabin's government in the 1970s.

IV

One useful result of the unity government is that threats of this
kind are not taken as seriously as they would be under a narrow
Labor coalition. But Ha'etzni's warning suggests how character-
less Israel's two major political parties have become and how
much they are concerned to appeal to a broad Israeli public that
is increasingly urban, youthful, influenced by television, tending

to concentrate more on short-term economic or diplomatic gains than on grandiose ideas of extending the reach of "Zionism." In the cities, Tehiya's exhortations to settle in holy land are becoming as irrelevant to middle-class Israeli families—whether of Sephardic or European origin—as Mapam's Labor Zionism of agricultural collectives and dedicated socialist schools.

The Mapam defectors from the Alignment, however, are justifiably concerned that a unity government will preserve a state of affairs that is more congenial to Likud's most strident supporters than to Labor's most moderate ones. Whatever may become of the ideal of Greater Israel, the fact of a greater Israel has persisted since 1967. The unity government gives no promise of fundamental change; its main immediate effect is a new atmosphere of hope that the country's divisiveness, which the elections only confirmed, will not now lead to riots among Israelis who have the deepest sense of grievance—among West Bank settlers, say, or in poorer quarters and hinterland towns. The uncertainty about how the government's economic policy will work has dimmed that hope somewhat. Still, *Davar's* Jerusalem bureau chief Danny Rubenstein told me, Peres and Shamir will find it increasingly impolitic for either of them to be the one responsible for breaking up the coalition.

Under the Likud, Israeli Arabs have lost ground while the Orthodox Jewish rabbis and religious parties have gained. By manipulating the public education law, the former Education Minister, the National Religious Party leader Zevulun Hammer, set up some twenty Orthodox national schools. He revised the curriculum to encourage Orthodox thinking. Begin's government gave greater scope for Orthodox law in civil courts, enacting laws against autopsies, for example. The unity government will keep all these changes intact. There is no prospect that civil marriage or divorce will be allowed in Israel.

The unity government leaders may agree to reform the electoral system in a way that will diminish the influence of the small religious parties. They could raise the minimum proportion of the vote necessary to enter the Knesset to, say, 4 percent, which would shut out Kahane and force all religious politicians into one camp. But a consolidated religious bloc in the Knesset would, in all likelihood, support the Likud. Navon may well call a halt to religious encroachments on secular education. But rule over 1.5 million Arabs is itself a kind of education for young Israelis and one over which he has no control.

During the campaign, I visited the development town of Yoqne'am Illit, in the Valley of Jezreel. Yoqne'am's residents are largely North African immigrant families who work in Haifa or in the well-to-do kibbutzim nearby or in the ammunition factory that the state set up there. An armored infantry base is a mile away. Labor's big rally was to take place that night with a speech by Navon, Labor's most prominent Sephardic politician. Yoqne'am's residents welcomed Navon enthusiastically when he was President of the state. Would they welcome him as a representative of the Labor Alignment?

"Look how they humiliated Navon," a young man said to me. "First he was President, then they made him nothing, number three." Who, I asked, were "they"? Alignment types— "*Ma'arachniks*"— the Ashkenazim, the well-educated, such as the members of the neighboring kibbutzim who once every four years—during an election campaign—turn out to demonstrate along the Yoqne'am roads. "Look at their demonstrations during the war," he went on. "Their signs were always full of English. What for? To embarrass the state in front of the Americans. If you had a wife and she publicly embarrassed you, would you keep her?"

He had read the Bible. He interpreted it as prohibiting the return of any part of Eretz Yisrael. "They'd give up the patrimony to others, like wicked brothers. They love the Arabs more than their own."

That night, a group from the high school came out to heckle Navon. I took a seat in the stands next to them, accompanied by an old friend who was born in a Mapai farming community nearby. My friend had had almost nothing to do with the Oriental Jewish town, though his daughter had just married an Iraqi boy she had met at Ben-Gurion University in the Negev. He told me that the overvalued shekel, which Likud had subsidized and with which Yoqne'am's residents had imported cars and television sets, had forced his neighbors to pull up and burn their orchards. Their crops could not be exported.

Navon came to the podium, clapping his hands to the Labor campaign jingle—a tune curiously like melodies to be found in the Sephardic liturgy. He started badly. Labor people, he said, had "opened the gates" to North African immigrants. The students took this as a provocation. "Who else would have done your dirty jobs?" a young man yelled back. Navon had doubtless heard this many times before, but it seemed to rattle him nevertheless. He was talking about the events of thirty years ago; Likud had governed for seven. Why did these young people believe that Labor was still *Ha'mimsad*, the establishment?

In fact, Israel's biggest industrialists—including David Moshevitz of Elite and Uri Bernstein of Amcor, both prominent in the Association of Manufacturers—strongly supported the Labor Party in these elections. Though the Labor Alignment appointed Israel Kessar, a Sephardi, as head of the Histadrut, the managers of Histadrut-owned industry—which still accounts for some 25 percent of GNP—have done little to dispel the idea that Labor's method of "socialist" development during the 1950s and 1960s became corrupted by patronage, by favors for "them," and discrimination against the Sephardic immigrants. (Just as the campaign was getting under way last June, Yaacov Levinson, the former chairman of Bank Hapolalim—the Histadrut's most glamorous and profitable operation—killed himself in the middle of a Histadrut investigation into his affairs. In his suicide note Levinson maintained his innocence and accused his colleagues of untold deceptions.)

Navon tried a different tack. As President, he grandly confided, he had met with Argentina's Raúl Alfonsín and they had talked about whose country's currency was losing value faster. "Argentinians count their money in the millions," Navon exclaimed. To which the young woman next to me responded mockingly, "You see, this is an international phenomenon!"

A boy of about eighteen interrupted Navon. Why had he called Arabs "brothers" in a television campaign spot? Why did he love the Arabs? Navon's face turned red. "What geniuses you are! What diplomats!" Navon shouted in our direction. "Can't you understand simple arithmetic? Why, the very point of Labor's

Zionist program is to have as much land as possible and as few Arabs as possible!"

My friend from the Mapai farm, who was appalled by the shouting, was hearing Navon make a familiar argument—for something like the Allon plan for "territorial compromise" with Jordan. But had these young people heard what he had heard? During his childhood, there was the struggle against fascism; during theirs, the wars of 1967 and 1973 and the struggle against Palestinian terrorism. When I talked to some of them later, Navon's reply only seemed to confirm their belief that the West Bank should be annexed and its residents expelled. Was Kahane, I wondered, doing no more than carrying to its logical extreme what had become the conventional wisdom during the Begin years?

Begin is gone, but not the borders, which Likud supporters take for granted as "realistic" and unchangeable. During the election campaign the party simply called itself the National Camp—Ha'machane Ha'leumi—and defended rule over "Judea and Samaria"; the PLO, scattered by Sharon's war, was no longer a matter for anxiety. For most young people in Israel, the territories seem as much a part of Israel as Arab Nazareth.

Likud's vote in the army fell by some 15 percent. But Likud, Tehiya, and Kach together got 45 percent of the vote in the army, 60 percent including the religious parties. Labor and the civil rights parties got about 39 percent. As if to corroborate the trend, a recent study by the Van Leer Jerusalem Foundation found that some 60 percent of Jewish high school students— two thirds of whom are of Sephardic origin—were unwilling to live in the same building as Arabs, and 40 percent were unwilling even to work with an Arab.* It is hard to see how the rightist groups will do worse with young voters once the IDF is out of Lebanon.

Young people whose families have been strongly attached to Labor are meanwhile confused and demoralized. In Labor youth movements, among the sons and daughters of the left-wing academic activists—even on the kibbutzim—one hears the ex-

*See Alouph Hareven's study in *Every Sixth Israeli*, Hareven, ed. (Jerusalem: Van Leer Jerusalem Foundation, 1983).

pression *"Ani masea rosh katan"* — literally, "I am carrying a small head," that is, keeping a low profile. This helps to account for last year's decline of volunteers for elite units and officer training in the army. If one thinks how aware young Israelis have been made of war, Greater Israel, death camps, and the Bible, it is hard to believe they would not eventually want something more stirring from national leaders than Peres's dream of high technocracy. If the unity government were to fall apart, Sharon's nationalism and Levy's populism would seem more powerful attractions.

V

Peres may still be right that Israel's leading high technology industries will respond to a period of strong government. The Haifa-based Elron group projects sales of $350 million this year, $100 million more than last year, and it has even set up a branch plant on Boston's Route 128. Greater Israel's population is about five million; its entrepreneurs have capital to invest, and they will likely benefit from the recently negotiated free trade agreement with the United States. There are many fine universities in Israel, though recent budget cuts have cut into their ability to meet the growing demand for computer engineers.

But Peres's plan for recovery may lack the political forces to carry it out. Likud, not Rafi, finally emerged as the party to challenge the power of the Histadrut and repudiate the old Mapai's state socialism. Can a Labor Party making itself over in the image of Rafi compete with Likud in the long run? The Likud includes, not only technocrats and the older Herut nationalists, but also a young guard of leaders such as Katzav and Meir Shitrit, the mayor of Yavne. Elections within the Likud have also brought forward Uriel Linn, an impressive young economist whose family emigrated from Morocco.

If they use their power competently, Peres, Rabin, and Navon may increase their personal prestige. If, as expected, there are new elections before the government's term expires, Peres might be a more popular candidate running as the Prime Minister, which is precisely why Sharon opposed the deal. But Labor is short of new leaders who can make the case for civil rights and territorial compromise to the new Israel. Jealous of its power, the central committee of the Labor Party has blocked the advance of such prominent liberal academics as Shlomo Avineri and Zeev Sternhel. Labor's most promising Sephardic intellectual, Shlomo Ben-Ami, has become estranged from the party.

The youthful head of the Jerusalem branch of the Labor Party, Uzi Baram—the son of the former head of the Jerusalem branch, Moshe Baram—told me that the decision-making apparatus should be "opened up." Perhaps, he said, Labor should adopt an internal primary system like the Likud's, in order to elect Knesset members from the rank and file.*

Reform is all the more necessary, other Labor insiders told me, since elections to the Histadrut general council are coming up next year. However embarrassing Labor's connection to such powerful Histadrut corporations as Bank Hapolalim or Koor may be, they have been important in financing the party's organization and electoral campaigns. Labor's control of the unions, moreover, provides the party with its main base from which to sustain and possibly increase its appeal to Israeli workers. Kessar may turn out to be more effective than Navon in bringing Oriental Jewish voters back to Labor. Still, David Levy and his Likud followers will pose a strong challenge to Labor if unemployment is high. A takeover of the Histadrut by the Likud would be a strong sign that Peres's gamble on unity had failed.

Would the party reform itself while its established leadership is firmly in government? This seems doubtful. Raising the minimum vote necessary for entering the Knesset will only strengthen the party bureaucrats. It will discourage the formation of smaller parties, such as the one Shulamit Aloni organized in 1973 to challenge Golda Meir. Ruling with the Likud for a while still may be the most dramatic way for the workers' party to restore a measure of legitimacy among Israel's have-nots.

*Peres is known to favor a new electoral system along Scandinavian lines, by which the country would be divided into three-member constituencies. Younger people who were elected would not be so tied to the party *apparat*. The plan suggests Peres's capacity for fresh thinking, but since it would antagonize the NRP, its chances of being adopted by the current Labor leadership are small.

VI

By November, it seemed clear that Labor and the Likud were willing to agree on a policy of withdrawal from southern Lebanon, with UN forces having a part in the arrangements for peacekeeping. How, during the coming months, will the unity government approach the question of the West Bank? Peres and Rabin clearly favor territorial compromise but have committed themselves to achieving a consensus with the Likud. Moshe Arens, who remains influential as the head of an inner cabinet coordinating committee, has often said that he favors annexation of the West Bank only because he would rather fight for "pluralism" in Greater Israel than fight terrorism from a smaller Israel. Does this mean that he and other Likud military technocrats might be more open to a negotiation with Jordan?

I asked Arens this summer how he could square pluralism with Israeli rule over 1.5 million more Arabs. His answer, I suspect, is the one we will hear more and more often. The West Bank Arabs, he said, don't present a problem essentially different from that of Israeli Arabs. "In either case, we must make it our business to be more open and pluralistic — though the effort could take a generation: they don't want us here."

Eventually, he said, the Israeli Arabs would have to be brought into the army. But he could not say when: "The younger generation of Arabs has undergone a process of Israelization. The same is true around Jerusalem. They have mastered Hebrew, want to be accepted and enjoy equality before the law. But nothing much can be done during a state of war. We have started by widening the circles of opportunity for minorities, such as the Druses in the army."

Some unpleasant questions lie beneath that reasonable-sounding talk. The Druses are recruited mainly for the border patrol, which is trained to keep the larger Moslem Arab community in line. And if "Israelization" means accepting Israel as a secular, Hebrew democracy, then what about all the young Jews who seem drawn to theocratic ideas — and the near majority who say they don't want to work with Arabs? Can Israeli Jews hope to develop a common language with Israeli Arabs so long as the country maintains an occupation of a million more Palestinians?

"We are a nation still dragging our roots around with us," he told me. "There may be more elegant laws than, say, the Law of Return, but this is still necessary so long as we provide a haven—for Russian Jews and others. We must rule out a return of territory so long as security is paramount. The Arabs would destroy us if they could. The Middle East is a dangerous place: look at what has happened to Lebanon."

Arens agreed that Israeli action in Lebanon has hardly made the region less dangerous, that the Shiite population has become inflamed against the Jewish state. In view of his concern for pluralism, I asked, would he favor negotiating with Jordan over the West Bank if Hussein's regime showed itself more flexible, liberal, attached to the West? "Absolutely!" he replied. He looked at me as if I were out of my mind.

Shimon Peres may be more sincere about the values of pluralism and is, in any case, more enthusiastic about negotiating with Jordan—though his views seemed identical to those of Arens when he served as Rabin's Defense Minister between 1974 and 1977. In 1982, however, Peres supported the Reagan plan and condemned Jewish settlement activity in the West Bank for the way it stifled development of the impoverished regions in Israel itself, particularly in the Galilee. Rabin has been even more forthright since becoming Defense Minister. In a private meeting with Gush Emunim settlers, Rabin warned them against any form of vigilante activity. Rabin may still have to deal with more such episodes as the recent rocket attack on an Arab bus in retaliation for the killing of a Jewish couple the previous week.

Sadly, however, the distinction between Peres's enthusiasm for an arrangement with Jordan and Arens's skepticism about it may not have much political importance today, though it might have made a difference when Sadat went to Jerusalem. Hussein has boldly re-established diplomatic relations with Egypt. But the Hashemite regime is dependent on the Gulf states, which have already cut his $1.2 billion subsidy in half this year. To make peace with Israel, Hussein needs not only the reassurance from Israel of a freeze on settlements—which the unity government has not given him—but also some indication that Israel will permit Jordan to re-establish Arab sovereignty over Arab Jerusalem. In short, Hussein wants a virtual guarantee that peace talks, once started, will succeed. Peres's Labor Party is uncompromising with regard to Jerusalem. His call to Hussein to negotiate directly "without conditions," reminiscent of Golda Meir's, will most likely lead to further stalemate; predictably, Hussein has already rejected it, although secret contacts with the Israelis continue.

The United States may intervene with some new plan for indirect negotiations. A senior planner at the State Department told me that the United States may try to revive negotiations for an agreement on disengagement of forces between Jordan and Israel—like the one that nearly came about in 1974. Peres could probably muster a narrow Knesset majority for an interim settlement, especially if the U.S. government made it clear that economic assistance will be coordinated with a comprehensive American Middle East policy. Some of the Liberals in the Likud—Arye Dulzin; the chairman of the Jewish Agency, Menachem Savidor; the former Knesset Speaker, Shlomo Lahat—have already called for a split with Herut. But like Israeli voters, the Reagan administration has been more concerned that the Israeli government solve its economic difficulties than risk any peace initiative.

That seems shortsighted. National unity certainly has advantages for Israel, and the country's possibilities for economic growth may, in another generation, make the divisions of 1984 seem as out of date as Ben-Gurion's Mapai. Yet Ben-Gurion's plan to partition the land is no less vital for Israeli democracy than before, and the Israelis of the coming generation seem less open both to partition and to democracy than their parents were. That may prove a greater tragedy for Zionism than six wars.

# 1988: The Elections Nobody Needs

*September 1988*

President Reagan has invited Israeli Foreign Minister Shimon Peres to meet with him — and with the Egyptian foreign minister, Ahmed Esmat Abdel-Meguid — at the United Nations on September 26. Both Israel and the United States will be holding national elections in early November; obviously, it is not Reagan who needs the photo opportunity.

Reagan wants Peres's Labor Party to win Israel's November elections, and who can blame him? Peres is the inspiration of Secretary of State George Shultz's peace initiative, which has been blocked by Prime Minister Yitzchak Shamir's leadership of Israel's deadlocked National Unity government. He has called for an international conference and has declared his willingness to swap land — including West Bank land, Eretz Yisrael — for peace. Though electoral polls now show Likud and Labor in a dead heat, other opinion surveys show a narrow majority of Israelis favor some form of "territorial compromise" — a principle at the heart of the Shultz plan. Is it too much to hope for a Peres victory?

To root for Peres is, alas, to miss the most salient fact of Israeli politics since 1984, which the Palestinian uprising has only reinforced. The National Unity government, preempting though it does the push and pull of democratic alternation, is *itself* an important buttress of Israeli democracy. Even if Peres were to win, it is hard to see how he could govern for long without Likud leaders — or, indeed, they without him.

Indeed, the most plausible outcome of an election—perhaps the best under the circumstances—is the continuation of the National Unity government for the foreseeable future. Labor must be in the government when Israel faces war, Likud when peace. Since the Palestinian uprising, Israel has been facing both at once.

Suppose that Labor wins a slim Knesset majority. Peres is not a popular or trusted leader, even in the peace camp he nominally leads. Even his promise to democratize the Labor Party has proven halfhearted. If Peres were to agree to halt Jewish settlement of the West Bank or attend a peace conference at which the PLO was represented (and at what conceivable peace conference would the PLO not be represented?), Ariel Sharon would be leading demonstrations in the streets of Jerusalem.

Jewish settlers on the West Bank would again take the law into their own hands, as they did during the tragic affair of Tirza Porat. Defense Minister Yitzchak Rabin, who is a leader of Labor, would opt for continuing the hard line against Palestinian youth. The popularity of the scripture hawks to the right of the Likud has grown, particularly among Israeli soldiers, who have been most burdened with putting down the uprising. In a time of strife, the young look to people who seem most comfortable with naked violence.

As the economy turns down again—as it must with so many managers, workers, and scientists tied up in doing reserve duty—Likud politicians in opposition benches would rail at Labor for funneling government funds into failing Labor enterprises and agricultural cooperatives. It is never very difficult to whip up anti-Labor populist feeling among North African immigrant families, the kind that swept Labor out of power in 1977.

But let us assume that Shamir will head a coalition including the ultra-right and religious parties. What would that be like? Sharon would likely re-emerge as Defense Minister. The upper ranks of the army—still mainly well-educated, closet Labor supporters—will be hard pressed to impose discipline among soldiers resentful of occupation duty and deeply confused by it. (One IDF general responsible for educational programs, including moral education, told me last winter that the occupation has undone twenty years of his work.)

Under Sharon, many combat officers, drawn disproportionately from Labor settlements, will refuse service in the occupied territory. Meanwhile, many Israeli lawyers and judges — the judicial establishment — will find themselves torn between the policies of the Israeli executive and their own consciences. Journalists from both the printed press and Israeli radio and television would be fighting daily skirmishes with the government over the right to report stories of IDF actions in the territories. The vast majority of university professors, writers, and popular artists would be undermining the authority of the government at every turn. On a smaller scale, much of this hard feeling began to emerge during the Lebanon war.

Israelis are, in short, so bitterly divided, so lacking in a sense of the future, that it would be folly to split the government just now. Israelis are quite capable of roughing each other up: settlers against peace groups, secularists against religious extremists. One feels repressed rages at every turn.

And split it for what? Shamir, it is true, favors the "unity of the land of Israel," Peres, some variation of "territorial compromise." Shamir is more xenophobic than Peres, and Labor is more instinctively pro-American. But if Shamir can be accused of refusing to budge, is Peres proposing anything likely to meet the expectations of young Palestinians halfway?

Peres remains as adamant as Shamir that an independent Palestinian state not arise in the West Bank and Gaza. Evidently, he does not dare challenge Rabin's rather brutal rule of the territories for fear of prompting the old rivalry. Though King Hussein has cut his ties with (and, perhaps disingenuously, renounced his claim to) the occupied territories, the thrust of Peres's diplomatic effort is still Jordan, which is totally unacceptable to the Palestinian young people now in revolt. Peres was Prime Minister from 1984 to 1986 and missed opportunities of his own.

Anyway, the real promise of the Shultz plan was all along that, once an international conference gets going, it would engender a peace process beyond what Shultz and Peres now say they envision, but which a majority of Israelis would probably ultimately accept. I mean peacemaking that begins with the reciprocal recognition of Israelis and Palestinians, a two-state solution based on new hard thinking about how to guarantee each state's security and democracy. Obviously, a peace of this kind would have to be strongly urged on Israelis and Arabs by the superpowers. An international conference might just have to be imposed.

And so the National Unity government would actually be better than any other Israeli government if American diplomacy finally made serious headway. There will be no peace unless the U.S. President takes the lead, and no Israeli government could spurn firm American leadership. Even under Shamir's Prime Ministership, Israel could not turn down a final American invitation to a peace conference: U.S. aid now amounts to 20 percent of Israel's national income. (Likud politicians representing the new Sephardic middle class know that their own people would be first to feel the pinch if American aid were curtailed.)

Curiously, Israeli voters seem to have figured all of this out, if only intuitively. In 1984, just before the last election, polls showed that 80 percent of Israelis preferred rule by a National Unity government to rule by either of the parties. Those were not unreasonable impulses. The Israeli government cannot negotiate peace without treading on the anxieties of large and powerful forces in the country. Better that the government be a broad coalition.

PART TWO

# ISRAELIS
# AND
# PALESTINIANS

# Zionist Colonialism:
# Myth and Dilemma

Mr. President, the roots of the Palestinian question reach back into the closing years of the nineteenth century, to that period we call the era of colonialism. . . . This is precisely the period during which Zionism was born; its aim was the conquest of Palestinian land by European immigrants, just as settlers colonized and indeed raided most of Africa.

—Yasir Arafat, speech to the UN
General Assembly, November 14, 1974

*Spring 1975*

The Dreyfus affair was, of course, not the ordeal only of Captain Dreyfus. Within a few years of his first trial, a collection of dissenting groups—liberals, socialists, and Zionists—had become his champions, primarily because they admired him for his enemies. The radicals who took up Dreyfus's defense perceived that they were equally vulnerable to the powerful alliance that, at least for the time, was aimed against the unlikely captain. This apprehension was intensified by a widely held conviction that the attack on Dreyfus was but the domestic side effect of a much larger and more ominous trend in international affairs. The "imperialists" appeared to be prostituting the foundations of democratic life in the Republic.

Government officials, easily bought off by "special interests," channeled national resources into the extension of empire and the support of brutal colonial administrations. All of Europe seemed torn from the liberal moorings so painfully acquired in the middle of the century. The great powers (even America!) were locked in a frantic competition to plunder the resources, labor, and economic surplus of African, Asian, and Latin American "natives." Armies and navies were mushrooming in the service of these imperial ventures; and the "war for steel and gold" (H. N. Brailsford's apt name for the European conflagration he foresaw) was already being plotted in an atmosphere of panic and chauvinism.

For weather-vane liberals such as Hobson, Morel, Clemenceau, and Emile Duclaux, the ascendance of reactionary forces, linked to repressive colonialist policies, shattered the image of a self-regulating market society that might encourage democratic practice. The "new imperialism" — as Hobson dubbed it — had neither progressive features nor Christian mission; its sole content seemed to be a savage labor discipline that had to be opposed if only on moral grounds.

Even those socialists who had been disposed to view imperialism with profound ambivalence began to reassess their attitudes.* Bourgeois societies were swaggering to the corners of the globe; but the dialectical possibilities for liberal progress in the colonies — free property relations, a genuine market in labor, an "end to national one-sidedness and narrow-mindedness" — that Marx had attributed to the imperial experience seemed little evident. Imperialism now seemed the project of huge cartels whose colonial agents aimed only at securing more profitable outlets for capital investments and "overproduced" commodities.

This new view of imperialism quickly became a conventional wisdom among socialists; every foreign adventure became suspect as a particularly rapacious business operation. And it was a short hop from this opinion to the revolutionary theories of Lenin and Rosa Luxemburg: European colonialism might be effectively challenged only by colonial liberation movements charged with a measure of socialist internationalism. Monopoly capitalism had forged an international division of labor and in

---

*As with Marx: "whatever may have been the crimes of England [in Hindustan] she was the unconscious tool of history in bringing about [social] revolution." *New York Tribune,* June 25, 1853.

so doing seemed to have rendered all narrow national concerns obsolete. So the socialist left began to argue, abandoning Marx's more cautious understanding of modernization and its slowly evolving conditions.

For European Jews, the period of the Dreyfus affair was a watershed of a different sort. Although it reinforced the suspicion of Europe's radicals toward nationalist appeals and colonial arrangements, the anti-Semitism unleashed by the alleged treachery of a Jewish officer drove thousands of Jews toward openly nationalist solutions and even colonial scheming.* If the time of imperialism provided the context for the Dreyfus affair, the anti-Semitism of the mob was its obvious content. Jewish nationalism and radical anticolonialism are thus the linked stepchildren of the same bleak history: both movements evolved political goals in response to the same historic conditions that aroused in democrats and Jews (often the same people) such bitter skepticism about the survival of democratic ethics in bourgeois, Christian Europe.

The despair that seized Herzl at the Dreyfus trial epitomized the widespread impatience of Western European Jews with what came to seem their failing attempt at assimilation. Herzl, who only a few years before had fantasized about a magnanimous conversion of Jewish children to Christianity, now watched despondently as liberal, cosmopolitan Europe seemed to collapse in a tide of racist hysteria. The Jewish question had suddenly returned.

It must be emphasized, however, that Herzl and most of the other early Zionists did not believe modern anti-Semitism to be terribly mysterious. They saw its recurrence as but a fragment of a larger problem whose universalist solutions, although compelling, seemed remote and utopian. The socialist Zionists, for example, were truly persuaded that the market society had staying power and would provide no solution to the social and economic vulnerability of the Jews. Market society, Borochov argued, was indefinitely mired in complex class conflicts, of

---

*See Hannah Arendt's fascinating account, "From the Dreyfus Affair to France Today," in *Essays on Anti-Semitism* (New York, 1946).

which anti-Semitic scapegoating was a predictable result. Jews would therefore have to take up the international struggle for socialism and democracy only after they solved their own special problems.

One recalls the poignant confrontation between Parvus, already a well-known Menshevik theoretician, and Nachman Syrkin, a mentor of Labor Zionism, which occurred while the two young men were studying in Berlin. Railing against Zionism to a Jewish student circle, Parvus held up his jacket and pronounced upon the new international order: "the wool in this coat was taken from Angora; it was spun in England, woven in Lodz; the buttons came from Germany, the thread from India," and so on, until Syrkin wryly observed that the rip in the sleeve had no doubt come from Kiev.*

The hatred of left-wing Zionists for all that was retrograde in bourgeois Europe was at the very core of their peculiar nationalism. These Zionists adopted with great enthusiasm the penetrating critique of Europe supplied by the radical milieu while swallowing, often apologetically, the profound contradiction implied in their separatist hunt for an overseas territory. In fact, until it became obvious that the symbols of Eretz Yisrael were indispensable for harnessing the energies of the Jews in Eastern Europe—still culturally fixated by the Orthodox liturgy, although more and more attracted to radical solutions —most "Zionists," including Herzl and Syrkin, were eager to take on any territory at all. Programs for settling in Argentina, Texas, and Uganda were promoted at various times. Clearly the aim, for the great majority of Zionists, was national reconstruction upon a territory and not—although this is being increasingly forgotten—the redemption of some historical "promise."

Not only the Labor Zionists were troubled by contradiction. No one articulated the fundamental incongruities of the Zionist position better than Herzl himself. He was a nationalist to whom nationalism seemed vulgar; he despised the kaisers and sultans whom he had to court and hoped to exploit. He was an avid

*See Marie Syrkin's memoir, *Nachman Syrkin* (New York, 1961), pp. 28–44.

promoter of colonization who was revolted by the inhumanity of existing colonial arrangements.

In his revealing work *Altneuland* (1902), Herzl emerges as a confounded Viennese "progressive" far more than a Jewish nationalist. His alter ego in the book, Dr. Lowenberg, is bitterly estranged from the decadence of the new imperial bourgeoisie yet remains loyal to the cosmopolitan promise of "European civilization." The hero's profound ennui results directly from his reflection upon the betrayal of equality and liberty by the bureaucrats running the Austro-Hungarian Empire. It was obvious to Lowenberg that the Jewish stake in the victory of democratic values cut deep; and Herzl's melodrama dwells broodingly on their apparent defeat.

By contrast, when Herzl finally gets down to his vision of the New Society — the name alone suggests the criteria by which he insisted the Jewish national home be judged — he exhibits all the monotonous righteousness of a Thomas More: economic development would be coordinated by a planning commission committed to the "national interest"; land would be publicly owned, workers' cooperatives encouraged, and private ownership controlled although market incentives would be retained. The New Society would be, moreover, a model of Millian democracy: a genuine meritocracy in which opportunity was equal, civil liberties safeguarded, and public service a reluctantly accepted privilege (like the secretaryship of a kibbutz?). Ironically, Herzl could not foresee any need for army service. After all, no private interests would foul the public good.

Nor did he neglect to grapple with the problem of colonialism itself. Clearly defensive about his advocacy of a new colonial project just when stories of horrible cruelty inflicted by whites during the Boer War were reaching the "salons," Herzl was eager to anticipate criticism. The New Society, he asserted, would be braced by proletarian virtues — self-reliance, discipline, and cooperation; therefore the exploitation of any native population would be impossible. Besides, Herzl maintained, Palestine was virtually "empty" — a contention that would later create great embarrassment for Herzlian Zionists but was at the time not all that far from the mark: Palestine was in fact greatly underpopulated at the turn of the century, largely because of the economic stagnation and political repression imposed by a Turkish administration wary of Arab sympathy for the "entente powers."*

The "emptiness" of Palestine was not crucial for Herzl, since the Jewish national home would anyway strive to be a paragon of cosmopolitan values. The great European languages would be spoken, while Yiddish (and presumably Arabic) would have to *earn* a status equal to them. There would be no Jewish colons; the Jews, on the contrary, would provide a model of self-determination for the Arabs of Palestine and even for the blacks of Africa ("all peoples need a home"). Social tranquility in Palestine would be underpinned by mutually advantageous business relations, assuring the progress of the Moslem inhabitants (such as Lowenberg's devoted friend, Reshid Bey), and Jewish science, prosperity, and liberalism would serve as a catalyst for Arab modernization.

Herzl's suspicion of conventional colonial models reflected not only a newly popular radical morality but also the disappointing experience of earlier attempts at Jewish settlement in Palestine. Although the lesson would be fully grasped only later on by the Labor Zionist settlers, even at this point such liberal Zionist leaders as Herzl and Nordau could agree about the basic reasons for the failure of the famous Biluim settlements. These had been founded in the 1880s and, even with Rothschild's extensive support, quickly became demoralized, losing many of their original members. The young Jewish pioneers, who had gone to Palestine to take up a national challenge, found themselves increasingly transformed into Arabic-speaking overseers of Arab labor and finally grew disgusted. Those Biluim who remained became preoccupied with the viability of their vineyard enterprises and lacked the social cohesion that would prove to be an indispensable condition for the revival of the national language, Hebrew, and of the Jewish culture for which Hebrew would be a major instrument. This insight was first articulated by Achad Ha'am in 1899, but Syrkin and his young protégés in Palestine—Ben-Gurion, Ben-Tzvi, and Shazar—would eventually transform it into the animating dogma of the Yishuv (Jewish population):

*See Desmond Stewart's "Herzl's Journeys in Palestine and Egypt," *Journal of Palestine Studies*, Kuwait University, Spring 1974, pp. 22–23.

i.e., socialism among Jewish settlers must presuppose the recon-
stitution of a Jewish nation in Palestine.* The prevention of
colonialist relations with the Arabs would be viewed as a pragmatic imperative as much as a moral ideal.

Herzl's *Altneuland* was therefore more prophetic than any document so unoriginal had a right to be. But with regard to the
reconciliation of Arabs to the Zionist project, no amount of "willing" could materialize the fable. The Yishuv was from its incep-
tion perceived by the Arabs of Palestine as a spin-off European
imperialism, and, no doubt, Herzl's grandstanding with imperial
potentates — whether the sultan or the Colonial Office — did little to dispel this perception. Few Arabs read *Altneuland*. The
Zionist settlers, unlike the large yet economically primitive and
politically inconspicuous Orthodox Jewish communities of Jerusalem and Safed, seemed strange and unwelcome intruders.
Palestine was a backwater of a dying empire where local "bourgeois aristocrats" were striving to replace the Turkish administration at the apex of a despotic, quasi-feudal pyramid and where
the political ambitions of the Zionists could not be easily har-
monized with those of Arab political elites.

It mattered little to these Arab elites that the Zionists came,
not as agents or allies of European imperialism, but as Jews
fearful that they were to be the chief victims of a Europe going
mad. The Zionist project was perceived as a European outpost:
a relic of foreign domination and a challenge to stirred-up Arab
xenophobia and nationalism. Nor can one deny the obvious fact
that the Zionist effort would probably have been quite futile had
Palestine not been subject to a foreign power. The penetration
of Palestine by independent Jewish settlers would have been
quite impossible in any conceivable sovereign Arab state, no matter how primitive.

This fact enabled leftist critics of Zionism, such as Maxime Rodinson,† to allege an inextricable connection between Zionism
and imperialism — in order to promote a critical perspective on

---

*Ben-Gurion's major theoretical work, *Memaamad Leam* (*From Class to Nation*), is
the defense of precisely this principle.
†*Israel: A Colonial Settler State?* (New York, 1973), pp. 45–51.

Israel within the Middle East conflict. Of course, "imperialism" dominated the fate of Palestine, as it did every other Middle Eastern and African country. But the Zionists operated within this political context no more comfortably than nationalist Arab leaderships and, on the whole, with far less success. Despite Weizmann's stubborn commitment to the "British connection," Arab elites were far more closely patronized by the Mandate government and the Colonial Office, and so indeed the Jewish settlers were finally driven to expel the British administration. Nor should it be forgotten that the mere promise of a Jewish National Home contained in the Balfour Declaration was promulgated during those same years that "British imperialism" actually created the three new Arab states of Trans-Jordan, Iraq, and Saudi Arabia, mainly as reward for the Hashemite clan's support in World War I, and that this support was no more sincere or decisive than that given the Jewish Legion during that war. Finally, the Balfour Declaration, granting as it did a virtual veto on Jewish immigration to the Arab leadership, was more the forerunner of anti-Jewish policies — such as the White Paper — than of Jewish independence.

But Rodinson's rhetorical connection between Zionism and imperialism is not quite as irritating as are his cryptic allegations about Zionist *"colonialism"* — based on the obvious fact that Palestine was "colonized" by Jews.* Having dispensed with the "imperialist link," I now want to argue that *colonization is not the same as colonialism.*

Rodinson stumbles onto an important insight — he could hardly have missed it — without appreciating its significance: the Zionists came, not to dominate the inhabitants of Palestine, but to control sufficient land to facilitate the creation of an independent Jewish society, i.e., one in which Jews would be a majority. Quite deviously, Rodinson stretches the term "colonialism" to account for this phenomenon, also invoking the example of the brutal colonization of the New World. But this will not do; by stretching the term he destroys its descriptive value.

The Pilgrim colonists, like the Zionist pioneers, were not "colonialist." Hobson and Lenin both understood the difference between refugees and imperial adventurers — the former com-

*Ibid., pp. 87–89.

ing to establish a self-sufficient community, the latter to dominate
and exploit an existing one for metropolitan benefit. Even if the
American colonists were moral cretins about the native population, this did not make them colons, certainly not in the sense
that Rodinson is trying to establish. The Yishuv can and ought
to be evaluated by the same moral criteria that made the American example so reprehensible. Since they obviously did not establish themselves as the colonialist masters of the laboring Arab
majority, did the Jews expropriate, slaughter, and destroy the
population they found in Palestine? But Rodinson would not
find such an evaluation to be a useful weapon.

The Zionists, of course, built the Yishuv through settlement
on the land and, in acquiring this land, displaced, by some estimates, as many as 30,000 peasant fellahin. No doubt, although
this displacement was achieved by legal land purchase from absentee effendi landlords, it created tremendous immediate suffering for the families involved. Most of these people, however,
were compensated by receiving other lands or became wage
earners in Palestine's newly energetic economy. The Peel Commission reports that all were successfully relocated within Palestine. Moreover, the Jewish National Fund purchased land at
such inflated values that many Arab small-holders who might
otherwise have lost their property found a new and vital source
of collateral for the purchase of labor-saving (and hence land-
saving) equipment.

This same point might be argued from a different angle. In
1938 the Palestine Partition Commission reported that the size
of the average farm of Arab tenant farmers was approximately
57 dunams, which, given their average technological standard,
was dangerously small for supporting a single family. Therefore the fundamental viability of traditional agricultural society
itself was greatly in question at the time of the Jewish National
Fund's major land purchases. Why else, indeed, were the effendis so eager to sell? It might be credibly argued, in fact, that
an imminent Palestinian Arab "enclosure movement," far more
devastating to small Arab peasants than the Yishuv, was fore-
stalled by these very purchases, and that those peasants who
retained their land quickly benefited from superior Jewish technology.

*

The image of a mass expulsion of Arabs from Palestine, so often promoted by modern critics of Zionism—and by hard-line Israeli politicians such as Dayan who require this image to justify annexations of occupied territory—is simply a fantasy. From 1922 to 1947 the Arab population of Palestine rose about 100 percent—from 565,000 to 1,200,000; the Arab population of the area that became Israel almost quadrupled between 1918 and 1947. Most Arabs were attracted to Palestine during this period because of the vigorous commercial and industrial life developed by Jewish immigrants and because of the lucrative Jewish market.* Moreover, the Arab population of Palestine enjoyed the highest birthrate in the Arab world, partly because of much higher wages, but also because of the Kupat Holim health care extended to them (while their reproductive rate remained that of a peasant society). The Zionists were neither colons nor cruel. One can only wish with Rodinson that this were really the point.

Rodinson and other Trotskyite critics, like Ernest Mandel and Isaac Deutscher, have in fact understood the issue exactly backward. The Jewish Yishuv came to be despised by the Arab leadership, and hence by the Arab masses, not because of Zionist colonialist practice, but precisely because of Zionist *anti*colonialist practice. The paradox of the Yishuv is surely that had the Jews attempted to penetrate Palestine as adventurer capitalists intent on the economic and political oppression of Arabs—the process for which the term "colonialism" was invented—they (the Jews) probably would have created little fuss.

The effendis and muftis would no doubt have been eager to accommodate such Jews in the "pores" of this quasi-feudal society, so long as these new settlers would reciprocate with recognition of the political preeminence and the religious-cultural authority of existing Arab elites—and, of course, with a piece of the economic action. This was actually a familiar pattern throughout the rest of the Arab world, where Jews were shown a measure of tolerance and respect. It is, on the contrary, because the Zionists did not come as profiteers to Palestine, because they rejected established exploitative relations, that traditional Arab

*Said B. Himadeh, *The Economic Organization of Palestine* (Beirut, 1938), pp. 228–29.

elites felt so deeply threatened. The displacement of some Arab fellahin was less important than the fear that *the traditional peasant society itself was to be displaced.* It was the separatist, socialist, and hence corrosive ethos of the Yishuv in Palestine that could not be accepted.

Rodinson therefore is driven to the argument that Jewish separatism was the definitive proof of Jewish colonialism;* but here he is both confusing and confused. Exhorted by their influential socialist theoreticians, the builders of the Yishuv determined to avoid the creation of a new South Africa, and they did avoid it—often at great immediate sacrifice. Separatism was an instrument, not an end in itself. Beginning with the formation of the *kvutzot*, the kibbutz movement, and the Histadrut (the general federation of Jewish labor) in the 1920s, and culminating with the struggle for "Jewish Laboring" in the mid-1930s, socialist leaders—Ben-Gurion, Ben-Tzvi, Katznelson—orchestrated with great skill and wide support the development of a comprehensive and cooperative Jewish productive base.

This plodding self-development was so genuinely impressive that Said B. Himadeh, an economist at the American University of Beirut, related admiringly:

> Economic and social activities of the Histadrut are performed by the following main organizations: the Workers Bank, which was established in 1921 with the aid of the Zionist Organization; the *Nir* Company, granting long-term loans to agricultural settlements; *Truva* cooperative society which markets all products of all Histadrut agricultural centers; *Hamashibir Hamercazi*, consumer cooperatives for Jewish workers; the *Mercaz Hacooperatzia*, the center for transport and industrial producers cooperatives; *"Shikum,"* which plans and executes workers' housing; Credit Cooperatives—loans and savings funds for workers; *Solel Boneh*, the contracting cooperative [which would become the largest construction firm in the Middle East—B.A.]; *Yakhin*, contracting for the plantation and management of citrus groves; *Kupat Holim*, health insurance; *Hasneh*, providing general insurance coverage; the employment fund for Histadrut workers; and, *Hevrat Ovidim*, the centralizing institution of economic and social branches.

The cultural and educational activities of the Histadrut are

---

*\*Israel*, p. 62.

undertaken by the *Mercaz Lechinukh*, the school system; *Mercaz Letarbut*, the adult cultural organization; *Davar*, the daily newspaper; *Ohel*, the workers' theatre; and *Hapoel*, the workers' sport organization.

Almost out of breath, Himadeh then half laments:

> Arab labor organization, as compared with Jewish, is still at an early stage of development. A number of Arab unions have been formed but few of them have been active. . . . The problem of cheap native labor was attacked in part by (Jewish) attempts to organize Arab labor, but . . . these attempts met with little success.*

What had been clear to Himadeh is fudged by Rodinson. Only after it became obvious that "fraternal cooperation" between Arab and Jewish workers could not succeed did the Zionist Labor movement adopt its new tactic—Avodah Ivrit (Jewish Laboring). Jewish capitalists who hired from the huge pool of comparatively cheap Arab labor were picketed and closed down by Jewish workers, often despite the intervention of the British army. No doubt the Jewish workers were motivated in part by the fear that, as in Russia's Pale of Settlement, they would be rendered superfluous by the illiterate and less demanding peasants.† But seen in the context of the other achievements and goals of the Zionist labor movement, including violently rebuffed attempts to organize Arab workers, Jewish Laboring made sense as a *revolutionary tool*. Most Arabs understandably saw Jewish Laboring as an exclusivist (even racist) plan to deny Arabs their livelihood. But this industrial strategy was rather a stubborn attempt to found a socialist society within the space of a traditional Arab society that did not share socialist aspirations, or, failing this, at least to spike the evolution of Jewish colonialist tendencies. Ironically, it was the very success of Jewish anticolonialism that proved to be the greatest historic impediment to peaceful Arab-Jewish relations.

When Nachman Syrkin visited an early kibbutz in 1920, he was startled to find that most members of the young settlement op-

---

*Economic Organization of Palestine*, pp. 290–99.
†See Ezra Mendelsohn, *Class Struggle in the Pale* (Cambridge, England, 1970).

posed producing an economic surplus in order to avoid the exploitation that was presumed to obtain in commerce with the neighboring Arabs. This was, of course, a vulgar interpretation of Marxian economics — exploitation occurs in production, not in exchange. But the attitude was an appropriate, if somewhat humorous, precursor of other self-imposed restraints by which the Jews sought to avoid the violation of the Arab communities in Palestine, earning instead Arab suspicion and contempt.

The anti-Zionist reaction that developed very early and gained great momentum in the 1930s was hardly an expression of revolutionary resistance to colonial domination. Many Arabs simply did not understand the Jewish settlers; those who did feared for their way of life. Secretary of the Higher Arab Council Jamal Husseini testified petulantly before the Royal Commission in 1937:

> As to the Communist principles and ideas of Jewish immigrants, most repugnant to the religion, customs, and ethical principles *of this country*, which are important and disseminated, I need not dwell upon them, as these ideas are well-known to have been imported by the Jewish Community.*

Not surprisingly, Jamal Husseini himself was no laborer.

The point of this analysis is not to provide some leftish moral sanction to Zionism and the Yishuv, but to probe to the nerves of the present conflict. The Jews, it is essential to grasp, were perceived as a foreign body, not because they came from another continent, but because they were the self-conscious catalyst of modernization in Palestine and so became the focus of reactionary resistance to it. This was far more perplexing than a conflict over land. It was a clash of two national movements, each promoting widely divergent images of human society.

The bitterness revealed in Jamal Husseini's testimony is therefore greatly revealing. For the openly condescending attitude of the Labor Zionists toward cherished Arab cultural values — fundamentalist and fatalist religious precepts, accepted notions of political legitimacy and class privilege — did not help matters.

*Quoted from Walter Laqueur, *A History of Zionism* (London, 1972), p. 246.

The Zionists often did not appreciate that social revolution encouraged by "foreigners" can easily be misconstrued as cultural repression. Many Jewish workers came to Palestine with all the arrogance of purveyors of progress, fantasizing about their common struggle with an imaginary Arab proletariat, and even inciting Arab mob reaction by publishing articles and pamphlets heralding the Arab revolution. Achdut Ha'avoda and Shomer Hatzair committed themselves to socialist binationalism—the latter abandoning this principle only in 1948. Rodinson unyieldingly concludes that this condescension was a feature of Jewish colonialism, forgetting that colonialist administrations, although their members privately denigrate the "natives," thrive precisely on the preservation of primitive practices. The British, unlike the Jews, made a great show of admiration for Arab political culture. The "myopia" of Zionists was rather generated by their all too enthusiastic acceptance of radical dogma, sanctioning only those national projects that promised to hasten democratic and socialist vitality.

If Zionist development strategy is to be criticized for the dislocations and injury it inflicted upon the Arab population of Palestine, it ought to be also appreciated for the miseries it prevented (another Algeria?) and the political possibilities it created. Jewish and Arab nationalisms were apparently fated to clash for reasons far transcending the concrete relations between Jews and Arabs in Palestine. European anti-Semitism helped provoke Jewish dreams of independence in Palestine just when Arab elites were becoming determined to kick out all Europeans.

Men do not make history just as they please; political choices are at best the decision to grapple with one set of problems and not with another. The Zionist settlers made a choice that, for all its shortcomings, has provided and still provides the two peoples of historic Palestine with genuine opportunity.

The separatist industrial strategy of the Yishuv concentrated on the construction of an independent Jewish political and economic infrastructure. The Jews determined to do their own work and avoid basing the economic viability of their Yishuv on cheap Arab labor. Were it not for this historical fact, the political autonomy of Jews and Palestinian Arabs would be impossible even in principle: How (unless one is the South African foreign minister) could one fathom the peaceful coexistence of two nations, each presumably exercising sovereignty and cultural independence to the extent that the modern world permits, if the two form a single productive structure in which one nation commands property and the other does the labor? Today, Arabs and Jews can still be reconciled to one another in historic Palestine precisely because the intended result of Zionist policies has been substantially achieved and class domination of one people by the other avoided.

This separation, moreover, need not preclude cooperative or federative relations between Israelis and Palestinian Arabs in the future. At present, Arab social and economic standards on the West Bank and in Gaza (and how much more so in the refugee camps of Lebanon) lag far behind those of Israel. The "law" of uneven development is operating: any premature integration of the two societies would guarantee "colonialist" relations. Indeed, the maintenance of separate political entities — assuming Palestinian Arabs are permitted and willing to get down to the painful task of economic development — is a condition for whatever "binational" harmony may someday be possible.

Since 1967 the Israeli economy has, to be sure, strayed considerably from the ambitious principles of Jewish Laboring. Israel today employs regularly about 70,000 Arabs from the occupied territories in construction, industry, and agriculture; and although Arabs were originally hired through labor exchanges guaranteeing equal wages, Arab wages are in fact not keeping pace with Jewish standards. The Israeli labor establishment appears exhausted and more eager to accommodate a politically strengthened Israeli bourgeoisie than to reimpose those restrictions upon which its power and moral authority originally rested.

Furthermore, the Israeli economy as a whole has become so dependent upon American government patronage and American Jewish capital that the pretensions of the early kibbutzim to self-sufficiency appear now as a cruel joke. Ten years ago, Israel produced about 80 percent of its needs. Today, after ten years of unprecedented industrial growth, only about 70 percent of domestic consumption (including military hardware) is produced in Israel. This puts the Jewish state in a class with Taiwan

with regard to American economic leverage. No doubt, this has
been largely responsible for the enthusiasm Israeli leaders have
shown—particularly before October 1973—for the protection
of other American interests in the Middle East.

Naturally these figures on employment and American economic leverage provide potent ammunition for leftish polemics
against the Jewish state (and make for sleepless nights among
Israeli socialists). But no matter how imperiled Israeli socialism
has become—mainly owing to the fitful industrial booms and
depressions, and labor "hard-hattism," resulting from periodic
wars—this has little to do with the reality of the Yishuv or the
ideological content of Zionism. War, not Zionism, is driving Israel step by step, expediency by expediency, to particular colonialist policies, though a new Zionism provides the rationale.
Still, Jewish colonialism is a distant nightmare and will not materialize except as the self-fulfilled prophecy of Palestinian max-
imalists who resist the very concept of Jewish national life.

Palestinian terrorists seem incapable of appreciating not only
the inherent morality but even the reality of Jewish economic
and social independence. But their attempt to ape Algeria's FLN
with revolutionary rhetoric and the more sensationalist motions
of "guerrilla war" is bound to be disappointed. Israelis are not
subject to the strategic weaknesses of a colonialist ruling class,
and one reason is that their fathers determined not to become
one. Israel will not be shaken out of Palestine like some ripe
olive from a tree. For better or for worse—for Jews, better—
Israel has elaborate roots of its own. Palestinian "guerrillas" reveal a macabre moral inadequacy when they attack schoolchil-
dren, but they reveal perhaps more sharply the insincerity of
their revolutionary claims. The victims of Maalot—Jewish and
Arab—were clearly not constituents of some exploitative apparatus. Their crime was that they were Israelis, not that they
were colons. But in a persistent flood of sophistry such distinctions blur. Children, if they are Jewish, may be killed in the name
of democracy; and the oil blackmail of the sheiks, when directed
against America and Europe (as a result of which millions of
Asians are starving), may be hailed as Third World anti-impe-
rialism!

There is, of course, no denying that the strategy of the Yishuv's leadership and (to a greater degree) the subsequent scourge of war have exacted a heavy toll from Palestinian Arabs. The refugee camps are a human tragedy and a political powder keg. Continued Israeli occupation of the West Bank and Gaza demeans Palestinian national potential. But instead of ascribing to the Yishuv a character it never possessed—indeed, set out not to possess—Arab leaders must come to grips with its concrete reality. Some form of repartition of historic Palestine—acceptable to Palestinian national aspirations and Israeli security considerations—must now be placed on the agenda in Geneva or elsewhere. And it is a fitting vindication of the obstinate, indispensable foresight of socialist Zionists that arguments in favor of political partition can still be put to work.

# In Cold Blood:
# On the Immorality of Terrorism

Though nothing can be immortall, which mortals make;
yet, if men had the use of reason they pretend to, their
Common-wealths might be secured, at least from perishing
by internall diseases. . . . Therefore when they come to be
dissolved, not by externall violence but by intestine disorder,
the fault is not in men, as they are the *Matter*; but as they
are the *Makers* and orderers of them.

—Thomas Hobbes, Leviathan

March 8, 1979

No terrorist will admit to "terrorism"—only to committing the
violence necessary for his presumably just struggle. Terrorism
is the more perplexing since many good causes—the abolition
of slavery, the subversion of the Nazi occupation, the founding
of the Jewish state, the destruction of European colonialism—
have been furthered by sickening acts of violence.

Of course the effectiveness of such acts may be exaggerated;
it is doubtful that the underground operations of the Irgun and
the Sternists would have had much impact on subsequent events

A review of J. Bowyer Bell, *A Time of Terror: How Democratic Societies Respond to Revolutionary Violence* (New York: Basic Books, 1979), Jan Schreiber, *The Ultimate Weapon: Terrorists and World Order* (New York: Morrow, 1979), and David Hurst, *The Gun and the Olive Branch: The Roots of Violence in the Middle East* (New York: Harcourt Brace Jovanovich, 1979).

were it not for the Histadrut's previous success in organizing an incipient Jewish state in Mandate Palestine. But even if some "terrorist" act does little to further the good cause it is meant to serve, the moral status of the action still gains. No one could think it an end in itself just to be terrifying. Underground fighters themselves prefer that their declared purposes—and not their murderous strategies—be the main subject of debate. Why not accept their view?

There are, as Michael Walzer* has recently suggested, good reasons for resisting it, although, like most of us, he is prepared to make some allowances. We might reasonably forgive the assault of the assassin, bomb thrower, kidnapper, or hijacker if his acts are a response to the active and violent repression of the lives and ideals of people opposing a tyranny—a cruel foreign imperial regime, for example, or police acting brutally for an intolerant majority. Second, the terrorist must convincingly be seen as working for a society in which one form of violent repression will not be replaced by another. Third, and here Walzer is more explicit, the assault must not be directed randomly against innocent civilians, but only against the officials and armed agents of the repressive regime, taking all precautions not to harm those who are neither. All these conditions are necessary. The Red Brigades, for example, cannot be exonerated merely because their victims are carefully chosen. The judges, prison officials, government workers whom they murder and cripple, enforce a constitution that provides effective political freedoms that the Brigades forgo. Only terrorism that is defensive and limited to the tyrants and their cruel agents is morally tolerable. And such actions are probably not best described as "terrorism" in the first place.

It is when underground groups take the offensive against civilians in a society that would otherwise suppress neither their ideas nor their nonviolent political organizing that we need an unequivocal epithet like "terrorism." Terror is clearly a moral violation in democratic societies, in which libertarian constitu-

*See his short discussion of terrorism in *Just and Unjust Wars* (New York: Basic Books, 1977), pp. 197–206.

tions and practices make violence superfluous to the pursuit of dissenting political objectives. In such societies the terrorist can be condemned by his tactics alone because, Walzer suggests, such tactics betray the revolutionary's "totalitarian" view of politics.

It should not be difficult to accept Walzer's conclusion that terrorism, particularly in its "current European and Palestinian manifestations," is intrinsically totalitarian and should be repudiated. These terrorists' strategies betray contempt for growth, reflection, articulate criticism — activities from which subtle and lasting commitments to social improvement derive. The terrorist can murder at random only if he repudiates the democrat's fundamental belief in the dignity of individuals, only if he reduces individuals to categories — "bourgeois," "imperialists," "Zionists," etc. — which he decides are disposable.

Only someone who believes that men are nothing but the products of their social circumstances (class, nation, race, etc.), and that their professed beliefs are no more than a cosmetic gloss on their intense drive for power, could take responsibility for the murder of people whose names, ages, occupations, and political opinions were not known in advance.

Bowyer Bell* and Jan Schreiber have undertaken to teach us about such calamities. They are social scientists who claim to be experts on terror and give advice on how to deal with it. Their separate books are nearly interchangeable, not only in style and concern but also as examples of how behavioral social science interprets the world — and might affect it, for they think in ways that bureaucrats will find congenial.

In particular, these authors have little patience for the kinds of moral argument I have just mentioned. They do not take us much beyond the vantage point of the voyeur. Their tone is casual and clear of indignation. Aside from some lively descriptions of the strange, even erotic, bonds which have at times evolved between hostages and their captors, they virtually ignore the effects of captivity on the victims. Bell and Schreiber want us to see terrorized people as a familiar part of the human condition; we should not single them out for special attention:

*See Conor Cruise O'Brien's review of Bell's earlier books on terrorism, *New York Review of Books*, September 16, 1976.

The many and the media [wrongly] perceive the dramatic slaughters of recent years, the machine-gunning of innocents, the no-warning bombs, the murdered diplomats, and the extended hijacking odyssey, as novel. . . . [Bell]

[P]arts of almost every major modern army must be considered terrorist organizations as well, for they have all burned villages, raped women, shot children and old people, destroyed hospitals and places of worship. [Schreiber]

These authors are frankly* more interested in aggression than in "shot children." Of course they profess concern for "innocents." But, like the terrorists they aim to comprehend, they see the people whose lives are disrupted or ended by terror as one-dimensional characters in a political melodrama or, as Schreiber prefers, "theater." And, since he and Bell usually cast terrorists in the leading parts in that theater, we find ourselves rooting for the bad guys if only for the sake of a satisfying climax.

Worse than their stoic attitude toward the suffering of others is Bell's and Schreiber's failure to provide any consistent moral criteria for judging terrorist activity. Neither raises the question whether such violence is a just means to a just end, but rather they take it for granted that we can recognize a "terrorist" by his violent manner and "radical" ideology. Two serious analytical weaknesses result. The first is the confusion of totalitarian-left undergrounds in today's Europe, Japan, and the Middle East with the old anticolonial national liberation movements of Africa and Asia. The success of Africans and Asians in the 1960s is taken by Schreiber to be a cautionary sign of the potential success of the urban terrorists of the 1970s and 1980s. Neither author asks what such different revolutionaries want — aside from publicity — or whether what they want can make sense to the people whose support they need, or whether their "terrorist" means will further these professed political ends.

The second and related consequence of Bell's and Schreiber's reticence regarding moral argument is even more troubling. Because they do not know why terrorism is wrong or how to distinguish it from justifiable revolution, they seem to believe

---

*Bell sees his book as yet another product of his interest in "revolutionary violence"; Schreiber is similarly interested in groups "for whom violence is a socially cohesive element."

that we should be detached and even-handed, even magnanimous, in the approach we take to terrorists. "What terrorists do
is appalling and should be stopped, but at the same time they
should be listened to: they have something to say." After all,
Schreiber concludes further on, should the economic decline of
the West continue, we shall be the "terrorists of tomorrow." In
the same vein, Bell argues that one man's terrorist is another's
freedom fighter.

The assumptions of such superficial moral relativism are worth
examining closely. Like Hobbes, both authors understand man
to be a calculating mechanism serving his own material interests,
which they see as underlying what Bell calls "dearly held beliefs,"
"desired futures," or, more quaintly, "cherished responses."
These are "rationally" pursued — even by terrorists — and are
acquired as a matter of routine in some subtle but automatic
process of social experience and indoctrination. The moral sense
of ordinary citizens is thus not vastly different from that of
terrorists once we see that the views of both are largely determined for them by the societies (nations, classes, etc.) in which
they live.

Our contempt for terrorist activity, Schreiber cautions us,
should be calmed by the professional social scientist's cool: "Positions which at first appear highly moral have a way of coming
down to issues of basic prejudice or personal or national ideology." Terrorists reflect the social conditions that produced them
much as we social scientists are influenced by our own backgrounds. And since it is we who are studying them, we must
especially resist "shaping analysis into advocacy" — an unfortunate tendency, Bell notes, of the academic mind.

Armed with these Hobbesian methods and sentiments, Bell and
Schreiber predictably extend their "use of reason" to "common-
wealths." They define the "state" as a monopoly of violence, itself
potentially "terroristic," which protects those who self-interest-
edly "subscribe to it" — to its predisposing but finally incidental
moral principles. The state "allows" its citizens only those freedoms that are consistent with its own survival. "States," Schreiber
observes, "may be tempered by democracy." But this is essentially
irrelevant to their origin in the embattled human impulse "to

acquire basic needs" in "safety." As with Hobbes, the sovereign's power derives from our reciprocal vulnerability.

Bell is never quite as explicit as Schreiber about libertarian political constitutions but, if we may extrapolate from his views on international affairs, he believes that "habits of law" develop according to the "balance of terror and the logic of greed." Nowhere do Schreiber or Bell find that democratic ethics or democratic states have any special moral value. In fact, they insist only that terrorism is a particular *technical* problem for democracies, in which the means of repression — secret police, administrative detention measures, etc. — are necessarily weaker than under authoritarian regimes.

In the political realm, then, men are mechanically self-interested, striving for scarce resources and for public "recognition," also in short supply. Laws and states assure these for some classes of men — i.e., the establishment — but not all can benefit equally. Thus, the rich believe in private property, the poor and their advocates in radical leveling. The moral ideologies of revolutionaries, Schreiber assures us, boil down to convenient claims of "exploitation" and emerge spontaneously from incidental social and economic conditions. When men cannot earn satisfactory means and "recognition" from these conditions they turn to revolution and, when frustrated, to terror.

Having analyzed the motives of terrorists as a matter of Hobbesian behaviorism, Bell and Schreiber proceed to fill chapter after chapter with second- and third-hand reports of terrorist operations and government reactions. These stories are often intricate, and we are apparently expected to be particularly fascinated by "hijacking odysseys." The chapters are headed and subheaded with slick titles devised to imply their authors' expertise in the art of crisis management, e.g., "Strategies of the Threatened" (Bell) and "Fear and Trembling: The Hostage Game" (Schreiber).

How are the crises to be managed? We are told, for example, that the "hard line" sometimes helps (as when the French police bloodlessly forced the capitulation of Croat nationalists who had hijacked a TWA plane to Paris), sometimes not (as when U.S. diplomats tried and failed to make a deal with the PFLP members who invaded the U.S. embassy in the Sudan). The apparent

willingness of state authorities to negotiate is sometimes a good
cover for eventual raids (Israel vs. PFLP in Entebbe), sometimes
not (Germany vs. Fatah in Munich). Capitulation to all demands
will sometimes save hostages (Austria vs. Fatah in Schönau),
while the satisfaction of some demands will sometimes save some
hostages (Canada vs. FLQ in Montreal). Storming the school-
house will sometimes succeed (Holland vs. South Moluccans in
Assen) and sometimes it will not (Israel vs. PDFLP in Maalot).

This advice is accompanied by bits of applied popular psychology: hostage-taking only works if officials are convinced that
the captors will kill the captives. Terrorists are unlikely to kill
hostages they grow to like. Terrorists are most nervous immediately after abducting hostages but should always be made to
feel respected, and so on. Schreiber even volunteers a variation
of the terrorism expert's riddle—a terrorist cannot kill the last
of many hostages without assuring his own capture, so how can
he kill the next to last? (etc.)—which he proudly solves, and
dismisses as a "nice academic joke."

At least some of their counsel is less obviously gratuitous.
Schreiber and Bell are openly hostile to the stated policies of,
say, Israel and Canada, which flatly* reject negotiations in principle. "Success means saving lives," Schreiber lectures, "not the
obliteration of the terrorist." Similarly, Bell cryptically warns
against "Pavlovian shootouts" which endanger lives that bargaining can save. Of course, Bell continues, "there is not yet
agreement how much bargaining should be done, how many—
if any—concessions should be made and how long the process
should take." But we must consider the hostages' welfare as
paramount until, presumably, other scientists can provide these
missing links.

This kind of science and humanitarianism will not do justice
to the real and terrible decisions that confront leaders of democratic governments when terrorists strike. The rules for crisis
management they offer cannot deal with psychological com-

---

*These policy statements may, of course, be disingenuous and promoted as an
element of strategy. Israel bargained earnestly with the PFLP during Entebbe
week; Canada likewise dealt with the FLQ cell holding James Cross to secure
this British diplomat's release.

plexities, which, as they show but do not acknowledge, arise in a different form in each case. How can government officials know whether their acquiescence in formal negotiation will not cause terrorists to raise their demands as the SLA did in San Francisco? Do conciliatory responses encourage further provocation later: Did the Schönau affair, for example, invite the Vienna raid on OPEC? Is it more risky to storm the terrorists than to allow them to repair with their hostages to renegade states such as Libya or Uganda,* states that ignore the international conventions that Schreiber painstakingly reproduces?

Bell and Schreiber show much concern with superficial tactical solutions to crises that are each inherently unique because they prefer to avoid the radical moral challenge posed by terrorism. The choice, of course, is not simply between saving hostages and killing terrorists; it is, as the English political writer Rosalyn Higgins recently observed,† between possibly saving hostages and probably subverting democratic practice. The leaders of democratic states might be more consistent in the face of terrorist blackmail if, instead of becoming preoccupied with their managers' efforts to psych out the culprits, they recognized that the preservation of abstract laws can be no less urgent than saving lives.

What makes terrorists bad is not merely that they resort to violence, but also that they use violence against forms of political life that have been devised to abolish violent intellectual and moral repression. I believe it can be wrong for elected governments inflexibly to risk the deaths of ordinary citizens for the sake of democratic ethics. Some compromises may be required; and if it would have saved my own cousins who were, in 1974, killed by Palestinian terrorists, I would have wanted to let the democratic rule of law be hanged. Still, this was not my reaction to the entreaties of the Moro family. In both cases it was probably best that the families were not taking the decisions.

---

*The complicity of Eastern bloc states with terrorist activity, particularly against Israel, seems to be increasing as well. According to one unconfirmed report, the East Germans are now heavily involved in the flow of arms to the PLO and have had a part in the training of terrorists in Eastern Europe ("Foreign Report," published by the Economist Newspaper Ltd., June 14, 1978).

†*The Listener*, May 4, 1978.

But for Bell and Schreiber the conflict in such cases is between the morally unexceptional state on the one hand and, on the other, its morally unexceptional opponents. "Innocents"—or as Schreiber prefers, "noncombatants"—are simply caught in the crossfire. He and Bell want us to save them at all costs not so much from compassion, but because they have so limited a conception of costs.

Bell and Schreiber profess to be concerned about "open societies," the origins and virtues of which they never explore, but which they admire—mainly, it would seem, because they have been living in them themselves. Both warn somewhat hysterically about the threats to "open societies" that are posed, not so much by terrorists, but by the paternalistic sovereigns eager to war with them.

Since, in their view, some "have-not" groups turn to revolution and finally to terror to get power—and defend their actions with claims for justice that are as good as any others—Western "have" societies are bound to come under attack. The governments which preside over these technologically advanced and functionally "open" societies are particularly vulnerable to terrorists for two reasons. First, "postindustrial" society presupposes such technological interdependence that a single terrorist act can affect many thousands. The stakes are dramatically higher when so many vital "nodes" of urban life depend on so many others, where nuclear terror is possible, etc.

Second, the sensation-hungry press and television in such postindustrial states give instant celebrity to terrorists and their messages. This, Bell and Schreiber explain, complements perfectly the terrorist's need for "recognition." Terrorist "theater" excites attention and spreads a new ideological vocabulary among the impressionable and the relatively disadvantaged masses; it may, Bell and Schreiber suppose, win new adherents or at least a dangerous degree of tolerance unless the state acts to destroy it.

And here, for these authors, is the difficulty. When the state suppresses terror it reveals its own paternalistic violence and invariably "allows" fewer of the civil liberties that had hitherto helped it to maintain its popularity. Like Italy and Germany, the state is damned if it is flabby and damns itself when it is not.* The inference we are to draw from all of this is sobering: "Terrorism works." And because it works it will always be with us in "open," "postindustrial" societies.

Another inference is also plain: we must be vigilant against those who would "close down open societies to make them safe." And the best way to keep alert is to adopt these authors' stoicism, that is, to remind ourselves that terrorism is finally to be seen as a natural catastrophe—"less deadly than hurricanes"—set in motion by the material conditions of history and grounded in man's widespread capacity "to do harm to his fellow man." This capacity, Schreiber consoles us, "is not merely latent in the human species." Hobbes also noticed, not without relief, that the natural condition of man was no worse than that of "Lyons, Bears and Wolves."

It is of particular interest that behavioral scientists concerned with terrorism should share so many methodological assumptions with the revolutionaries they study. That Bell and Schreiber describe terrorists in much the same language as the latter describe themselves is evident in the recent interview with the German terrorist Michael ("Bommi") Baumann in *Encounter*, September 1978. Here too we find the paternal state, the cavalier attitude to democratic ethics, the lure of press and television attention, the simple-minded view of "exploitation," etc. Given such shared premises, it is not surprising that Bell and Schreiber should conclude that terrorism works.

If these social scientists were not, like terrorists, so intent on ignoring the processes of thinking behind political action, they might realize that to kill in cold blood and to presume that such actions will be vindicated by "science" and "history" is not to act by reflex from social conditions: terrorists view the rest of us as mechanically produced and so we can be random targets; they

---

*Better informed and more thoughtful writers than Bell and Schreiber have written perceptively about this dilemma. See Alberto Ronchey's unsettling article "Terror in Italy, Between Red and Black," *Dissent*, Spring 1978, and John Donberg's analysis of Germany's "anti-terrorist right" in *Saturday Review*, June 10, 1978. By contrast, Bell's section on the Red Brigades is uninformative, and Schreiber's comments on West Germany's battle with the Baader-Meinhof group uninformed.

view history as programmed, hence capable of being manipulated by their own special violence, which they view as inevitable. Such views are not derived from common sense.

Moreover, behind terrorists' (and, I daresay, Bell's and Schreiber's) apparent indifference to argued analyses of right and wrong—and necessary to that indifference—is in fact an argument about right and wrong, namely, that what has come to seem necessary, in view of the frequency or intensity of its occurrence, action, etc., also has claims to be right. Whatever their pretensions to acting merely by response to history's stimulus, terrorists could not have begun to speak their "scientific" language without having absorbed moral and epistemological views that have a long history.

This becomes clearer when we inspect terrorists' statements and backgrounds. The Red Brigades' leader, Renato Curcio, called the killing of Aldo Moro "the highest act of humanity possible in a class-divided society"—not an offhand remark. Walter Laqueur reminds us, sardonically, that the Tupamaros were said to require a Ph.D. from prospective members.* This is not to say that terrorists are smart; but we should realize that their actions cannot be explained by theories about unreflecting drives for power, competition, and aggression born of "desperation." In fact, most terrorists are the products of the middle class, with university backgrounds, and have developed imaginative and elaborate schemes to "free" us from the "oppression" maintained through "capitalist" and "imperialist" violence by counterviolence.

Terrorists, as we have often heard, may also be deeply disturbed by their frustrated searches for specialized employment, by bureaucratic corruption and persistent social poverty. Particularly in countries like Italy and Germany, they may be driven by repressed shame for the murderous regimes that they identify with their parents. In creating their own subterranean international network, they appear to have had various kinds of help from the Middle East as well as from Cuba and Czechoslovakia.†

---

*See his essay in *The Terrorism Reader*, which he recently edited (Philadelphia: Temple University Press, 1978).
†See Claire Sterling, "The Terrorist Network," *Atlantic Monthly*, November 1978.

It is also likely that the rigors of underground life drive them to a bloody-minded paranoia. But although they would now deny us this privilege, terrorists are above all erstwhile participants in endless arguments about the nature of mankind and its future. We have little hope of talking students out of their totalitarian philosophic and historical premises once they have become disciplined, nervous murderers. But Western universities have, for two generations, been filling up with teachers like Schreiber and Bell, who did not know how to do so when they had the chance.

Nor have such social scientists been able to teach us very much about the virtues of democracy, for all their assumptions about the superiority of "open societies." No democracy that I know of is the happy accident of the "balance of terror and the logic of greed." Democratic institutions aim to provide what Mill called the moral and psychological climate for exerting our highly individual capacities in art, science, moral philosophy, and production. Hobbes's sovereign would guarantee only our consumers' rights to property. And if we cannot distinguish Mill's principles from those that simply want to maximize power in the market or maintain the security of property, we shall have little with which to reproach Renato Curcio.

If they are to be successfully supported, democratic institutions must be understood as having been established by *opposition* to the kings, Whigs, and tyrants who willingly provided security for the pursuit of market power.* Such institutions derive their strength from commonly held ideas of personal rights and the public good; they are not now so fragile that they cannot be defended without being destroyed, as Bell and Schreiber suggest. Warring against men of violence is, Michael Walzer implies,† an irony but not a paradox.

Bell and Schreiber seem helpless and even resigned when they point out, quite rightly, that the fight against terrorism may endanger civil liberties: Italy has recently enacted laws permit-

---

*For a study on the development of democratic programs in opposition to prevailing bourgeois-utilitarian constitutions, see C. B. Macpherson's new book, *The Life and Times of Liberal Democracy* (New York: Oxford University Press, 1977). †*Just and Unjust Wars*, p. 327.

ting emergency search, seizure, and detention; Canada's RCMP has apparently practiced illegal surveillance of the Parti Québecois since the War Measures Act lapsed in 1971; and Germany and Israel have established secret anti-terror squads whose practices should be chilling to civil libertarians. But few civil liberties would survive the abuses of government officials if they were not vigilantly protected. The "SWAT teams" set up to fight terror do not present challenges to citizens of democratic society that are different in kind from the ones citizens face in controlling arrogant police and intelligence officers, high-handed bureaucrats, and megalomaniac leaders.

Nor does the claim by these authors that terrorism works well now because modern societies are technologically interdependent seem relevant to the moral dilemma facing democratic governments. The choices are the same whether the hostages or potential victims number 100 or 10,000, whether terrorists close down an airport or kidnap a judge. But the practical implications Bell and Schreiber draw from high technology seem to me wrong in any case. The cost and sophistication of high technology can be of advantage to democratic states in dealing with terrorists. They are in a better position to use it for their own defense than are terrorists to use it for attack; no El Al flight has ever been successfully hijacked. The terrorist's threat to knock out one power station in a "grid" can hardly seem as terrifying to us as the poisoning of a village well did to medieval peasants.

Bell and Schreiber are, finally, in awe before the power of television. Terrorism works, they think, because it can always get attention on television—now the key, they seem to believe, to all political action. Were it not for television, how many would have learned of Croatians or south Moluccans, or even Palestinians? But while it is true that terrorists are encouraged by publicity, how much in fact do viewers learn about them or their struggles, and to what effect? Here the authors could use Susan Sontag's insight into modern image making, that it may convey nothing more than a momentary shock, or an illusion of knowingness, lacking in historical perspective and having no coherent result. I doubt that television is an effective political weapon even for those terrorists who make it to Barbara Walters's interviews.

Nor have journalists always pandered to those terrorists whose demands or actions seriously threaten democratic practice. In Quebec during the October crisis and in Italy during the Moro affair, television turned the public against the FLQ and the Red Brigades. Television can undermine the allure created by the rumor and mystery surrounding terrorists; it can also make suspects recognizable on every street corner. And if television does give a "high recognition factor" to some terrorists, such as "Carlos," Curcio, and Lelia Khaled, it can also numb the public to their strident rhetoric. If you've heard one hijacker, the rest will offer few surprises. Flashes of publicity for violent actions are still no substitute for achieving real political power.

This last point is germane to the case of the PLO and its most recent champion, David Hurst of the British *Guardian*. His book surveys the Arab-Israeli conflict "from its roots" in 1921. He is concerned to deflect criticism of PLO terror by arguing that the violence of the emerging Palestinian movement was matched by the violence of Jews and Israelis. He recalls the Zionists' part in the early riots, in the events that led to the Arab revolt, in Deir Yassin, and, more recently, in the Israeli air force's brutal retaliations in southern Lebanon. What is striking is that he ignores how useless the PLO's terror has been from the first. He does not ask how the PLO can expect bombings and massacres to obtain for them anything more than the professional attention of "experts" like Bell and Schreiber.

Hirst reluctantly accepts the permanence of Israel as a majority Jewish state and endorses a Palestinian state on the West Bank and Gaza Strip. But he fails to draw the conclusion that PLO terror will prevent such a state from emerging rather than establish it. The only purpose such terror can achieve is a general, ruinous war, one that will have no victors. Israelis are not *pieds noirs* who will be driven by terror from historic Palestine as the colonists were from Algeria. Israelis have too many roots in their land and their language for that; and they carry a vivid image of their collective vulnerability. As the Camp David agreements suggest, the PLO will not gain in thirty years at underground war what Sadat accomplished in thirty minutes at Yad Vashem — Israel's memorial to Europe's Jews.

Instead of continuing to sabotage the Camp David agreements, the Palestinians would have much to gain by formally recognizing Israel and working to achieve real autonomy in the West Bank and Gaza. Chaim Weizmann and the Labor Zionists pursued a similar policy for thirty years before they achieved a Jewish state, and they did so under less propitious conditions than those now facing the Palestinians. By withholding recognition of Israel and refusing to renounce terror, the PLO leaders and intellectuals are not withholding crucial bargaining chips. On the contrary, recognition and commitment to peaceful methods are far more likely to bring the Palestinians into a position where they can bargain strongly over repatriation of refugees, political relations with neighboring states, borders, water rights, security, etc.

For over a decade, a popular slogan of the PLO said that an enemy cannot be defeated with roses. The underlying premise, now more than ever, is false. There are moments in history when one can defeat an enemy with roses, but only after deciding not to destroy him.

# Whose Peace Now?

---

*Washington, D.C., November 15, 1979*
The indefatigable editors and sponsors of *New Outlook*, the monthly of Israel's peace camp, convened an international symposium in Washington on October 27. "Eminent scholars and statesmen," as the announcement put it—Israelis, Palestinians, and Americans—were invited to talk about solving the Palestinian problem. As with an earlier *New Outlook* conference in Israel, this one was intended to show that a dialogue between Israelis and Palestinians could and should take place. To have prominent Israelis talking to Palestinians in Washington might impress American politicians and American Jews, might suggest that the Begin government is partly responsible for the siege against which it is struggling. The participants were expected to do what Begin will not do—endorse Palestinian self-determination, insofar as this would be consistent with Israeli security. In full view of President Carter and the Zionist Organization of America, they would discuss the kind of two-state solution that Israeli and PLO officials might eventually negotiate.

*New Outlook*'s first conference, held in November 1977, was widely viewed as a success since it seemed a "prelude," as the *New Outlook* editor Simha Flapan grandly remarked, to President Sadat's "historical visit to Jerusalem" later that month. Unfortunately, history's cunning of reason was not on the side of Flapan's little magazine this time. The conference had its poignant moments, but these mainly pointed up the deep dilemmas that have already stalled the Camp David autonomy plans and that were bound to leave many of the conference participants bitterly divided.

As for the participants themselves, it must be said that they were not exactly what the conference organizers had in mind. One purpose of the symposium had been to find a way to bring together West Bank mayors (e.g., Karim Khalaf, Faid Kawasmeh), well-connected Palestinian intellectuals (Walid Khalidi, Edward Said) and others loyal to the Fatah leadership in the PLO, and the centrist doves of Israel's Labor Party. Such dovish Labor Party politicians and intellectuals as Abba Eban, Yossi Sarid, A. B. Yehoshua, Uzi Baram, and Micah Harish have met with West Bank Palestinians in the past. But a meeting in Washington, unlike one in Nablus, would be seen as a move toward mutual recognition by Labor and Fatah leaders. For even if all the participants came as individuals, even if neither side claimed to speak for its movements, it would still be clear that they would not have come to Washington without the approval of people higher up. An important precedent would have been set. Or so the *New Outlook* organizers hoped.

Those who showed up at Washington's International Inn for this wedding of sorts, however, were immediately discouraged to find neither the bride nor the groom present. Just before the meeting was to begin, it became clear that neither the West Bank mayors nor the Labor Party doves were coming. Conspicuously represented instead were young people of the Israeli Peace Now movement, which is not a political party and is mainly concerned with protesting new West Bank settlements and calling for an end to Israel's rule over Palestinians. "The government of Israel," it holds, "should conduct negotiations with any Palestinian body which accepts the path of negotiation as the only means of solving the Middle East conflict." Endorsing this view in Washington were people from Mapam as well as the civil rights leader Shulamit Aloni and some prominent academics. And there were also the leaders of Israel's Sheli Party, including Lova Eliav, Mati Peled, and Meir Pa'il, all of whom have broken with the Labor Party and advocate a bolder policy: direct talks with the PLO and peaceful coexistence with a new Palestinian state.

But neither the Labor Party nor the PLO would allow itself to be represented at the conference. Professor Hisham Sharabi, the editor of the *Journal of Palestine Studies*, and the fiery West Bank Palestinian writer Raymonda Tawil came; both are known to have good connections with Fatah leaders. But they appeared at the meeting expressly to denounce any attempt to circumvent that leadership and to attack the conference's strategy—of inviting West Bank mayors to come as individuals—as an insulting attempt to do so. So even before it began the symposium failed.

Why will Labor and the PLO not put themselves into position to conduct serious talks? In Labor's case, the reason cannot be as simple as PLO terrorism, for Shimon Peres is known by insiders to have discussed with Austrian Chancellor Kreisky the possibility of contact with Fatah officials last year.* The newer problem seems to be that Labor has picked up the scent of power, and Peres (along with Chaim Bar-Lev, Yigal Allon, Chaim Tzadok, and the other leaders) does not want to provoke potential coalition partners in the National Religious Party, or, for that matter, the hawks in his own party—those, like Amos Hadar, who favor West Bank settlements and whom Amos Elon neatly called the "agrarian reaction." The presence of Labor doves at *New Outlook*'s conference would be all the more provocative to them, since Sarid and Baram will be active in running Labor's election and Yehoshua has accepted the job of writing the party platform in elegant Hebrew.

Peres and his brain trust may be correct in estimating they can return to power in 1980 or 1981 and shrewd to show concern for saving appearances. Begin was seriously embarrassed in October when Foreign Minister Dayan's resignation was followed by the Supreme Court's ruling against some of the government's plans for new settlements. Dayan, for all the admirers he disappointed in the 1973 war, has continued to be a model of political "realism" in Israel. This reputation is partly owing to his own history—his childhood in Labor Zionism's first moshav, or farming cooperative, his youthful association with Ben-Gurion and the new army, his presentation of himself as the

*A UPI report of November 12, 1979, from Cairo suggests that another attempt was made to arrange a meeting during the recent conference of the Socialist International in Lisbon.

Israeli who is most at home in his land and, unlike the old-style Jews, in his skin. All this has combined to create an image of Dayan as the man who can tell his generation what is and is not naive for them to believe.

When he abandoned the rest of Begin's feuding ministers, Dayan carried with him no faction, only his own vote. But he has denied the Mandate of Heaven to their annexationist designs on the West Bank. The Supreme Court's condemnation of the government's expropriations of private Arab land only reconfirmed this to the Israeli public, over 60 percent of which (according to a *Ha'aretz* poll) had, even before Dayan's resignation, declared themselves ready to forgo the West Bank to solve the Palestinian problem, and negotiate to that end with *any* authoritative Palestinian group that is prepared to renounce terrorism.

Defense Minister Ezer Weizman is openly sympathetic to such sentiments. He has himself threatened to resign if the government defies the order of the Supreme Court to evacuate the illegal settlement at Elon Moreh—a defiance shockingly advocated by Agricultural Minister Sharon—or gives its approval to Sharon's newest blueprint for Greater Israel. Like the ailing Yigael Yadin, whose lame duck Democratic Movement is necessary for a government majority, Weizman could sink the Likud and have much popular support in doing it, particularly in view of the government's mismanagement of the economy it was elected to save. (Meanwhile members of the ultra-Orthodox Agudah bloc, for whom the borders of Israel are Jehovah's business, are currently pressing the weakened government for still more concessions to ritual laws. If they continue to be frustrated—as they were on November 11 when their bill to restrict abortion failed in the Knesset—they may save Weizman and Yadin the trouble of bringing the government down.)

Begin has tried to restore his government's internal cohesion and strengthen its waning support among the poor, mainly Sephardic, second Israel, which is the hardest hit by the 100 percent inflation rate. He has sacked his cantankerous Finance Minister, Simcha Ehrlich, and replaced him with Yigael Hurwitz, a passionate, brilliant, and intolerant industrialist—the brother of Amos Hadar—who is best known for having been the only min-

ister in Begin's first government to resign over the return of the
Sinai settlements and the other terms of the Camp David accords.
Hurwitz's prestige as an economic czar—he is bragging that he
will trim the government bureaucracy down to its "live flesh"—
and hawkish views on settlements may firm up the cabinet majority just enough to let it ride out its term beyond the American
elections. Neither Weizman nor Yadin seems eager for noble
retirement. But should Peres soon be fighting an election, he
knows that however open-minded Israelis may appear to be regarding the Palestinian question, the PLO still conjures up for
them and their daily press all the bloodthirsty goys who they
fear would kill the Jews as a matter of principle.

Which brings us back to the *New Outlook* conference. By refusing to allow the West Bank mayors to come to Washington,
the PLO deliberately missed an opportunity to allay just such
fears in the Israeli public. It is true that Sharabi and Tawil came
to the symposium endorsing the two-state solution. But all the
higher Fatah spokesmen—Farouk Kaddumi, Abu Iad, Shafik
al-Hout—have publicly, though inconsistently, supported
roughly the same approach since 1975, and it has not led to a
relaxation of the terror directed at Israelis, or to any manifest
demonstration on the part of the Fatah leaders that they would
hope to live with the Jewish state in peace—a hope some of the
West Bank and Gaza mayors would likely have expressed if they
had come. (More recently, all of the mayors resigned in response
to the military government's decision—sanctioned by Begin's
Ministerial Defense Committee—to deport Bassam Shaka, the
mayor of Nablus, who had, it was charged, expressed views sympathetic to PLO terrorist attacks. But the mayors' collective resignation was in protest against such unwarranted curbing of their
political activities, not a show of support for Shaka's hard-line
views.)

This reluctance to deal with the Israelis politically seems the
more inexcusable since, as Professor Sharabi admitted to me
after his smooth speech, the letter of the Camp David agreements
plainly favors the emergence of a Palestinian state from some
stage of transitional autonomy. But it is America's and Egypt's
attempt to negotiate over the heads of the PLO leadership as
such—not General Sharon's shaky settlements on the West

Bank—that makes the PLO so opposed to the prospect of a transitional stage. Of course, Sharabi stressed that suspending the West Bank settlements would be "helpful" to PLO moderates. And surely the settlements should be stopped for the sake of Israeli democracy, if for nothing else. But Sharabi would not even state flatly that an end to the settlements would bring a corresponding end to "armed struggle." That, apparently, would be missing the point.

The point, Sharabi left me to infer but would not himself acknowledge, is that the PLO leaders in Beirut intend to "take power" in the West Bank and Gaza as a group. They are not interested in winning out through some democratic or transitional exercise in which potential rivals—say, Anwar Nusseibeh of Jerusalem's electric power corporation—can emerge. The Fatah leaders make up a tightly disciplined authoritarian group that has for ten years suffered and acted daringly together and now is winning one diplomatic victory after another. They have fought off bloody challenges from rival groups and from Arab states that see them as excessively independent. For all their carping at the "Camp David process," they clearly believe themselves to be on the verge of winning recognition from the American government. Their actions on behalf of the American hostages in Iran, their courting of American black leaders, and so on, show their confidence.

Moreover, Arafat seems to prefer the prospect that his personal organization—the Fatah cadres loyal to him—would become the Palestinian representative in any settlement imposed by the superpowers: he does not want to see this network of cadres deteriorate during a drawn-out transitional regime or during the negotiations over Palestinian autonomy. The Fatah leaders are not going to be kept from their places in the promised land if they can help it.

To the PLO, this approach may seem dictated by its needs for internal discipline and its chain of command. It seems to me a formula for deadlock. Arafat may prefer this deadlock and the machinations of high diplomacy to the responsibilities of running the schools and collecting the garbage in the West Bank towns. That he is indispensable to peace seems clear enough since the West Bank has lined up behind him. What is not clear

is whether he is willing to risk the uncertainties of political negotiations, on and off the West Bank, with the same determination that he risks death from Iraqi, Syrian, and PFLP assassins.

The *New Outlook* conference was probably too minor an occasion to take such risks, but there may well be more propitious
ones in the next several months. Professor Sharabi hinted
broadly to me that a more suitable chance for PLO diplomacy
would be created by an amendment, or clarification, of UN Resolution 242 to the effect that the Palestinians are a nation with
rights and not merely a "refugee problem." Such a change would
open the way for the PLO's implicit recognition of Israel. Since
the resolution already endorses security and recognition for "*all*
states in the area," PLO acceptance of the amendment would
also open the way for American mediation.

Andrew Young, we recall, resigned after meeting the PLO
representative to ask for a delay in amending 242 because he
knew its importance but thought the attempt premature. The
efforts to amend the resolution will, however, likely continue
this winter. For even if Sharabi is wrong to expect the PLO to
support an amended version of 242, the new version will be seen
as an opportunity to call the Palestinians' bluff. And, although
the Israeli government has opposed any tampering with 242
since Rabin extracted a promise from Kissinger to leave it intact
in 1975, fair-minded Israelis will point out that the clauses of
the Camp David accords devoted to Palestinian "legitimate
rights" go well beyond anything envisioned by the Security Council in 1967.

The activities of Israeli doves and American Jews seem pertinent to just this question because their support for American
politicians may be essential if the United States is not to be intimidated by the anger of the Begin government. A change in
Resolution 242 is in Israel's interest, for it could present the PLO
with a diplomatic challenge from which there is no return. On
the other hand, there seems no reason why Israel's friends
should help the PLO win victories in America until that organization agrees to be bound by Resolution 242 as amended. A
recent *New York Times* poll showing 42 percent of Americans
willing to deal with the PLO now should be cautionary to those
in Israel who, in their enthusiasm to oppose Begin and the legacy

of Golda Meir's Labor regime, inadvertently give the PLO more prestige in America than it has.

Which brings me to some final observations about the *New Outlook* symposium. Perhaps the most nerve-racking confrontation at the event took place, not between Palestinians and Israelis, but between some of the members of Israel's Sheli Party, Lova Eliav and Uri Avnery, and American Jews such as Irving Howe and Arthur Hertzberg—the former president of the American Jewish Congress—who support the more broadly based, and less strident, Peace Now movement. Eliav and his colleagues have, of course, been trying to promote a more forthcoming approach to the PLO in Israel for many years, and Eliav has himself recently shared a prize in Vienna with Isam Sartawi, a PLO intellectual who is often described as a moderate and with whom Eliav has had many contacts. For years now Eliav, Peled, Avnery, and the others in Sheli have been standing up to attacks for having met with the PLO and advocated a deal with it. But their dissident passion seemed overintense in Washington. From the start of the proceedings, the Eliav group did not hide its impatience with Peace Now and its American supporters, who were themselves openly annoyed to be facing, not West Bank mayors with a mandate from the PLO, but people who, on behalf of the PLO, were delivering blasts at Camp David, Sadat, the Carter administration, and the conference itself.

The bad feeling between Peace Now and the Eliav group came to a head in a session devoted to American Jews. Howe and Hertzberg debated testily with Eliav and Avnery over the propriety of appearing to credit the PLO as a partner in future peacemaking efforts when, despite its growing power, that group has been so reluctant to pay more than lip service to peace. In fact, it was precisely the PLO's growing power in America, along with anti-Jewish feeling, that seemed to put Howe and Hertzberg on guard and make them more committed than before to the circumspect attitudes of the Peace Now group, whose influence has been growing rapidly. In Israel, Peace Now has recently been able to mount demonstrations of 80,000 people against new settlements and continues to get support from a remarkably wide range of people, including retired generals, kibbutz members, business executives, and scholars such as Gershom Scholem. The leaders are now trying to make their case to American Jewish groups.

What was most troubling about this unresolved dispute was, however, that the specific disagreements reflected a more profound and rarely acknowledged difference between Israelis and American Jews. Eliav, for all his bitter dissent from Begin and the Israeli establishment, remains an Israeli, a Hebrew, the builder of the famous Lachish development, much as Peled remains the brigadier general who was quartermaster of the Six-Day War. Both men also know that they are a telephone call away from rejoining the same Labor Party they now oppose but once believed in all too earnestly. One may indeed have to be from a political establishment to know how to hate it, but Eliav cannot expect American Jews to join him without reservations in his crusades against it. His free-lance diplomacy, after all, can be seen as one of these crusades. By contrast, many American Jews live a Jewish life so attenuated, so barely strung together by vicarious political Zionism and pro-Israel institutions, that they view dissent from official Israeli policy on the Palestinians as a breaking of cultural and institutional vessels for which there are no replacements. Professor Sidney Morgenbesser of Columbia put the problem sharply when, appealing for unity, he cautioned the more activist Israelis that support for Israel has become the center of American Jews' ethical sense.

Peled complained to me after the conference that he had never before understood how much the American Jews were an obstacle to peace. And the American Jewish leaders have been all too willing to be uncritical of Israel's diplomacy, particularly since 1967. But Peled is wrong to assume that American Jews are an obstacle to peace just because they will not rally to Sheli's political program the way they rallied to Golda Meir. In fact, the pronouncements and performance of the Begin government have caused many American Jews to be more open to dissent from Israeli policies and more nervous about the effects of those policies on their lives—especially as they watch the PLO gaining ground and foresee the day when they may be blamed for the harsh economic consequences of a Middle East stalemate. According to a recent Harris poll, almost two thirds of American Jews now favor an end to new Israeli settlements and a return of the West Bank as part of a general solution to the Palestinian problem. This majority could support the principles of Peace Now — as it could also support an amendment of Resolution 242 endorsing Palestinian national rights. It remains to be seen whether American Jewish leaders will ignore such opinions, as they ignored the *New Outlook* conference.

# Friends and Enemies: New Books About the Palestinians

*February 1981*

By "the Palestinians," the British television journalist Jonathan Dimbleby means the hundreds of thousands of people in south Lebanon — what Israelis call Fatahland — who are the children of the refugees who fled Palestine in 1948. They are the main body of the national movement whose vanguard is the PLO. Having spent their lives in harsh camps, or working in Gulf states that denied them citizenship, the Palestinians in Lebanon are now men and women who set themselves apart from the rest of the Arab nation as people who have witnessed their own catastrophe. It is Dimbleby's unreserved sympathy for them that makes his book worth reading. Through interviews and photographs, he presents their history as they see it.

Just when (he tells us) the Turks were repressing the Palestinians' own first challenge to Ottoman rule during World War I — by ruining their traditional economy and hanging their leaders — the British army marched in. But British politicians only replaced the Ottoman Empire with their own duplicitous colonialism. Notwithstanding Sir Henry McMahon's commit-

A review of Jonathan Dimbleby, *The Palestinians* (New York: Quartet Books, 1981), Amnesty International's *Report and Recommendations of an Amnesty International Mission to the Government of the State of Israel, 3–7 June 1979*, and Ann Mosely Lesch, *Arab Politics in Palestine 1917–1939: The Frustration of a National Movement* (Ithaca, N.Y.: Cornell University Press, 1981).

ments to the Hashemite Sherif of Mecca in 1915 and early 1916, the secret Sykes-Picot Agreement between England and France during 1916 detached Palestine from its cultural and political center in Syria, which the French sought to control. This accord prepared the ground for British administration of Palestine under the League of Nations Mandate, which formally endorsed Lord Balfour's promises to the Zionists in 1920.

The imperialism of some Europeans, Dimbleby continues, thus promoted Zionism in Palestine even as the racism of other Europeans menaced Jews, driving them to Zionism. Nor were the Jews all that grateful for refuge; they barely concealed their ambition to have a state within their ancient borders. They set about dispossessing Palestinian farmers of traditional holdings, only to establish upon them farms and industries that actively discriminated against Palestinian workers. Forced from their land, vulnerable in the cities, the Palestinians thus saw their country bought up, fenced in, transformed, by swelling waves of Jewish immigrants. Peaceful political action was useless while their own desperate use of force brought on British and Zionist terror. The Zionists finally drove them out, harassing Arab families who clung to their land.

Suddenly homeless, reviled by the imperialist West, at war with Israel, the Palestinians were also misused by reactionary Arab regimes and patronized by UN relief agencies. The writer Yahya Rabah told Dimbleby:

> We came to realize that we were nothing without a homeland. . . .
> A homeland is not only land and security. It is songs and happiness. When we ate bread or drank water, our first thought was that the bread of our country was better, the water tasted more sweet.

Dimbleby wants readers to share the ideology that most Palestinians derive from this special version of their history. But he does not appreciate what he's revealed: that the galvanizing force in the lives of the Palestinians of Fatahland, of the PLO leadership, seems to be their political rage and not the defense of some more distinct cultural tradition, as one finds with, say, the Québecois. The Palestinian nation, according to its current leaders, is not the product of the Palestinians' particular language, civilization, or religious practices. Rather, Palestinians are Arabs whose Arabic is indistinguishable from that of the Syrians and who claim to remain pan-Arab nationalists in the tradition of Nasser. Most also profess the faith of Sunni Moslems or Christians, for there are no sects peculiar to Palestine. So their national movement seems to Palestinians in Lebanon a political response — to Zionists who are held to have caused the Palestinians' recent suffering and to the events that culminated in their "exile."

As a result of the intensely political origins of their nationalism, the Palestinians in this book now seem to take military power to be an end in itself. Salah Tamari, a PLO commander in south Lebanon, offhandedly told Dimbleby that he did not consider himself a human being until he took a gun in his hand. He and the other PLO fighters Dimbleby talked to make it clear that the common identity of Palestinians centers on the political goals and military methods that promote their cause — the "Return," the destruction of Zionism, the foiling of imperialism. For this reason Palestinian leaders may find it especially difficult to compromise on any part of that cause for the sake of tactical gains, or even peace. What is not clear from *The Palestinians* is how people like Tamari can consider peace proposals with "Zionists" and still, by their own definitions, think themselves Palestinians. Of course, peace would eventually empty the camps, and PLO leaders should welcome this. But since, as Tamari puts it, the Palestinians view their struggle as "between two wills, two existences," won't the PLO leaders or West Bank politicians who take part in some compromise solution be risking violent opposition from armed radicals who believe in the conventional Palestinian wisdom? (In November, for example, Mohammed Abu-Wardeh, a Palestinian of little influence but noted for his pro-Egyptian views, was murdered in Gaza.)

Part of that wisdom, one gathers from *The Palestinians*, is that the Jews are to be viewed as a "religious" community which can be incorporated in some secular Palestinian state. In fact, most Israeli Jews see themselves as part of a secular Hebrew culture that has emerged from the Zionist settlement; so Donald McCullin's pictures of them as Orthodox men, praying at the Western Wall in side locks and *talesim*, seem intentionally misleading. "Religious" rights will not satisfy most Israelis now as they might have satisfied the pious Jews of the Meah Sha'arim quarter in Jerusalem under the Turks. And portraying the Israelis as a people in the grip of religious obligations obscures the opposition of a great many Israelis to the Begin government's messianic settlements on the West Bank. Poll after poll reveals that most Israelis favor trading more land for more peace. Dimbleby's book says nothing about which Palestinians would be willing to take steps toward coexistence. As Tamari succinctly put it, "If we get that Palestinian state, we will have initiated the decline of the state of Israel. I do not see their leaders permitting such a thing of their own free will. We cannot afford a crack in our unity. . . . We must fight."

For all of this militarism, it may no longer be possible to exclude the PLO from negotiations for a settlement. The Western European governments have already drawn this conclusion. Notwithstanding the preference of most Israeli moderates (such as those in the Labor Party) for some Jordanian administration on the West Bank and Gaza, Palestinians under occupation now owe allegiance to Fatah, however different their experiences from those of the refugees in Lebanon.

This sentiment does not testify to Fatah's diplomatic success. The PLO during the last six months has been dominated by Syrian military power and diplomacy, while the Saudi leaders who largely finance the PLO strongly oppose Assad's increasing reliance on Soviet aid to defend his regime. Arafat and other Palestinians may now regret his support for Khomeini and his bloody rivalries with the Iraqi-sponsored ALF within the PLO. King Hussein, moreover, may now reassert his claim — repudiated both by himself and the other Arabs at Rabat in 1974 — to negotiate on behalf of the Palestinians, and he may do so with the backing of Saddam Hussein of Iraq. But Fatah's status in Israeli-occupied territory seems undiminished just because the occupation has, after thirteen years, become economically distressing and politically dangerous to West Bank residents, whatever their social class.

Nor have the Israelis acted to undermine the PLO's popularity. Quite the contrary. The West Bank has been absorbed into Israel's economy in a manner that has stunted the industrial base of its Palestinian residents: today, 90 percent of West Bank imports originate in Israel.* Before the October war, Palestinian merchants and thousands of unskilled laborers prospered because they suddenly had access to Israeli markets; the GNP in the occupied territories quadrupled from 1968 to 1973. But Israel's erratic, inflation-ridden economy since 1973 has been hurting not only businessmen and traders on the West Bank who must use Israeli currency, but also construction workers — now estimated at 75,000 — who have no unions, are underpaid, and are the first to be laid off during Israel's recessions.

The more immediate cause for alarm is, however, the continuing flow of Jewish settlers. Those who belong to Gush Emunim, around 14,000 of them, now claim 29 percent of available West Bank land. According to reliable reports in the Israeli press, some of them have been organizing an underground to resist any efforts to move them out. A counterterrorist organization called TNT (Terror Neged Terror) was reportedly responsible for the bombs that maimed Nablus Mayor Bassam Shaka and other West Bank officials in September after Fatah terrorists had attacked and killed Jewish settlers in Hebron. For Palestinians and Jews the West Bank thus remains tense, polarized, and full of risks — fertile ground for pro-PLO sentiment.

It is this context, the collapsing order on the West Bank, that makes Amnesty International's report on Israel's treatment of people arrested on grounds of security all the more troubling. Here, in AI's brief, one can find a summary of the tragedy of Israeli society since 1967: the state, as represented by its policemen, soldiers, and legislators, retreating by stages from the democratic standards that most of Israel's judges, lawyers, and citizens would wish to maintain. A recent Israeli law, for example, which AI could not consider, empowers the Minister of the Interior to cancel the Israeli citizenship of any person who "illegally" takes residence in an Arab country or who has performed an act "which constitutes disloyalty to the state." The law even provides for disenfranchising that person's minor children.† As

---

*Claiborne and Cody, *Washington Post*, September 30, 1980; Brian Van Arkadie reports the figure for 1972 as about 60 percent. See *Benefits and Burdens* (Carnegie Endowment for International Peace, 1977), p. 79.
†*Ha'aretz*, July 31, 1980.

for AI, its most important criticisms concern the practices of Israel's military police and intelligence services when they detain suspects for questioning—at times up to eighteen days without a warrant—before charges are made. Palestinians have complained they are violently threatened, questioned for hours, sometimes beaten.

AI's specific recommendations aim to cut down opportunities for such physical abuse or for the other forms of intimidation that Israeli forces are accused of having used to extract confessions from Palestinian suspects. Not that the report is unequivocally damning. AI does not allege that Israel uses systematic torture or that suspects are killed or maimed—or disappear. Israel's respected Attorney General, Yitzchak Zamir, acquits his government, in the report's appendix, of many of the suspicions that AI representatives have honorably raised. He seems especially convincing where he points to Israel's good record of cooperation with the Red Cross, which is allowed to visit convicted prisoners, and to the military government's regular practice of reducing sentences.

Yet one will miss the political significance of the report if one concentrates only on its grim details. The issue is not simply whether Israeli forces are brutal to the Palestinian suspects they arrest but that so many young Palestinians have been arrested. The military governor admitted in June 1979 that, during the previous six months, some 1,500 had been taken into custody, 70 percent of whom were between sixteen and twenty-three years of age. We hear about Palestinians fired at in the legs by Israeli soldiers and not about thousands more who have been routinely questioned or simply frightened by Israelis in uniform. Their capacity for organized resistance should be kept in mind when we read of official Israeli reprisals: the closing of Bir Zeit College on the West Bank; the sudden deportation of leaders such as Mayor Faid Kawasmeh of Hebron and the mayor of Halhul, Mohammed Milhelm; the censoring of *al-Fajr* and *al-Shaab*, Arab newspapers openly sympathetic to PLO leadership; the banning of artworks in Ramallah;* and so on.

And the most compelling part of AI's prose is what is left

---

*Ma'ariv*, September 3, 1980, p. 4.

between the lines. I mean the liberal democratic principles implied in the face of so much mutual hostility—principles necessary for peacemaking. Not only any Israelis, but leaders in Jordan as well as Palestinians—families with property and independent intellectuals in the West Bank and Gaza—will want to endorse liberal democratic institutions, hoping that open elections and impartial judges enforcing civil rights will provide stability for any future settlement. But the principles of democratic life also seem essential as criteria by which Palestinian and Israeli leaders will have to negotiate that settlement. They will have to agree on a partition, and to do so on the assumption that the land and the city of Jerusalem are resources to be used by separate societies. Each group will want to maintain its own majority state but will also have to guarantee within its borders the civil liberties of the other's national minority. Loose talk about "mutual recognition" and "self-determination" can obscure the fact that, to live with each other, Israelis and Palestinians will also have to be tolerant of each other.

Which is why *The Palestinians* seems to me a further disappointment. For all of Dimbleby's professed sympathy for the suffering of the Palestinians, he never sees them as complex people capable of divided feelings or unexpected thoughts; the only question seriously posed by the book and its photographs is whether one is for or against the PLO cause. Dimbleby's most obvious moral simplification is his failure to condemn PLO terror. He does not even try to compare it with that of the Irgun's former commander, Menachem Begin, whom he dismisses as "terrorism's philosopher"; that Begin's old slogans sound close to the statements he quotes by Tamari escapes him. *The Palestinians* celebrates PLO militarism: twenty-two large photographs in the book are of boys and young men in uniform or brandishing weapons; the newborn are called "babies for Fatah." By contrast, there are just two pictures of girls and young women in groups—they stand "in silent anticipation" at the edge of a political meeting where "fighters" are seated, or else they are shown wailing over graves.

Dimbleby criticizes the Western nations for closing their doors on Jewish refugees from Hitler; he attacks the Israelis, with justice, for their failure to confront the misery of the Palestinians and to offer to resettle or compensate those in camps. Nowhere, however, does he examine the record of Palestinians or of any Arabs with regard to Jewish refugees, whether before the Final Solution or after. Was, for example, the Evian Conference, at which the Western powers refused to raise their Jewish immigration quotas, more discreditable than the Cairo Inter-Parliamentary Congress—also held during the fall of 1938, just after Evian—at which Arab leaders friendly to Haj-Amin appealed to Britain to close Palestine completely? Are the material claims of 800,000 Jewish refugees from Islamic countries after 1948 to be disregarded just because these people have not been kept in camps?

Dimbleby's most ingenuous argument is advanced, paradoxically, to excuse the terror of the PLO not against Israelis but against other Palestinians. When Ali Salim, the leader of the Palestinians resisting both Falangist attacks and the Syrian siege in Beirut, became outspokenly critical of Arafat's leadership during those bloody days, the PLO chairman had him executed. Far from being friendly to Israel, Salim thought Arafat too soft, too enmeshed in diplomacy. But Dimbleby defends his execution: "He [Arafat] must preserve his position in the quasi-democratic institution which he leads and ensure that his freedom of tactical manoeuvre is not unduly restricted by minds that are not as free of naiveté as is his own."

That one of Britain's "most prominent journalists" could become so cynical about civil liberty seems relevant to his fascination for what he sees as the Palestinian way of life before it was contaminated by the Zionist "invasion": he admires powerful men who stick to the land, trust in their fathers, breathe clean air. He seems drawn to their "common code of honour . . . upheld by the ritual of revenge." This enthusiasm for an idealized virile past prevents Dimbleby from discussing the questions about the history of Arabs and Zionists that Palestinians will have to ask if they look beyond the catastrophic version of history that was put to Dimbleby by PLO spokesmen. To what extent were Zionists responsible for modernizing Palestine—for cities, secularism, technological advance, and egalitarianism? And is the catastrophe of Palestinian history partly the continuing failure of their own intellectuals and political leaders to face these changes constructively? Dimbleby may regret that Zionism was ever invented, but he cannot expect Palestinians who view themselves only as victims to "work out their joint salvation" with Israelis.

The new study of Palestinian politics before World War II by the American scholar Ann Lesch raises just these questions, but for the purpose of showing how Palestinians failed to organize opposition to the Zionists. Lesch has little sympathy for Zionist goals, but her research will be no comfort to advocates of the PLO who ignore how Palestinians themselves helped to frustrate the emergence of an effective national movement in the 1930s.

Lesch gives much attention to the class divisions among Palestinians, which thwarted their efforts to speak with one national voice. In fact, the very idea of a Palestinian nation must have seemed fanciful, even subversive, to most of the leading Palestinian families in the cities — notably the *hamulas,* or clans, of the Khalidis, Nashashibis, and Husseinis — who felt secure enough in the Ottoman Empire to serve in its diplomatic corps and central administration. With Ottoman backing, they also controlled their own municipalities, religious institutions, and schools. Lesch could have added that the urban notables, or *áyan,* had also abused their power to carry out the Ottoman Land Law of 1858, registering large stretches of *miri* land — land that is state-controlled but farmed by peasants — under their own names.* Such corrupt practices, which were tolerated by the Ottoman authorities, increased their power as rich absentee landlords.

Lesch's arguments thus put in a new light the long-standing claims of Palestinians that the Turks oppressed them. But similar reservations seem warranted even with regard to the more common charge that they were betrayed by the British. This view has been accepted among supporters of the Palestinian cause since George Antonius published his influential *Arab Awakening* in 1938. It is true, as the Palestinians claim, that the British secretly annexed Palestine to their empire, although the territory

---

*See Y. Porath's succinct discussion in *The Emergence of the Palestinian Arab National Movement* (Frank Cass, London, 1974, and International Scholarly Book Service, Forest Grove, Ore.), p. 11.

had been promised by McMahon to Emir Hussein, the Hashemite Sherif of Mecca. But Antonius himself argued that, as late as 1920, no specifically Palestinian nationalism had taken shape except in the imaginations of some intellectuals and Christians who were inspired by their teachers in missionary schools before and during World War I. After the war, the Palestinian notables were faced with a prospect of Hashemite rule from Damascus, guaranteed by British arms, or the Mandate. No one asked the fellahi what they preferred.

In fact, many of the elite families in Palestine were highly educated and resented the prospect of being ruled by a Bedouin whom they regarded as a desert king; this was Hussein's son, Faisal, who in 1919 had already made a deal with Weizmann along lines more favorable to the Zionists than those envisioned by Balfour's declaration. No wonder some urban families, such as the Husseinis, turned to the Syrian nationalists in Damascus, who soon forced Faisal to repudiate his cooperation with the Zionists. Other families, such as the Nashashibis, seemed positively drawn to the Mandate.

Lesch shows that this was a time of great political confusion and that the Palestinians and British each, with some cause, saw themselves as betrayed by the other. In fact, all the important Palestinian families turned against the Mandate when its power could not be used for their own private purposes, and the Husseinis were no exception. The pro-Zionist High Commissioner, Sir Herbert Samuel, went beyond traditional rules in order to appoint the anti-Zionist leader Haj-Amin al-Husseini as mufti of Jerusalem just after Arab disturbances there in 1920. But in 1922 Haj-Amin, unlike the Nashashibis and others, rejected British proposals for a legislative council in which Jews would have been in the minority, although Weizmann had accepted them. The mufti claimed that by accepting, he would only confirm the same illegitimate Mandate authority that had appointed him in 1921.

Nevertheless Lesch demonstrates that the politics of Palestinian nationalism were mainly frustrated by the rivalries among the powerful Palestinian clans, who stirred up peasant fears of Zionism — which was, to most fellahin, the major threat to their proprietary rights in land. Dimbleby, who seems so impressed by the peasants' style of life before the arrival of the Jews, would find from Lesch's book that by 1930 the average fellah owed Arab bankers from the leading families a sum roughly equal to an entire year's revenues, often at a usurious rate of interest — as much as 30 percent. Just such indebtedness led to the many foreclosures that made land available for sale to Zionists.* The largest single land purchase by the Jewish National Fund — the one for the Valley of Jezreel in 1920 which, in uprooting over twenty Arab villages, helped touch off the Jaffa riots of 1921 — had been concluded only because the Sursoq family in Beirut had been eager to rid itself of insolvent tenants. The great *hamulas* sincerely opposed Zionism's atheism, socialist rhetoric, and exclusivist farming of land. They increasingly tried to organize opposition to the Mandate on that account. But it was the British who organized new, easy credit for fellahin during the 1930s.

Lesch also describes the illiteracy of the Palestinian peasants, their primitive technology, and their religious authoritarianism in order to explain why they could not prevail on their own elites and British diplomats to block Jewish immigration and land purchases. That the Palestinians during the 1930s lacked a large, confident, and literate middle class — such as now exists in the West Bank — helps to explain not only the ineffectiveness of Palestinian opposition to the Mandate but also, ironically, the small number of Palestinians who might have settled for partition in 1938, or when Ben-Gurion offered it in 1946.

Lesch is reluctant to endorse the principle of partition, even in retrospect. She certainly does not approve of the plan of 1937, which would have given the Jews a mini-state — no Jerusalem, no Negev, no western Galilee — and the Palestinians the Hashemite rule they had been denied in 1919. This plan called also for a large Arab minority in the Jewish sector, and there was some British talk about transferring Arabs elsewhere so as to accommodate the Jews expected from Germany and Poland. Were these sufficient reasons for the Palestinians to mount a revolt in order to scuttle the proposals of the British Peel Com-

---

*See Said B. Himadeh, ed., *The Economic Organization of Palestine* (Beirut: American Press, 1938), pp. 496–97. Also, Lesch, p. 69.

mission for partition? Lesch seems to think so; but she also shows that whenever compromises were proposed, right up to 1948, the Palestinian national movement came under the domination of fanatic traditionalist groups wholly opposed to all dealings with the Zionists—the Istaqlal organization, for example, and the Husseinis. These silenced, at times violently, the more moderate voices, including members of the Nashashibi clan and some of the merchants of Haifa, who were cautiously advocating negotiations.

Like Dimbleby and the PLO fighters, Lesch considers the Histadrut, the Zionist labor organization, discriminatory and seems to approve of the Palestinians' defiant attitudes toward it. She is right that the Labor Zionist leaders exploited the vulnerable Arab political economy to establish a foothold in the land. Except for those who joined small Zionist groups like the one called Brit Shalom during the thirties, they showed little enthusiasm for contact with Arab intellectuals. But Palestinians could not have overcome their difficulties by defeating the Histadrut. On the contrary, because of Labor Zionism's "movement for Jewish Laboring," which kept Jewish industries and collectives from hiring landless Arabs, both groups avoided a colonialist pattern in which Jewish employers would have been seen as exploiting Arab labor.

Certainly the growing numbers of peasants who were becoming part of an Arab proletariat resented Zionist unions for keeping them out of jobs. But Lesch has the advantages of writing in retrospect, as Jewish leaders once had those of foresight. A more liberal Histadrut would have established a society where Jewish settlers found themselves trying to dominate a hostile mass of Arab workers. A pale copy of such colonialism now exists on the West Bank and is a major source of tension.

Ben-Gurion, it must be said, was not as much concerned with avoiding colonialist labor relations with the Arabs as with keeping Jews working in Hebrew collectives. But his socialist-Zionist policy nevertheless preserved an Arab economy largely distinct from the Jewish and the possibility of partitioning the land between two states. It also encouraged the growth of the very class of Palestinian merchants, industrialists, and intellectuals who gradually built up Palestinian nationalism.

Lesch's closely argued history of the failures of Palestinian nationalism raises the question of how moderate and progressive people in Lebanon or the West Bank can now change that history in spite of the strident position of the PLO leadership and in the face of the Israeli occupation. Dimbleby deals perfunctorily with the position of Palestinians who seek social progress while coexisting with Israel; he writes instead of Fatah's modest attempts to establish schools, factories, and hospitals in Lebanon. But such influential Palestinian intellectuals as Walid Khalidi, now professor of political studies at American University in Beirut, have argued forcefully and openly that political compromise will be indispensable. Khalidi has already advocated what Dimbleby will not: that the PLO recognize Israel and negotiate for a virtually demilitarized Palestinian state on the West Bank and Gaza. Khalidi now seems an isolated figure. If peace does become a serious possibility, how many Palestinians will know what to do with it?

# Do Israel's Arabs
# Have a Future?

*February 19, 1981*
For Israelis, one of the most disturbing facts of life is that so
many of the 500,000 Arabs who are Israeli citizens are increasingly militant supporters of the PLO. In the elections of 1977,
over half of them voted for Rakah, Israel's pro-Moscow Communist Party, which claims to be anti-Zionist and openly favors
a PLO state in occupied territory. When the party planned an
Israeli-Arab political congress in Nazareth for December 6, the
Begin government banned it from taking place. Arab student
organizations at the Hebrew University and other universities
have refused to stand guard duty on their own campuses, though
these have been the targets of terrorist attacks. Students' groups
have issued statements endorsing the PLO as the sole representative of the Palestinian people. So has Tufik Zayat, the communist mayor of Nazareth, who told me not long ago that such
sentiments are only the surface signs of deep disaffection.

Four books have been published recently to account for the
estrangement of "Israeli" Arabs from their state. Each seems

A review of Elía T. Zureik, *The Palestinians in Israel: A Study in Internal Colonialism*
(London: Routledge and Kegan Paul, 1981), Sami Khalil Mar'i, *Arab Education
in Israel* (Syracuse: Syracuse University Press, 1981), Ian Lustick, *Arabs in the
Jewish State: Israel's Control of a National Minority* (Austin, Tex.: University of
Texas Press, 1981), and Yoella Har-Shefi, *Beyond the Gunsights: One Arab Family
in the Promised Land* (Boston: Houghton Mifflin, 1981).

complementary to the others, which is remarkable in view of the diverse origins of their authors. Elia Zureik is a Palestinian scholar who lived in Israel until he graduated from high school and was thereafter educated in England. His book is the most bitterly polemical of the four, but also the most daring work of social theory. *The Palestinians in Israel* recapitulates the relations of Jews and Arabs in Mandate Palestine in order to show that the Arabs are casualties of Zionism's "internal colonialism."

Zureik's main evidence for this thesis is the current social condition of his former community. About half of Israel's Arabs still live in nearly isolated towns and serve as a work force for Israeli Jewish industries. A quarter work on Jewish farms and construction sites. Zureik's figures convincingly show that the Israeli Arabs are "dependent upon and dominated by" the Jewish economy; that Arabs have become a segregated industrial proletariat in Israel and will remain one unless some of Israel's political institutions are reformed. The other books under review recognize the force of Zureik's facts.

But Zureik's attempt to use the Arabs' current problems to discredit Zionism under the British Mandate as colonialism is something else. It seems to me not only insupportable from the historical record, but to obscure the intense cultural conflicts among the Israeli Arabs themselves. In 1948, the 175,000 Palestinian Arabs who stayed in the territory that became Israel were almost all peasant farmers. Unlike the professional people, merchants, workers, and other urban Arabs who fled cities such as Haifa and Jaffa in panic, or were driven out of towns such as Ramle by the Haganah, the Palestinians who became Israeli citizens lived mainly in rural villages in north-central Galilee or the Little Triangle between Haifa and Nablus, where the fighting did not quite reach. With the exception of Christian Nazareth, these were among the most backward places in the country that became Israel.

Zureik knows this, but he refuses to acknowledge that the changes in the social conditions of the Arabs in these regions are more usefully considered for the period after 1948 rather than for the one before. He does not want to write about these Israeli Arabs apart from the Palestinian nation as a whole. He does not consider that the flight of urban Palestinians in 1948 could be understood as a consequence of sudden war—but rather wants to portray it as the culmination of Zionist "colonialism," which presumably still exists. To prove his case against the state, Zureik tries to show not only that Israel's Arabs have been "proletarianized" since 1948—this, after all, might suggest that they made some advance—but also that their leading commercial classes have suffered as Jewish commerce gained. To do so, he cites evidence to show how, in 1944, about 11 percent of the Arab population was employed in "commerce and services," as compared with only 8.2 percent in 1963. What Zureik omits to say—at least here—is that most of the urban Arabs who had commercial jobs fled in 1948. Nor does he recall that a great many working in "services" in 1944 were clerks in the Mandate bureaucracy. By contrast, the number of Arabs working as "traders, [commercial] agents, and salesmen" in Israel, according to his own statistics, actually doubled from 1963 to 1972 and was roughly equal to the proportion of Jews doing the same work during the same years.

Not that such comparisons could anyway tell us much about political power in Israeli society. In 1972, most powerful Israeli corporations, collectives, and unions were largely ruled by an old-boy network of Histadrut managers and Labor Alignment politicians, few of them Sephardic Jews or sympathetic to them, let alone Arabs. The crucial disparity between Arabs and Jews was this: nearly 40 percent of Jews had technological, administrative, and clerical jobs in 1972—most of them not in private commerce—and only 6.7 percent were unskilled laborers. But only 12 percent of Arab workers were employed in such privileged fields. To grasp the implications of such facts, which could have made a stronger case on behalf of the Israeli Arabs, Zureik would have had to undertake a much closer analysis of Israel's complex political economy; and he would have had to raise the question of the resistance of rural Palestinians to modernization.

Sami Mar'i is prepared to do both, which does not make his book less challenging to those who would wish Israel well. Mar'i was, like Zureik, born and educated in Israel, but he attended the Hebrew University and finally decided to stay. He is currently one of a handful of Arabs teaching social science at Haifa University, the only university in Israel to admit a substantial number (over a thousand) of Arab students. Few writers are in a better position to survey the dilemmas of Israel's Arab citizens, and few have done so more persuasively.

Mar'i's main subject is the education of Arabs in Israel, and this leads him to consider the larger situation that determines the personal and political attitudes of Arab students. His central point is plain: Arab citizens will have to have far greater social and economic opportunities in Israel if their children are to feel loyal to the state and their teachers are not to feel like quislings. Mar'i believes that the Arab educational system ought to be run by Arab educators, that it should teach more about Palestinian national culture and history. He leaves open the question whether cultivating Palestinian identity will inevitably lead to anti-Zionism by calling for an "Arab national identity which *is not* and *should not* be anti-Jewish." If this seems evasive, it is typical of a book that is devastating in its facts, yet concerned to promote conciliation between Israeli Jews and Arabs.

Mar'i also makes clear what Zureik had implicitly denied: that most of Israel's Arabs regard the Jewish majority and Hebrew culture with some ambivalence. While Israel to them is conquering, humiliating, and hostile, it has also been a source of rapid progress for some Arabs in their knowledge of technology and their sense of women's rights, economic liberty, and the values of individualism. Much that they want to know about the modern world is written in Hebrew.

But of course any such guilty feelings of admiration for Israelis do not outweigh their contempt for the state. Israel's Arabs have had bitter claims against their government, arising out of the years of bloody conflict during and after the founding of the Zionist state. Quite apart from the antipathy Palestinian peasants felt to Zionism, and to Jewish soldiers, the state took actions immediately after the 1948 war that were bound to cause deep anger among its Arab citizens. Instead of democratic elections, military government was imposed on the Arab towns, and this was only withdrawn in 1966 under the liberal regime of Levi Eshkol. Between 1949 and 1956, moreover, the state expropriated about half of all Arab land for Jewish settlement, often resorting to specious claims that this land was abandoned or was required for state security. In mitigation of this record, officials point out that Israel was vulnerable to the raids of Palestinian *fedayeen* throughout this period and was frantically settling hundreds of thousands of Jewish refugees from Arab countries. But Israel's Arabs bore the brunt of this turmoil for a generation and do not forget the violence done them by Israeli forces.

For example, during the Sinai war in 1956, forty-three people, including some women and children, were summarily executed for breaking the curfew at Kfar Kassem. The Israeli commanders were court-marshaled and later pardoned. In 1976, six young men were killed by soldiers during demonstrations against new Israeli plans to expropriate land in the Galilee. The government would not hold public inquiries into these killings. Mar'i shows in detail, moreover, that in addition to expropriating land, state officials discriminated against Arab municipalities and public schools during this period, denying Arabs the funds that might have helped them catch up to standards in the Jewish sector. He is particularly hard on the record of the state's Arab Department, which reports directly to the Prime Minister and the Defense Ministry but claims to be a bureaucracy set up to serve the Arab community.

Mar'i's book is poignant because he senses the contradictory situation in which young Arabs find themselves. Whatever their current enthusiasm for the "Palestinian cause," Arab students, he writes, became part of a modern society in Israel. They have ceased viewing membership in a powerful, patriarchal clan as central to their lives and have grown accustomed to coeducational arrangements outside school as well as within it. Compared with children in West Bank schools, Israeli Arab children became impatient with rote learning and have shown, according to research Mar'i cites, a much higher predisposition for independence and "creative" thinking.

And Mar'i reminds us that these students have absorbed such tendencies in Hebrew. During four years in high school, Arab students have to study 768 hours of Hebrew language and literature (including Bialik, Alterman, and leading Zionist writers), as compared with only 732 in Arab studies. Yet these students don't unequivocally despise the culture they have had to master. It seems no exaggeration to call them Israelis even though the standard dogmas of both the Arabs and the Israeli Jews would deny that this is what they are. Still, Mar'i's most discouraging finding is that 90 percent of the Arab students he interviewed in 1977 doubted they had a future in Israel. Some 40 percent of young Israeli Jews concurred with this assessment of Arab prospects.

Such attitudes might change if progress can be made on peace between Israelis and the Palestinians beyond Israel's borders. But another finding shows the severe obstacles that would exist for Israeli Arabs even if peace should become possible. Arab high school seniors who major in science believe their future in Israel will be especially grim; and some 90 percent choose to major in the humanities. At first this seems odd: the students, as Mar'i found, consider the humanities curriculum in Arab schools degrading, with its heavy load of Hebrew culture. Besides, one would expect the young members of a minority to advance most rapidly in technical jobs, where knowledge of mathematics and science would count for more than the loyalties of the majority. To explain their reaction, Mar'i takes us back to Zureik's claim: that Israeli Arabs lack the independent industrial base that could absorb their young scientists and professionals. The Jewish managers of Israel's advanced industries will not hire Arabs, whether because of misplaced feelings of patriotism, fear of espionage, or common racism.

Moreover, technical schools are very expensive to develop. Arab municipalities, which carry little weight with Israeli political leaders and have a small tax base, cannot afford them, even though a majority of Arab parents, albeit a small one, favor technical training for their children. Mar'i's conclusion, that students choose the humanities because they've grown resigned to a career in teaching in their own towns, seems inescapable. Arab students expect, and accurately, that they will be excluded from respectable positions in Israel's urban economy. Recent promises by Begin's adviser on Arab affairs, Benyamin Gur-Arye, that about $30,000 of Moslem trusteeship (Waqf) funds will go to gifted students and that school overcrowding will be eased over the next ten years seem unlikely to change their minds.

To understand their social frustration, one can usefully turn to Ian Lustick's book. A professor of government at Dartmouth, Lustick seeks to show how Arab dissatisfaction derives from the

basic pattern of the Israeli political economy. He first analyzes
the various methods by which Israel's Labor bureaucracy and
the state's Arab Department have broken up the Arab community by encouraging the preeminence of local *hamulas*. To
that end, Israeli leaders have made separate and unequal arrangements with the Druse communities and resorted to high-
handed "security regulations" to suppress the emergence of any
national Arab party—like el-Ard (Land) Party of the early
sixties—which might field candidates for election to the Knesset.

The historical inability of Israeli Arabs to organize on a national scale interests Lustick most. Israeli Arab workers are not
only subject to repression by the government, they must also
depend on the quasi-socialist and private industries run by Jews
for their livelihoods. During the 1960s and 1970s, the established
political parties gave small numbers of the most promising young
Arabs jobs in the government and the Histadrut, where they
would have to be politically circumspect. But such sinecures have
run out. That the Rakah Party receives an independent subsidy
from Moscow has thus helped to make it a singularly effective
forum for Arab dissidents, who would otherwise have no sympathy for communist social theory. But Lustick points out that
Rakah's Jewish leaders, such as the old Stalinist Meir Wilner,
have exercised subtle constraints on Arab dissidents, keeping the
Rakah members tied to the communists' binationalist program.

Lustick's most pointed argument is that Israeli citizenship is
of no advantage to Arabs who want to live in Israel so long as
the governing apparatus will not reapportion the power held
by the semi-official Zionist institutions established during the
years of immigration before statehood. These bureaucracies—
the Jewish Agency, the Jewish National Fund, the organized
rabbinate—routinely violate the democratic standards that must
be upheld for the Arabs if they are to gain anything like equality.

The problem Lustick shrewdly identifies is not that Israel is a
Zionist state. It is, rather, a democratic state that accords some
important civil rights to all, but in which the old Zionist institutions still reserve the principal economic benefits only for the
Jews. The Jewish Agency has, for example, spent some $5 billion
to develop the Jewish economy and advance the prospects of
Jewish families since 1948, resources to which no Arabs can have

had access. Land expropriated from Arabs by the Israeli land authority for "public use" is casually consigned to the Jewish National Fund in order to, say, "Judaize the Galilee." According to that fund's regulations—once justified by Zionist officials as means of developing the Jewish economy independent of that of the Arab majority—this land may never be leased by non-Jews, even when no Jewish settlers will have it. Such regulations create hardship for Israeli Arabs in towns such as Nazareth and Acre that are critically short of housing.

Lustick's criticisms of such policies imply that Israeli Arabs, if only they had the chance, would want to take an active part in the life of Israel while receiving a greater share of social benefits as they did so. But the growing separatist sentiment among Arab majorities in central and northern Galilee puts this in doubt. Lustick gives Israel moral credit for the democratic standards it has achieved despite the hostile feelings of Arab communities and for the state's traditional refusal to draft Arab men into the Israel Defense Forces to fight other Arabs. But he points out that Israeli Arab youths have paid a high added cost for their exemptions, since national service is not only the prerequisite for being socially accepted in Israeli cities but is also necessary for benefits upon discharge, such as low-interest mortgages, jobs that require security clearance, and so on.

Lustick's excellent book has some flaws. His data are often taken from the 1950s and 1960s, and the lives of Israeli Arabs now seem both better and worse than his book anticipated. Better, because the Israeli economy has been liberalized during the last several years and shaken by inflation. Like many Sephardic families in petty commerce or on moshavim, Arab merchants, contractors, drivers, and farmers have prospered by comparison with most other Israeli wage earners during this time. Yet, like members of kibbutzim, Arab workers who live a semirural life have been insulated from the disastrous inflation affecting Jewish workers in Israel's large cities. The Arab birthrate is now almost twice that of Israeli Jews and is unlikely to decline in such rural areas as it might in the cities. While tens of thousands of Israeli Jews are emigrating, few Israeli Arabs feel they must.

On the other hand, since the Begin government's election the political climate has become much worse for Israeli Arabs. The

Arab Department no longer operates under the comparatively benign regime of Labor appointees such as Shmuel Toledano. Rather, the infamous Koenig Report, calling for systematic impoverishment of Arab municipalities — secretly prepared during Rabin's term by an Interior Ministry official and then put aside — now seems official policy. Tufik Zayat has charged, for example, that the Arab part of Nazareth now gets less per capita than one third of the revenues going to Jewish Nazareth. Lustick shows that the Green Patrols, under the influence of Agricultural Minister Ariel Sharon, have been harassing Negev Bedouins whose lands are being expropriated for new air bases. And Sharon has for years openly threatened Israeli Arabs with expulsion if they show themselves hostile to his view of Israel's interests.

Not that Sharon speaks for most Israelis or that his threats have intimidated Israeli Arab leaders. In fact, the latter now seem much less susceptible to the "cooptation, segmentation, and economic dependence" for which Lustick has tried to account. Rakah, led by such men as Tufik Zayat, seems to be emerging as the Arab national party Lustick could not find when he began his study. Mar'i's view seems to me more nearly right, that circumstances have forced more and more Israeli Arabs to decide between, on the one hand, the PLO and, on the other, their fading prospects for combining cultural autonomy and integration into economic and civil life under the Likud regime. Should the Labor Alignment regain power in the forthcoming Israeli elections, the new ministers will have to act quickly to shore up those prospects and to engage the cooperation of young Arab activists and intellectuals in and out of Rakah, however this may rankle Labor's old guard, especially from the moshav movement.

It is to the reasons why such efforts are necessary that Yoella Har-Shefi devotes her new book. She uses the form of a historical novel to describe her own relations with a well-known Arab family whose identity she conceals but that most well-informed Israelis will immediately recognize. In doing so, she suggests the thinking of those Jews who are struggling for democratic treatment of Arabs. The narrator of her book often seems naive, especially in her touching, crusading tone, which brings to mind

Gotthold Lessing's hero in *Nathan the Wise*. She is justifiably hard on the Orthodox rabbis whose legal authority made it impossible for a son of the Arab family to marry his Jewish lover in Israel. Har-Shefi is a tough-minded journalist, a survivor of the death camps — I. F. Stone identifies her as an outspoken ten-year-old on the Haganah ship he wrote about in *Underground to Palestine* — and, like Stone, she has become a muckraker. She gained prominence by attacking the self-censorship of Israel's dailies, which now do not give her steady work.

Her book is also a chronicle of the doubts common among Israeli liberals and secularists — e.g., A. B. Yehoshua or Amos Elon — who worry about condemning Jewish politicians while Palestinian leaders do not stop threatening their country's survival. But Har-Shefi also harbors a more terrible fear: that Israeli Jews, so many of whom are from premodern Arab countries, may not have the will to bring off the Hebrew democratic revolution that European Zionists were once so confident would take place. Har-Shefi's support for the Israeli Arabs therefore derives from an embattled sense of her own moral survival. Their success would be evidence that she is living in a free country.

# The West Bank:
# The Road to Disaster

I

*June 10, 1982*

"There are two camps on the West Bank today," the Bethlehem journalist Jamil Hamad told Rafik Halabi after the Camp David accords were signed: "PLO supporters and PLO members." In *West Bank Story*, his chronicle of the relations between Israeli authorities and local Palestinian leaders, Halabi reluctantly arrives at much the same conclusion.

Few observers are in a better position to write about the occupation and its future. Halabi is an Israeli Druse who studied Hebrew literature and Jewish philosophy at Hebrew University, and has covered the West Bank for Israel Television since 1974. He kept his job in spite of efforts by General Sharon and other Likud politicians to censor his reports. Those efforts began to succeed after the Begin government appointed Yosef Lapid — a reactionary columnist from the daily *Ma'ariv* — to direct the Broadcasting Service in 1979. Halabi now expects he will be stopped from reporting on the West Bank and will have to resign. Yet his book shows neither fear nor spite, and few traces of self-congratulation.

What makes his account particularly sad at a time when each

A review of Rafik Halabi, *West Bank Story* (New York: Harcourt Brace Jovanovich, 1981).

passing week Israeli soldiers fire on Palestinians is that it can be read as a history of lost opportunities. During the June 1967 war, some 1.1 million Palestinian Arabs living in the West Bank and Gaza came under Israeli rule.* Most of the 750,000 people on the West Bank had become citizens of the Hashemite Kingdom of Jordan, although some had long-standing grievances against King Hussein's regime. Abdullah, Hussein's grandfather, forcibly annexed the territory during the 1948 war. In 1949, West Bank lawyers tried to petition the UN peace conference at Rhodes to found a Palestinian state, as was authorized by the Partition Resolution of 1947. The Jordanians shunted them aside. Israel's Labor government tried and failed to gain international recognition for its post-1949 boundaries. Even Begin publicly dropped his Revisionist Zionist ambition to expand the state's borders to those of ancient Judea so that his Herut Party could run with the Liberals as the Gahal bloc in the 1965 elections. If Hussein had decided to stay out of the 1967 war, he might control the West Bank today.

In occupying the West Bank, Israel took over an area roughly equal to that of Israel itself without the Negev Desert — some 2,270 square miles. Its six small cities — East Jerusalem, Hebron, Ramallah, Nablus, Jenin, and Bethlehem — had not been doing well under Jordan. Between 1952 and 1961, the size of East Jerusalem's population of 60,000 people stayed the same while Amman grew from 108,000 residents to a quarter of a million. Eighty percent of the population of the West Bank lived in 396 villages and 40 percent of the labor force worked in agriculture. They fared no better than the Palestinians in the cities. Hussein preferred to develop the East Bank. When the occupation began, officials counted only sixty-seven tractors in the area. Of the 200,000 people in UN refugee camps, half fled across the Jordan to the East Bank during the six days of fighting in 1967.

But most of the West Bank's leading urban families and vir-

---

*Useful supplements to the cursory data supplied by Halabi are Brian Van Arkadie's *Benefits and Burdens* (Washington, D.C.: Carnegie Endowment for International Peace, 1977); and *Judea, Samaria, and Gaza: Views on the Future*, ed. Daniel J. Elazar (Washington, D.C.: American Enterprise Institute, 1982).

tually all of its rural clans cooperated with Hussein. Two of the most prominent East Jerusalem Palestinians, Anwar el-Khatib and Anwar Nusseibeh, became ministers in the Jordanian government. Sheik Ali Ja'abri, the influential mayor of the more rural, and more pious, town of Hebron, allied himself and his considerable following with Hussein. Only in Nablus, the largest city outside Greater Jerusalem, did serious anti-Jordanian feeling emerge. A few months before the June 1967 war, Hussein's forces put down antigovernment protests in the city, killing twenty young demonstrators. The mayor, Hamdi Kenan, was quick to grasp that feelings of Palestinian nationalism might intensify once Israeli tanks moved into the town.

On the Gaza Strip, on the other side of Israel, the 350,000 Palestinian residents, with the highest density of population in the world, were ruled by an Egyptian administration much worse than Jordan's. Denied Egyptian citizenship, Gaza residents were stateless, and they needed little encouragement to hate the Israelis from Nasser's officials, who turned a blind eye to raids by *fedayeen*—Palestinian terrorists—on southern Israeli settlements. In 1964 Nasser helped to set up the Palestine Liberation Organization, which was led from Gaza by Ahmad Shukeiri until Fatah emerged after the June war. (Shukeiri, a fanatical and untalented lawyer from Acre, is now remembered for having threatened to "push the Jews into the sea.") The 150,000 refugees from Israel in Gaza were much poorer than those in the West Bank and were treated with contempt by the permanent residents of Gaza City and Khan Yunis. The prominent Gaza families were not inclined to provide political leadership under Nasser's regime and left to the UN the work of housing and educating the refugees.

Fewer than 20 percent of the Palestinians in Gaza could make a living from the land. Conditions were far better under Hussein on the West Bank, where 50,000 agricultural families farmed about half a million acres. Hussein's police sharply restricted liberties but judiciously created a civil service for West Bank teachers, postmen, clerks, etc. No doubt the more prosperous West Bank residents resented Hussein's discrimination: in 1965 the West Bank contributed to Jordan 2.4 million more dinars toward indirect taxes and public services than it got back. But these families nevertheless owned enterprises accounting for 40 percent of Jordanian GNP in industry, banking, and trade. By contrast, Gaza's industry was as feeble as its agriculture. Twenty percent of family incomes came from welfare payments. However, owing to UN schooling, the rates of literacy among all refugees were high.

So it is not surprising that after the Israelis took over the West Bank, Palestinians tended to be peaceful while Gaza was seething with violence. Rafik Halabi was at that time working in the administration of Jerusalem's mayor, Teddy Kollek, and could follow closely what happened in each of the occupied zones. Hamdi Kenan and Sheik Ja'abri, he recalls, seemed to take the occupation in stride, in spite of Kenan's submerged Palestinian nationalism and Ja'abri's Jordanian connections. Both mayors and most of the Jerusalem notables assumed Israeli rule would be temporary until some new arrangements, favorable to their autonomy, could be worked out with Hussein. Moshe Dayan permitted the bridges across the Jordan to remain open. Still, in 1967 alone, Israeli officials conducted some 1,100 trials for various security offenses on the West Bank, and in Gaza there was frequent, bloody violence. In 1970, 106 of its residents were killed, 94 by terrorists and 12 by Israeli forces. Of some 1,200 young people arrested during the disturbances, half confessed to guerrilla activities.

Israeli forces finally regained control of Gaza by cracking down harshly under General Sharon, then commander of the southern front. In 1972, Rashad a-Shawa, a member of Gaza's most prestigious family, became mayor, and he has since used his non-partisan relations with Jordan, Egypt, and the PLO to provide the competent leadership previously lacking. Moreover, by 1973 about a third of Gaza's labor force—including many children—were employed on Israel's farms, factories, and construction sites. This contributed to calm, but, as Halabi notes, it also led to new kinds of resentment. About 50,000 workers were commuting from the West Bank by this time.

Between June 1967 and September 1970, Israeli authorities had to deal with more than 5,000 attacks and bombings of one kind or another in the occupied territory. What Halabi shows, however, is that leaders such as Dayan allowed those attacks to prevent Israel from forming a coherent policy toward the Palestinians as a whole. In much of *West Bank Story*, Dayan appears as something like a modern pharaoh who, facing a plague of terror, inflicts hardships on his alien subjects, inflames their desire for freedom, and increases the prestige of the radicals among them. (Halabi notes that in 1968 Yasir Arafat was an unlikely guerrilla, crisscrossing the West Bank on a motorcycle while trying to build an underground network of young nationalists.)

Immediately after the 1967 war, the Israeli Knesset annexed East Jerusalem and the army destroyed several Israeli-Arab villages, claiming that their location made them potential threats to the Latrun highway to Jerusalem. The government built new Jewish neighborhoods in Jerusalem, displacing Arab residents. Protests from the West Bank leaders and intellectuals were turned aside. When they requested Dayan to allow them to organize their own political parties independent of hostile Arab states, he replied, "Not under the Israeli flag." Under Dayan's rules, local leaders were expected to help keep order but were severely restricted as a political group, not allowed to travel freely or to hold open political meetings.

Dayan, moreover, set up the policy of collective punishment by which the security forces have routinely destroyed the homes of relatives and neighbors of convicted terrorists. No doubt such punishment intimidated many of the older people, but, as Halabi points out, it only stiffened the resistance of those young men drawn to radical politics. By 1968, Hamdi Kenan said openly that were he a young man he would join Fatah; and Fatah denounced the other mayors and leaders for their fecklessness, their ties to the old feudal order.

But Dayan's policy also undermined the traditional urban leaders and landlords by promoting quick economic development as a way of quieting Palestinian restlessness. Not only had tens of thousands of peasants and refugees started to work in the Israeli economy by 1973, but the gross product grew by 14.5 percent annually between 1968 and 1973 in the West Bank and 19.4 percent in Gaza. Agriculture was rapidly being mechanized: the number of tractors had risen from sixty-seven to well over a thousand. The typical peasant was becoming less isolated, more dependent on urban mechanics and merchants. The landscape of his town was becoming dotted with television antennas; his children were seeing doctors—infant mortality was reduced by half—and more of them were attending school.

Halabi observes that between 1967 and 1980 the number of classrooms in the West Bank doubled, from 6,167 to 11,187. The student population rose from 250,000 to 400,000, a change that no doubt had the effect of reinforcing radical politics. In 1967, Halabi recalls, Arab banks were closed and merchant classes began to face Israeli competition. High per capita growth stimulated the integration of the occupied territory into Israel's economy. Even under Labor governments, by 1977 the West Bank was exporting 91 percent of its commodities to Israel. But there was little capital investment in the West Bank economy itself. If local manufacturing had been encouraged, the old Jerusalem and Nablus middle class might have evolved into an industrial leadership independent of the largesse of the Gulf states and able to deal with Israel's new entrepreneurs. But the Israeli banks that controlled (and still control) credit refused loans for West Bank industrial ventures by Arabs.

Between 1974 and 1978, when the Israeli economy went into recession following the costly war with Egypt and Syria, the West Bank's rate of growth sharply declined to 5.1 percent and Gaza's to 4.5 percent. Subsequent recessions hit Arab workers first.

The difficulties of their economic and therefore their social position undermined Kenan and Ja'abri, el-Khatib and Nusseibeh; but so did other Israeli policies which, though justified by officials as a response to terrorism and PLO rejectionism, seemed to be more the product of Israeli military and political complacency, at least until the October war in 1973. After "Black September" of 1970—when Hussein killed many Palestinians and drove the PLO leaders and tens of thousands of refugees to south Lebanon—the West Bank remained relatively calm. Two years later the Jordanian regime proposed a federal plan for the territory which Israel turned down, mainly because Hussein insisted that East Jerusalem and the mosques come under his sovereignty. During the October war, the West Bank, again, did not become violent.

Hussein tried once more to initiate negotiations for the territory, hoping for an agreement on disengagement similar to ones that Israel had just made with Egypt and Syria. The new Rabin government showed some interest during the spring of 1974. But Dayan's heart had been hardened by terrorist attacks such as the one at Maalot and by the accusations that he had failed to prepare for the 1973 war, which drove him from the Defense Ministry. He led the Knesset in rejecting Hussein's overture. The extremist settlers' organization, Gush Emunim, founded the year before, circulated a petition ruling out all negotiations for "Judea and Samaria." Dayan, along with a majority of members, signed it.

This was a crucial mistake. Later in 1974 the Arab states, in their meeting at Rabat, stripped Hussein of the right to negotiate for the territory and endorsed the PLO instead as the sole representative of the Palestinian people. Arafat triumphantly addressed the UN General Assembly in November. Gush Emunim's settlements helped to bring about this victory for the PLO; they became, in Halabi's view, the main impediment to improving relations with the new, more nationalist politicians who emerged on the West Bank, once the old guard of pro-Jordanian leaders like Sheik Ja'abri had been undermined by the decision at Rabat.

By 1976, more than half of the sixty-eight Jewish settlements that are now implanted on the West Bank were already set up. At first they were ramshackle affairs led by religious zealots, like Rabbi Moshe Levinger, who illegally moved his followers to Hebron in 1968. The Meir government eventually rewarded Levinger for his persistence, permitting him and some of his group to establish the Qiryat Arba settlement outside the city. Levinger and other settlers seemed to capture the imaginations of old Labor leaders looking back to the golden age of the thirties and forties, when settlements meant security and security made possible the Zionist revolution.

That precedent proved decisive. By the time Meir left office in 1974, many other settlements had sprung up, with and without the government's approval. Rabin's foreign minister, Yigal Allon, put forward his own plan for a string of settlements along the Jordan River and around Jerusalem; these were supposed to provide security if and when the rest of the West Bank was returned to Hussein. But Hussein had already refused to be a party to any deal that would not include Jerusalem. Any possible compromise, such as Israel's sharing Jerusalem as a guaranteed open city with Hussein, was unmentionable in Israel—and might well have been rejected by Hussein anyway. More annexationist settlements followed, such as Kadum and Elon Moreh, which, Halabi explains, were founded by the Gush Emunim in the spaces between the West Bank's most populous cities.

In the spring of 1976, Shimon Peres, the Israeli Defense Minister, nevertheless decided to hold on the West Bank the municipal elections that had previously been scheduled under Jordanian law. Since the October war, resistance to the occupation among Palestinian youth had been rising. In 1974, soon after the Bir Zeit College was set up near Ramallah, Peres expelled its president, along with some other of the younger West Bank nationalists. He also stepped up repression of the increasingly influential Arab newpapers *al-Fajr* and *al-Kuds*. Now Peres wanted to reassert the authority of the Palestinian old guard, and he assumed that the PLO would boycott the elections as it had all other Israeli initiatives in the past.

He badly miscalculated. Pro-PLO candidates ran for mayor in every major town, and all but one—in Bethlehem, where the pro-Jordanian Elias Freij was re-elected—were swept into office. Even Ja'abri was replaced by an old Nasserite rival, Faid Kawasmeh. The mayor elected in Nablus was Bassam Shaka, a former Syrian Ba'athist, whose views were close to those of the Palestinian rejectionists calling for the liquidation of Israel in favor of a "democratic secular state." This was the position of the Popular Front for the Liberation of Palestine terrorists, who carried out the Entebbe hijacking just after the elections.

Halabi believes, however, that taken as a group the mayors represented a new opportunity for Israeli diplomacy. He came to admire Kawasmeh for his humane attitudes, shrewdness, and moderation. Except for Shaka, all the new mayors—Mohammed Milhelm in Halhul, Karim Halaf in Ramallah, Ibrahim Tawil in el-Bireh, and Kawasmeh—joined Freij and a-Shawa in Gaza in endorsing a Palestinian state at peace with Israel in spite of their PLO connections.

Halabi argues persuasively that the mayors were close to the

PLO but not simply its tools. They appeared to speak as the authoritative voices of the modernizing Arab society that Israeli policy had inadvertently produced, and Sadat's trip to Jerusalem in November 1977 gave them new importance. In 1978, they formed a National Guidance Committee, which, it seemed, might have a useful part in carrying out the transitional "autonomy" plans that were discussed after Sadat's trip and became serious possibilities at Camp David in September 1978. Since "full autonomy" seemed an obvious bridge to some kind of independent Palestinian entity acceptable to both Israel and Jordan, the mayors seemed a likely group to preside over that transition, an alternative to the Fatah leaders—Arafat and Farouk Kaddumi —with whom it appeared premature, if not impossible, to negotiate.

## II

Those now seem to have been better days. West Bank and Gaza politicians, intellectuals, students, and merchants are now mobilized as never before. The new civilian administration, headed by Professor Menachem Milson, was installed by Sharon last November, a month before the government made its de facto annexation of the Golan Heights. Thousands of demonstrators took to the streets this winter to protest when Professor Milson carried out his new policy, previewed in *Commentary** last May, by deposing the pro-PLO mayors of Nablus, Ramallah, and el-Bireh (Shaka, Halaf, and Tawil) and by dissolving the mayors' National Guidance Committee, which still includes moderates such as Freij and a-Shawa, who have stayed apart from the PLO. Milson has also closed down two Arab newspapers and Bir Zeit University, now a center of Palestinian national sentiment. The protests against these measures seemed like eruptions of boiling anger; but then, in April, after a murderous Jewish fanatic attacked the Mosque of Omar, the West Bank and Gaza Palestinians were able to organize the most effective general strike since 1936.

*"How to Make Peace with the Palestinians," *Commentary*, May 1982.

At this writing, at least seventeen Palestinians have been killed, some of them while attempting to assault Israeli soldiers or settlers. Eighty have been seriously wounded. No longer will either Israelis or Palestinians be able to explain the violence of Palestinians as isolated acts of ruthlessness or despair. Palestinian youths at rallies have defiantly shown the PLO flag, although it has long been banned. The Israelis have sent paratroops to break up these rallies and to arrest organized gangs of rock throwers. Jewish vigilantes from Gush Emunim settlements, armed by the government, have fired on Arab students in el-Bireh, and some have been warning farmers against building on their own land. A group of students at Bir Zeit University attacked one of Milson's officials and publicly burned his yarmulke.

Such extreme nationalism and violence are unprecedented, but they will not surprise readers of Halabi's book. The pro-PLO sentiment that brought the mayors to power has only grown as the Begin government transformed the incoherent policies of the Labor governments into one of outright annexation. Since signing the Camp David accords, the Israeli government has more than quadrupled the number of Jewish settlers—there may now be, Halabi recently estimated, as many as 35,000 of them. Begin's regime has built huge new military bases, and along with them extensive roads, and electricity and water lines that provide services for civilian settlements and could easily be turned over to civilian administration. Rabbi Levinger now occupies the heart of the Hebron casbah.

A good many other new Jewish settlers are subsidized by low-interest mortgages and funds from Sharon's Defense Ministry. About one eighth of the land, some 175,000 acres, has been expropriated by the government as "state" land; but more has been acquired for "security reasons" or by agents acting on behalf of Israeli developers, especially around Jerusalem. The moderate Ramallah lawyer Raja Shekhadeh estimates that 30 percent of the land is now in Israeli hands. Moreover, the Jewish settlers, armed as reservists, go out on patrol. Two Palestinian youths who died recently were shot by Jewish settlers, not by soldiers. Many settlers have been organized by Elyakim Ha'etzni, a lawyer from a Jewish settlement near Ramallah, into vigilante groups. There have been detailed charges—but no proof—that other settlers have recklessly engaged in terrorist activity themselves, placing the bombs that maimed Mayor Shaka and Mayor Halaf in June 1980, a month after PLO terrorists killed six Jewish settlers in Hebron.*

Begin's government has used much harsher collective punishment against incidents of Arab terror than did Dayan. After the attack on Jewish settlers in Hebron in May 1980, Mayor Kawasmeh was finally deported, the whole town was placed under curfew for a month, travel was banned, and telephones were cut for forty-five days; all the men were interrogated, and many house-to-house searches led to beatings. Some 1,100 books have been banned, including works on Islam by the French Jewish leftist Maxime Rodinson, although most contain anti-Semitic material.

A ghastly cycle of retribution has set in. Friends of mine who have recently done reserve duty in the West Bank note a sharp rise in aggressiveness among Palestinians. Israeli patrols are increasingly the targets of Molotov cocktails thrown by cocky gangs of children. And Arab death squads have been active against dissident Arabs. Two men who opposed the PLO—Hamdi el-Kadi of Ramallah and Hashem Khuzandar of Gaza—were murdered after expressing support for President Sadat.

Professor Milson claims to be acting against the mayors to prevent the rise of the PLO's power and its violence. And certainly the PLO's attacks on other Arabs prefigure a militant and authoritarian style of politics that Halabi, like any thoughtful Israeli, despises. But Milson's claims seem disingenuous, for they ignore Israeli policies that have undermined West Bank leaders, including some mayors, who now fear they will become PLO victims. The expansion of Jewish settlements, as Halabi argues, soured any opportunities for compromise after the Camp David accords. When, for example, Aziz Shekhadeh, the respected Ramallah lawyer, joined Nusseibeh, Freij, and a-Shawa in endorsing an autonomy plan that would lead to a Palestinian state, Kawasmeh, at first, would not condemn them.

*The West Bank and the Rule of Law, Report of the International Commission of Jurists, Geneva, 1980.

Halabi's point is that settlements must be understood as political events and not merely as abstract numbers of Jews to be compared with numbers of Arabs. Ultranationalist settlers such as those at Elon Moreh seemed determined to show that Israel would annex the West Bank just at the time Sadat and Carter were asking Palestinians to live through a five-year period of transition. The aim of the Camp David accords was to make security depend not simply on land but on reciprocal acts that would build trust over a considerable period of time. Yet the settlements, and the religious and historical rhetoric of the ministers and movements responsible for them, raised bitter and plausible suspicions that Israel would use the time to grab the land: i.e., would destroy the Palestinian claims to sovereignty over the West Bank by putting as many as 100,000 Jewish extremists in every corner of it. The settlements confirmed a grasping version of Zionism in the minds of young Palestinians. And they continue to do so. The Begin government inaugurated eleven new settlements on April 28, Israel's Independence Day.

It is true that the Fatah leadership rejected any idea of a transitional period leading to autonomy well before Begin made it clear that the government was willing to put peace with Egypt at risk in a drive to incorporate the West Bank and Gaza into Israel. But this fact will not discredit the PLO in the eyes of the West Bank Arabs today. So Milson now has to administer the territories without any authoritative West Bank leadership favoring, as most of the mayors did, a Palestinian state arrived at through peaceful diplomacy.

The key to Milson's intention to "root out the PLO from its bases on the West Bank" is nevertheless an accelerated plan to discredit the mayors, at least in the eyes of the rural village people whose leaders once seemed more inclined to a Jordanian solution than a separate state. Milson evidently believes that the people in the rural villages are less radical and more susceptible to control than the more sophisticated and militant urban Palestinians. Since November, he has been organizing an association of village leagues, led by the clan patriarch Mustafa Dudin, who served in the Jordanian government and openly broke with the pro-PLO mayors. Clearly Milson would like to reinvent a leadership composed of men like Sheik Ja'abri, whom he described in *Commentary* as "willing to work within the necessities and constraints of reality." This is not a new idea and, on the face of it, it was not necessarily a bad one. As early as 1969, the Hebrew University professor Shlomo Avineri suggested that Israel try to cultivate an independent Palestinian leadership. But the timing is now sadly wrong. Even if Sharon will permit Milson to encourage a pro-Jordanian leadership—and Sharon will not—Milson will more easily find candidates for the army's patronage and power than reinvent the world in which Ja'abri wielded his.

Milson has cut off the municipalities from the Saudi funds paid out by a joint Jordanian-PLO committee created after Rabat. He has been giving the village leagues some funds from the defense budget. He has even distributed small arms to Dudin and his followers, who will now need to defend themselves: the PLO assassinated Yusuf al-Katib, the head of the much less influential Ramallah Village League last November, and in March it attacked Kamal al-Fataftah of the Tarquimiya League. Dudin has himself been taking the offensive, roughing up opponents such as a dean of Bethlehem University who tried to prevent his men from entering the campus. The Jordanian Prime Minister, Mudar Badran, has denounced Dudin and declared that all the leaders who participate in the leagues would be subject to the charge of treason should they fall into the hands of the Jordanian authorities.

Since about 70 percent of the West Bank population remains in the villages, Milson may hope to make some gains nevertheless. But the changes in culture and demographic structure brought about by Israel's economic policy work against him. About as many villagers today have jobs in Israel proper as farm their land. And Halabi shows that Israeli expropriations of land for Jewish settlement have had their most adverse effects on the villagers—the lands from Rujeib (near Nablus) were used, for example, to build Elon Moreh, those from Tarquimiya (near Hebron) to build Kiryat Arba. The villagers may not be of the modern world, but they know they are in it when they see Jewish settlements enjoying the modern roads, electrification, and water mains they are themselves denied. They are not searching for new effendis.

Milson seems likely to have more success repressing the political leaders in the cities: keeping the pro-PLO mayors under house arrest, deporting security offenders, and, as Abba Eban has charged, creating conditions that will encourage more and more of the educated Palestinians to seek their fortunes in the Gulf states. The Israelis I have talked to believe that Milson does not expect a final defeat for the PLO on the West Bank until the Israelis can deal a serious blow to PLO leaders and their forces in south Lebanon, something Defense Minister Sharon obviously favors. Prime Minister Begin has described practically every anti-Israeli act—including the murder in March of an Israeli diplomat in Paris—as a violation of the cease-fire worked out last year by Philip Habib. Fatah disclaimed this murder; but on April 21, Israeli jets retaliated for it by raiding PLO bases in south Lebanon, killing twenty-three people. Moshe Arens, Begin's confidant and the new ambassador in Washington, has called a more serious strike against the PLO forces around the Litani River in Lebanon "a matter of time."

Those forces have meanwhile been organized into the kind of armored battalion that is vulnerable to Israeli air power. And Sharon may have even more ambitious plans: he has lately been insisting, as he has intermittently done since 1973, that Israel cannot hope to solve the Palestinian problem without toppling Hussein in favor of a Palestinian regime willing to take in the exiles and refugees. In any case, Sharon's evident conflict with Milson on this question gives substance to recent speculation that Milson's tenure may not last long.

Based in refugee camps, the PLO's leadership will for its part continue to press for a version of self-determination that still makes irredentist claims on Israel proper. And it seems that those claims are inciting separatist feelings among the Israeli Arabs themselves, especially those in Nazareth, who have been citizens of the state for a generation. On March 30, some 10,000 Israeli Arabs marched to commemorate Land Day, when expropriations took place in 1976. Six Arab youths were shot and killed by Israeli police. Here again the Palestinian flag was shown.

\*

### III

Such sentiments among Israeli Arabs make *West Bank Story* the more valuable as an appeal for tolerance from a unique vantage point. Halabi grew up in the Druse villages of the Carmel Mountains in a minority Arab community whose eclectic and esoteric faith diverged from Islam in the tenth century. The secret dogmas of the Druses are said to be inspired by the Persian prophet Zoroaster and by classical Greek philosophers — Pythagoras and Plato — as well as by Asiatic influences predating Islam. So although the Druses are Arabs, they have tended to view with favor Israel's civil liberties. Israeli Druse intellectuals have learned about modern life in Israel's Hebrew culture, not unlike the thousands of Jews who came to Israel after 1948 from backward countries such as Yemen. And unlike other Israeli Arabs, the Druses serve in the army, especially in border patrols and antiterror squads.

Halabi is himself a reserve officer in the army and tells how a Druse acquaintance of his, the demolition expert Suleiman Khirwabi, was blinded dismantling a bomb meant for Ibrahim Tawil — the man whose firing led to the most recent explosion of violence. Halabi is perhaps the only Israeli who can claim relatives in the Ramle prison on both sides of the bars: some are security offenders, some jailers. Since he is regularly threatened by Jewish and Arab fanatics, democratic rights for him are a matter of life and death, not to mention daily work. Perhaps the most memorable moment in his book comes when he describes how his colleagues at the broadcasting service rallied to support him when Sharon began to impugn his patriotism. It is from just such circles of libertarian sentiment and private affection that, in my view, many more Israelis will have to draw political conviction if the country is to survive.

But these are the very circles that are most vulnerable now. The current violence may recede, but the war will remain. One might think that more Israelis would now see the occupation, not simply as a prop of "security" or the climax of a "Zionist" saga, but as a continuous series of risks to be compared with those of a Palestinian state. But on the whole, the violence is silencing the voices of moderation, especially in the big-circulation dailies *Ma'ariv* and *Yediot Acharonot*. And the realization that the occupation poses risks is as useful to Milson, Sharon, and Begin as to their critics.

However much they would want to crush the PLO by invading Lebanon, they may not have their way. The Reagan administration has been insisting, at least publicly, that they hold back on the northern border. Two former Israeli Chiefs of Staff, Chaim Bar-Lev and Mordechai Gur (both now in the Labor Party), have publicly opposed such an invasion. Begin's prestige — though not Sharon's — was damaged by the Sinai settlers who fervently denounced the Camp David accords. So it is not clear that Begin could lead the country to war in Lebanon in the absence of flagrant PLO provocation, which the PLO evidently tried to avoid, even after the air strike of April 21.

Still, Begin now controls events more effectively than his Labor opponents and American allies. On May 9, the Israeli air force launched another attack on PLO bases. This time PLO forces responded by shelling Israeli settlements in the north. As I write, Begin has taken his cabinet into emergency session, and pitched battles seem closer than ever.

The prospect now is that Begin's government will present Israel's own increasingly militant voters with the choice between war against the PLO — "without end, without reservation," in the words of Foreign Minister Yitzchak Shamir — and a PLO state that will seem to most Israelis a Trojan horse for terror. And for Sharon the possibility of such a state must be eliminated soon, since Mubarak will be tempted to embrace the Saudi peace plan if the autonomy talks break down permanently. That plan calls for a PLO-run state within six months, with none of the transitional arrangements likely to allay Israeli apprehensions about PLO terror.

And Begin, sick and increasingly remote, would like to unite the whole land of Israel before he dies — or so it would seem from such gestures as his recent claim that Peace Now demonstrators who carried placards referring to the West Bank as occupied territory should be charged with treason. His recent references to the West Bank as "Western Eretz Yisrael" have revived the revisionist notion that the "historical land of Israel also included the east bank of the Jordan." General Sharon's power in the cabinet is growing as Begin's energy declines, and although Sharon is not a likely successor to the Prime Minister, few in the Likud dare to challenge (as they did last summer) Sharon's huge power as Minister of Defense.

What has been missing in this frightening impasse is a clear policy from the United States, which was responsible for the Camp David process in the first place. Instead of pursuing the autonomy negotiations, the Reagan administration has allowed them to fade into obscurity. Instead of addressing the Palestinian issue by exploring the possibilities of Camp David's shrewd transitional arrangements, the Reagan administration has dismissed the PLO as a species of international terrorism to be crushed like any Soviet surrogate and, at the same time, applauded the Sinai plan, which calls for a PLO state within six months. Nor has Reagan pressed Israel to stop its annexationist policies: rather, he continues to maintain that the settlements are not illegal, and he failed to prevent the annexation of the Golan. Finally, instead of calming the war fever by reducing arms sales to all sides, Reagan has been increasing Israeli fears (and Begin's antigentile conceits) by selling advanced warplanes to the Saudis. Some in his administration have been campaigning for such sales in Congress with allusions to the power, presumably unwarranted, of American Jews.

No doubt, Deputy Secretary of State Walter J. Stoessel and Philip Habib will continue to try to keep a lid on hostilities in the weeks to come, but last-minute shuttles are no more of a policy than were Kissinger's perfunctory visits to Middle Eastern capitals before the October war. Should a war break out in southern Lebanon, Assad's Alawite regime in Syria cannot be expected to stay out, especially after it has just suppressed the Jihad-prone Muslim Brotherhood in the Syrian town of Hama, killing thousands in the process. And the war might spread further. Iraqi and Iranian leaders might see a battle in Lebanon as a pretext to end their own. And if the Syrians determine to make a stand against the Israelis and Christian militias in Lebanon, can the Soviets let Assad fail or let Syrian cities be bombed yet again?

The Israeli daily *Ha'aretz* reports that the European Economic Community is on the verge of endorsing a Palestinian state. If

Reagan is capable of a coherent policy, he should at least try to work with America's European allies in pursuit of a comprehensive plan before a new war overtakes the peace that might still be created from the remains of the 1973 war. A good first step might be that the United States endorse an amendment to UN Resolution 242 so that Palestinian national rights are not obscured by the vague references to "refugees" that appear in the 1967 document. Professor Walid Khalidi of Harvard and the American University in Beirut, who is close to the PLO, continues to insist that the Fatah leadership would be prepared to recognize Israel if the PLO were recognized in reciprocal negotiations. According to Khalidi, "Arafat would accept a permanent peace with Israel and stringent transitional arrangements that lead to a Palestinian state." Every nation concerned, including Israel, should be exploring this possibility. If the PLO shows itself willing to accept Resolution 242, then the autonomy talks could still succeed. But even such an Israeli moderate as Meron Benvenisti, the former vice mayor of Jerusalem, now fears that Camp David has been made obsolete by Begin's annexationist policies. The fate of the West Bank rests with Palestinians who believe that time works against Israel, and Israelis who believe that they can make time work against the Palestinians. Both are right.

# Looking Over Jordan

*April 1983*

Last September President Reagan called for "self-government by Palestinians in the West Bank and Gaza in association with Jordan." He did not refer to the PLO except to acknowledge its forced "evacuation" of Beirut. For a while Reagan's proposals seemed to be having some success, notwithstanding Prime Minister Begin's immediate rejection of them. After King Hussein visited Washington in December, he made it clear that he was interested in Reagan's plan if it could be subject to "Arab agreement and coordination." He asked for support from the PLO and met several times with Yasir Arafat in Amman. State Department officials hinted during the early part of January that the King would enter the "peace process" by March 1. Hussein himself seemed to accept the deadline: after it, he said in a speech in Amman, "U.S. leaders have other things to preoccupy them," an obvious reference to presidential politics. A White House official told me then that he hoped the King would make a bold, dramatic announcement recognizing Israel according to the provisions of UN Resolution 242 and offering to negotiate the future of the West Bank and Gaza directly with Israeli officials.

But later in the winter prospects for this seemed to grow dimmer. Israel would not withdraw its forces from Lebanon until the Lebanese government agreed to "normalize" relations, which Amin Gemayel refused to do. In February, at its meeting in Algiers, the Palestine National Council conceded only that the PLO might consider some federal arrangement with Jordan —

*after* the Palestinians have established an independent state. This was hardly the endorsement Hussein had been waiting for. The PNC also said that Arafat could continue meeting with Hussein, and as I write, at the end of March, Arafat is expected in Amman for what has been described as a "final round of talks." These are supposed to decide whether the PLO will, at least for now, endorse Jordan's plan for Palestinian representation in possible talks with Israel: that Palestinian leaders who have been close to the PLO, but not members of it, would form part of a Jordanian delegation. If Arafat says yes, the way would be open for Hussein to pursue the Reagan plan. If he says no, or continues to procrastinate, is the plan "still-born"?*

My own recent visits to Jordan, Israel, the West Bank, and Washington—including an interview with Crown Prince Hassan, the King's younger brother and confidant—have made me doubt that peace can come except through the administration's proposals, whatever Arafat may do. Hussein and the PLO have obviously disagreed over who should control any negotiations. Hasn't this betrayed a much deeper disagreement over the kind of settlement such negotiations would produce, a disagreement obscured by each side's talk about "federation"? If so, can Jordan take the initiative from the PLO on the West Bank and Gaza and contain Palestinian nationalism within some new arrangement of its own? Does Hussein now have stronger reasons than ever to try? The answers I found to these questions suggest that Hussein now holds the Arab key to peace, and knows it.

I

This has taken a long time to come about. From the 1974 Rabat conference, at which the PLO gained the right to represent Palestinians in the Arab League, until last summer's war in Lebanon, the PLO's claim to be waging "armed struggle" from the north against Israel both provided the impetus for West Bank nationalism and diminished the prestige of the former Jordanian ad-

*See Fouad Ajami, *New York Times*, February 18, 1983.

ministration in the occupied territories.* Jordan continued to pay the salaries of teachers and civil servants. But the memories of "Black September" 1970, when thousands of Palestinians were killed by Jordanian troops and hundreds of thousands were sent into exile to southern Lebanon, have remained strong.

Before the Rabat conference, during the summer of 1974, King Hussein conducted fruitless secret negotiations with Prime Minister Rabin. He got no concessions regarding Jerusalem. After the Rabat conference, some members of the Hashemite court—notably Crown Prince Hassan—argued that it was time for the King to cut his losses. Palestinians already made up the majority of Jordan's population on the East Bank. Two hundred thousand remained in refugee camps. Had not the PLO threatened his regime in 1970? Was it not time, as an American diplomat in Amman put it to me recently, to "steer clear of the juggernaut across the river"?

By then Hussein needed little persuading, though staying apart from the West Bank was, from all accounts, painful to him. He took hard the loss during the 1967 war of the territory that his grandfather Abdullah had won in 1948. The great-grandson of Emir Hussein of Mecca, T. E. Lawrence's original champion of the "Arab nation," the King yearned to regain Arab rights in Jerusalem. But Hussein was disgraced at Rabat in 1974, and he knew a threat when he saw one. He had been with Abdullah when a Palestinian extremist killed him on the steps of the Mosque of Omar in 1951. Later, in 1957, after he had forced Abdullah's mentor Sir John Glubb (Glubb Pasha) from the country, he allowed the free election of Suleiman Nabulsi—a Palestinian from a leading Nablus family—as Prime Minister. Soon after, when some young officers attempted a coup, he met with them and forced them down. Caution regarding the Palestinians had long been necessary for Hussein's survival. His brother's advice made sense. The Hashemites would prevail only by emphasizing their willingness to cooperate with the surrounding Arab nations; they would have to follow the consensus of the Arab League.

---

*This point was made forcefully in a paper by Professor Walid Kazziha of American University, Cairo, at the Lehman Institute on March 2, 1983.

Hussein drew closer to the Saudis, blood enemies since Ibn Saud threw Hussein's family out of the Hejaz in 1925. He even moved to coordinate military command with the Syrians, though President Hafez Assad had sent tanks to help the PLO bring Hussein down in 1970. (Those tanks did not turn back until the Israeli government, at American urging, threatened to send its own aircraft against them.) When President Sadat traveled to Jerusalem, King Hussein joined with other Arab League nations in Baghdad to oppose him.

Hussein's accommodation to the consensus favoring the PLO paid off. "His neighbors had oil and he had a natural resource that was nearly as good," a former American diplomat to Jordan put it to me. "This was his long border with Israel." The Saudis and Iraqis supported him with enormous grants in aid, amounting to over $1.1 billion in 1982; and at the beginning of its war with Iran, Iraq's contribution was more impressive still. Most of this money has gone into supporting Hussein's military. But even larger sums have been accumulated by as many as 400,000 educated Jordanian citizens who now work in the Gulf states as technicians, engineers, accountants, clerks, and contractors. Their remittances in recent years have helped to finance the prosperity that both Palestinian and Jordanian families have shared.

The boom has certainly lessened tensions in Amman itself, which has grown from a city of 250,000 people in the sixties to more than a million today. There is a saying among Palestinians in Amman: "The King has made a social contract: he rules, we make money." Prince Hassan, who has much to do with economic planning, made the same point less bluntly: "The politics of economic legitimacy" — i.e., of open economic opportunity for all, including the Palestinians — "has fostered Jordan's existence," he told me. He would like to move beyond this, but nobody close to the Hashemites is quite sure how to do so.

Between 1978 and 1981, the Jordanian GNP doubled, from $2.6 billion to $4.9 billion. But Jordan's economy is a commercial bubble dependent on foreign politics. Only 10 percent of the national income is earned in manufacturing; only one third is agricultural income, which, proportionately, is declining. The country has some tourism — the ruins at Jerash and Petra are among the wonders of the world — but Jordan exports nothing but a little potash and a great many people. The potash works will be swamped with water if Israel goes ahead with its Mediterranean–Dead Sea canal. More important, Amman will be swamped with unemployed people if the Gulf states decide to retaliate against Hussein.

The Israeli Labor Party officials who, before the Lebanon war, predicted that Hussein would be willing to negotiate a "territorial compromise" with a Labor government ignored this fundamental difficulty. They justifiably contended that Israel could not expect to demilitarize the West Bank and Gaza if there was to be an independent and hostile Palestinian state there; but they did not make it easier on Hussein by persisting in denying any Jordanian rights in Jerusalem. The King in any case could never have dared to act like Sadat. "Egypt," Sadat said, "*is* the Arab world." Hussein could only envy his confidence. Jordan's economy, whose prosperity is necessary to domestic peace, is "raw human material that has to be attached to larger economic engines," as one American diplomat put it to me. As oil revenues have declined, Hussein's Arab brothers have not needed much provocation to cut him off. Could American aid or large deals with Israel underwrite Hussein if he broke ranks?

But there is more at stake here than money. Jordan's prosperity during its continuing "state of war" has produced a growing urban middle class in which once sharp national differences between "Palestinians" and "Jordanians" have been blunted. Those differences are nothing like the deeper contrasts between, say, Russians and Poles: Jordanians and Palestinians speak the same Arabic, are likely to be Sunni Muslims (95 percent of Jordan is Sunni Muslim), and show to some degree the influence of British colonialism.

Nevertheless, Jordan has been a country where families prize their origins. The Hashemite monarch, his extended family, his tribal connections, and his top army officers are mostly descended from Bedouin stock. The Palestinians, on the other hand, are descended from the settled people on both sides of the Jordan. Many educated Palestinians never quite grasped the point of having a Hashemite king of Transjordan in the first place. Abdullah was, after all, set up in Transjordan by Winston

Churchill, the colonial secretary, in 1921 as compensation for his brother Faisal's loss of the Iraqi throne. Faisal claimed that throne by traditional right after the French threw him out of Syria. Educated Palestinians, moreover, had never considered Amman to be much more than a watering station between Jerusalem and Damascus.

Still, this odd country has shown a remarkable ability to survive. Palestinians lived under Hashemite rule and English protection until the 1948 war. Hundreds of thousands crossed over into Jordan after 1948, when Abdullah annexed the West Bank, and more than 300,000 have come since the 1967 war. Today there are well over 1,250,000 Palestinians on the East Bank, and a good many of them are among the Jordanian citizens working in the Gulf. Thousands of Palestinians hold important positions in the Jordanian civil service. The Minister of Information, Adnan Abu Odeh—often described as one of the most influential men in Jordan—is a Palestinian. It is true that those who recently arrived from the West Bank are likely to resent Hussein, not only because of his high-handed ways before 1967, but because he exploited their region to build up the East Bank. Between 1952 and 1962, while Amman was doubling its population, that of Arab Jerusalem held steady at 60,000. Few forget Black September. One still sees the Palestinian black and white *kaffiyeh*—or headdress—proudly worn in Amman, contrasting with the red and white Jordanian one. Still, fewer and fewer heads of households wear the *kaffiyeh* at all.

One Palestinian with whom I spoke, Dr. Carlos Diemas, a physician from Beit Jallah who now runs a hospital in Amman, seemed typical of the new era: "Our differences with Israel—and with each other—will slowly dissolve. This is the most opportune time in our history for a healing peace." Dr. Diemas is also a member of the King's appointed National Consultative Council that has been set up to replace the elected lower house, the Council of Deputies, which has been suspended since 1974. But about 70,000 Palestinian refugees still live in camps in and around Amman, some in the shadow of the symbols of Jordan's progress: the airport and the huge satellite dish receiver that feeds Jordanian television.

Social advances can themselves create frictions, since the economic boom has created the kind of commercial opportunities that make traditional family connections all the more valuable. One remembers one's relatives when deals are made; Jordanian Abu Jaabers remember Abu Jaabers, Palestinian Zorbis remember Zorbis. (There are also closed circles of Orthodox Christians and Circassians.) An economic crisis would certainly confirm hundreds of thousands in what an American official calls the "theology of Palestinism."

Nevertheless, the question of identity is more fluid than national labels suggest. "Some Palestinians deny this," Prince Hassan told me, "but the trend toward 'similitude' is strong among Palestinians and Jordanians both." Of course, this trend is also a matter of who is perceived to be winning. A Palestinian professor in Amman put it this way: "If the King gets Jerusalem we are all with him. If he gets less, Arafat claims the right to be the Palestinian leader he got at Rabat. If he gets nothing we raise hell." But the Crown Prince seems essentially right. It is impossible to look back on the West Bank from the East, to think of the ties between them, and to imagine a Palestinian "entity" that is both at peace and separate from Jordan—or what Jordan can become.

I do not mean by this Ariel Sharon's macho fantasy of toppling the Jordanian regime in favor of some Palestinian junta and then, little by little, driving the people on the West Bank across the river. Jordan cannot be confused with Palestine in this way. Loose arguments in pro-Begin advertisements and polemics that "Jordan is Palestine," and that Jordan's territory is actually "77 percent" of the original Mandate Palestine, neglect to add that less than 5 percent of that 77 percent is not desert.* The heart of the Palestinians' homeland is now the Jordan Valley, bounded by Jerusalem in the west and Amman in the east. (What would Israelis say if Palestinians offered peace on condition that all Jews move to Beersheba and the Negev, "70 percent of Israel"?) But there are over a million people on the East Bank who consider themselves Jordanians.

*See the ad on the Op-ed page of the *New York Times*, March 28, and also Sidney Zion's Op-ed page piece, "Is Jordan Palestinian? Of Course," *New York Times*, October 5, 1982.

Prince Hassan said he hoped that the Jordan Valley could be turned into a pilot project of cooperation and industrial development between the two populations on both sides of the river: "Israel could certainly participate." With the Prince's backing, Rami Khouri, a Palestinian editor of the *Jordan Times*, made a study of the possibilities for Jordan Valley development. Khouri estimates that from one large dam project alone Jordan could gain about $90 million in annual benefits from irrigation networks, another $30 million in municipal water supply, and about $3 million in electrical power.* But Khouri told me that he mainly wants gains for national unity. "Palestinians and Jordanians are already closely meshed in geography and demography. The point is to create one constituency."

These hopes are betrayed—if nothing else—by the map included in Khouri's book that shows the *entire* area west of the Jordan as "Occupied Palestine." Still, more such studies are needed. Economic cooperation is one of the most serious approaches to the conflict between Jordan, Palestine, and Israel. And Israelis do no better than Khouri's map when they plan a canal connecting the Mediterranean and the Dead Sea as if Jordan weren't there either.

## II

The Camp David accords are an even more serious way of solving this triangular conflict, however, which raises the question why Hussein condemned them. The question is the more disturbing when one considers that Reagan clearly—and rightly, in my view—based his new proposals on the Camp David agreements. In fact, Hussein's condemnation was not quick. According to President Carter's account, Hussein secretly conveyed to President Sadat at Camp David that Jordan was "willing to help implement the agreement" as Sadat understood it. On January 1, 1978, Hussein had told Carter in Tehran that he "would give Sadat his support," that UN Resolution 242, calling for a retreat to "secure borders," should prevail, and that he would consider

*See Rami Khouri, *The Jordan Valley* (London: Longman, 1981), p. 216.

"minor modifications" of the 1967 border: "The people of the West Bank–Gaza should have the right to self-determination but not the right to claim independence."*

Only after it became clear—or so a Jordanian official recently insisted to me—that Begin's promise to Carter to "freeze settlements for the period of the negotiations" meant merely that he would accept a freeze for three months (that is, during the negotiations with Egypt), and not for five years, as President Carter announced to a joint session of Congress, did the Jordanian government repudiate the accords. Does this mean that Jordan was—and still is—open to Camp David's most important provision, that of a period of democratic transition in which West Bank Palestinians and Israelis could work out "autonomy" before more difficult issues such as sovereignty and Jerusalem are negotiated? The answer remains unclear. The agreement the Arab League made at Fez last December demanded a greatly reduced period of transition, a demand that Hussein faithfully transmitted to President Reagan in December.

When I put these contradictions to the Crown Prince, his answer was unexpected. "The concept of transition is a virtue after fifteen years of occupation. It will revitalize political life where now Israeli extremists and PLO leftists exclude everybody else. . . . Some democratic formula is necessary for the process of disentanglement." I suggested that it would be better to negotiate the status of Jerusalem in a climate of peace that would grow as Arab autonomy became a reality. He agreed, though Jordan understandably insists that the East Jerusalem Arabs participate in autonomy elections.

But then I asked Hassan how he squares the Jordanian call for Palestinian "self-determination" (as in the Fez agreement) with the spirit of Camp David, or even with the Jordanian interest in growing "similitude" between Palestinians and Jordanians. He replied, "Self-determination implies structure, process, protection, elections—not just the urge to independence." He warmed to the subject: he has written a book about it.† The PLO,

*Jimmy Carter, *Keeping Faith: Memoirs of a President* (New York: Bantam, 1982), pp. 300 and 404.
†*Palestinian Self-Determination: A Study of the West Bank and Gaza Strip* (Quartet Books, 1981).

he said, has taken over the "nationalist middle ground" in the face of Israeli attempts to suppress it. "Self-determination, whether Israeli or Palestinian, must be mutual, complementary, and not exclusive of the rights of Jordanian society. . . ." He talked of a "cantonal evolution within a constitutional framework that could give a more effective expression to nationalism than a narrow mosaic of ethnic-territorial divisions." Self-determination, he concluded, "must be based on the aggregate rights and freedoms of all sides of the Jordanian, Palestinian, and Israeli equation."

This is surprising talk from an Arab Prince whose King actually rules. Elections, rights, constitutions, cantons. Jordan is not Switzerland. Nor — one does well to keep in mind — is Hassan his brother. Hassan has an honors degree in Oriental studies from Oxford and reads the Hebrew-language press. His elder brother is a product of Sandhurst — an autocrat who is willing, I was told by diplomats in Amman, to hear earnest arguments for democracy from few people other than Hassan. The point of Jordan's emphasis on mutual rights, or so Hassan assured me, is not to exclude PLO members and supporters. It is to demonstrate that self-determination is not a matter of having an organization but of working out a way of life.

The widow of the former Prime Minister and now a member of the National Consultative Council, Mrs. Laila Sharaf, was more concrete about what might happen on the West Bank. "Jordan will send in no military governors. West Bankers should manage their own affairs — not defense or foreign affairs — and govern themselves on the municipal level. The PLO can have a part in the peace process. Some PLO people will be mayors or governors and can look forward to a role in the central government. But there will be no direct rule by the PLO as such." Then she added quietly, as if merely stating a logical conclusion: "At the end of the peace process, there should be no PLO." A diplomat who had been a high official in the Carter State Department confirmed this attitude: "The Jordanian view of the PLO's role is to help absorb the shocks of the concessions that will have to be made to Israel — and then disappear." I said to the Crown Prince that he wants the PLO to play Garibaldi to Jordan's Cavour. He just smiled. But there has been no upgrading of the PLO's military or political status in Amman since September.

Can that minimum of parliamentary self-rule be restricted to the West Bank? We can put aside for the moment the other problems — for example, the appeals from refugees in Lebanon that they not be abandoned and the violent opposition that may come from what Mrs. Sharaf called the "extreme and negative" factions of the PLO. A different and basic question is how the moderate East Bank Palestinians will respond to the prospect that, across the river, their relatives may enjoy greater freedoms than they do. Can one imagine a federation between an incipient republic and an absolute monarchy? Of course not, which is precisely why Prince Hassan's interest in constitutionalism should be taken seriously. "We should have a liberal, constitutional monarchy," he told me. "The latent potential of Jordan's existing regime to initiate a successful, peaceful process of internal constitutional development is hidden from view by the deadlock over an Arab-Israeli-Palestinian settlement." The Crown Prince was evidently angered and appalled by Israel's continuing annexation of the West Bank. But he observes that "Israeli society, notwithstanding the apparent current triumph of extremism, has progressed more than its neighboring Jordanian-Palestinian societies along the path of political development." Nasserism has failed. Radicalism has failed. The "totalitarian" fundamentalism of Khomeini's Iran looms ahead. Jordan, he thought, could eventually work out a democratic framework reciprocally with Israel. Later he clarified this. "Instead of our proximity becoming a cause of friction and conflict over water and mineral resources, transport and routes, markets, a plan that guides the coordinated development of these resources can lead to further interdependence and collaboration."

I tried to reconcile what I heard from Hassan with my other impressions of Amman. It does not seem to be a heavily controlled place, but every visitor can sense that order is being firmly kept. "The mosques take over where the King leaves off," a resident foreigner told me. Government drivers shuttle businessmen and invited journalists between the royal palace and the prosperous modern quarter called the Third Circle, where you find the Intercontinental, the American embassy, the Ministry of Information. You drive in a loop around the university, the sports complex, and the cultural center, rare public spaces dominated by square sentry boxes and minarets. Uniforms are not everywhere, but it is taken for granted that some of the security forces—especially the agents of the king's Muhabarat —are not in uniform.

Foreign newsstands, found only in hotels, sell *Newsweek*, the *International Herald Tribune*, and the *Jordan Times*, which, like Jordanian television news (in Arabic, English, and Hebrew), is polite and predictable: His Majesty arrives, departs, receives. On the street you hear Oriental and pop music from cassettes, also car horns and loud calls to prayer. In the city center, every other block is an obstacle course of little concrete mixers, planks, hoses, and dull-eyed Egyptian laborers loading cinder blocks and sweeping away the dust. Here a house is going up or being added to, a handsome stone building in the Arab style. Next door a new office building, scarcely bigger than the house, is being built for an insurance agent, a contractor, an importer of German cars or of Japanese calculators or of Dutch butter. Upper-class women are in the shops. But you must walk beyond the city center to see many women in the streets. Most of them are accompanied by children; the birthrate is about 3.75 children per family. And women from the Philippines or Sri Lanka wait on tourists. At night, there is no brightly lit quarter to go to, few nightclubs or cinemas, and little by way of theater. The fathers take over where the mosques leave off.

Still, when one gets beyond the threshold of someone's house in this city of houses, one is astonished to find people who talk as freely as did Dr. Diemas or Ibrahim Abu Nab, a Palestinian filmmaker and editor of a family magazine. Every question about the regime and its future can be raised, even in conversation with a foreign professor one has no reason to trust. It is true that these are not hard times, that the King can afford to be magnanimous. But there seems to be something more to the openness in Amman, perhaps having to do with the elite's inherited legacy of English tolerance, the effects of foreign education, of travel. A UN diplomat pointed out to me that Palestinians who work in the Gulf may become fed up with the sheikdoms that employ them, about which they can do little or nothing. "They voice their complaints where they can, at home in Jordan."

"Our sons are drafted into the army," Abu Nab told me, "our taxes are levied, there are thirty-four emergency regulations.

There are government bureaucrats who will even tell me how much to charge for my magazine." He changed the subject. "Elections here will explode the myth of the merit, power, and cohesiveness of the old Jordanian families, of the tribal obligations." He said he respects the King's efforts to solicit criticism, as he does in meetings throughout the country, following the traditional custom. But could the problems of his magazine be settled over a feast of roast lamb? No, Amman has outgrown such rituals. "If the economy declines, the Hashemites are in trouble. Palestinians can acquire 'Jordanian consciousness'; but democracy for the West Bank will not be contained there." Later, in criticizing the findings of the Kahan Commission report on the Beirut massacre—in an article in the *Jordan Times*—Abu Nab nevertheless lamented that "we lack any kind of commission of inquiry into anything."*

What I found more astonishing is that Mrs. Sharaf, who had married into one of those "old Jordanian families," substantially agrees with Abu Nab's views. "You cannot isolate your people from ideologies from the outside," she told me earnestly. "They travel, get newspapers, grow in sophistication, learn foreign languages." (Her son, in sweatshirt and jeans, was playing rock music in the next room.) Her late husband, Abdul Hamid Sharaf, Prime Minister in 1979 and 1980 and the founder of the National Consultative Council, had, she said, persuaded the King to accept the idea of a new "national covenant." "The 'covenant' was to encourage voluntary associations. It would have meant the decentralization of power, virtual freedom of the press, and the organization of political parties—not communist parties but welfare-state parties would be approved." In fact, Jordan already has a Federation of Trade Unions, including seventeen syndicated unions—for workers in the power company, the banks, hotels, and docks—and 120,000 members. The federation's deputy secretary, Khalil Abu Kurmeh, has stated in an Amman paper that he hopes "to bring pressure to bear on employers and, eventually, to influence the political decisions of the government in favor of the interests of labor."†

*

*Jordan Times*, February 20, 1983.
†*Jerusalem Star*, December 2, 1982.

Mrs. Sharaf struck me as a charming, reticent woman, concerned to uphold her husband's principles: "The King addressed the National Consultative Council. I was one of those asked to respond to his welcome. He said, 'How good it is to have the council,' and so on, and I said, 'No, it is not right to say this; the council is temporary, because of the emergency.' We want to have our parliament again." Will the King, whom she obviously adores, agree? "It is not a matter of choice. The King knows that it is inevitable."

This prospect, according to well-informed Americans I talked to, is arguable. It is doubtful that Hussein would want to submit to Parliament anything but economic legislation, and there will be much less money all around if the process of both integrating the West Bank and liberalizing the regime should alienate the Gulf states without quickly producing new economic opportunities for the emerging middle class. The boom, after all, is the result of the state of war. Still, Abu Nab and Mrs. Sharaf are their own best evidence that Jordan's approach to Palestinian self-determination can be more generous and constructive than what PLO spokesmen in the West have implied. Why shouldn't there be some decentralization of power in the whole of Jordan? Why shouldn't cantons evolve on both sides of the river — separate Palestinian cantons around Nablus, around Hebron and Jerusalem, a canton for the Jordan Valley, a Jordanian canton in Amman or Irbid? Why not draw up a liberal constitution? A former American diplomat in Amman put it this way: "It would be an elite politics. But it is an elite pluralism you have here. There is the Orthodox club, the Circassian community. There are East Bankers, tribal Jordanians, West Bankers, transplanted West Bankers. And there is always the chance that political parties will be bought off by Syrians or Saudis. But a constitutional monarchy will only give institutional expression to the openness that already exists here."

### III

It is hard to say what chance the Jordanian approach would have on the West Bank today, and whether the anger and dejection of the Palestinians living there are great enough to cause a decisive majority, already drawn to the PLO, to embrace Hussein. Of those who realize that this implies a choice, few are aware of Hassan's ideas. "We have learned something from you," Ziad Abu Ziad—an editor of the nationalist Jerusalem daily *al-Fajr* —recently told Amos Oz. "We want to live in an open society, a pluralistic and democratic one. This will not materialize so soon in Jordan. We remember the Hussein of old."*

Nevertheless, a recent poll revealed that while 90 percent of West Bank Palestinians consider the PLO to be their "sole legitimate representative," 80 percent also favor Hussein's offer to act on their behalf.† Such ambiguous opinions reflect a sense of desperation. Danny Rubenstein, the well-informed West Bank reporter for *Davar*, recently reported that new orders from the Israeli military governors declaring uncultivated land to be "state land" will make it possible "to seize about a third of the West Bank."‡ A high-ranking Likud politician told me casually that Israel already "controls 80 percent of 'outstanding' land," by which he apparently meant land for which there is no existing private title. And Israeli construction in the territories is continuing steadily. Meron Benvenisti, the former deputy mayor of Jerusalem, whose careful report on the political economy of the territories was mentioned to me by nearly every Jordanian and West Bank Palestinian I spoke to, told me he expects that the Begin government could have more than 100,000 Jews settled on the West Bank by the end of 1986. Already Jewish settlers have municipalities—not to mention roads, power lines, and military encampments—similar to those of Jews in Israel proper. They purchase their apartments for approximately one third of what they would have to pay inside Israel, thanks to various government incentives.

Moreover, the vigilantism of the 11,000 or so Gush Emunim fanatics is increasingly felt in Arab towns. The smaller and more virulent Kach movement of Meir Kahane is thought by Israeli police to be responsible for at least two shootings into houses in

---

*Davar*, January 7, 1983.
†Peretz Kidron, National Public Radio, February 18, 1983.
‡*Davar*, January 11, 1983.

Hebron. Of course, the situation is grim as well for Jews traveling in the West Bank: stonings and other acts of violence from Arab youngsters have become so commonplace that the new Minister of Defense, Moshe Arens, recently warned that "the time has not yet come when Jews can move about freely in Judea and Samaria without firearms." He also warned Jews not to take the law into their own hands. But that cannot reassure the peaceful majority of West Bank Arabs, who consider the occupation and de facto annexation of their land no less than an act of naked force.

Furthermore, the Lebanon war has clearly made a difference. Last spring the West Bank was violently protesting against General Sharon and the civilian administration of Professor Menachem Milson for firing the pro-PLO mayors of the major towns. A poll taken at al-Najah University then revealed that less than a quarter of the population—as compared with four fifths today—was willing to consider Jordanian representation. A group at *al-Fajr* itself recently organized a petition to the Algiers conference asking that Arafat go along with any realistic diplomatic efforts. A similar petition was sent by eighty-seven leaders of unions and professional associations in Nablus. Rashad a-Shawa, the deposed mayor of Gaza who was always sympathetic to Hussein but close to the PLO, told the Israeli Druse journalist Rafik Halabi that he regrets ever having gone along with the "armed struggle." Such talk used to be taboo among West Bank Palestinians.

Abu Nab, who was director of PLO broadcasting in 1964, told me in Amman: "The people want peace. The war has given us a chance to express this." After leaving the PLO in 1965, Abu Nab, a Jerusalemite by origin, lived and worked in Qatar, then in Beirut—where he saw the start of the civil war—and Cyprus; he came to Amman in 1978. "The PLO leader," he said, "lives a different style of life. He gets money and prestige from the struggle, so why should he climb down from his ideologies?"

> The mere idea of a state gives him almost complete relief. He has the opportunity for organized work, for political excitement. Just pursuing the ideal is enough to cure him of his moral sickness which is the consciousness of inferiority. And the higher and more distant the ideal, the greater the power of exaltation.

These are not the words of Abu Nab about Arafat. They were written about Theodor Herzl by Achad Ha'am, the Zionist thinker whose more pragmatic approach influenced Chaim Weizmann. So Sharon and Begin, in trying to prepare the way for annexation last summer, may actually have prepared the way for Hussein. No encounter demonstrated this so vividly as an interview I had with Bassam Shaka, the former mayor of Nablus. Shaka has remained close to the PLO rejectionists since 1976. After the massacre near Haifa in 1978, in which almost forty civilians were killed, he refused to condemn the Palestinian terrorists. Two years later, when a bomb planted by Jewish terrorists blew off his legs outside his house, he refused the offer of treatment from Israeli hospitals. At the same time, he condemned more moderate mayors (such as Bethlehem's Elias Freij) for being seduced by Camp David's autonomy arrangements. When he was fired by Milson last year, tens of thousands of young Palestinians took to the streets in protest.

Today, Bassam Shaka says flatly, "We are ready for partition, for peace: we should recognize Israel and Israel should recognize us." (Rafik Halabi, who interpreted for Amos Elon and me, has known Shaka for years. "He is very choked up," Halabi whispered to us in Hebrew. "He has never said this to journalists before.") I asked Shaka about Hussein's initiative. "The PLO must decide," he said, "but the armed struggle should give way to diplomatic efforts. We look forward to quiet. Israel has always exploited our radicalism. The PLO should cooperate with Hussein. We cannot reject Hussein's initiative, but it must be endorsed by the PLO."

While we were speaking, his teenage son appeared. They embraced warmly and the boy sat down next to his father. Only after a few minutes did it become clear that he had been released from prison just an hour before and that he was home for the first time in two months. We asked him the charge. "Incitement." Was he tortured? No. Was he interrogated? No. His conditions? Fifteen young prisoners lived in a room of about seventy-five square feet with only a few blankets, no books, virtually nothing but time to talk about "the struggle." His face glowed with pride. "But Hussein will get nothing," Shaka interrupted, as if suddenly recalling our talk earlier. "Hussein cannot change the facts al-

ready established. There is no minimum Hussein can get that will let others in the PLO go ahead."

Some of those "facts" are particularly striking in Nablus, a city of some 70,000 Arab residents nestled in a valley and surrounded by seven eroded mountains. There are Jewish settlements on every summit today. Some are pathetic, isolated outposts, to be sure; Halabi, Elon, and I drove up to a new settlement called Bracha A, where we found a few concrete barracks, fewer families, some troops, and a flag. We also found a private contractor who drives here every day from Ashdod to oversee his prospering business. Would he ever live here? "Never." But the roads leading to the settlement are more impressive than the housing, and one road is already cut to Bracha B. They entirely bypass the Arab towns and are portents of a Jewish presence that does not so much annex the territory as graft a thin layer of control over the top of it. In Nablus, some of the Gush Emunim faithful have taken over the "Tomb of Joseph," yet another symbol of their misguided "Zionist" messianism. Next to it is an Arab school, and fights often take place. On the wall nearby, "Death to Collaborators" is painted in red Arabic letters. And, in fact, since Shaka's firing no West Bank Palestinian will take the post of mayor. Nablus is now run by a low-ranking Israeli Druse officer. Public housing construction has been stopped. Roads are deteriorating. Families who protest by not paying their taxes soon find their electricity is shut off.

## IV

Shaka may be right about PLO attitudes, but he may yet be proved wrong about Hussein. The lack of a clear PLO endorsement is only one of Hussein's difficulties, and it may not be his most urgent one. Jordan also has a northern border. The Syrians mobilized against him a year before the Lebanon war, and their new SAM-5As threaten the skies over Amman even more than those over Tel Aviv. Iraq's resistance to Syria's Iranian allies can never be certain either. And Hussein knows that, for the first time since 1948, there is a government in Jerusalem that would not send aircraft to defend him and would prefer to see the Hashemites fall.

This is why the first demand Hussein made of President Reagan in December had nothing to do with Israel. Rather, he insisted on, and got, a guarantee that the United States would mount a police action to support his regime should he face, again, a Syrian challenge like the one of September 1970. In all the stale speculation whether the PLO will give Hussein a "green light" or an "amber light," it should not be forgotten that we ignore the lights when a cop appears and waves us through.

Nor should we conclude that a lack of "progress" in the talks concerning Israeli withdrawal from south Lebanon will necessarily prevent Hussein from going ahead. Obviously, the King would like some clear sign that the United States is prepared to press its will on Israel. He asked again on March 19 that the Americans do something to "enhance their [i.e., his] credibility."* He has also requested advanced weapons from the United States. But the King cannot be sorry to see the Syrians pinned down in the Bekáa Valley while the Israelis stay on. An American diplomat told me: "Hussein would never give the Syrians a veto over the peace process by linking his initiative to some withdrawal on all sides." Uppermost in his mind is whether he can maintain Saudi backing for the first step toward discussing a settlement with Israel. "He wants to be sure that the check is in the mail." And it is hard to believe, at least in this diplomat's view, that Hussein would have come this far in support of the Reagan plan without the Saudis behind him. That would not be like him.

Just why the Saudis should be willing to go along with a move by Hussein is harder to understand. They have made clear their skepticism about the Reagan administration's intention to force concessions from Israel. They do not share a border with Syria and, according to one UN diplomat, are anxious that Israel withdraw from Lebanon. They are leery of PLO radicalism in the Gulf but usually try to keep their friends close and their enemies closer. Their last quarterly subsidy to the PLO, some $30 million, was paid in full and on time before the PNC meeting in Algiers.

*Boston Globe, March 20, 1983.

Assad gets a check too. But now we are getting to the heart of what distinguishes Hussein's "initiative" from his permanent interests. Nobody I talked to in Jordan, Jerusalem, or Washington expects that a statement by Hussein to the effect that he is willing to recognize and negotiate with Israel will produce serious talks with the Begin government. The Jordanians have no more illusions than do the Saudis about U.S. intentions or Begin's plans for "Judea and Samaria," no matter how open-spirited, dramatic, or popular with the West Bank Palestinians Hussein's long-awaited statement proves to be.

Hussein's aim would be to sharpen the differences between Israel and the United States over settlements. He wants to test the administration's power—what Reagan calls resolve—and, for this, a good number of Palestinian moderates are prepared to wait and see. Hussein's willingness actually to sit down with the Israelis will be conditional on a freeze of settlements, at least "for the period of the negotiations," to borrow the Camp David language, and a move by Hussein might be dramatic enough to force the Reagan administration to consider what has until now been unthinkable: real pressure on Israel to freeze settlements. "He wants to put the ball in our court," a White House official told me.

Of course, this is also the way for Hussein to prove that he alone can end the occupation, which is precisely why PLO hardliners at the Algiers conference were opposed to giving any opening to him whatever. One PLO representative I talked to in Washington conceded: "Whoever controls the diplomacy will also control the configurations of power in the future." Yet no Palestinians who want peace—Arafat may now be among these—could justify obstructing the test of the U.S. government that Hussein may undertake during the coming year.

The Begin government is transforming the land. So its policies have, at least in the short run, been to Hussein's advantage. Anyone can see that there will be nothing about which to negotiate with Israel beyond, say, two years. Hussein must know that it is also in his interest to stop Israel's annexation before it goes much further. Every Palestinian expelled from the West Bank is likely to be added to the East. And Hussein must wonder if he can control the "hell" that will be raised by Palestinian radicals whose ranks grow as the homeland is lost.

# Wounded Spirits:
# Shipler's Israel

The best books, we are told, put our scattered thoughts in order;
they help us to recognize our convictions. David Shipler's *Arab
and Jew* confuses our thinking about Palestinian Arabs and Israeli
Jews, and this is its great virtue. His foil, clearly, is the over-
wrought imagery that is too easily transformed into all kinds of
political conviction, "Jewish religious fanatics," "Palestinian terrorists," West Bank "notables," Israeli "siege." He searches, plausibly enough, not for answers but for questions.

Shipler is not very smug about his sophistication; he is his own
best evidence that stereotypes give way only slowly, in sweaty
conversations and lasting friendships. He got to Israel (so he
used to joke in Jerusalem) "by mistake." His editor at the *New
York Times*, Abraham Rosenthal, wanted to signal that the newspaper's famous reluctance to send a Jewish reporter to cover the
Jewish state was over. And so Rosenthal appointed Shipler, the
Moscow Bureau chief, whose name was obviously Jewish — only
to discover that Shipler was Protestant.

This is not to suggest that Shipler was completely innocent of
the country when he got there. His father-in-law, the late Professor Harold Isaacs, had spent some time in Jerusalem during
the early sixties and had published a book about American im-

A review of David K. Shipler, *Arab and Jew: Wounded Spirits in a Promised Land*
(New York: Times Books, 1986).

migrants. But that was Israel under the old regime of the Labor
Party and Histadrut (the Federation of Hebrew Trade Unions).
When Shipler took up his post, Menachem Begin had been
elected Prime Minister, and a good reporter had to scramble to
make sense of the new forces Begin represented, of their consequences for the Arab-Israeli conflict. He began to interview
people: politicians, vendors, university professors, cabdrivers.
He visited West Bank settlements, veteran kibbutzim, West Bank
towns; he read up on Israeli and Palestinian history. *Arab and
Jew* is the emptying of perhaps the best notebook ever compiled
on the subject.

Shipler's most original chapter, I think, is the one he calls "Religious Absolutism: Isaac and Ishmael." Religion, Shipler writes,
gives the national tension "an added sense of scope and an aura
of inevitability" — not an original statement in itself, but a good
example of the elegant way Shipler often puts things, and he
assembles many novel pieces of evidence — bigoted school texts,
strident theological treatises — to clinch the point. What really
makes the chapter fresh, however, is the way Shipler breaks off
his analysis to take us places, usually to the homes of people he
knows well enough to cross-examine. In *Arab and Jew*, strong
positions are defended by strong people, who are the more memorable for their contradictions.

Shipler takes us to the cluttered study of an Orthodox rabbi,
Professor David Hartman — as it happens, my old rabbi in Montreal. Hartman used to insist that Jewish Law was inherently
civilizing and that West Bank settlers were "cooperating with
destiny." Now Hartman talks earnestly about the need for "pluralism" in Israel and in Judaism. Can one be a liberal and Orthodox at the same time? Hartman is obviously exasperated.

"Religion is the source of Utopian dreams," he declares, compulsively adjusting his skull cap. "It is fundamentally reactionary,
not pluralistic." Yet a moment later, as if to demonstrate the
action of a subtler Jewish impulse, Hartman mocks himself for
the "Utopianism" that he obviously thinks helped bring about
the Lebanon war (a war, it may be noted, in which his own son-
in-law was killed): "The land had become an idol, violence had
become a means, and those embracing it were the victims of a

tragedy in which Judaism has failed to evolve in its new context, that of state power."

Only about 11 percent of Israeli Jews are Orthodox, though their influence greatly exceeds their numbers. David Hartman, Shipler concedes, is hardly typical of Orthodox sentiment. But neither is this talent for self-criticism typical of Jerusalem's Moslem community—a point that becomes chillingly clear when Shipler sits us down in the immaculate reception room of a leader of the Moslem Waqf in Jerusalem, Sheik Akrameh Said Sabri. In contrast with Hartman's anxious talk, Sabri speaks serenely about how Islam is already a religion of perfect tolerance. Jews, he says, have always been created "equally and gracefully" in Islamic society. What then is the source of enmity between Jews and Arabs? The Koran, Sabri instructs (there is not a trace of irony in his voice), reveals the answer, which is that the Jews rejected Mohammed: "An Arab fulfilled all the criteria written in the Torah; the Jews were disappointed and shocked."

The last word, perhaps, goes to a soft-spoken Palestinian professor, Sari Nuseibah, who reminds Shipler that not many Palestinians of his generation read the Koran in any case: "[Some] want to defend the position that the Israelis are terrible, the end is near, and they go to a passage from the Koran that says how terrible the Jews are."

Upon reflection, that wry comment of Nuseibah's prompts a most disturbing thought, which seems the very point of Shipler's search. Let us say it is true that young Palestinians do not much read the Koran, and that only about 11 percent of Israeli Jews are Orthodox. Why then do so many people, Arabs and Jews, resort to religious myths and prejudices? Why all the pious extremism?

What Shipler seems to be getting at here is that the conflict is itself now shaping the thinking of Arabs and Jews more than any positive sense of their national self-determination. Especially among young people, the wars have seemed to produce *cultural* patterns much stronger than those once inspired by the old national movements—Labor Zionism and Istaqlal, say—movements that, in effect, were the first to spill blood.

It is exactly fifty years since the Arab Revolt of 1936. By now,

Arabs and Jews prepare for war with the resignation of people conforming to the laws of nature. They strive to keep faith with their dead—Jews in Days of Remembrance, Arabs in poetry and songs. Jews will justify preemptive cruelties against Arabs and vice versa; people on each side will depend on stereotypes —religious stereotypes, surely, but also historical and sexual ones —to assure themselves of the other side's ruthlessness. Some of the people Shipler interviews—Israeli General Rafael Eitan or Palestinian "fighter" Adnan Jabber—define their victories merely in terms of the other's losses. Arabs and Jews are "wounded spirits," Shipler writes. "They will not escape from one another. They will not find peace in treaties or in victories. They will find it, if at all, by looking into each other's eyes."

And yet precisely this insight, however poignant, produces the book's fundamental weakness, which is one of structure. Taking the conflict as his point of departure, Shipler divides his material into chapters about the response of the psyche to the years of war. His titles read like a catalogue of reciprocal fears (e.g., "The Primitive, Exotic Arab," "The Alien, Superior Jew," "Sexual Fears and Fantasies") or of categories of bigotry (e.g., "Nationalism," "Terrorism," "Segregation and Class"). This may have seemed a good idea at the time. Each chapter offers only a *slightly* different vantage point from the chapter before. There is a great deal of repetition and overlapping of interview material.

*Arab and Jew* need not be a short book. But it need not feel so long. How, in the context of an interview, can national images be detached from religious and sexual ones? How can being "alien" be divorced from being of a certain alien class? Shipler presents people such as Hartman and Nuseibah in fragmentary comments spread over two or three chapters—putatively about distinct subjects—and he intercuts them with the comments of many others. I think it would have been more satisfying—and so much easier to spot the contradictions—had we read everyone's views without interruption. Amoz Oz composed his important book, *In the Land of Israel,* virtually without a narrative line; though Shipler's people seem more interesting, the impact of Oz's book seemed stiffer.

And if he must interrupt his interviews, then why not to provide more historical background? Arabs and Jews may well be fighting more now over the compounded results of war than over any past nationalism. But American readers are still in need of the history, of a way of sorting out which claims (and counterclaims) are most nearly true. (The exemplary way Shipler handles the matter of terrorism suggests he would agree.) After all, Arabs and Jews who look "into each other's eyes" may see only a reflection of themselves. What in this play of images is not merely projection and misapprehension and fear?

As it is, *Arab and Jew* is too much written in what can only be called the *New York Times Magazine* style: a statement about someone's perception, an anecdote or two (or three) to illustrate why the perception may be plausible, perhaps a poll to evaluate how widespread this perception is. *Are* Jewish archaeological digs, as some Palestinians charge, a kind of cultural warfare? *Is* Palestinian nationalism more superficial and reflexive than Zionism? These are not questions to be settled by the search for questions.

Shipler's concluding chapter includes a narrative about a weeklong encounter between Arab and Jewish teenagers in Kibbutz Neve Shalom. It is not to be missed. The dialogue gives weight and a climax to everything that comes before. The youths meet and slowly peel away each other's suspicions. At the end of the week, Shipler notes, Salman has fallen for Ricky, "a Jewish boy is looking lovestruck over an Arab girl." Shipler describes their parting touchingly, as if exhorting the friends he leaves behind to watch out for them, to keep working for the democratic tolerance that would protect them.

And so, for all the professional caution, *Arab and Jew* is a brave book. It is about individuals, innocence, and liberty. Which is another way of saying that it is a very American book. In the Middle East, it is impossible to think like an American without suppressing the fear of sounding like a fool.

# The Forty Years' Crisis

*April 1988*
"This is not a strike but a lockout; the Arab merchants of East
Jerusalem are locking out the Jews." I was driving in late winter
with Avi, my old neighbor from the French Hill, to the kitchen
of his catering business in Atarot—an industrial park for Israeli
businesses, planted on the hills northwest of Jerusalem—leap-
frogging the Arab suburb of Shu'fat, on the road to Ramallah.
Once a leftist Zionist leader in Mexico—"Zapata," his wife calls
him—Avi has been supporting peace groups since 1972. Now,
he says, one lives from "day to night": he makes this trip morning
and evening.

We used to linger for pita and pottery on this road; this time
we drove through, windows up, without stopping. "Nobody is
going hungry here," Avi said, not in solidarity but with resigned
admiration, pointing to the Arab duplexes. "The teenage boys
who work for me say that trucks pass from house to house in
the middle of the night, disturbing food and cash so that the
demonstrations can go on during the day. It's no secret who's
organizing the thing. They're in touch by telephone." He meant
the Palestine Liberation Organization, which most Israelis assumed to be instructing the underground organization of the
Palestinian uprising—an exaggerated assumption, as matters un-
fold. (The army subsequently put an end to international telephone calls.)

We drove deeper into Shu'fat, which looked deceptively serene
—as on the Sabbath. Only this was Thursday afternoon. The

main road to Ramallah was full of traffic; on either side we saw
block after block of closed shops, cream-scrabble Jerusalem stone
buildings shut up with maroon steel-plate doors. A few young
men (but no women) milled around on the sidewalks. The most
striking change was the graffiti, which were spray-painted everywhere, even on the courtyard walls of Shu'fat's most elegant
houses.

"At night there is border patrol every 200 meters." Avi passed
an intersection. "There was an Arab woman shot and killed here
two weeks ago, and a riot. She just happened to be standing in
the wrong place, but the soldiers then had to move in." He looked
at me blankly, caught between disapproval and apprehension.
His son is nearly fifteen, three years away from conscription. His
wife speaks of returning to her native Argentina. A police van
stood at the intersection where the woman was killed; an army
truck was parked less conspicuously, about fifty meters beyond.

When we finally reached our destination there was a different
sort of drama. I've come to see it as more revealing of Israel's
grim crisis, the Jewish state's crisis, than the drive over had been.
We pulled up to a concrete slab building and Avi honked the
horn. A genial Arab youth named Hana opened the door, and
we drove into a damp, grimy space, half garage, half kitchen.
Another Arab youth was sleeping out back on a soiled striped
sofa. We walked around and Avi was suddenly in distress. "Why
did you let the fire go out?" he chastised Hana, like an older
brother who's discovered the evidence of mischief just when
parents are expected home. He ran over to the wall and me-
thodically lit an oversize gas pilot at the end of a long rubber
hose.

It turns out that the *mashgiach* — the supervisor appointed by
the rabbinate to certify the food as kosher — had warned Avi
about his Arab cook, an older man who's worked with Avi for
ten years. Avi explained, "Jewish law requires that if a non-Jew
does the cooking, the stove must be lit by a Jew." Avi's main
clients are government agencies, which serve only kosher food.
Since kashrut certification is legally up to the rabbinate, Avi had
lit the gas. He is an atheist, but his state identity card reads
Yehudi, which is good enough for the *mashgiach*. "The rabbinate
charges me 1,000 shekels [$625] a month for 'supervision.' "

The preoccupations of the Orthodox rabbinate struck us as sadly amusing. A couple of months before, he told me, Jerusalem Arab workers at an Israeli food-processing factory had been caught pissing into huge vats of hummus they were preparing for the restaurant trade. On the ride back to West Jerusalem, Hana rode with us, and we asked him to translate the slogans spray-painted on the walls: "Yes, to the Palestine Army!" "Fatah, Fatah!" There were also slogans by supporters of the Moslem fundamentalists, he said, but he couldn't find the Hebrew words for them. I wondered if he was being tactful. I wondered what Hana thought of that kosher flame. I wondered most about what that sleepy youth had been doing during the night.

Seventy percent of Palestinian residents of Gaza are under age twenty-four, and about 60 percent of West Bankers are. It is precisely because of youths like Hana that many Israelis are re-examining their attitude toward the occupation. Since Moshe Dayan's time most Israelis, really, have thought of the occupation as an obvious gain for Israeli defense — "security borders," Dayan called them. Since December young Palestinians have imposed a kind of partition of their own on the land. The road to Judea goes through Bethlehem, the road to Samaria through Shu'fat.

Ehud Olmert, a Likud member of the Knesset close to Prime Minister Yitzchak Shamir, told me that Israel should now accord the Palestinians autonomy unilaterally, even if this cannot be negotiated with the local inhabitants — an impractical suggestion, perhaps, and reminiscent of former Defense Minister Ariel Sharon's frustrated effort to set up collaborationist "village leagues" in 1981. Still, it was revealing of his defensiveness. "American Jews failed us," Olmert said. "We held the land for twenty years and they didn't come."

And yet the peace camp would be wrong to find in Olmert's disquietude anything that is very reassuring. While many Likud supporters are openly disappointed in the occupation, only about half of Israelis surveyed favor the Shultz plan, and that most callous of hard-liners, Ariel Sharon, is getting stronger within the Likud, not weaker. Polls taken since the uprising started last December show the ultranationalist Tehiya Party winning eight to ten Knesset seats in the next elections and Rabbi Meir Kahane's Kach Party as many as four.

Why has the collapse of hawkish security arguments about the occupation not led to a corresponding surge in public enthusiasm for Labor and "territorial compromise"? Israel's claim of sovereignty over a united Jerusalem—over the mosques, the Arab quarter, the Jerusalem of gold depicted in the El Al posters—is becoming an abstraction. If young Palestinians are going to impose de facto partition of the land, why not try to negotiate a more peaceful de jure partition, one that satisfies the Palestinian hunger for self-determination but incorporates new and formal guarantees for Israeli security?

The simple answer is that Jews and Arabs loathe each other. After fifty years of war, defeat of the enemy has become for Israelis and Palestinians alike something more compelling than the pristine nationalist strivings that got the conflict going in the first place. Right-wing leaders appear more at ease with naked violence than their rivals. There is also persistent suspicion among the less well educated Israelis that peace intellectuals are blindly idealistic about the human race, that they are *yefai nefesh*, or "pretty souls," the equivalent of bleeding-heart liberals.

This kind of charge always has some truth to it. "Peace Now people go to Gaza," Meron Benvenisti told me. "They see the squalor and report it to the press. But they disregard the hatred, the explicit Palestinian intention to 'return' to their homes. Does any Arab youth talk about what Labor means by territorial compromise? Does anyone in Gaza even mention Jordan? And do Peace Now people acknowledge the racism that has emerged among the soldiers? How ironic, this hatred! It turns out that your victim is even more hateful to you than your oppressors!" He let it sink in. Power was teaching Jews unexpected lessons.

Benvenisti picked up *Ha'aretz* and noticed a Peace Now advertisement, a call to a demonstration. Read it, he commanded. I stumbled; he snatched it away. "Look at this Hebrew: you can't read it because it's goddamned poetry!" His voice was thundering. "Who can understand this? How many young people go to the Hebrew University? Are Likud advertisements like this?"

Still, there is more to the failure of the peace camp than Arab stones and poetic ads. And here we get back to the heart of the crisis. Greater Israel may not be possible as the Israeli right has envisioned it. But the response of Israeli Arabs to the uprising has raised some unsettling questions about "smaller" Israel—questions the Israeli left, especially the leaders of the Labor Party, have tended to disregard.

Israeli Jews have often said that they do not intend to return to the borders of the pre-1967 state. Israeli Arabs, in their support for the Palestinian uprising, have shown their unwillingness to return to the pre-1967 state of affairs—whatever the borders—back to an Israel that was the product of revolutionary Zionism. After 1967, after all, the dominant rejoinder of the Labor Party's left to Dayan's argument about "security borders" was not an argument in favor of reciprocal Palestinian and Israeli national rights. Rather, it was Finance Minister Pinhas Sapir's assertion of a danger to a Jewish majority in Eretz Yisrael. Sapir, who died in 1975, pointed out that the Arab birthrate, including that of Israeli Arabs, was much higher than the Jewish one. If the territories were not returned, he said, Israelis would soon be living in a country whose "Jewish character" was lost.

Presumably, if Jews were in the majority, they would continue to have the historic right to turn the country into something Jewish. What if the Arabs were the majority? Would not protections for Jewish national rights be rescinded?

Political scientists close to Labor developed the argument further, taking Sapir's essentially cultural fears and putting them into the context of Israeli electoral politics. Shlomo Avineri, professor of political science at Hebrew University—who, like Olmert, has chastised American Jews for not being Zionists in action—insisted that if the occupation continued, Israelis would be forced to choose between living in a Jewish state or a democratic one. He wrote that an emerging Arab majority might well mean a majority for PLO leader Yasir Arafat in the Knesset. That demographic argument has been reinforced in recent months by the work of Haifa University geographer Arnon Sofer, who found that in 1985 there were 365,000 Jewish children under four years of age living in Greater Israel and 370,000 Arab children.

Of course, all this begs the question of just what Avineri, Sofer, and others actually mean by "Jewish character" when they speak of the Jewish state. There are problems with the term "majority" too. Israeli Jews are not a single bloc of people. They are themselves split into dozens of approaches to Jewish theology and history, modern intellectual styles, cultural and ethnic camps. In any case, if the trip to my friend's catering business did not bring home to me how confusing all of these terms have become since 1967, then another visit did.

While I was in Israel, a cousin of mine in Haifa—a man strongly in favor of territorial compromise—invited Professor Sofer to his house to speak before forty guests, some with annexationist views and some, like him, in favor of partition. Sofer made a forceful presentation of the demographic facts. My cousin was astounded to discover that people who were opposed to territorial compromise before his talk were even more opposed to it when Sofer had finished.

This was not perverse stubbornness on their part. A majority of Israelis see and dread something that people on the left—those who think of the Jewish state merely as a state with a Jewish majority—often overlook. What, in practical terms, does living in the Jewish state mean? How does the demographic argument play in the Israeli Arab community?

No Israeli nervous about demography—not Sapir, not Sofer, not even Avineri—ever seriously considered giving the Palestinians of the occupied territories the right to vote. Therefore, the growth of the population of West Bankers or residents of Gaza never really threatened to change the Hebrew atmosphere of Israel or the electoral balance of the Knesset, whatever the impact of the occupation on democratic values.

In contrast, many of the institutions and ideological principles supported by the Jewish state are deeply vulnerable to the claims of the 750,000 Arabs who are citizens of Israel. These people have demanded serious changes in the legal and bureaucratic structure of the state, changes having little to do with demographics. The Palestinian uprising has swelled the desire of Israeli Arabs for full, meaningful civil equality—in Hebrew, if necessary—and they see no reason why the state should fail to grant this equality simply because they constitute 17 percent of the population and not 51 percent. At the same time, there are perhaps 100,000 Arabs from the occupied territories working in Israel mainly in low-level jobs in construction and tourism, many of whom want to be treated as permanent residents.

What changes? Though Israeli Arabs vote, Israel is legally held to be the state of "the Jewish people," not merely of its citizens. Traditional Jewish Law is used to determine citizenship rights under the Law of Return: a Jew is anyone born of a Jewish mother or converted to Judaism by a rabbi. The Orthodox rabbinate has established jurisdiction in supervising marriage, divorce, aspects of child custody, burial—and food catering. Entrenched privileges have been accorded the Orthodox rabbinate and leaders of state-supported Orthodox educational institutions. Incidentally, a philosophical friend told me that there are now as many yeshiva students in Israel (partly supported by the state) as there were in Poland before World War II, some 30,000.

Old Zionist development institutions, which were not retired after the state was founded, still bestow economic rights on individual Jews—people whose nationality is legally designated as Jewish on state identity cards. The old Zionist land development corporations, Keren Hayesod and Keren Kayemet, are in effect organs of the state land authority; the Jewish Agency is an organ of the Ministry of Immigration when it comes to disbursement of loans to new immigrants and settlements. So have the public corporations, agricultural settlements, and welfare agencies of the Histadrut labor federation remained national Jewish institutions.

Israeli Arabs, the Druses excepted, do not serve in the army, as if military loyalty presupposes loyalty to the Jewish people and not to the democratic state of Israel. Israel has no integrated system of public education, no civil marriage, no Bill of Rights to protect non-Jews against discrimination in housing or employment, and, indeed, no protections for secular Jews against the encroachments of Orthodox politicians.

Israeli Arabs will thus never settle for an unreformed Israel, which is precisely what Labor intellectuals have promised to get back to. The Labor Party is identified with the proposition that partition will rescue the Jewish state from fundamental Arab challenges. But it is now clear that even in the context of a peace process, even if a Palestinian state were to be established, there could be no return to the "Days of Binyamina" (as Chava Alberstein's nostalgic song evoked the years between 1948 and 1967): no return to the years when the principles, battle cries, and costumes of the Zionist movement engendered a revolutionary Jewish national life. Some new federation is logically inescapable.

To be sure, 1949 was a stirring time for any Jew, a time of unfamiliar, heady patriotism, of pride in the harvest, the biblical land, the people's army. But the Israeli state apparatus created during these years was afflicted by compromises with rabbinic theocrats, by constitutional stopgaps, privileges for a labor aristocracy, separate administration of Arab villages—the seeds of the current inequalities. Meir Kahane has understood, evil genius that he is, that the demographic problem of *this* state can be solved most logically by expelling all Arabs. In Kahane's view —God knows how many Israelis now share it—such expulsions would only pick up where the 1948 war left off.

When the Palestinian disturbances started last December, Israelis were stunned. But they were more deeply alarmed by the general strike Israeli Arabs carried out late that month to show sympathy for the uprising. Then came another shock, in January, when Labor's most important Arab member of the Knesset, Abdulwahab Darawshe, left the party to form a new party, led by Israeli Arabs, committed (so his young cousin and political strategist Mohammed Darawshe told me) to a Palestinian state on the one hand and complete civil equality for Israeli Arabs on the other. It is worth noting in this context that the Land Day demonstrations that convulsed the occupied territories during the last week of March were to commemorate a bloody confrontation in 1976 between the Israel Defense Forces and Israeli Arabs in the Galilee, not West Bankers.

For most Israelis now, the Palestinian uprising means a kind of return to 1947, a struggle over the very existence of a state derived from revolutionary Zionism. Ari Shavit wrote in the February 24 issue of the weekly *Koteret Rashit,* "The slogan-warning of the Israeli right, 'Today Shechem [Nablus], Tomorrow Jaffa,' is not less ominous because it is used by demagogues. One should not conclude from it that we should stay in the occupied territories. But we must be careful that our withdrawal does not produce a domino effect." That is a sentiment approved of in the Israeli heartland.

I visited a friend on Kfar Yehoshua (a cooperative farm in the Jezreel Valley), a moshavnik and a Labor supporter literally from birth. "I would be for a Palestinian state today," he told me earnestly, "but that will not be the end of it. The Palestinians are a majority north of Safed, in the upper Galilee. They are a majority down the road, in the Little Triangle. Why won't *they* want a state?"

Because, I responded as best I could, Israel will not relinquish the territory, and the Israeli Arabs know it is strong enough not to. Besides, they are not demanding national rights for themselves. The creation of a Palestinian state will probably mitigate their national or separatist impulses. They could then enjoy Israeli citizenship and enjoy Palestinian nationalism vicariously. They are modern in Hebrew; they like the political and sexual freedom of Israeli civil life.

"What do you mean, 'citizens of Israel'?" he asked skeptically. "I know many Arabs: they are building contractors and farmers — we got along. But they'll never want to be citizens of a Jewish state! They'll never sing 'Hatikvah' [the Zionist anthem]; they'll always be unhappy. We'll start with a Palestinian state, and then the Arabs here will want to go to the army, and they'll want Israel to be like any other state, a multinational state, like America. Then what will it have all been for?"

Some of this fear, I would still maintain, is the result of not having thought things through. If Kfar Yehoshua is any evidence, then the Zionist movement's great achievement was precisely to lay the foundation for a secular, Hebrew democracy, not a "Jewish state." The Hebrew language predominates in historic Palestine. Even young Palestinians in the West Bank and Gaza have, for economic reasons, been forced to acquire its rudiments.

Nor would Israel be much changed in the everyday sense if it were to become the more complete secular democracy — like "America," or at least more like Canada — that Israeli Arabs and a growing but small minority of Israeli Jews want. The Israeli Arab intelligentsia will still be drawn more to Hebrew literary culture than to the village. If you want to see how Israel is not

a democracy, look at the way Arab writers live; if you want to
see how it is, listen to the way they speak. They understand the
beauty of federalism in their bones.

Israel at forty is hardly a revolutionary Zionist society. If Israelis were to acknowledge the post-Zionist Israel in which they
live, Tel Aviv would still be steamy, the Hebrew University would
offer the same courses, the lyrics of Matti Caspi's songs would
still reveal a wry Yiddish wit, the Moroccan Jews would still
celebrate the festival of Mamuna. Most Israeli Jews, including
the largely middle-class Sephardic supporters of the Likud, are
hardly religious fanatics and would find themselves quite at
home in a country where civil marriages were permitted and in
which the buses — not just the soccer players — ran on the Sabbath.

Besides, the tremendous growth of the Israeli Arab population
in the upper Galilee only underscores how foolish the Israeli
state has been to squander its resources on populating the West
Bank. The settlements are no security asset; Defense Minister
Rabin has openly criticized the citizenry for making the army's
job more difficult.

Nevertheless, even if the transformation of Israel from a Jewish state to a Hebrew republic federated to Palestine would not
prove so very traumatic, Israelis are not open to making changes
just now. People are living from day to night. Most active Israeli
politicians are in their sixties. They are mainly veterans of the
army during David Ben-Gurion's era or third-level leaders and
bureaucrats of old Zionist parties. They are nationalists. The
hardest-boiled Zionists, even in Labor, think of liberalism as
Sapir did, as a return to the delusions of the German bourgeoisie
or to the frustrated romanticism of prewar Poland.

Even for many of Israel's peace intellectuals, liberalism has
never been fundamental to Zionism but has rather seemed a
kind of cherished, imported luxury, a competing "theology" —
or even worse, a concession to historic forces opposing Zionist
socialism and nationalism, a dropping of the guard. Young Israeli Jews cannot tell you why Chaim Weizmann is remembered,
but they have absorbed old Zionist principles in the form of
forceful clichés about the nobility of Jewish settlement, the
chronic betrayals of the gentile world, historic Jewish rights to
the land of Israel.

In spite of their admiration for America, few young Israelis think of liberal institutions and federal as nonviolent routes to settle disputes that would otherwise be intractable. In consequence of the occupation, most of them (and young Palestinians, for that matter) have come to see Arabs as a dominated class, power as something that speaks from the barrel of a gun. Today, 60 percent of Israeli Jewish youth would reduce, not enhance, the rights of Israel's Arabs. Israeli soldiers and Palestinian rock throwers are routinely in the grip of an atavism that outpaces political science.

As for my friend on Kfar Yehoshua, a serious, compassionate, utterly charming man: he has as much difficulty envisioning a pluralist Israel as white residents of Little Rock, Arkansas, had envisioning the New South in 1958.

# The Logic of the
# Belated Shultz Initiative*

April 1987

Too often, one reads about George Shultz's Middle East diplomacy as if this were merely the product of fellow feeling, an old labor negotiator's effort to come up with a complex formula others would not see without him—the diplomatic equivalent of resolving "pi." Some prominent commentators, George Will and William Safire among them, write that his plan is a kind of meddling. If the Israeli government—or at least the bigger half of it, controlled by Prime Minister Yitzchak Shamir—does not want an international peace conference, why push the idea on an ally? Is Israeli security anybody else's business?

No doubt, the Palestinian uprising that began in December, escalating daily, is horribly intimate for Israelis—and Palestinians—in a way it cannot be for outsiders. In principle, people should have to live with the consequences of their plans. But consequences are precisely why Shultz is right to press on with his plan this week, despite Shamir's opposition: the violence between Israelis and Palestinians cannot be indefinitely contained to the West Bank and Gaza.

In fact, Shultz is a firebreak against a conflagration that not only could engulf Israel and its neighbors but also has the potential to draw the superpowers into an unprecedented round

*Written in collaboration with Avner Cohen.

of nuclear brinkmanship. The U.S. government has, in this sense, as great an interest in focusing on the Israeli-Palestinian dispute as it does on arms control. Why work with the Soviets to reduce the store of dynamite and then do nothing about the blasting caps?

## THE WEAPONS FACTOR

Mordechai Vanunu, the nuclear technician who was recently tried and convicted of treason in Israel for revealing Israeli nuclear secrets to the London Sunday *Times*, has inadvertently shed light on why Shultz is right to proceed with urgency. According to Vanunu, Israel may currently have as many as 100 nuclear weapons. Less widely noted, but more chilling, are claims inferred from Vanunu's press briefings that these weapons are distinctive for their small yield — as little as .5 to 5 kilotons. They are tactical weapons, by implication, designed for plausible Middle Eastern battlefields. They represent a departure from Israel's better-known nuclear capability, which former President Ephraim Katzir acknowledged in 1974 — the country's deterrent of last resort.

Vanunu has revealed that the Israeli research and development effort includes experiments with tritium. This suggests that Israel has been working on enhanced radiation devices — such as the neutron bomb. Israel may well have the capability of delivering nuclear shells. It is widely believed, moreover, that Israel has tested the Jericho II missile this past summer, the range of which falls within the categories prohibited by the INF Treaty. We know that the Soviet Union has warned Israel not to deploy Jericho II; the missile has the power and accuracy to threaten Soviet territory. (Israel also has Lance missiles from the United States.)

None of this is to imply that Shamir is itching for a fight. Not at all. The point is that the Middle East is always drifting toward war for reasons bigger than any individual leader's will. If the Palestinian problem does not quickly become a subject of political negotiation, or if the Israeli government continues to deal with the uprising with an "iron fist," Arab states neighboring Israel

would soon find themselves under pressure from their own political insurgents to become more deeply involved. This is particularly true of Jordan, the East Bank, where Palestinians make
up 65 percent of the population — a quarter of a million of whom
are in refugee camps.

The Israel Defense Forces have already killed more than a
hundred Palestinians. What if the Israeli government tried to
expel, despite its reassurances to Jordan, a large number of the
thousands of Palestinians it has detained? What if Israel's decision to keep newsmen away from the scenes of rioting leads
more Palestinians to abandon nonlethal forms of protest? What
if more Israeli soldiers are killed by Palestinian gunfire? What
if, again, a Molotov cocktail burns to death a Jewish family on
a day trip? What if a group of Arab youths in a West Bank town
try to take revenge against the IDF by attacking a Jewish settlement? People are feeling swept up.


### PRESSURE FROM WITHIN

Pressure on Jordan may come directly from Israel, moreover.
Likud leaders are speaking more positively than ever before
about Ariel Sharon's idea of "transferring" more Palestinians to
Jordan or toppling the Hashemite monarchy so that a Palestinian
state can arise across the Jordan River. When Israeli hard-liners
says "Jordan is the Palestinian state," this is what they mean.

For now, at least, the Hashemite monarchy is firmly in charge
of Palestinian camps and neighborhoods around Amman. The
Hashemite throne is well armed, and it has the loyalty of tens
of thousands of Bedouin soldiers, bureaucrats, and tribesmen.
But it might not be able to remain in control indefinitely. The
Palestinian uprising across the river could eventually precipitate
civil war in Jordan. If the Jordanian regime looked vulnerable,
Syria would have as good a reason to intervene as it did in
Lebanon. Israel and Syria would have to confront each other
again, and they face each other on the Golan with as many tanks
and planes as Germany and the Soviet Union during World War
II.

Israel still has significant superiority in the air. This time, however, the Syrians have SS-23 missiles that could blow out the runways of northern airfields. The Syrians have actively pursued a program of chemical warfare in order to match Israel's nuclear deterrent. Meanwhile, the Egyptian leadership is mocked by Islamic fundamentalists for holding to the Camp David accords. Missile installations in Saudi Arabia and Iraq are increasingly spoken of as a target for an Israeli preemptive strike.

In short, Israel may not start a war, but it is hard to see how an Israeli government would not consider using nuclear weapons to try to end one. A longer, more drawn out, or inclusive regional war would mean thousands of Israeli casualties — a price the Israeli military will not want to pay. The Palestinian uprising has made Israeli military difficulties much sharper than ever before. According to Lieutenant General Dan Shomron, Israeli Chief of Staff, the IDF has had to increase its forces in the West Bank and Gaza by four to five times just to keep Palestinians at bay. Many of the IDF's training programs have been disrupted by so much occupation duty. The uprising has undermined the deterrent forces of Israel's conventional forces.

If the IDF were to take heavy casualties on the Golan, or if, in the course of war with Syria, the Egyptians were to introduce a large armor force into the Sinai, what good choices would Israeli leaders be left with? In the case of a fast-developing war, would the Israeli government be able to stick to conventional weapons, particularly if the Syrians surprised the IDF with chemical weapons carried by its own missiles, just as Iraq surprised the Iranians with a gas attack in Iraqi Kurdistan?

And who, then, would be in control of Israel's nuclear arsenal? The army? The Defense Minister himself? The cabinet as a whole, which has never been involved with matters of nuclear strategy? The tiny coterie of nuclear technocrats shaped by Yuval Neeman — the leader of the ultra-right Tehiya Party?

These are hard questions, but they are not farfetched. How many politicians or analysts, so many of whom cautioned Israel to preserve the occupation "until there are Arabs to talk to," imagined that the West Bank and Gaza would be in revolt today? How many predicted the 1973 war in 1972?

Israel's nuclear force could, of course, be seen as an asset to peace forces in Israel arguing in favor of the Shultz initiative.

In the event of a peace treaty negotiated at an international conference, it should give Israeli leaders confidence that no combination of Arab states could ever risk trying to "push Israel into the sea." But Israel's nuclear deterrent is by itself hardly enough to bring serious peacemaking about. Only the concerted efforts of the superpowers can do that—with the United States reassuring and cajoling Israel and Jordan and the Soviets restraining Syria.

How, then, is Shultz doing? It is a relief that he is doing something. In February 1985, a weakened Yasir Arafat agreed to join King Hussein in a subordinate role in a joint delegation to peace talks, accepting the Jordanian formula of "land for peace" and buying into Shultz's "Reagan plan." At that time, Shimon Peres was the Prime Minister of Israel, West Bankers were looking for any way out of the occupation—and Shultz did nothing.

No one would hold Shultz's former inaction against him if his diplomacy were to succeed today. But though his sincerity cannot be questioned, what we know of his plan leaves one wondering if he is not just taking a five-foot leap over a seven-foot pit. According to the letter he wrote to Shamir, Shultz is still trying to work within the logic of previous peace formulas, the principles of Camp David or the Reagan plan. His plan calls for "providing for the legitimate rights of the Palestinian people"—not self-determination—for a period of transitional rule (albeit a shorter one than Camp David). It also calls for an international conference to which the Palestinians would come as part of a Jordanian-Palestinian delegation. The PLO is not mentioned.

Shultz has, in effect, adopted Shimon Peres's line just when it has become anachronistic. Peres and Shamir have themselves been at odds, sincerely and publicly, over Shultz's initiative. But if Shamir can be accused of refusing to budge, is Peres proposing anything likely to meet the expectations of young Palestinians halfway?

The Jordan option made sense in 1985. But the riots have sealed off the unexploited opportunities of the Reagan plan, and Labor's hope that Jordan will lead the Palestinians to a conference has been frustrated. The implicit purpose of that plan, after all, was to create conditions for King Hussein to reinstall Jordanian rule in the territories, gradually and in the context of a federal system; Palestinian self-determination was not to be denied in principle, Crown Prince Hassan explained in 1984, but it was to be "expressed" in essentially cultural and regional institutions.

And the unstated assumption of the Reagan plan was that Greater Israel would otherwise remain intact, that the West Bankers and residents of Gaza would settle for Jordanian rule, if only transitionally, in order to rid themselves of an occupation even more hateful to them than that of the Hashemite King.

Now Hussein has told Shultz that Jordanian leadership of Palestinian diplomacy is impossible. The West Bank and Gaza Palestinians will not have him. Hussein has stated, not for show, that the PLO must come to an international conference on its own — not as part of a Jordanian-Palestinian delegation.

This is not to say that Hussein has lost interest in keeping Palestinian nationalism under control. He is anxious about disturbances spreading to Palestinian refugees on the East Bank. Some kind of confederation between the East Bank and West Bank has always been inevitable for commercial reasons if no other. Still, the Palestinians in the territories will not stand for any other representation but Arafat's. They now have the power to stand for something.

### WHAT OF THE PLO STANCE?

If the Jordan option is dead, is the PLO giving Shultz any kind of opening? During February, in Jerusalem, he tried to meet with Palestinians close to the PLO, and they snubbed him before scores of TV cameras. Then one of Arafat's terror squads hijacked a bus to Dimona's nuclear facility, and three Israelis were killed — the day before Peres tried, and failed, to persuade Shamir to bring Shultz's plan to a vote in the cabinet.

About the immorality, the criminal folly of killing people at random, just to frighten others, there is little more to be said. It is precisely to undermine the perverted rationale for such cruelty by PLO cadres and Israeli soldiers that the peace process is so necessary. But why, if it is interested in peace, did the PLO leadership snub Shultz at this critical moment?

In fact, the PLO did not snub him and has not snubbed him since. It is true that none of the West Bank and Gaza Palestinians whom Shultz invited to the American Colony Hotel showed up. But they did not reject Shultz's initiative—as distinct from his plan—nor reject the prospect of negotiating with Israel on the basis of mutual recognition. What they did reject was the prospect of being forced to participate in the peace process *as part of a Jordanian delegation.*

One Palestinian who was close to Arafat during negotiations over the abortive meeting in Jerusalem, Khalil Jashan—the current chairman of the Council of American Arab Organizations—explained in an interview that the executive committee of the PLO was willing to have Palestinians who were anything but "PLO cadres" meet with Shultz in Cairo—of all places, the home of the Camp David accords. The point of this counteroffer was not even to demand a direct role for PLO officials right now, but at least to establish that the Palestinians are not "local" inhabitants of some future Jordanian territory.

Nor were the "diaspora" Palestinians whom Arafat proposed advocates of murderous hostility to Israel's existence. On the contrary, his list was composed mainly of Palestinian scholars living in America who have often and emphatically called for mutual recognition: Walid Khalidi, Edward Said, Rashid Khalidi, and others. These people have spoken and written movingly about their desire for peace with Israel, alongside Israel, about Jewish national rights and about the appalling victimization of Jews during the Holocaust. More recently, Arafat explicitly told the *New York Times*'s Anthony Lewis that the PLO accepts UN Resolutions 242 and 338, which entail recognition of Israel. Professor Said and Ibrahim Abu-Lughod willingly met with Shultz in Washington just last week.

Perhaps Shultz should stop circulating drafts and start making American interests more explicit. Harvard's Nadav Safran has argued cogently that Shultz and President Reagan should exploit the upcoming summit in Moscow to thrash out not principles but the crucial matter of who has the right to participate in the process. According to Safran, Shultz should induce the Soviets to re-establish diplomatic relations with Israel and make a new gesture on the question of Soviet Jewish emigration. This would help mitigate Shamir's and American conservative opposition to Soviet participation—which Peres endorses. As a quid pro quo, Shultz should enter into talks with representatives of the PLO —not only meet with Palestinian-American scholars in their capacity as American scholars.

Participation is not merely a procedural matter, of course. If the United States established diplomatic contacts with the PLO, it would send a strong signal to everyone that, ultimately, it would view with favor the creation of a Palestinian state that did not prejudice the security or sovereignty of Israel and Jordan. In this spirit, the Reagan administration should refrain from closing down the PLO mission to the United Nations.

Of course, U.S. contact with the PLO may mean going beyond Peres's stated policy. But most leaders of Israel's peace camp— some say Peres, too, at this point—look forward to the United States sending just this tough message to their government and to young Palestinians now in revolt. Just over half of Israelis polled support the Shultz initiative. Yet the peace camp has despaired of winning a decisive electoral victory while the occupied territories are consumed by bloodshed—not against rightwing leaders who seem so much more comfortable with naked force than they do. Most Israelis want the National Unity government to stay together if only because they fear the consequences of either party trying to rule a bitterly divided Israel alone.

And so the time has come for Shultz to support the participation of the PLO in the peace process and for the rest of us to support the participation of Shultz. His diplomatic activism may be the best hope to transform Israelis and Palestinians. Peace is, in any case, too important to await the transformation of Israel's unity government or the fractious PLO.

# PART THREE

# IMAGINING THE NEW JEWISH PEOPLE: ISRAEL AND AMERICA

# The Jewish State
# in Question

*January 1975*
King Hussein's humiliating defeat by Arafat at Rabat, followed
by the PLO leader's more glamorous, although politically less
significant, appearance at the General Assembly, has appeared
to settle for a while the question of who represents the diplomatic
interests of the Palestinian people. Even more distressing for
Israelis, perhaps, is that recent demonstrations of support for
Arafat on the West Bank seem to indicate that this issue is being
settled for the Palestinian Arabs in the occupied territories as
well.

The attempts of the last six months by Rabin and Kissinger
to entice Sadat into serious bilateral negotiations have been
stalled, eclipsed by the Palestinian question. But, even if most
Israelis were now convinced that the PLO is a genuine party to
the conflict, the PLO is giving little evidence that it intends to
be a party to a settlement. Despite veiled hints to the contrary
by a few PLO spokesmen,* Arafat remains adamant in his refusal

A review of Noam Chomsky, *Peace in the Middle East? Reflections on Justice and
Nationhood* (New York: Pantheon, 1974).

*The Israeli paper *Ma'ariv* reported (on November 4) that a meeting of Israeli
academics and PLO representatives in Baden, Austria (under the auspices of
"Pugwash"), produced a resolution calling for mutual recognition by Israelis and
Palestinian Arabs of the other's national rights. Borders were not discussed.
More significant however has been the conspicuous purge of PFLP terrorists
which Fatah seems to be carrying out in Beirut—culminating in the proposed
show trial of the Tunis hijackers.

to respect either the principle or the reality of Jewish national existence, let alone renounce his claims to all of old Mandate Palestine.

However, the new legitimacy accorded the PLO, compounded by the depressing threat of war, have led various writers, among them some Israelis, to reconsider the historic raisons d'être of the Jewish state.* Noam Chomsky has been troubled by these justifications for many years, and he now could not have a more dramatic political backdrop for publishing his conclusions. His new book is so timely, in fact, that one wishes that it were better.

The young Karl Marx once complained about the many socialist theorists in his day who seemed to believe that water flowed downward because men were possessed of the idea of gravity. Chomsky's essays are heavily burdened by a similar idealism. This is unfortunate; for Chomsky's sustained attack on Zionist impediments to brotherhood detract greatly from his otherwise valuable and periodically prophetic observations about Israeli society. So, too, does the way he uses the principle of socialist binationalism as a deus ex machina that could resolve the conflict.

Chomsky argues repeatedly that insofar as Israel is a "Jewish state" it cannot, in view of its substantial Arab (and Druse?) minority, also be a democratic state. On this premise he bases his conviction that binationalism is the "right" ("just," "correct," "better") method for the residents of historic Palestine to organize themselves. By "binationalism" he does not mean simply that two peoples would live as separate entities in one mutually convenient political entity, but that this state would reflect fraternal relations of Jewish and Arab workers. Chomsky also has been persuaded that the claims of both Palestinian Arabs and Israelis to the *whole* territory of Mandate Palestine are equally cogent; so any formula to share it must imply some binational arrangement. Both of Chomsky's premises seem to me misleading and contradictory.

Israel can be a democratic state to the extent that it impartially

*See Nahum Goldmann's searching and eloquent reappraisal in *New Outlook*, November 1974.

and strongly guarantees civil liberties for all of its citizens, has publicly accountable government institutions, and makes it possible for everyone to have enough of a share of common resources so that all can carry on decent lives. The "Jewishness" of Israeli society, although surely not beside the point for Jews, is beside the point for democrats; indeed, to the extent that the Israeli state apparatus falls short of democratic standards, Jews, Arabs, and Druses may all suffer directly. Jewish society in Israel is itself anything but monolithic, and Jewish democrats — who have been active in most of the political parties (from the Liberals on the right to Mapam on the left) but who increasingly belong to independent civil rights groups — have a sharp sense of their stake in constitutional liberties and in diversity.

Chomsky knows this. Although he is skeptical about their cause, he admires Israeli civil libertarians and realizes they have a powerful forum in the newspaper *Ha'aretz*. But Chomsky's book mainly ignores their struggle and is based instead on a tidy, casuistic syllogism — that a Jewish state plus a large Arab minority implies an undemocratic society. For him, a Jewish state apparatus can only be the product of a crass nationalistic movement that intends to exclude Arabs from the national life. To show that Zionism has become such a movement, he makes a brief historical argument recalling the romantic and martial doctrines of the right-wing Revisionists, who under Jabotinsky's leadership were the bitter opponents of the Labor Zionists in the 1930s and 1940s (and whose heirs can be found in the Likud today, led by Menachem Begin).

The Revisionists, it is true, wanted nothing less than a Jewish *risorgimento* in the whole land of the ancient tribes of Israel and were generally indifferent to Palestinian Arab national rights. The state, in their view, would have to foster "Jewish destiny" in a way reminiscent of — but less morally scrupulous than — Orthodox Jewish messianism. The Arabs would only be guests of the Jewish state (the liturgy instructs magnanimity to "strangers"), labor "freely" in the Jewish economy, or conveniently move elsewhere. Moreover, when Revisionism evolved into the Irgun underground during the Holocaust (under Begin's leadership), its fatalism and militarism were merged into an ideology.

Chomsky is right about, although gratuitously nasty to, right-

wing Zionism;* but he neglects to analyze in any depth why the
Revisionists and the Labor Zionists were so bitterly opposed even
*after* Ben-Gurion and his dominant Labor faction decided that it
was necessary to have an independent state. In fact, Chomsky
tendentiously suggests that when, at the Biltmore Hotel conference in 1942, the Labor Zionists (except for Mapam) abandoned
their deliberately vague claim to a Jewish "homeland" and demanded in effect a Jewish state, they stealthily took over the precepts of the Revisionists. This was a time when the Labor Zionist
army, the Haganah, was stalking the Irgun in Palestine, and the
Revisionist movement was in a shambles following Jabotinsky's
death. Nevertheless, the Biltmore conference for Chomsky was
the turning point: Zionism has been slipping down the slope of
chauvinism ever since. Nor, in his view, could this decline have
been avoided. A Jewish state ipso facto means Jewish "privilege"
that is incompatible with democracy because, if the state is to
have a Jewish character, it simply has to discriminate against
Arabs. Now, as in the forties, he sees no alternative.

The Labor Zionists, however, did seek an alternative at the
Biltmore Hotel, although most knew it was far from perfect. In
the 1930s, when they were trying to secure only some Jewish
"homeland," they promoted any number of binationalist ideas
—all of them stubbornly opposed by Palestinian Arabs. Even at
the Biltmore conference, convened a few months after the tragic
sinkings of the *Patria* and *Struma* (ships laden with Jewish refugees which the British turned away from Palestine), Mapai,
Ben-Gurion's own party, first abstained on his motion for a state,
while Chaim Weizmann, on his right, and the Mapam Party on
his left opposed it on the grounds that some binational solution
must still be found. The Revisionists were not invited to participate.

---

*For example, he buries in a footnote that it is still "generally assumed" that the
Revisionists murdered socialist leader Chaim Arlosoroff in 1933. This issue has
been laid to rest long ago by persuasive evidence (including the testimony of
Arlosoroff's wife and, more important, the testimony of a Jewish policeman
involved in the investigation) that he was killed by Arab thugs and that the
Revisionists arrested were framed. In any event, the charge is certainly not
"generally assumed" any longer. Also, he ignores the Irgun's courage in fighting
the Nazis and its contribution to the fight against the British.

Moreover, although Ben-Gurion was devoted to Jewish culture he did not derive his political convictions mechanically. He was an admirer of Spinoza and Marx no less than of the Torah. His romance with the Jewish community in Palestine (the Yishuv) was not a matter of irredentist claims or commitment to some Darwinian nation-state. He adopted the goal of a Jewish state as a pragmatic and limited instrument to deal with a series of dilemmas that Chomsky doesn't really consider: the British administration favored the Arabs and the latter steadfastly opposed Jewish immigration to Palestine even during Himmler's most murderous days; the United States and the Western democracies maintained "closed-door" immigration policies; even later, after the trauma of Nazi genocide, there was the question of what was to be done with the tens of thousands of Jewish DPs still in European camps. If there was a way for Jews in Palestine to protect themselves and to secure the safety and dignity of those Jews desperate for Palestine without an independent state apparatus, neither Chomsky nor anyone else has suggested how this could have been done.

The Labor Zionists' idea of a Jewish state thus meant something quite different to them from the chauvinist strawman Chomsky makes of it when he speaks of a "tension in Zionism"—between, on the one hand, the universalist idealism he would admire in such Zionists as Martin Buber and, on the other, the vulgar nationalism of which Biltmore was presumably the first of many triumphs. This abstract way of putting things avoids considering the actual political battles fought out among the Zionists themselves. In fact, the struggle between the Revisionist Irgun and socialist Haganah culminated precisely in the dispute over the nature of the Jewish state. The Irgun insisted upon Jewish sovereignty in the whole of Mandate Palestine; it took part in the slaughter at the Arab village of Deir Yassin—an act the Haganah condemned with revulsion—which terrified Jerusalem Arabs and caused thousands of them to flee.

By contrast, Ben-Gurion accepted partition in 1947; he was prepared to settle for a much smaller state on various tracts of territory where substantial Jewish majorities were already living or would soon be after the arrival of refugees, a settlement that Palestinians such as Fawaz Turki now regret the Arabs rejected when their armies attacked. The Labor Zionists made it clear that their idea of a state was practical, limited, and devoid of ambitions to dominate Arabs. Ben-Gurion backed this up with force, preventing the Irgun from carrying on independently with the arms they were to have obtained on the ship *Altalena* and by putting this group under the command of the new Israel Defense Forces in 1948. But these actions were in no way inconsistent with the Biltmore resolution, which had demanded that "Palestine be established as a Jewish Commonwealth, integrated in the structure of the new democratic world."* Indeed, six years later, when the Yishuv was invaded and the Arabs of Haifa were fleeing in panic, the mayor pleaded with them in vain for thirty-six hours by loudspeaker to stay. One would know none of this from Chomsky's book.

Nor did the setting up of the state after 1948 spell the end of the commitment of Labor Zionists to democracy, although the year of slaughter that launched the state certainly made the new Israelis—many of whom had barely escaped the Nazis—preoccupied with security matters. Chomsky rightly decries and documents many abuses of the principle of "national security" in the confiscation of certain Arab lands by the Israeli government from 1950 to 1953. Israeli leaders should have shown more concern for the Palestinians who left, should have offered just compensation and allowed more of them to return. But in this context Chomsky says nothing about the attempted invasion and the hostile encirclement by the Arab states or, indeed, about the confiscations of Jewish property by these states which occurred during the same period.

The state of Israel was thus conceived as a democratic-socialist entity with a large and growing Jewish majority, offering citizenship to Jew and Arab. Ben-Gurion expected the Jews to remain a self-reliant community that would not exploit the labor of Arabs but would extend to them what were, at this time, very considerable social services. The groundwork for this policy was already laid by the anticolonialist industrial and social strategy of the Histadrut during the 1920s and 1930s.

*See Christopher Sykes, *Crossroads to Israel* (New York: World, 1965; Bloomington, Ind.: Indiana University Press, paper, 1973), p. 236.

But from the outset Ben-Gurion had to enter into parliamentary coalitions with the religious parties in order to govern. The latter have not really been out of government since, and they have greatly distorted the development of Israeli civil law. Chomsky believes this alliance goes deeper than coalition politics, and no doubt there have evolved personal ties between Labor and National Religious Party functionaries that have become difficult to break. But Rabin's first government excluded the NRP—over the question of "Who is a Jew?"—and did so with suppressed relief. There is no shared spirit of Orthodox legalism lurking at the roots of this alliance.

Ben-Gurion wanted the state to provide a modern center of Jewish culture and a dependable refuge from European anti-Semitism, goals that could be reached only if the state were to have a Jewish majority and that were severely hampered, to put it mildly, by the "binationalism" of the Mandate. The state of Israel need not be presumed, however, to embody "Jewish national values"—as if this were some closed body of dogma—but rather to protect Jews and foster a common language and an eclectic Jewish culture. These aims do not necessarily prevent the Jewish state from doing the same for minorities and their cultures or, conversely, from encouraging their assimilation.* Even if, as Chomsky claims, Israel has wholly failed on both counts regarding its minorities—something I would dispute—this is not because the Jews of Israel have become "possessed of the idea" of a state.

Chomsky is surely right to perceive and condemn the vulgar

---

*Michael Walzer's criticism of Chomsky in the *New York Times Book Review* (October 6) fails on this point. Although Chomsky is very casual about the need that Jewish refugees have had (and from the Soviet Union still have) for the Law of Return, he is right to insist that legally and administratively there can be no such person as a "real Israeli" (i.e., "Jew," according to Minorities Adviser Shmuel Toledano); that in practice absorption of non-Jews into Israeli society should not be impeded by the legal definitions of Jew that the rabbis jealously guard. Walzer's reply that "an Arab can become a French citizen but not a Frenchman" is clearly false (except for periods of French history hardly worthy of emulation). This kind of "political realism" is no substitute for democratic standards. See Chomsky, p. 127, and Walzer, p. 6.

Jewish nationalism that became an element of Israeli foreign policy after the 1967 war — the swaggering Sabra mythology that was promoted by figures such as Dayan or the writer Moshe Shamir and that served to reinforce a callous disregard by many Israelis for the civil rights of Israeli Arabs or for Palestinian national aspirations. But Ben-Gurion's modest notion of statehood, although compromised by Israel's greater financial dependence on the support of American and European Jews, is still strong in Israeli Labor politics.

One typical example of this was the celebrated alarm of the Mapai Party boss Pinhas Sapir over the so-called demographic problem. Sapir feared, and was widely supported in his view, that the Jewish character of the state would be ended if Israel held on to occupied territories and the one million Arabs living on them. One may marvel at his characteristic shortsightedness. He seems to think that having an equal Arab population would pose an entirely new challenge for Israel's national identity, while a 20 percent Arab and Druse population poses none at all. Nevertheless, Sapir's criteria are consistent with original Labor Zionist convictions that the "character" of the state turns on numbers, a point of little concern to, say, Menachem Begin. (Such convictions have been strengthened, I believe, since October 1973.) Israel is a Jewish state in that it is a democracy dominated by Jews, who, not accidentally, have a large majority; they have not done so well during this century without it.

But Chomsky is right nevertheless when he argues that Israeli democracy since 1948 has seriously failed with respect to the Arab population and, for the Jews themselves, is far from satisfactory. Israel suffers from many discriminatory institutions and practices, many of them deriving directly from the Mandate period. Those who are not legally defined as Jews are excluded from the lands owned by the Jewish National Fund and from access to the funds of the Jewish Agency. This means that some of the most desirable lands in Israel are closed to Arab farmers and home builders, neither of whom could now be said to pose any threat justifying such discrimination. Rabbis elected by Orthodox rabbinic councils still control important parts of the civil law. Israeli laws of censorship and preventive detention — both inherited from the British — have been particularly hard on dis-

sident Arabs. The electoral laws favor the despotism of the party
bosses.

Nor, as Chomsky would rightly insist, have these discrimina-
tory practices been seriously challenged by Jewish democrats.
There was little protest from Jews in the early fifties when the
Israel Land Authority expropriated the allegedly "abandoned"
Arab lands, just as there is very little protest today when Israeli
Arab political agitators are expelled from the country as if they
had no rights at all.* Chomsky justifiably criticizes these injustices
in much detail. But he is only partially accurate about their cause.
The series of wars Israel has been fighting since the Arabs rejected the 1947 partition have done much more damage to democratic life in Israel than has "vulgar Zionism." Israeli Jews are
haunted by the prospect of a huge fifth column among Israeli
Arabs and have been understandably cautious about permitting
them to participate fully in the national life. This fear is exacerbated by the terrorism of the *fedayeen*, who have been an important weapon of Arab encirclement for thirty years. One might
expect that Chomsky would be inclined to appreciate those democratic standards that Israelis have kept up in spite of the obstacles they have faced.

Chomsky has no such inclination. That the Druses and the
Arabs in Israel feel estranged from the Israeli state† — although
certainly not from Israeli Jews — is, for him, evidence only of
the state's repressiveness. But the frustrations and anger of the
Arabs and Druses can also be taken as evidence of the considerable political, technological, and educational advances that
they have made in Israel and that encourage them to step up

---

*A notable exception to this indifference was the movement, widely supported
by Israeli academics and writers, to permit the expelled Maronite Arab residents
of the towns of Biram and Ikrit to return to their homes during 1972–73. Dayan
balked, on grounds of "security considerations," but the movement continued
to grow until it was undermined by the October war. Chomsky refers to the
expulsion but not to the backlash (p. 32).

† Sol Stern, writing for the *New Statesman* in December 1972, wryly observed that
the Syrian spy ring that had just been exposed and that created such a sensation
because it included two Jewish kibbutzniks should have created a far greater
sensation for its large number of Israeli Arabs; though ignored by the press,
the latter represented the far greater challenge to Israeli society.

their wholly justified demands for equal opportunity in housing and employment and for equal attention from the state bureaucracy.* Israel now faces a crisis over civil rights within its *old* borders because, despite the government's authoritarian and politically expedient policies, it has nevertheless ended for most Israeli Arabs and Druses the illiteracy, the numbing poverty, the primitive social services, and the domination by religious-aristocratic elites that were so characteristic of the communities that stayed put in 1948.

Indeed, except in Nazareth, most Israeli Arab leaders believed the modernizing influence of Jewish society to be highly threatening and a state policy of "benign neglect" to be more congenial. But precisely because a new generation has enjoyed a good many democratic rights, Israeli minorities, particularly young people, are now finding it all the more repugnant to be denied the full privileges and responsibilities of citizenship. In fact, a recurring demand of Arab civil rights groups—such as the small one at Abu Ghosh as late as 1972—is to be conscripted, like the Druses, into the Israel Defense Forces (which they see as a means of integrating themselves into Israeli society).

Such a demand would make no sense to Chomsky. He wants to equate the discrimination against Israeli Arabs with the outright denials of political rights to the Palestinian Arabs in occupied territory. This serves the rather elegant argument he makes in favor of binationalism, but it severely distorts the democratic and secularist possibilities of the Israeli state. The latter certainly is in need of further liberalization, for Jews as well as for Arabs and Druses. And one may plausibly look forward to a federal arrangement with Palestine and Jordan. But one would have hoped that Chomsky could channel his energies into a defense of, say, Shulamit Aloni's proposed bill to have the "nationality" designation removed from Israeli ID cards rather than denigrating the very possibility of democratic values in Israel— a denigration that encourages those who, unlike Chomsky, hypocritically attack the quality of Israeli democracy but really want to destroy Jewish national life.

---

*The numbers of Arabs and Druses attending school in 1948 was 10,000; in 1972, 117,000. They had five agricultural machines in 1948; in 1972, almost 1,000.

But refuting Chomsky's argument against any specifically "Jewish" state on these grounds may be irrelevant to the image of justice implicit in his book. I suspect that Chomsky is unsympathetic to those who need and cherish their national culture and, worse, who act politically to preserve it. He would, I think, be uneasy about any society whose citizens were very different from the culturally neuter "internationalists" of his socialist utopia in Palestine:

> Any individual will be free to live where he wants, to be free from religious control, to define himself as a Jew, an Arab, or something else, and to live accordingly. People will be united by bonds other than their identification as Jews or Arabs (or lack of any such identification). . . . The society will not be a Jewish state or an Arab state, but rather a democratic, multinational society.

Chomsky seems not to realize that men are seldom "free" to define themselves as Jews, or Arabs, or "something else," in the same way as they choose graduate schools; that their particular language and culture are their indispensable means for working out their lives; and that to lose them can be no less dispiriting and tragic for a man than the loss of his land or his tailor shop. Recognizing this is what, after all, animates both Jewish and Palestinian nationalists; not the sophistic image of a "multinational society" in which "human bonds" are as purely metaphysical as in liberalism's "state of nature."

Considering his distaste for national feeling, however, Chomsky's second major argument for a binational state is baffling; for he also maintains that the most uncompromising territorial claims of Jewish and Arab nationalists have equal moral validity — that "Palestinian Arab and Israeli have equal rights in the whole territory of Mandate Palestine."

This is unworthy of Chomsky's considerable talents. Surely he would not have us adopt a faith in binationalism so that we may, presumably, reconcile the inflated moral claims of Palestinians, typified by Arafat's address at the UN, to those of the Likud demagogue Menachem Begin, both of whom demand the entire land of Mandate Palestine and deny the other's right to national existence. I suspect that most of us would prefer rather more utilitarian standards in order to promote the humanism that Chomsky professes; i.e., we would ask how elementary human suffering can be minimized immediately and how the irreducible cultural and economic needs of both sides can find satisfactory political and territorial expression in the longer run. Applying these criteria, reasonable men could dismiss the brutal demands of Arab or Jewish extremists, but they would also have to discriminate among conflicting moral priorities; i.e., they could recognize both the claims of the Zionist settlers in 1936 for a home and refuge in Palestine, despite Arab hatred, and the claims of Palestinians in 1974 for a home and refuge on the West Bank and Gaza, despite right-wing Jewish irredentism. (The equally powerful claim of Palestinians to the *East* Bank is not in Israel's hands to satisfy.) It is regrettable that Chomsky should have missed this chance to be reasonable.

But like a lawyer so wrapped up in his argument for a client's case that he seems indifferent to his client's real welfare, Chomsky himself seems only perfunctorily concerned about the lives of real people. Short of "socialist binationalism," even peace itself seems, for Chomsky, hardly worth a great deal of effort. He denigrates first partition, then the Rogers Plan (just another Pax Americana), and lately the principle of an independent Palestinian state on the West Bank and Gaza, which would merely result, he contends, in the "Balkanization" of the Middle East. He does not quite ignore but he does not seem strongly concerned about the immediate horrors of the Palestinian refugee camps, of the situation of the Jews still living in Arab lands, of the terrorism and bombing that stalk sleeping children in a climate of insurmountable mutual hatred between two embattled and wounded peoples.

Chomsky would have us reject — from a "radical perspective" — the prospect, however risky, of two independent, self-developing states in historic Palestine. He contends that a West Bank Palestinian state would not be economically workable; and even if it were, it would be "dominated" by Israel, Jordan, and "U.S. imperialism."* Such a state would be a "repressive" and "irre-

---

*Some might argue that so much "domination" would promote the survival of such a Palestinian state. Both Israel and Jordan would each be intent on keeping the other's army out of this territory, while it is clearly in the interest of the United States to stabilize an area so close to the Persian Gulf by providing the Palestinians with aid and suitable guarantees for their security.

dentist" society in a Middle East already full of these. Perhaps. But he neglects to add that this would still be a substantial improvement.

The economic argument that an independent Palestinian state would be "nonviable" is a mysterious one. It seems to be based on the physiocratic notion that the land is productive only up to a point and no further while ignoring the striking industrial example of Israel next door. Palestinian Arabs could likely count on development capital from the sheiks and on a million "freed" industrial workers from the camps; these would seem plausible conditions for undertaking modern economic development.

Moreover, I don't understand how Chomsky can argue that the underdeveloped economy of the West Bank is an obstacle to genuine Palestinian independence and yet not see this same underdevelopment as an obstacle to binationalism. Surely, under current economic conditions no binational arrangement in Palestine could avoid turning it into another Algeria—with Jews in the situation of the French—particularly without strong labor movements (and institutions) willing to cooperate on both sides. Socialist binationalism is more easily imagined than constructed.

To his credit, Chomsky acknowledges the "absence of a common program" between Israelis and Palestinian socialists. But he fails to see that for a common program to have some political significance there must be some symmetry in the social and political composition of the societies that are presumably expected to support it. This symmetry is lacking between Israel and Arab Palestine and makes Chomsky's "principle of economic integration" irrelevant. The Palestine Arab mayors, lawyers, village leaders, and other elites are only now contemplating modernization and industrialization; their society on the West Bank is still "traditional," despite the economic advances since 1967, and socialism, let alone binationalism, remains for them a threatening and alien concept. It will be difficult enough for Palestinian Arab economic elites—even with the participation of the PLO—to persuade the Palestinian masses to turn from traditional, small-holding agriculture to industrial production. Only by organizing West Bank agriculture on Stalinist lines could Palestinian socialists expect to emulate (i.e., caricature) the kibbutz model that

Chomsky admires so much. And Arab socialists are themselves hard to come by.

Chomsky tries to dispel these differences between Israeli and Arab economic practice by digging up the vague binationalist pronouncements of obscure Arab figures and by counterposing them to Jewish binational programs from the Mandate period. As he acknowledges, the Mapai leadership (Ben-Gurion, Ben-Tzvi, Katznelson), the left-wing leaders of Shomer Hatzair (even at the Biltmore conference), Weizmann, Ruppin, Magnes, Buber, and others, were all at various times proponents of binationalism. But these men dominated the political life of the Yishuv. By comparison, courageous Arab martyrs to the cause of binationalism (although I doubt socialism), such as Fawzi Husseini, the Mufti's nephew, will likely be remembered mainly for their having been mentioned in Chomsky's book.

Chomsky has ironically overlooked something that is obvious to anyone who has visited Israel since 1967 (as Chomsky has not), namely, that the improved relations between Israeli Jews and West Bank Arabs are primarily the result of market relations. The relatively anonymous and self-interested transactions of buyer and seller in West Bank bazaars and Tel Aviv department stores have provided many Israelis and Arabs with their first person-to-person contacts with one another, however superficial and suspicious these encounters have often been.

Imagine, by contrast, the frustrations of nationalist-minded Arab and Jewish workers' parties trying to forge a "common program" even before any of the banal mutual interests that one would hope could evolve between them first exist, as they now do exist, for example, between Arab and Jewish taxi drivers in Jerusalem or between Jewish electricians and the Arab construction workers who were only recently organized by the Histadrut, or among intellectuals in the universities and cafés.

The Arabs of Palestine are not interested in socialist binationalism; and even the Israeli left has long since become contemptuous of it, particularly when Israeli children are killed in its name. (Naif Hawatmeh flaunted a policy resembling binationalism a few weeks before his group attacked at Maalot.) This is not to insult the often exciting visions that Chomsky proposes: he wants genuine national autonomy for a new state that will be free of great-power meddling. He hopes for cooperation between Jews and Arabs, perhaps under some mutually advantageous federal structure, a greater degree of cosmopolitanism, etc. Perhaps if peace talks ever materialize, Chomsky's suggestions for transnational economic arrangements and greater cultural understanding and contacts will become irresistible; more than a few Israelis are already hungry for the latter. But if "vulgar nationalism" might be an early victim of peace, still, the *ideas* of socialism and internationalism will not help much to bring peace about.

# To Praise Zionism
## and to Bury It

*October 1977*
Now that in the wake of anti-Zionist slanders by the Kremlin
and the General Assembly we have all become defiant Zionists
again, it may be somewhat indelicate to ask: Do we need Zionism
and Zionist ideas today? Defiance offers a kind of satisfaction,
especially for Jews a generation after the Holocaust, but it can
also be counterproductive; the best defense of Zionism may well
be a grateful and loving epitaph. So, at least, it seems in light
of the increasingly evident circumstance that the *only activist*
"Zionists" of our day turn out to be a group of right-wing fundamentalists whose passion masks their own slipshod understanding of what Zionism once was and what it has achieved.

### OLD ZIONISM: THE RISE

In 1893, four years before the first Zionist Congress, Theodor
Herzl openly proposed the mass conversion of Jewish children
to Christianity. For Herzl, the Jews were people of fate, inherently cosmopolitan individuals reluctantly drawn together by the
chronic hostility of the gentiles. Achad Ha'am (Asher Ginzberg)
thought otherwise: he knew his East European Jews to be an
organic people, united in the exercise of their unique religious-
cultural heritage, language, and social institutions—of which,

he rightly suspected, Herzl was pitifully ignorant. Achad Ha'am believed that assimilation was itself the looming threat to Jewish life, and he despised men like Herzl who came to Zionism only because assimilation was not working.

This dispute between Achad Ha'am and Herzl precurses the major tension in Zionist thought, a tension that would plague the movement for the following half century—between "cultural" Zionism, primarily concerned with modernizing Jewish life, and "political" Zionism, concerned mainly with saving Jewish lives. Not that the two were in principle incompatible; Chaim Weizmann would achieve a kind of synthesis between the two in subsequent years. But early on, these two approaches were at odds in practice.

Herzl, for example, opted for the vigorous pursuit of an imperial charter that might enable Jews to migrate en masse to Palestine—or to any available territory. He believed that Jewish cities, diplomats, bureaucracies, and flags would make the Jews more "progressive," more dignified, and more "acceptable" by conventional European standards—the only standards he respected. And since he could not understand what held the Jews together apart from gentile anti-Semitism, he thought the Jews' state could be situated anywhere—even thousands of miles from historic Eretz Yisrael.

Achad Ha'am, on the other hand, represented those Zionist priorities deriving from the still vital—but already withering—Jewish life of Eastern and East Central Europe. He saw in Zionism a method of Jewish self-development, a way of keeping the Jewish people together even after the halachic glue had come unstuck. For Achad Ha'am, the gradual, "organic" development of a Jewish nation in Palestine would provide the basis for a viable Jewish civilization after theological categories were no longer persuasive. Final political structures were of less interest to him than the process of nation building; vitality for Judaism in a rapidly secularizing world was as important to him as safety for Jews in a continuingly hostile world. And building a new Jewish society was something Achad Ha'am saw as very different from acting out the panicky frustrations of assimilated Viennese-Jewish dramatists.

Quite apart from the substance of this disagreement, it highlights the most conspicuous feature of early Zionism: dissension. In its formative years, especially after Herzl's prestige began to wane, the Zionist organization was regularly torn apart and pieced together by an extraordinary variety of groups: socialists, anarchists, liberals, advocates of cultural as well as political-territorial Zionism, and even a few religious mystics. Consensus was unlikely; for the most part, they behaved (to Achad Ha'am's suppressed delight) as if their movement were not about some abstract notion of Jewish power or solidarity but rather about the concrete ways in which Jews ought to be living in the modern world. Zionism was widely presumed to be about living, not just resisting, a perception that invited no end of dispute about the look of the living space.

Preoccupied as they were with the challenge of creating some national, hence novel, way of living as Jews, and buffeted as well by the ideological crosscurrents of the Europe of the day, Zionist theoreticians, especially those from Eastern Europe, were as various as they were intolerant. Indeed, the vitality of the movement was manifest in its discord. Though Herzl soon tired of his quarrelsome army of *Ostjuden*—in his diary he dismisses them as "schnorrers, boys, and schmucks"—the followers of Achad Ha'am, such as Weizmann, recognized in their own dissension an exuberant desire for "self-expression and not merely for rescue."

Like his contemporaries, Herzl had also been proposing a radical—even spectacular—redirection of Jewish life. But it was not his exotic nationalism that prevailed. Instead, it was the politically more modest but culturally more ambitious strategy of Achad Ha'am, reinterpreted by men like Weizmann. And this was because the priorities of cultural Zionism appealed to the movement's only reliable constituency, the one from which would come the pioneers who would actually attempt to live in Israel. Between 1881 and 1914, two million Jews left the Russian-Polish Pale of Settlement: only 40,000 attempted settlement in Palestine. These were mainly workers, students, and petit-bourgeois intellectuals whose Orthodox origins had become something of an embarrassment to them. Yet, in contrast to Herzl's analysis, these were men and women whose feeling for Jewish language, ethics, and aesthetics made the prospect of assimilation unthinkable.

Of course, a substantial number of early Zionists, mainly the Western, already assimilated variety that idolized Herzl, were most concerned about anti-Semitism, vulnerability, the "degradation" of Jews in Western societies. They were, consequently, moved by Herzl's elegant vision of Jewish corporate power: the Jewish state, employing Jewish statesmen and Jewish ministers who exert the power and ape the savoir-faire (Herzl insisted that Nordau change into a morning coat at the Basel Congress) of Austro-Hungarian officials. Herzl played on these dreams with great panache, "calling on" the Sultan, the Kaiser, the British Colonial Office. But in the end, Herzlian Zionism did not really inspire anyone to build much of anything. The heroic and macabre images of political Zionism would be eclipsed until the more tragic 1930s, when Jabotinsky would revive them in the Revisionist movement.

The Zionism that did inspire foundation work was, as I have already suggested, the Zionism of men who thought primarily in social and cultural categories, not political ones. Such men and women wanted to be culturally self-determining, scientific, secular — and Jewish. Life in the Pale had taught them that such national goals can be pursued outside the realm of high politics. So the land of Zion represented, in the first instance, not so much the chance to exercise national power as to engage in what might be called national therapy. Most early Zionists thus rejected Herzl's emphasis on purely political solutions, agreeing instead with Achad Ha'am's rebukes (1897):

[For] the emancipation of ourselves from the inner slavery and spiritual degradation which assimilation has produced in us . . . Judaism needs at present but little. It needs not an independent state, but the creation in its native land of conditions favorable to its development: A good sized settlement of Jews working without hindrance in every branch of culture, from agriculture and handicrafts to science and literature. Thus Jewish settlement, which will be a gradual growth, will become in the course of time the centre of the nation . . . and when our national culture in Palestine has attained that level (the highest degree of perfection of which it is capable) we may be confident that it will produce men . . .

who will be able, on a favorable opportunity, to establish a state
which will be a *Jewish* state and not merely a state of Jews.

We may observe a subtle principle in Achad Ha'am's argument, one that was to become central to Zionist ideology once
Herzl's diplomatic house of cards collapsed in 1904. Not only
were purely "political" questions to be relegated to the margins,
but it would in any case be the socioeconomic and demographic
and cultural facts created by Zionist pioneers that would ultimately determine the *political* outcome. Achad Ha'am then, and
Weizmann later, saw that there was an intrinsic connection between social relations and political structures. If high-minded
and disciplined Jews would go to Palestine to work on themselves
and on the development of a Jewish society, *they* would eventually
become the decisive political fact—naturally, organically; not
artificially, not by fiat.

Herzl left behind a brilliant example of sacrifice, a bureaucracy, and a bank, but he died a failing, brooding hero. It was,
instead, the politically astute and culturally attuned Zionists,
those whom Weizmann came later to call the "practical" Zionists,
who in fact created what Herzl had barely willed. Achad Ha'am
and Weizmann created the ideological and institutional framework in which the plodding and revolutionary work of Labor
Zionism could be initiated. Achad Ha'am's contribution was to
provide the guiding principles for the evolution of a Hebrew-
speaking culture, principles that were both gradualist and anticolonialist (i.e., refraining from the employment of Arab labor).
Weizmann's contribution was to transform the Zionist organization into a financially solvent and diplomatically agile sponsor
for Labor Zionist settlements.

This was the great alliance, the alliance between "practical"
Zionism and socialist pioneering, that gave rise to the state of
Israel in due course. The theory required men and women who
would have a personal stake in modest practical achievement,
who wanted to be "rebuilt by rebuilding," as an early song put
it, who could draw inspiration from a revolution that was to take
place one dunam (a quarter of an acre) at a time, who could also
persuade themselves that growing Arab resentment was but an
aspect of a world soon to be superseded. And, beginning in 1905,

they came. Gordon, Katznelson, Ben-Gurion, Brenner, and the others, rejecting New York, undertaking collective settlement, fashioning a Jewish-socialist polity within the Mandate state, constructing a Jewish society that was not only economically independent and militarily defensible but also culturally distinctive. It was this society that was able to absorb thousands of Polish and German refugees when the crises of the 1930s became terrifying. It was this society that was to prove itself a substantial political fact.

Herzl's followers—those who had been consumed from the beginning by a vision of the Jewish state—never had the patience to create it. Indeed, most of them abandoned the movement just when it stopped making headlines and began making history.

Political sovereignty was not the primary concern of the practical Zionists. It was not until 1942 that the Labor Zionists decided to struggle for sovereignty, and then it was not because they had converted to the more strident Revisionist approach to Zionism but because of the radical change in Jewish circumstance. Europe had simply become so grotesque that the political agenda had become not only compelling but also realistic. When Ben-Gurion demanded a "commonwealth" at the Biltmore conference in 1942, it was because he could now feel sure he had behind him a solid national community that was capable of organizing a state and of protecting authentic Jewish interests. The Zionism that had built this Yishuv was a movement of social revolution, not of political reflex.

## OLD ZIONISM: THE DECLINE

More recently, it has been a symptom of the Zionist movement's eventual triumph that disharmony, activism, and social experiment appear superfluous. The land has been settled, and so have the old debates. The Holocaust, apart from murdering practical Zionism's organic constituency, caused an endemic preoccupation with defense and rescue; the advent of statehood in 1948 and the struggle for its preservation since then have made debate of the old kind irrelevant. The new "Zionist" purposes became self-evident, beyond debate: hold off the Arabs, expand the economy, integrate the North African Jews who were arriving, and tax the North American Jews who were not.

Few thought it worth pointing out that these were not Zionist purposes but post-Zionist purposes. Revolutions finally exhaust themselves, in new institutional problems and old banalities; the Zionist revolution hatched Israel and inevitably inherited the consequences of its own success.

Little wonder that for most Israelis the word Zionism— *Tziyonut*—has come to mean showy moralism or patriotism. It is the word they expect in editorials but not from friends. This is because Zionism has commonly become a term that merely suggests how right it is for children to be raised on the Hebrew language and for the trees in the Valley of Jezreel to be green. When professed too vigorously, it is taken as a cheap form of self-congratulation.

In the West, moreover, "Zionism" now comes even cheaper. Like Winston Churchill, who confessed "Zionism" to Weizmann in 1948, anyone with a decent concern for Israel's survival calls himself a Zionist. And Western Jews conspicuously display such decency today at fundraising dinners, at rallies, or on their car bumpers. I do not mean to denigrate such sentiments or to dismiss lightly the formidable political apparatus they have engendered. The Israel lobby and the fundraising network of the UJA are tapping deeply felt devotion and are highly accomplished instruments of Israeli policy. For many Western Jews, vicarious "Zionism" is a serious (and final?) mode of Jewish expression, and anyway, their money is indispensable. But this activity and these sentiments ought not to be confused with historic Zionism. For today's universal "Zionism" no longer provokes Jews to search out new forms of Jewish culture and social enterprise—to rehabilitate their lives within a national setting—but merely to applaud and support the Jewish state's existing achievements. The "Zionist idea" has conquered the Jewish world in this generation by transforming itself into a celebration.

There is, of course, a healthy streak of realism in this diluted "Zionism." For the two fundamental promises of the Zionist movement—to modernize Jewish cultural life by means of a cooperative, national experience and thus to end the peculiar vulnerabilities and fears of Jews in class-divided, Christ-avenging

Europe—have more or less been delivered upon. In fact, the achievements of historic Zionism are so obvious that they are often overlooked. We would thus do well to have another glance. No doubt, Israelis still have far to go before meeting the standards of their culturalist mentors. But whatever its other failings, a modern and deliberately Hebraic Jewish life is growing splendidly in Israel and has been since the 1930s. A synthesis of traditional Jewish practices with modern values and aesthetics is being worked out. Israeli society is eclectic yet unmistakably Jewish; this was, as we have seen, the very point of the Zionist project.

The recurring complaint, voiced mainly by American Jewish visitors to Israel during the 1950s and '60s, that Israel is not "Jewish" enough, not sufficiently committed to traditional religious authority and legal principles, thus betrays a profound misunderstanding of original Zionist goals. The Zionists enjoined Jews to emancipate themselves, first of all, by employing new categories—those of Enlightenment history, philosophy, and sociology—in defining themselves as Jews. There could no longer be for such Jews an established body of Jewish concerns, Jewish belief, and Jewish liturgical practice. There could be only a Jewish "spirit" embodied in a language, a literature, a complex of symbols, and a scientific understanding of Jewish history; a "spirit" that could only make sense in the context of a national-territorial experience. The rabbis of Bavaria knew what they were about when they conspired to prevent Herzl from holding the first Zionist Congress in Munich, and much of modern Israel would vindicate their fears.

But it is less clear, particularly since the 1973 war, that historic Zionism has delivered so well on the promise of ending Jewish vulnerability. The physical dangers and economic adversities now faced by Israeli Jews seem today far more stark than anything they would encounter in Western democracies. The traditional Zionist's hope to furnish Jews a "refuge" has become increasingly ironic ever since 1948. Beleaguered Russian and Argentinean Jews now acknowledge this openly by their actions. The former are moving to Canada and the United States in far greater numbers than they are moving to Israel. Israelis who stay put do so despite the danger that surrounds them, and most Israelis now cling to the classic Zionist conviction that all Jews

should come to Israel. This conviction, however, arises not out
of fear for the destiny of Western Jews but out of fear for their
own.

But finally secure or not, when Jewish state power was consolidated in Israel, the question of the vulnerability of the Jewish
*nation* — the specific European vulnerability to which Zionism
addressed itself — had been transcended. At least and at last, the
question of Jewish vulnerability had been transformed into a
military and diplomatic matter. The Jewish people of Eastern
Europe had been murdered; the nation in Palestine had a state.
There was nothing left for Zionists to say about the security of
the Jewish nation except to admonish the Israeli government to
be brave and wise. As Ben-Gurion suggested twenty-five years
ago, political Zionism has become a truism within the Jewish
state and an affectation without.

This is why Ben-Gurion believed that Jews could perform —
must perform — only one last Zionist act: namely, come to Israel.
But regarding the *aliyah* (ascent to Zion) of Western Jews, the
traditional claims of the Zionist movement reflected in Ben-
Gurion's imperative have become increasingly unrealistic. Israeli
society can no longer entice Jews with some vague promise of
"self-determination." Israel can only be what it is: a complex,
already determined society to be mastered.

It is thus the legacy of the Zionist movement, the great west-
ward emigration after 1881, and tragically, that of the Third
Reich, that the choices for free Jews have not been more plain
for a century: one lives in Israel or one does not; one satisfies
one's needs within the culture and institutions of the Jewish
nation as constituted in Israel or one remains an active, vigilant
Jewish participant in Western democracies. Israel has not proven
to be a more effective refuge than North America; neither does
Israeli society possess some unique and forceful moral charm.
Israel is, gratefully, too real to be the darling of utopian mor-
alists.

The old attraction of the Jewish Yishuv in Palestine has dis-
sipated along with the utopian élan that is possible for a revolutionary resistance movement whose future is still before it.
Zionism's future is behind it. The Jews in Israel are a nation
"like all others" today, not because of their government's exercise

of military and diplomatic power, but because the nation in Israel is now too intricate to be readily transformed by any person's revolutionary will. Too many wills have already run their course. Israel has become, as it were, "natural." Living there requires an act of mature love, not an act of moral excellence.

And as to love, in spite of their overtly Zionist sentiments, Western Jews yearn for Zion a good deal less than they used to. It is not simply the material comfort and political security of North America that is an issue, but the very authenticity of North American Jewish life. Regardless of what Achad Ha'am would think about them, Western Jews can deal better with their English-speaking, pluralist surroundings than they can with any intensely Jewish ones. And even if this is a road to assimilation, the Jews who are on it are hardly troubled by "self-effacement." Alex Portnoy thought it prudent to ask his mother if "Jews believed in winter." But writers like Philip Roth are not similarly distressed. We think we know that America is good for the Jews; even the historian Salo Baron has called postwar America the Jews' first real experiment with "emancipation." But we do not know how long "Jewishness" will be persuasive to Americans of the Jewish persuasion. Irving Howe once remarked to me that this depends on how long American Jews can live on their questioning; and this may be a long time indeed, at least for a self-conscious minority. But genuine Zionist questions are no longer among those being posed by American Jews. Zionism today is all answers.

And why not? Who needs Zionist heroes? Jews can get along without them as easily as they can do without the peculiar cultural crises and historical horrors that provoked Zionist heroics. If there is nothing creative left to the Zionist movement, that too is a measure of Jewish relief.

### NEO-ZIONISM

But heroic Zionism is back on our minds, even on our agenda, put there as a consequence of the occupation. The status of the West Bank has opened a new chapter of quasi-Zionist discourse. Those who argue most vociferously for its retention—Gush

Emunim and the Land of Israel Movement—couch their claims in attractive and familiar terms: the land of Israel, promised to the Jews by God, has always been the central object of the Zionist revolution. To give up a substantial portion of the land, especially now that it is under Israeli control, is to diminish Zionism; to give up the West Bank entirely is to betray it.

This cult of the land is, of course, reinforced by security considerations in the face of a bloody-minded PLO. But the equation of land with redemption, and of both with "Zionism," is nevertheless a powerfully new ideology, which speaks an old and visceral language to Israelis and to Jews abroad. There is more at play here than some dry deliberation over diplomacy and defense. Begin's victory has made this much obvious. And so it is that hard-line annexationists like General Ariel Sharon call now for a "Zionist" revival. And so it is that ultranationalist and flamboyantly religious groups such as Gush Emunim claim to be reviving Zionism by agitating for settlements on the West Bank, and settling them. Even bitter critics of such policies and practices grudgingly acknowledge the "idealism" and "Zionism" of the settlers, referring to them as the "new *chalutzim*," "heirs" to the authentic tradition. In a society otherwise grown so urbane, so middle class, so normal, it is easy to confuse passion with pioneering. But it is a parody of Zionism to propose that annexationist agitation is an extension of the practical Labor Zionism of old.

*That* Zionism never placed at its center a cozy relationship with God's will. *That* Zionism was secular, pragmatic, preoccupied with the moral and social dilemmas of modern Jews. *This* "Zionism" is based on and encourages religious-mystical attachment to the land, post-Holocaust cynicism, and messianic militarism. For such sentiments, the prestige of Zionist history is just a convenient smokescreen.

It is true that these sentiments were never completely absent from the Zionist movement; they were mainly promoted by the Irgun and Sternist undergrounds after Jabotinsky's death. But those undergrounds were consistently ostracized by the movement's mainstream leadership and were cautiously accepted—and temporarily—by Ben-Gurion and his associates only when the pressures of the Mandate government became intolerable.

The "common front" that was thus forged did not even last beyond the War of Independence. It is a perverse reordering of fact and a disservice to mainstream Zionism to make what was a splinter into the main plank. Gush Emunim and its supporters can lay claim to a historic tradition, but it is not the tradition of the Zionist movement or of the *chalutzim*. Zionism and the *chalutzim* were primarily and explicitly concerned with rebuilding a people, not a land. Historic Eretz Yisrael was a means, not an end in itself. The pioneers needed the land; by and large they earned it, and inflicted a minimum of injury on Arab residents when they appropriated part of it. They never promoted some casuistic "historic right" to the whole of it.

Nor were the leaders of Labor Zionism long indifferent to the practical necessity of seeing the land in conjunction with those Arabs who lived upon it. As early as 1931, at the 17th Zionist Congress, Ben-Gurion made a spirited defense of the principle that the land had to be shared by two peoples. The neo-Zionists who wishfully call the Arab city of Nablus by its ancient Hebrew name, Sh'chem, or display similar affectations do not get us a jot closer to Zionist aspirations. On the contrary, they obscure the fact that historic Zionism held out the promise of a new Jewish civilization, not an old one.

But today there are no mainstream Zionists left to oppose the mystical and militarist appeals that, since 1967, have monopolized Zionist images and prestige. Mainstream Zionism, as I have already suggested, was exhausted by its own success. The Labor Zionist leadership whose third generation is now trying to figure out what it means to be an opposition may have been born to parents knee-deep in Labor Zionist activity, but it is more readily the offspring of the modern Israeli army and state bureaucracy. For them, the kibbutzim and moshavim look like farms, the Histadrut looks like a trade union, and the Hebrew University looks merely pompous. These perceptions are sensible and even useful: Israel has outgrown the Zionists' awesome sense of history, and Israelis, like their Arab neighbors, must now come to terms with the fruit of the Zionist revolution.

But since the terms of the old Zionist debates are no longer thought relevant, then the vocabulary for the new Zionist debate is, sadly, fixed by the new Zionists. Men like Peres and Rabin feel that it would be impolitic openly to abandon Zionist professions, even though they have long since transcended Zionist practices. But when it comes to making sense out of these professions, the leaders of Labor Zionism end up debating the issues raised by their historic opposition, now the government: how to give up as little of the West Bank as possible; how to appease but not integrate the huge minority of Israeli Arabs; how to keep diaspora Jews in line. And when they propose a more pragmatic approach to, say, the occupied territories, they appear to be suffering a failure of nerve. Is it not ever so much bolder, more visionary, even more authentic, to speak of *liberated* territories?

Moreover, the Labor Party leadership cannot very well lay claim to a different Zionist tradition when it was that very tradition over whose dismantling it so comfortably presided for so long. They preferred economic expansion to socialist planning; coalition politics to constitutional reform; religious concessions to Kulturkampf; bureaucratic regulation to voluntaristic expression. Perhaps they had no choice, but the consequence is that severe class divisions now tear at Israel's social fabric and the inflated Orthodox bureaucracy has found new champions. Even more unfortunately, the traditional policy of Labor Zionism toward Palestinian Arabs was greatly subverted after 1967. That policy—partition—was the outgrowth of a commitment to a Jewish society based on Jewish labor. But now, of course, over 100,000 West Bank Arabs work in the Israeli economy—virtually all in industrial and construction jobs—so that there has come to be a substantial economic interest in retaining the present arrangement. Partition today (read "return of the territories") would involve "return" of a critical element of Israel's labor force.

So the Labor Zionists cannot have much to say about old-fashioned Zionism. It would be hypocritical of them to praise it, and they lack the courage to bury it. Instead, they allow the Likud and Gush Emunim to redefine it, and the "Zionist" debate comes to be about solidarity vs. subversion, land vs. cowardice, Judaism vs. apostasy.

There is also a more subliminal origin to our current Zionist malaise. The battles of the Six-Day War ended with Jewish control of sites so ancient and so powerfully symbolic that strident and atavistic redefinitions of Zionism became virtually irresistible. This was a new problem for Israel, but as far back as 1881 the Zionists had expressed their apprehensions regarding the "spiritual traps" of Eretz Yisrael, regarding the very atmosphere of the country and the permeation of that atmosphere by atavistic memory. The apprehensions were well grounded: we have finally reached the time when the only serious "Zionists" are those who view the redemption of the land as a prelude to some millennium, when the only plausible Zionism is one that sets goals inherently beyond its reach. The vast majority of Israelis are secularists and remain moderate and open-minded about the status of the occupied territories. But that majority has long since lost the ability to make its case in Zionist terms. It thus becomes easy to represent it as flaccid, played out, purposeless. Begin, Sharon, and Zevulun Hammer will give us all a last fling at "Zionism"; we shall not be better for the experience.

The images of Zionism today have been appropriated by a resilient and dangerous dogma that Zionism had historically repudiated. The traditional elite of Israel is either unwilling or unable to refute this dogma. Is it not, however, time to acknowledge openly that for Western Jews, at least, Zionism was a revolution with coherent goals that have been substantially achieved, and to insist that the present debate be about what it is in fact about—annexation, peace, decency, security—and not about Zionist authenticity?

## POST-ZIONISM

Jews are, after all, living in an uncertain, post-Zionist age. Yet Zionist slogans, ideas, and symbols are fetters on our current possibilities. The Arab world, for example, must be made to admit that a vital Jewish nation in Israel *already* exists and is an end in itself. But it is difficult to persuade the Arabs of this if we have not yet persuaded ourselves. We cannot expect the Arab world to approve of historic Zionism any more than we can expect any Jew to denounce it. But the argument today is no longer an argument about historic Zionism. It is not an argument about the justice of the Jewish coming; it is an argument about the Jewish staying. It is an argument not about ideology fulfilled, but about genocide contemplated. Israel is a sovereign nation, not a movement, and it is time for that sovereign nation to put aside dogmatic and clearly obsolete rhetoric and to deal with more urgent matters: drawing final borders, developing the economy, writing a constitution. These priorities are not put forward for the sake of wooing Arabs—what do Khaled or Sadat care for moderation or democracy?—but for the sake of Israelis, who deserve something better than interminable territorial and constitutional confusion.

Moreover, if neo-Zionist ideas and rhetoric are persistently employed to justify the occupation of the West Bank *in principle* —that is, apart from legitimate security requirements, in the name of some higher truth—the consequences could be diplomatically disastrous. For if Jews inside and outside Israel persist in stressing the view that Israel's borders are not yet final because the Zionist revolution is not yet over, they will squander twenty-five years of international recognition of the 1948 borders. The neo-Zionists, including Likud's leadership, argue that they cannot renounce their claim to Hebron without renouncing their claim to Tel Aviv. "If we are usurpers in the West Bank, then we are usurpers in Tel Aviv, for the justification for our being anywhere in the Holy Land is our justification for being everywhere in it." But Israel's democratic supporters are not likely to be impressed with God's promises. They may well derive a very different conclusion from that which is intended: indeed, they may say, the right is no different in the one place than in the other, and it is no right at all. The same logic that holds that "because Tel Aviv, therefore Hebron" can readily be turned inside out and made to read "because no Hebron, therefore no Tel Aviv"—or, more likely, "no Nazareth."

Nor is it only the diplomatic community that would be reassured by a recognition that Zionism has long since achieved its fundamental goals, and that, therefore, the future of the West Bank should be determined on the basis of security and diplomatic considerations alone. Israelis themselves should be reassured that if a way can be found to end the occupation consistent with Israel's security requirements, withdrawal from the West Bank will involve no repudiation of Zionist principle. The spectacle of Western secular Jews now becoming fundamentalist neo-Zionists is not ludicrous; it is dangerous. It is not clear that Israel owes Western Jews anything; it is certain that it does not owe them the West Bank. Such Jews who choose to live in the Jewish state will not want to do so in order to make their homes in Hebron. Israel is entitled to bargain with the Arabs on the basis of its own social priorities and on the basis of what Israel is, not on the basis of what some right-wing activists, inside and outside the government, insist it has still to become.

# You Can't Go
# Home Again

---

If Napoleon wins, the better for the Jews; if he loses, the
better for Judaism.

— Scheneur Zalman of Lyadi (1804)

*November 1977*

American Jews will be disturbed by Hillel Halkin's articulate
and nervous "letters" from Israel. A former American himself,
Halkin prophesies that "Jewish life in the [American] diaspora
is doomed." He believes that "such life has a possible future only
in an autonomous or politically sovereign Jewish community
living in its own land, that is, in the state of Israel."

We notice immediately that Halkin is ascribing only a "possible
future" to Israel, not a very optimistic statement in view of his
otherwise glad tidings for the doomed. He tells us that his mis-
givings are the product of the Yom Kippur War, which "frightened the country with a glimpse of its own mortality." What
Halkin would probably not concede is that his very determination to contrive some plausible, tough-minded version of Zionism
for American Jews derives similarly from this war's aftermath —
when most Israelis were anxiously counting their dead, their
enemies, and their leaders' corrupt mistakes. But Halkin's barely

A review of Hillel Halkin, *Letters to an American Jewish Friend: A Zionist's Polemic*
(Philadelphia: Jewish Publication Society of America, 1977).

repressed and typical anxieties aside, his arguments are succinct, intriguing, and deserve the serious attention they have already commanded.*

Since Jewish life is fated to vanish in American and not — or not necessarily — in Israel, Halkin's argument continues, any American Jew "who is committed to his Jewishness" ought to emigrate to the Jewish state. Those remaining behind will lack endurance and "authenticity," and they should realize that they are fossils of historic forces beyond their control.

To anyone modestly acquainted with classical Zionism, Halkin's polemic has a familiar ring to it, one that will nevertheless be jolting to most American Jews. For all their professions of "Zionism" during recent years, American Jews have been more inclined to ask searching questions of gentiles than of themselves. American Jews' daydreams are still crowded with images of the Final Solution, the more intense for the ease with which they have been reassigned to the Israeli-Arab conflict since 1948. Here, ostensibly, are still the genocidal threats to Jews. The accusations by the enemy of Jewish moral failings seem once again inspired by anti-Semitism. And here, once more, is the prospect of Western appeasement, preceded by diplomatic ostracism. "Hitler never died," I was told as a child, "but swam to Egypt and became *nasser* [wet]."

Such cheerless puns do justice neither to Israel's ability to determine its fate nor to the complexity of Arab enmity. But they do betray the American Jew's strangely enervating conviction that, after Auschwitz, after *Exodus*, being a Jew requires little more than a sense of oneself as victim in the goy's indecent world and a corresponding sense of Jewish solidarity to survive it. "Survival" itself seems to have become less the self-evident objective of a vital community than the binding neurosis of an otherwise disintegrating one.† Philip Roth, whose renderings of

*See Robert Alter's essay in *Commentary*, August 1977, and Ruth R. Wisse's review in *Moment*, September 1977.

†As a recent United Jewish Appeal poster put it: ". . . as Jews we stand alone . . . if we are to survive, we must stand as one . . . the rest of the world is anxious to forget [injustice to Jews]. Hold on to it. . . . We are one." (*Canadian Jewish News*, September 23, 1977.)

American Jews have been much maligned, has warned that most of his critics are so preoccupied with the dilemma of the Jewish victim that they are embarrassed by Jews who confess to their merely human wants or, worse, who in trying to satisfy them display aggressiveness toward other Jews.*

Halkin is no admirer of Philip Roth, but he certainly shares Roth's intuition that a great many American Jews are trying, and failing, to live on a kind of moralistic spite now that the more resilient bonds of language, faith, and folk culture have been gradually dissolving during four generations. However willingly most American Jews profess their mutual solidarity, or rally to Israel's and their own defense, Halkin recognizes that their practice of Jewish culture is, "to be kind, not great: a smattering of Yiddish or Hebrew remembered from childhood, a nostalgia for a parental home where Jewish customs were still kept, the occasional observance of an isolated Jewish ritual, the exclusion of nonkosher foods from an otherwise nonkosher kitchen, a genuine identification with the Jewish people combined with a genuine ignorance of its past history and present condition."

In this light, Halkin implies, American "Zionism" is merely a consoling (and vicarious) celebration of Jewish power. More directly, it is a chance to work off some of the "residual guilt" that sinks so many American Jews as they contemplate the terrors they have themselves been regularly spared, and the tradition that other Jews have suffered for and that they have let slip through their fingers nevertheless. It is this advanced assimilation, not physical violence, that seems to be on Halkin's mind when he proposes that American Jews are doomed.

He also makes an ingenious case for the imminent decline of Jewish political influence in America—a decline resulting from a falling birthrate, intermarriage, the steady abandonment of northeastern urban centers where Jewish votes were hitherto concentrated, and so on. He also speculates about the demoralization of Jewish leaders who will soon have to preside over a community that is increasingly divided by American diplomatic pressure on Israel and, more urgently, that will progressively

---

*See Roth's essays on American Jewish self-images in *Reading Myself and Others* (New York: Farrar, Straus and Giroux, 1975).

lose interest in existing Jewish cultural and social institutions. He sees these stresses precipitating a kind of "crash." But, to his credit, Halkin is aware that it is precisely their loss of interest in Jewish life that will erode the Jews' political power, not vice versa. So one must first understand that diaspora Judaism is wearing thin if one is to appreciate the loss of political élan among diaspora Jews.

At this point Halkin proves himself a most faithful and persuasive disciple of classical Zionism, echoing the views stated in 1897 by Achad Ha'am, the founder of cultural Zionism.* Halkin recalls that the political emancipation of Jews in "enlightened" Western societies posed a more serious threat to the traditional culture of the Torah than any posed by Christ's avengers during the Middle Ages:

> As religious belief and identification waned among the native populations in whose midst the Jew lived, so it declined as well among the Jews, who were increasingly forced to ask themselves ... in what sense were they still to accept the hardship of being a Jew at all? At the same time, ceasing to be Jewish ... became an easier and less painful step to take since there were now, especially in the large urban centers of Europe and America, secular gentile societies ... which the assimilating Jew could join without having to feel a traitor to his ancestral past.

So it was that most Jewish immigrants to, say, Berlin, Vienna, Paris, and London throughout the nineteenth century—and to New York at the onset of the twentieth—made for the "neutral" ground of their hosts' secular and liberal nationalism.† This is what Achad Ha'am had in mind when he wrote about "Judaism coming out of the Ghetto also" and when he argued that the old defenses of Jewish life were "overturned" by those modern societies whose political freedoms and scientific gifts were bestowed only on those Jews who would first adopt the languages and habits of Western nationals.

---

*See his essay "The Jewish State and the Jewish Problem," in a collection of Achad Ha'am's most perceptive essays, *Ten Essays on Zionism and Judaism*, part of a new series on modern Jewish thought. (Leon Simon, ed., Arno Press, 1973.)
†See especially Michael Marrus, *The Politics of Assimilation* (Oxford: Clarendon, 1971).

Achad Ha'am—and Halkin, who writes in his shadow—cherished Zionism as the saving movement of newly secularist Jews who, though hankering after "modernity," were loath to secure it at so high a cost to their own distinctive and still flourishing Jewish culture. If the prospect for Jewish life had become bleak in the post-Enlightenment world, caught as it was (in Halkin's phrase) between "the Scylla of assimilation and the Charybdis of anti-Semitism," then the Jews must fully transform themselves into a separate, secular nation, living in its ancient homeland. There the Jews' traditional religious symbols and their old folk culture would have counterparts in a new and modern social life; there confident, rooted writers could ask radical questions in Hebrew.

So much for Halkin's impressive reproduction of the Zionists' view of history. What is lacking, however, is the Zionists' feeling for politics. Achad Ha'am, for example, emphasized that the Jews for whom Zionism was a real alternative were not some abstract world "people" but a vigorous and immanently national community in the East European Pale of Settlement. These were the four to five million Jews who spoke and wrote Yiddish and Hebrew, who were turning in ever-increasing numbers to their own "national" (literary, cultural, and political) vanguard movements such as Hibat Zion and the Labor Bund and away from the rabbis. They did so, moreover, in lively new centers of Enlightenment Judaism such as Odessa, where Achad Ha'am himself edited the leading Hebrew journal *Hashiloah*. These cities, on the other hand, were increasingly ominous places for the Jewish merchants, small tradesmen, and their masses of dependent workers, who were being hard pressed by the industrialization policies, and the anti-Semitism, of the czarist bureaucracy.*

Achad Ha'am denied that Zionism would be a serious option for his so-called brothers in Western Europe. Hence his contempt for Theodor Herzl's melodramatic and predictably ephemeral leadership. The assimilating Jews of Germany, France, etc., had already lost the cultural fluency, and standards, upon which the Zionist revolution would have to be grounded. Of course,

---

*See Ezra Mendelsohn, *Class Struggle in the Pale* (Cambridge, 1970), and David Vital's *The Origins of Zionism* (Oxford, 1976).

Hitler eventually made reluctant Zionists out of many assimilated Western Jews. But we should not be misled by their tragic
choices; Anne Frank left behind pinups of Shirley Temple and
Ray Milland when the Gestapo finally took her. If, in spite of
the Holocaust, Halkin is convinced that assimilation is politically
possible in America — and he is — he should also have concluded
that his own Zionist exhortations to American Jews would fail.
His weighty evidence for the eventual collapse of Jewish life in
America — so reminiscent of Achad Ha'am's survey of Jewish
life in France and Germany* — is also evidence that few American Jews will even read his book, let alone move to Israel.

What would such unlikely Jews achieve for themselves by moving? Halkin's rejoinder is that they will participate in "Jewish
survival." But, surely, he is begging the question: Jews will survive for the sake of being Jewish; they will not be Jewish for the
sake of "survival." And being Jewish, at least in the sense Halkin
admires, means being in command of the many perspectives,
practices, and habits that make up a seriously Jewish way of life,
a life that, as Halkin knows, most American Jews have abandoned.

Halkin has apparently been confused by the guilty lip service
American Jews earnestly pay to the importance of "Jewish survival." It is as if he need only prove that Jewish life in America
will eventually disappear for significant numbers of American
Jews to react by moving to Israel as Zionists. Perhaps he has
forgotten that the conspicuous declarations by many Jews of
concern for "survival," for "solidarity," are less resistance to assimilation than a symptom of it.

Halkin plays on American Jewish guilt more shrewdly, with his
evocative and undeniably moving account of life in contemporary Israel: he describes the economic austerity, the rounds of
reserve duty, the terrorism, and the political uncertainty. If
American Jews will not be persuaded that they need Zionist ideas,
at least, Halkin supposes, they can be made to understand that
Israelis desperately need American Jewish recruits. The country

*See Achad Ha'am's essay "Slavery in Freedom," in *Selected Essays*, Leon Simon,
ed. (New York: Atheneum, 1970).

is at war—a terrible, inescapable war—and American Jews dare not allow Israelis to carry the burdens alone.

Quite apart from the serious objections one might raise with respect to Halkin's argument that war with the Arab world is inevitable, I cannot see what his alternately inspiring and depressing anecdotes can achieve other than to speed up the pace of American Jewish breast-beating. How, after all, can even what he calls "hard-core"* American Jews be expected to help beyond writing checks and backing their lobbies in Washington? Moving to Israel is not like joining the Jewish Defense League. Unless one grows up, as Halkin did, in a home steeped in Hebraic tradition, moving to Israel requires a leap into a radically new way of life. It means struggling three years with the mysteries of a new daily newspaper, learning a new politics and new customs, and sending one's children off to schools that turn them into strangers. Such transitions are not impossible, of course; American Jewish parents and grandparents were immigrants too. But for all his thoughtfulness, Halkin avoids the most obvious problem for anyone with old-fashioned Zionist aspirations: that Israel has by now become such a complicated and molded society that it can hardly accommodate the "self-determination" of American Jews. Of the few thousand Americans who have tried to "ascend" to Zion since 1967, over 70 percent have returned—not because Israel is less than a good country but because they have evidently decided not to be reborn.

The Zionism that Halkin celebrates once offered Yiddish- and Hebrew-speaking youths from the Pale the chance to escape the pogroms and fill up the empty spaces of Palestine with their ambitions. The "Zionism" of today offers English-speaking (Bellow-reading, Dylan-humming, Wheaties-eating, world-hopping) American Jews the chance to be "good material" for Israel's society and good soldiers in Israel's army. Early in his book, Halkin remarks that "the Zionist movement always had little taste

---

*Halkin supposes that out of five million Jews in America, only about one million are "hard-core" Jews who put Judaism—its practices, sources, and community institutions—at the center of their lives. These, by the way, are mainly Orthodox Jews who would, presumably, not need the Zionism of Achad Ha'am, or who would resent Israel's incipient secularism, something Halkin does not consider.

for the tragic antithesis latent in its own success." One such tragedy has been the crumbling of the cultural unity that once characterized the Jewish people in the Pale. As the fictitious "American friend" to whom Halkin's book is addressed tries to tell him (and it is curious how often his answers evade the strongest questions raised by his fictitious foil), Israelis and American Jews are different. If the latter are to be Zionists, they must also be self-denying; and this is not the same as having moral excellence.

But Halkin resists the evident differences between Israelis and American Jews. He clouds our perceptions of their respective ways of life with novel, and bad, arguments. To take his second point first, Halkin tries to convince us that Israel has no secular Jewish culture of its own as yet, a conclusion that, if it were true, might make the prospect for American Jews in Israel considerably brighter. If Israel had no real culture to master, then American Jewish newcomers would presumably have substantial room to work out their own ambitions.

To make his case, however, Halkin relies on a triple confusion. First he presumes that there will eventually develop in Israel some ideal, organic, and embracing folk culture, the absence of which he now regrets. He then surmises that, until such time as this appears, Israel will have "no culture" at all. Finally, he blames its absence on the cultural pluralism that has marked Israeli life as it has grown more sophisticated, less dominated by the institutions and practices of Labor Zionism, and as it has been made more fractious by the antagonisms between the Sephardic immigrants and the old Ashkenazi pioneers.

Some of Halkin's insights into Israel's cultural history are brilliant. He is right, for example, that many esoteric folkways of immigrants from Islamic lands were lost during Ben-Gurion's misguided campaigns to achieve a cultural consensus by fiat in the 1950s and 1960s. He is also right that Labor's constituents put their own fragile and pristine culture under great strain in this failed attempt to integrate the newcomers. The result has been, for both groups, an often thoughtless emulation of Western bourgeois standards in a country that cannot afford them, especially by those in the new middle class.

But Halkin's reasons for recounting this convincing history

are simply wrong. Those who would now join him in his quest for a Jewish (or any other) folk culture will be chasing the past—and, thank goodness, will also be few and far between. If Halkin wants to live in an Israel that will be as "Jewish" as the *mir* is "Russian," as the *souk* is "Arab," this is his affair; some of us would find the prospect stifling. (Those who like Israeli rock music, as I do, would be as remote from Halkin's idea of folk culture as those who like the music of Stravinsky.)

But the absence of a single, thick Israeli folk culture is obviously not the same as "no culture." Israel's pluralism is a mark of its maturity, not of its prolonged infancy. As a matter of fact, this is precisely the conclusion Halkin might have drawn from his own analysis of Israel's cultural history. The ethos of Labor Zionism—its music, dress, moral heroes, literary styles—has been superseded by an urbane eclecticism drawing on Sephardic, Orthodox, and Western sources as well. Yet the "language and the land," Halkin knows, are still Jewish, still vital, and still open to new possibilities. Israel's cosmopolitan style of life is not as cozy as what Halkin, it seems, had in mind when he went there. But its peculiar cultural anarchy is what secular Judaism is all about. I need not add that new immigrants will have all the more difficulty adjusting to Israel because of its confusion.

Halkin's misunderstanding of, or distaste for, secular Judaism in its less fantastic forms leads him to carp at the "inauthenticity" of American Jewish reformers even before he tries to take on Israel's "nonculture." This is Halkin's second fresh point. Why is the "new" American Judaism that one finds on college campuses —secular but often intensely concerned with moral and political issues—"inauthentic" in addition to being so vulnerable to assimilationist pressure? Again, he resorts to good history and bad argument.

Halkin explains, cogently, that non-Orthodox American Jews who have nevertheless retained some positive attitude toward Jewish practice have—like German Jewish reformers in the nineteenth century—tended to reduce Judaism from a total and demanding pattern of life to an *ethical* tradition that can be reconciled to Western civil experience. But such reforms are absurd in principle, Halkin asserts, because "there is and can be no such thing as Jewish ethics." Why? Because "ethics are uni-versal. They deal not with Israelis or Palestinians but with men as men; as such there can be no more a Jewish ethics than a Moslem or Navajo ethics, which is why there is always a potential tension . . . between owing one's allegiance to a particular tribe, people, or nation, and being an ethical human being." This state-ment is so wrong-headed one can only marvel at it.

In the first place it is philosophically unsound. Ethics, at least since Aristotle, have been a conscious *attempt* to set moral stan-dards for the whole human species. But we generally acknowl-edge the existence of Jewish ethics or Navajo ethics, liberal ethics and socialist ethics, because we perceive no species-wide agree-ment about what a human being is. Moreover, different cultures will disagree about a man's needs, endowments, and his corre-sponding social claims. Cannot Jews have some unique things to say about right thinking, right living, and cannot American Jews distinguish themselves, however subtly, from other American citizens by saying them? Of course they can, and will, at least until they disappear. It is all the more galling that Halkin should take so unwarranted a slap at this last face of American Judaism when, less than forty pages later, he shows very eloquently how Jewish ethics would differ from that of the so-called American counterculture.

Halkin's implication that loyalty to one's people or "tribe" is bound to contradict one's ethical obligations is not only wrong but dangerous. Defense of the particular society through which one develops one's capacities — one's language, ethics, aesthetics — may itself be ethically warranted; this is why today most of us acknowledge claims to national self-determination. Of course, one may have to decide on conflicting ethical priorities, as in war. But a man who thinks he must defend his society without regard to his own sense of ethics — as if generals ever fail to point out the "justice" of their cause — is losing himself in love. Halkin's formula cannot be right; but it does inadvertently pro-vide a refuge for scoundrels.

Halkin's denial of "Jewish ethics" is revealing apart from its failures of logic. For his identification of Jewish interests with some form of tribal loyalty, along with his contention that the

Israelis are a "community of faith" whose interests may clash with the self-evident ethics of humanity, leaves one doubting whether Halkin knows how, or wants, to be a secular Jew at all. In fact, he has reproduced, albeit without Jehovah, the fundamentalist belief of some Orthodox Jews that ethics are natural laws that, as Maimonides claimed, all men would eventually promulgate for themselves had they not been revealed at Sinai. The Jews, in this view, are set apart from a potentially righteous mankind by their keeping of God's special and finally inscrutable commandments to them. No wonder Halkin dismisses as "inauthentic" any Jew who will not view the tradition as a "divine trust." (He is so oblivious to his own syncretism, by the way, that he does not even bother to use quotation marks for such religious categories.)

Halkin's shuttle between classical, secular Zionism (the cultural consequences of which he dislikes) and Orthodox Judaism (the God of which he rejected in his youth) would be more poignant, and less annoying, if it did not finally carry him into the camp of the "scripture hawks," who now resist any plan to end Israel's occupation of the West Bank for "historic" reasons irrespective of the state's security requirements. Although his "Zionism" pretends to promote a revolutionary, secular Jewish culture, Halkin's wants at the same time to accommodate notions such as "holy land" and "promised land," which, he does not see, subvert such a culture. The result is an ideological mélange that may well persuade him and many other Israelis that their national rights in Palestine derive from God's will and not from the UN's recognition of their modern self-determination. Such rhetoric may also convince them that they will betray "Zionism" if they agree to redivide sovereignty in the "promised land."

Halkin, in fact, has shown that he can himself fall into his own intellectual trap. In an article in *Commentary*, he complains that if Jews do not have rights in such West Bank Arab towns as Nablus or Jenin, he "is not sure" what rights they have to Tel Aviv and Haifa. He cannot imagine a Jewish state "from which the heartland of Jewish historical experience" has been excluded. Unfortunately for Halkin, his new and syncretic "Zionism" has blinded him to the elementary importance of Zionist history. The new heartland of "Jewish historical experience" is obviously in Tel Aviv, Haifa, and the Valley of Jezreel, not in Arab cities built on ancient Jewish sites. How can Israelis expect Arabs to recognize the modern Jewish state if they will not do so themselves?

Still, I suspect that Halkin's is a self-inflicted blindness motivated, as I suggested at the outset of this review, by the trauma of Yom Kippur 1973. If Halkin were to admit that Zionism is merely what it was to Achad Ha'am, Weizmann, and Ben-Gurion—a cultural revolution and political refuge for Jews who needed both—he would also have to admit that Jews are living in a post-Zionist age. With the challenges of war still heavy on his mind, this conclusion could be understandably painful to him.

Israelis are anxious about their enemies and the condition of their civil life—about their collective durability—and want badly to believe that new waves of Jewish immigrants from America will not only help to resolve their economic, political, and military problems but give their enormous sacrifices a special meaning. They want Zionism to be still magnetic, still heroic, though it is thirty years since their state's founding and thirty-five years since Hitler murdered the large remnants of Zionism's natural constituency in Eastern Europe.

Israelis want immigrants and are afraid to abandon the word —Zionism—that they think is their major draw. To give this word meaning, however, is no longer a simple matter. This is why so many sensitive and overtly secularist young Israelis like Halkin are tempted to promote the only Zionism that, it must seem to them, cannot be made obsolete by history. This is the messianic and righteously chauvinist "Zionism" of Gush Emunim and Menachem Begin, which sets itself goals inherently beyond the reach of politics; a "Zionism" that promises God's redemption and anoints its faithful with the prestige of pioneering martyrs.*

It is convenient for the new "Zionists" that their language is

---

*Menachem Begin's popularity among the young—whose sense of history is most likely to be acquired at second hand—is still astounding. *Ha'aretz* (October 3) reported a poll in which Begin was given a high rating by 70 percent of young Israelis, even after his unsatisfactory performance in Washington and his controversial (some say politically motivated) pardon of a bank embezzler with connections to Gush Emunim.

one that a good many American Jews can understand — namely the "hard-core" Jews Halkin refers to, though they are not potential immigrants. And it is the more convenient that their squatter settlements on the West Bank — now endorsed by the government itself — appear as a manifest demonstration of their integrity and "realism" just when the more moderate voices of the Labor movement have discredited themselves in corrupt administrations. Only Carter's peace initiatives seem inconvenient.

The recent Soviet-American communiqué is unprecedented in that both superpowers, supported by several Arab states, have jointly agreed that Israel can be expected to negotiate not merely to end the state of war but for "normal peaceful relations" and on the basis of "sovereignty, mutual recognition, territorial integrity, and political independence." The Israeli government cannot be reckless in pursuing these objectives. It would be right — as the Brookings Institution report supported by the Carter administration concedes — to demand open borders, formal treaties, and convincing demilitarization of evacuated territories. Still, it would be ironic if a "Zionist" revival now became an obstacle to the progress of these negotiations. When learning from history, Halkin might have considered that those Frenchmen who would not, by 1848, give up on the "revolution" helped clear the field for Louis Napoleon.

# The Arts in Israel:
# Rebirth

*May 1979*

There has been more, and less, to Israel's cultural patrimony than seems congenial to the writers, artists, composers, and critics who are currently revamping it. More collective purpose, less honest virtuosity. This paradox is not unlikely considering the purpose. Israel's cultural life did not exist one hundred years ago. It was created by the Hovevei Zion, a loose federation of Hebrew writers and culturalists who began organizing settlement activity in Palestine after 1882, and, more decisively, by the Labor Zionists, socialist pioneers who built the country's political life from their collective agricultural settlements. These forerunners made up the modern Hebrew arts in Mandate Palestine more or less as they went along, usually at odds with their own most intimate details and affinities. They were immigrant revolutionaries, uncertain about how or, more poignantly, whether to be themselves. Although most were the products of Eastern European *Yiddishkeit*—Yiddish and liturgical Hebrew were their mother tongues—they arrived in their "Land of Israel" still pondering the dreams and aesthetic sensibilities they had acquired in Odessa, Bialystok, Budapest: cities that had taught them to be modern in Russian, Polish, German.

These people were, moreover, overwhelmed by common struggle. They delighted in that folk culture that celebrated their politics but, in retrospect, could hardly have been expected to survive them. Theirs was a pioneering culture, bigger than its constituents and enjoining their individual discipline for the sake of the progressing social effort. One was expected to be *be'seder*: restrained and OK. So, as individuals, the pioneering Zionists emptied few of their private tensions into the public realm. Their cultural products — songs, plays, stories, pictures — now seem correspondingly empty, especially to the newer intellectual vanguard of this little country, which has subsequently grown so urbane, plural, and bourgeois.

The reticence of Israel's first cultural innovators cannot, however, be blamed on Zionist designs. The willful young Jews who got the Jews' colonizing enterprise going at the turn of this century held their writers and other artists in high esteem as a matter of principle. Achad Ha'am — a pen name for Asher Ginzberg, the Zionists' most articulate mentor and editor of *Hashiloah*, the most important Hebrew journal of the day — pleaded for the development of a new Hebrew culture — in magazines, journals, art schools, universities, collective agrarian settlements. He did not expect this to be mere embellishment for the presumably more urgent rescue operation that his failed rival, Theodor Herzl, was proposing but, rather, the very point of the Zionists' exercise.

Rescue — which had anyway been beside the point so long as American immigration laws remained liberal — seemed less essential to most early Zionists than the working of a novel Jewish culture in the pores of Palestine. They hoped for one that would cope more successfully with the modern world than could the traditional Eastern European Jewish orthodoxy into which they had been born. The practice of Halacha — the tight web of culture deriving from Talmudic law — and the binding version of God that this practice had engendered now appeared to these early Zionists to have been superseded by scientific method and secularist ideals. Zionist construction, they supposed, would provide their incipient Jewish nation with a chance to be modern and civil in their own language, their own land, in touch with their own history.

Their pedigree in such "cultural Zionism" explains a good deal of the Labor Zionists', and then the Israelis', consistent — even astounding — promotion of their own culture-makers over the years. Three million Israeli Jews still read, per capita, more books, magazines, and newspapers than any other society in the Western world. They support scores of galleries and three lively art museums. One of these, the Israel Museum in Jerusalem, has consciously undertaken to be the leaven for Israeli plastic art (and, according to critics of its senior curator, Yona Fischer, the too-high-minded conscience of it). Israelis also support two philharmonic orchestras—the Israel Philharmonic is, by any standards, one of the best—and several chamber orchestras and groups. They enjoy five established theater companies, including the prestigious Habima, and four dance companies: the Israel Ballet (classical), Inbal (folk classical), Batsheva, and Bat Dor (both modern). Government agencies, which have at various times supported all these enterprises, now also supply seed money for several commercial film companies. Behind such activities grows a large constituency for the arts in Israel's seven universities and two art schools: institutions built with deliberate vision. The most important ones, the Hebrew University and the Bezalel School of Art, were inspired by Achad Ha'am's polemics and established before he died in 1927.

Still, all this realized enthusiasm for the invention of Hebrew culture has not much diminished the obstacles to inventing it in a manner worthy of the Zionists' original intentions. The impressive quantity of past Israeli culture-making can obscure the fact that much of what was produced—especially in the high arts—was meant to satisfy the imported tastes of Europeanized German and Polish refugees who arrived in Palestine during the 1930s—a group to which I shall presently return. Moreover, the very political ambitiousness of the earlier, more radical Zionists' culturalism was, as I have implied, something of an obstacle to enduring works. So many people were, in the 1930s and '40s, prepared to link arms and dance to cheerful, redundant melodies or to sing—not without self-congratulation—the banal lyrics of the collectivist revolution that their art now seems to have been sacrificed to their élan.

From 1890 on, the earliest Zionist poets and writers—Bialik, Tschernikovsky, and later Agnon—expressed the halting confusions of the Jews' Jewish problem in Europe. But the Labor Zionist settlers, along with city-dwelling fellow travelers like Natan Alterman—the poet and songwriter who was Labor Zionism's poet laureate during its high time in the thirties and forties — expressed mostly the certainties of the Palestinian Jews' socialist and nationalist solutions. Their work, it must be emphasized, broke the most ground in modern Hebrew culture, but it now seems, like the reminiscences of old kibbutzniks, pristine and slightly autistic.

Contemporary Israeli artists, especially after the absurd and murderous Yom Kippur War, know that there are darker, clumsier sides to men — Jews included — than the celebrated virtues of the Golden Age. These artists are similarly wary of the reactionary politics (Alterman, before he died, joined the Whole Land of Israel Movement, which aimed to annex to Israel all the territories later captured in the Six-Day War) that such heroic art engenders. As the writer Amos Elon described it to me, writers associated with the War of Independence midwived the birth of the Jewish state — a state trapped by a language that was suffocating, nearly totalitarian in its corporatism, banality, and sanctimoniousness.

There are, of course, other obstacles to making a Hebrew culture that can stand up to the subtlety of the Western world for which it was first contrived. The traditional Jewish societies of Eastern Europe, which the Zionist pioneers rejected but from which they nevertheless sprang, had had a long history of proscribing idols, of idol-making, and of radical individualism. Plastic art, poetry, and melody-making were not considered ends in themselves by Israelis' grandparents — or, certainly, by their great-grandparents. Young artists and writers (such as Mauricy Gotlieb, I. L. Peretz) were obliged to create their imminently national, hence heretical, culture unschooled by any evolved tradition of their own. Moreover, they had to vie with the fabulous investments — words, music, liturgical decoration — already made in God's personality. At the same time, they were rubbing up against the stifling, loving communitarianism imposed by rabbinic Orthodoxy and gentile prejudice. It had been hard to be a Jew and harder still to be a Jewish artist.

This absence of modern Jewish cultural tradition — an absence the Zionist enterprise was deliberately supposed to end — is still painfully felt by Israeli writers. A. B. Yehoshua, Israel's foremost novelist and writer of short fiction, underlined this point to me by addressing the problem of choosing Hebrew words and phrases for his stories: words and phrases that are neither loaded with extraneous biblical associations nor scented with the ersatz of dictionary makers. His challenge is considerable. Imagine trying to write Latin without sounding like a Roman, a priest, or a prig. Of course, Yehoshua can now go to the fairly normal streets of Tel Aviv and Haifa (Jerusalem is never normal) to find koshered words—words made fit by common use: a refreshing advantage that has not been lost on him. But the people in the street have not been figuring out what they're about in Hebrew for very long. Even without the politics of the old Zionist revolution, they have had to talk much—too much—about grand, national preoccupations. Next to these, individual anguish pales.

The Holocaust. The War of Independence. The forced immigration of Sephardic Jews exceeding the number of Ashkenazi veterans. The Sinai campaign. Arab encirclement. The erosion of socialism. The Six-Day War. The American "diaspora." The conflict between orthodoxy and secularism. Jerusalem. The occupation. The October war. Sadat's promises. American government support. Political scandal. What Israeli writer can ignore problems that weigh on the public's mind like an Alp? What writer of fiction can compete with their theater? More intriguing perhaps: How are Israelis in the street to discover the words to express the subtlety of their individual feelings and perspectives while they are continually assaulted by "historic" events? Israelis' Hebrew, for example, still has only one common word for "sadness"—not because their lives are without trials, but because of the nature of those trials. It is no wonder that Yehoshua's latest novel, *The Lover*, like that of Israel's other most admired author, Amos Oz (*The Hill of Evil Counsel*), seems to surrender to the problems of living out overpowering events.

Yet Yehoshua and Oz, along with other writers such as Yehuda Amichai, Yoram Kaniuk, Dan Ben-Amotz, Avi Cohen, and journalists such as Amos Elon and Amos Kennan, have represented a genuine watershed in Israeli cultural life. Unlike the "Palmach generation" against which they consciously revolted during the 1960s, these established authors do not allow political history to flatten their heroes. On the contrary, they use it as a foil for the ambitions, quirks, contradictions, sexuality, and anxieties of private life. These writers take their place in their language and their land so much for granted that they can attempt to author universal drama—the point of departure, ironically, for good national literature. They represent the new and newer generations of native Israelis who are growing conscious of their own distinctiveness, of their country's unique mode of discourse, of its irrepressible pluralism (since the Sephardic immigrations of the 1950s). These native Israelis are aware, too, of Israel's particular moral and physical climate on the Mediterranean, its proximity to the Arab world, its—let's face it—aloofness from Americans and Europeans of Jewish origin whose "Zionist" professions are treated with tender cynicism.

I have concentrated mainly on the new Israeli literary establishment because it has been responsible for the country's earliest and most comprehensive artistic statements. But the development of an Israeli style by men and women who, in spite of their country's contretemps, are secure in their own power has not been restricted only to letters. Plastic artists, playwrights, and composers have also, increasingly, undertaken to solve very personal artistic problems that, they consciously assume, could not have presented themselves quite the same way in any other country.

This case is most difficult to prove in the plastic arts. Painters, sculptors, and printmakers work in the most cosmopolitan and translatable of media and usually train by rehearsing the methods of schools that are remote in place and time. For example: the still-popular precursors of the Israeli artistic community, if not of Israeli art—Agam, Ardon, Yanko, Rubin, Bergner, and others—all acquired their spiritual loyalties and technical strategies in various European movements well before coming to Mandate Palestine. Israel is an address for them much more than a problem.

Some artists, it is true, became fascinated with the land—with the austere, iridescent quality of its colors, with the elementary humanism of refugee families, with the ultimately quaint routine of pious Jerusalem neighborhoods. The black and white Judean Hills drawings of Anna Ticho epitomize, I think, this self-conscious love affair between immigrant Jewish artists and their exotic new surroundings. But Ticho's celebrated, ostensibly Israeli mysticism has seemed to me most easily deciphered when accompanied by some Brahms. And there has been no dearth of immigrant musicians to play for her.

Since Bronislaw Huberman formed the forerunner of the Israel Philharmonic Orchestra in the late 1930s, Israel's substantial community of *yekkes* (German Jews) and urban Polish refugees of the same era have been able to indulge their appetite for *kultur* (purged, understandably, of Wagner and Richard Strauss). They and their children, along with new immigrants from Russia, constitute a loyal audience for "serious" music in Israel, over which that most righteous (and charismatic) of gentiles, Zubin Mehta, now presides. Israel has also nurtured more than a few virtuosos of its own: Itzhak Perlman, Daniel Barenboim, the young and coming Shlomo Mintz. But this kind of musical genius—even that of Israeli composers such as Partos and Seter—seems to me finally irrelevant to the distinctively Israeli experience. It appears rather to be the conscious, nostalgic reappropriation by European Jews of that Europe which could never have betrayed them: the music that helped to unleash Jewish energies in pursuit of an older, outpaced version of emancipation and enlightenment. The seductions of such music are great, but its following appears not to be growing.

On the other hand, more popular forms of Israeli artistry, made by the living counterparts of Yehoshua's stories, are thriving, particularly within Israel's urban and increasingly integrated middle class. This is a streetwise, personal, skeptical art, implicitly critical of the dissonance between the standard values of common experience—army, job, claustrophobia, traffic, debts—and the lingering Zionist rhetoric echoing within anachronistic political institutions that still run so much of daily life. It is the art of sculptors such as Yigal Tumarkin, painters such as Rafi Lavie and (perhaps the only really talented one so far) surrealist Shmuel Bak. Beyond lies a younger and even more radical group of Abstract Expressionists and Minimalists who seem to resent these other artists' preoccupation with the street: Joshua Neustein, Benni Ephrat, Aviva Uri, Reuven Berman, Tamar Getter, and some even more enigmatic Conceptualist artists whose highly technical works, though hardly classifiable as Israeli per se, seem to express that evasiveness into which so many Israelis would like to escape.

Such fascination with technique among young intellectuals is, arguably, their most radical defiance of a society whose conventional wisdoms appear decreasingly wise but from which the Arab siege precludes open revolt. This trend is by no means confined to the plastic arts: departments of philosophy in all Israeli universities are now making disproportionate room for young, home-grown analytic and linguistic philosophers who seem very pleased to be abandoning the push and pull of political philosophy for the more elegant abstractions of logic and esoteric epistemology.

Such evasions are, however, not plausible for those Israelis — the majority — who are uninitiated into their curious satisfactions. Rather, the pop music, theater, and film that Israelis particularly admire express the contradictions of social transition in the manner of Bak, through surreal images and comedy. This trend is probably most pronounced in the songs of Danny Sanderson and Matti Caspi: cocky, iconoclastic, confessional, raunchy singer-songwriters whose music has, since 1973, eclipsed the more conventional and slightly unctuous folk rock of, say, Chava Alberstein and Arik Einstein. Sanderson — the most remarkable, I think — blends traditional Jewish musical phrases with good-natured slang, social criticism, and soft rock in irresistible concoctions. Sometimes the songs are deadly serious, sometimes satirical, usually heavy in irony and jaded idealism. This is music for smart young people to indulge themselves by — an indulgence that, they know, grows in the shadow of the cybernetic military machine they will soon be required to operate.

In the wake of the brilliant musical synthesis of Sanderson and Caspi has come also a much larger group of Israeli singers and musicians aping American pop culture and commercialism, abetted by the preponderance of American programming on Israeli television. The result is an Israeli schlock pop that is truly exquisite in its unoriginality; the kind of music that can only be sung earnestly by Hebrew youngsters proud of their Oklahoma State University T-shirts. This music, along with straight American rock, has a broad appeal in Israel — as do most things American: for example, Israel's entry in this year's Eurovision Song Contest, "Hallelujah," seems destined to become the regional theme song for Coca-Cola. But I suspect that this music excites no very deep loyalties among young Israeli WASPs (white Ashkenazi sabras with *proteksia* [connections]): certainly no such loyalties as those that attend Sanderson and Caspi and more veteran performers such as smooth and chunky Yehoram Gaon—the uncrowned king of the Sephardic community—or Naomi Shemer, the durable folk-singing spokesman for Six-Day War sensibilities.

Surrealism is particularly marked also in Israeli comedy, led by the wicked satire of the Gashash Hachiver trio. Sephardic Jewish immigrants to Israel—much like the Jewish immigrants to America at the turn of the century—learned about the foibles and hypocrisies of existing political elites much more thoroughly than the children of the establishment ever could. Gashash Hachiver has been airing these discoveries to the sons and daughters of both ethnic communities for many years with remarkable wit and versatility. The trio has become a pillar of the new Israel and is expected to entertain on television even between reports of national election results. Although they have no real counterparts in the "nicer," old European Israel, the *shlemiel* satire of Shakie Ofer, Gadi Yagil, and, more recently, Dubi Gal carry on a long Eastern European tradition here.

One must be tempted to account for the abundance of comedy-making in Israel in psychoanalytic terms. Israeli Jews, after all, have had a lot to cope with. But the content of Israeli comedy betrays much more than some conspicuous defense reflex. It is, I believe, the most striking evidence for the self-critical and sincere humanism of the Israeli public. Within Israeli satire gestates the political sophistication, realism, and decency of a people that often seems so much more full of guile than its government.

A much more savage form of this satire can be found in the idiosyncratic plays of Chanoch Levin, whose most recent work, *The Rubber* [Condom] *Merchants*, is being produced this season by the Habima theater. An earlier play, *Queen of Baths*, which spoofed what Levin considered to be the growing militarism in Israeli political culture, caused so much outrage in the late 1960s that it was finally closed. But theatergoers now seem to be getting used to him. In fact, it is not his politics that make Levin an interesting cultural phenomenon so much as his highly personal exposure of himself. Even more than Yehoshua and Oz, Levin wants you to know that he thinks it is permissible for Israelis to wash the dirtiest, most semen-stained linen in public. He is a breaker of taboos, much as Philip Roth has been for American Jews: a product of his generation's defiant confidence in itself.

So is director Danny Wachsman, whose new film, *Transit*, promises to revolutionize Israeli filmmaking. The premise of *Transit* is novel: a German-Jewish refugee decides, after twenty years in Israel, that he wants to go back to Berlin; but instead he spends a week with a local madman in a Jerusalem hotel. This film will be very different from the lightweight slapstick and soap opera fare that has hitherto dominated the Israeli industry. Wachsman wants to deliver that shock of honesty which announces the tense integrity of Israeli life—and he seems likely to succeed.

Israel, the society like the state, was the product of ingenious and tragic politics. But those who are working out its self-accounting, self-advertising culture now know their country to be not a cause but a home. Like all social attitudes in Israel, this one is not without important political ramifications. Almost every artist and writer in the country's fresh, secular culture is a dove of varying intensity, anxious to exchange land for peace and to settle with the Palestinians on the basis of mutual recognition. This should come as no real surprise. It is easier to make peace with someone who would know what to do with it.

# Breaking Faith:
## *Commentary* and American Jews

*Spring 1981*

In 1963, the young editor of *Commentary*, Norman Podhoretz, astonished his readers by appealing for "the wholesale merging of the races in the United States"—ending racism through "miscegenation." His article, "My Negro Problem—and Ours," seemed the more remarkable since, to secure the premise that too much hatred attaches to color for civil integration ever to succeed, Podhoretz confessed to the fear, envy, and contempt with which he had grown up in Brooklyn under the siege of "Negro gangs." Those streets still seemed to him world-historical ground:

> There is a fight, they win, and we retreat, half whimpering, half with bravado. My first nauseating experience with cowardice. And my first appalled realization that there are people in the world who do not seem to be afraid of anything, who act as though they have nothing to lose.

In retreat with him were other young American Jews, barely digesting their parents' veiled reports of catastrophe abroad and also faring badly against the fascinating brutes on the block. His own packs, or so Podhoretz insisted, could not be ruthless to the end. But Negroes would play hooky, swallow candy, and hit you in the face; Italians had surrendered only somewhat less to the state of nature.

Such imaginings of Jews and gentiles may have been gleaned

more from the new literary life—from, say, Saul Bellow's novels
—than from memory: our own Louis Lepke, "Bugsy" Siegel,
and "Gurrah" Shapiro are not so easy to forget. Nevertheless,
Podhoretz seemed not to think his recollections just embellish-
ments of some firmer cultural identity: his primal identity as a
Jew meant getting pushed around.

In fact, Podhoretz's "Negro problem" now seems most revealing when viewed as but a complication of "our" Jewish one,
of our lack of positive reasons for Judaism's survival, which is
something he wanted to concede in the article despite his old
gang's defiance: "In thinking about the Jews, I have often wondered whether their survival as a distinct group was worth the
hair on the head of a single infant."

Why survive indeed if, say, the Jews' "dark and surly" foils
took his advice, married whites—among whom, as a matter of
"duty," Podhoretz refused to exclude his own children—and
melted into the pot? Could the Jews then claim to be holding
back just to nurse the discontents of civility? Besides, ruthlessness
could not have seemed all that unkosher to the "precocious"
writer who, in *Making It* just four years later, announced that
the world's choices resolved into giving orders or taking them,
grasping for money or having none, getting fame or dying in
obscurity. Podhoretz was understandably vexed: "I think I know
why the Jews once wished to survive (though I am less certain
as to why we still do): they not only believed that God had given
them no choice, but were tied to a memory of past glory and
a dream of imminent redemption." He thought it unnecessary
to add that his own cohorts are not bound in this way. They
are now afflicted with choices, not the least of them how—or
whether—to make something out of Jewish origins once in Man-
hattan, away from the Manichaean street fights of an immigrant
childhood.

## INVENTING AMERICAN JEWS

Far from being discreditable, Podhoretz's reservations about the
point of Jewish survival in America seemed to drive him, and
*Commentary*, into a unique position of Jewish cultural leadership.

The magazine succeeded brilliantly as a force for American Jewish life, especially from 1963 to 1968, because its gifted editor consciously charged it with the eclectic voice to which, he knew, thousands of educated, ambiguous American Jews could respond. Like Podhoretz, such people were "neither especially religious nor much Zionist" but were strongly drawn to the divided ambitions and political tragedies of our parents and grandparents, of our European relatives haunting us in snapshots. We had no corporate loyalties apart from the abstract obligations of citizenship, yet as individuals knew we had in common the moral confusions of being Jews. So we keenly awaited *Commentary* every month as if it were a public realm in which Jews were permitted to live on the questions.

These were good questions, and the magazine treated them with deliberate skill, organizing the intellectual standards of the American Jews' increasingly suburban and attenuated communities. *Commentary* established itself as our mail-order polity; one could, it seemed, be actively Jewish just by reading about the Jews' history, debating the place in culture of Jewish ritual law, or discerning the American "emancipation" in the elegance of the magazine's prose. And one could hope to be a good Jew by writing with virtuosity about issues that were on our minds. If such sentiments were vain, the pretentions to leadership of the Conservative and Reform rabbinate seemed far more so. Only *Commentary* seemed to demand that American Jews put the record of historic Jews on our cluttered cultural agenda, and this when the practice of historical analysis — research, publish, debate — already seemed to surpass in virtue the halachic obligations no one (who was anyone) was willing to fake.

I've been rereading the volumes published during Podhoretz's early years at *Commentary* and I'll review, briefly, the apparent purposes of his editorial leadership. This seems necessary since, in spite of its greater conspicuousness, the magazine has not been generating much enthusiasm among Jewish intellectuals in recent years, which probably accounts for its declining number of subscribers — 60,000 in 1970, 38,500 today.

Consider, for example, *Commentary*'s response to American Jewish writing in the sixties. It did not merely publish criticism of new novels and stories by American Jewish authors, it also provided them with an established forum to try out new material. Saul Bellow, Isaac Bashevis Singer, and Bernard Malamud each published new fiction during those years, as did younger writers as wildly different as Elie Wiesel and Mordecai Richler. Moreover, the pages were rife with responses and attacks by equivocally Jewish novelists who, while not publishing original fiction here, used the magazine to clarify their critical strategies: Philip Roth, for example, first defended his depictions of Jewish aggression here, in an essay that was itself a bright attack on bond-dinner heroes. Norman Mailer wrote a series of idiosyncratic exegeses on Martin Buber's newly published Hasidic tales.

The magazine indulged such writers, took them to express the most original inventions of American Jewish experience. Podhoretz would later acknowledge that, anyway, the writing of Mailer, Roth, Bellow, and others was "culturally all the rage in America"; but trendiness could not account for the care with which *Commentary* charted its development and subjected it to the criticism of writers whose essays were themselves reasons for raised expectations about "Jewish" possibilities in America. Irving Howe wrote regularly, covering even the opening of a play, *Fiddler on the Roof*. Other regular critics were Alfred Kazin, George Steiner, Theodore Solotaroff, and Lionel Abel, as well as more senior members of Podhoretz's "family," Lionel Trilling and William Phillips. *Commentary* also was giving a start to Robert Alter. Of course, Steiner's pieces were very different from Howe's: the former was claiming to see "Judaism" plain between the lines of Western European humanist philosophy, while the latter might write to evoke the values and materials of East European Yiddish culture, enjoining "dignified silence" from those incapable of mourning it with him. Very different voices, and their juxtaposition neatly made Podhoretz's point.

No less, pluralism characterized the magazine's approach to theological matters even when this required a good deal of moral courage. In the July 1963 issue, for example, Marc Galanter wrote a passionate dissent on the case of Brother Daniel, the Carmelite monk of Jewish origin to whom the Israeli Supreme Court had denied "Jewish nationality"—an important legal designation in Israel—because he had converted to Catholicism during the war. Arguing that the Orthodox center could no longer hold the Jews' "spiritual dispersion," Galanter charged that the court's verdict seemed to repudiate the new Jewish world the Zionists had themselves helped to create:

> The Jews have developed an identity much richer than a religion, a nation, or a culture—a kind of brotherhood through history that crosses unprecedented barriers. . . . No Jew or group of Jews is able to partake of all of it. The complexities of this heritage should not be reduced to the more manageable or presentable dimensions of nationality or religion, but should be kept open to the complexities of our changing experience—including the enrichments of such Jews as Brother Daniel.

Surely, Galanter—and Podhoretz—would also want to keep that heritage open even to various enrichments of the Upper West Side.

Those enrichments appeared in *Commentary* as philosophical arguments and theological styles. Martin Buber wrote about the Hasidic masters while Gershom Scholem published his initial research on the "false" messianism of the cabalists. Leo Strauss published twelve terse pages of "introductory reflections" on the distinctions to be derived from Judaism and Hellenism, while Hans Jonas needed less space to pose, in a stunning polemic, the tensions between Jewish- and Christian-inspired ethics and the contributions of both to the Western tradition.

*Commentary* published pieces by the Marxist Albert Memmi, the Freudian rabbi Richard Rubenstein, and others who were inclined to give it a rough ride. The point is that *Commentary* aimed to achieve some consistency between American Jewish identity and the actual, various voices of American Jews: however inimical the concept of a Western tradition seemed to the Orthodox Jewish one—Leo Strauss had frankly posed these as options—the magazine could not pretend to deny the blandishments of the West at a time when most of its writers and readers were resorting to the categories and analytic methods of Western social science and cultural criticism. It was in this spirit, to take yet another example, that the anthropologist Erich Isaac considered the "enigmas" of circumcision and the dietary laws.

This is not to say that traditional Jewish modes of argument were excommunicated. The exegetic tradition was represented in Midrashic essays by Emil Fackenheim, Robert Alter, and Milton Himmelfarb, who provided our best view of former rabbinic standards during the Haskalah, the period of the Jewish Enlightenment. But orthodoxy was not, it is true, given authoritative prominence. On the contrary, so much prophesy in one magazine—as if Judaism were a load of texts dropped at the feet of highly individual critics—struck the yeshiva masters of Flatbush and Mount Royal as profound heresy. Yet the understandable outrage of the Orthodox community seemed a risk worth running: from the play of Mailer or, somewhat later, Harold Bloom issued our otherwise unlikely re-examination of those texts, of Torah and Talmud, Midrash, and Hebrew language. For Americans of Jewish origin, prophecy seemed not to be the culmination of traditional learning but its first step.

Another reason *Commentary* was getting Judaism the respectful attention of intellectuals was the hard-headed, exacting way Podhoretz acquired articles on Jewish history. Avoiding martyrological apologia, Podhoretz published pieces that displayed the Jews as people who could also confound themselves by vain hopes, failing ideologies, and malice. I have already mentioned the magazine's publication of Scholem's work on the movements of Jewish mystics; he also wrote about the Jews of Germany in *Commentary*, and with the measured and distant compassion of one who had made a once painful and misunderstood choice: leaving Berlin for Palestine. His work, like that of Cecil Roth on the biblical period and of Arthur Hertzberg on the modern, corresponded to what seemed an overt editorial injunction against "sentimentalizing the Jews," depicting them in Robert Alter's phrase as "a continuing parade of holy sufferers, adepts of alienation, saintly buffoons, flamboyant apostles of love." So where Yigael Yadin would be asked to proffer the political Zionist symbolism of Masada, H. R. Trevor-Roper was invited to challenge the simple-minded lessons from which, he thought, so much of modern Jewish nationalism derived.

*Commentary*'s approach to the Jews' literary, legal, and historical products had a profound political impact on thousands of young Jewish students and scholars. It seemed to us not merely refreshing to recognize historic Jews as participating agents of their fate; this also inspired a good deal of timely action. In Montreal, for instance, a number of Jewish students (including Ruth Wisse, and, several years later, me) worked to establish a pilot program in Jewish Studies at McGill University—by challenging both the existing priorities of local Jewish philanthropies and the high-minded resistance of McGill's academic committees. I do not think it an exaggeration to say that in our mind's eye was the example of *Commentary*'s writers, the lure of emulating its subversions and reconstructions of Jewish life by standards worthy of our academies. I doubt that this experience in Montreal was unique: dozens of similar groups sprang up at other colleges and universities during the late sixties. Their faculties have, by now, virtually eclipsed the rabbinate as the arbiters of Jewish moral life in America.

I think *Commentary*'s influence on American Jewish practice during the 1960s may itself be put in some historical perspective and usefully compared with the cultural Zionist monthlies in, say, Odessa during the 1890s, the first time the people of the book, coming to a modern city, became the people of the magazine. But *Commentary*'s record in the sixties corresponds to the Zionist monthlies in another crucial respect since, like the cultural Zionists, *Commentary* supposed that historic Jews' communitarian traditions, their moral standards issuing from lapsed theology and collective vulnerability, make Jews natural candidates for modernism, for scientific discourse, for "progress" in politics.

I'll not recapitulate here the politics of such Zionists as Achad Ha'am and his disciple Chaim Weizmann, nor do I mean to press the analogy with *Commentary*'s newer Jews too hard since the Zionists would not have viewed with favor attempts to modernize Jewish life in any language but Hebrew. Still, it seems revealing that in turn both Jewish intelligentsias, distant in time and space, took for granted a tradition with incipient political commitments to democratic tolerance, peace, and social improvement. *Commentary* during the 1960s took social action to be the vocation in America of people who might preserve what Achad Ha'am had called the Jews' "spirit," their "moral genius." Which is not to say that competing moral ideologies, like those of laissez-faire conservatives, seemed indefensible. Rather, *Commentary*'s writers strongly implied what the Zionists stated: that such ideologies could not serve the needs of Judaism. Jews, rather, belonged with the utilitarians, the socialists and democrats, with people who took the emerging social good and not the individual's sensuous pleasure as the preeminent moral problem. It also seemed Jewish, I shall argue later on, to endorse the apparent goals of the Democratic Party since Roosevelt, and this as a matter of principle, not merely out of some immigrant habit to be shed along with economic distress.

That the Jews stand for something did not mean that *Commentary* should support every program a reform-minded Great Society Congress proposed: as early as 1963, the magazine was publishing perceptive articles by Nathan Glazer that anticipated the difficulties of reforming urban and educational institutions — even the minimal reforms being suggested by such other *Commentary* writers as Paul Goodman, Jane Jacobs, and Edgar Friedenberg. (Especially notable were the writings of Paul Goodman, to whom Podhoretz gave special encouragement; writing in an unsectarian radical spirit, Goodman helped initiate what was best in the political upsurge of the early sixties.)

Yet the democratic impulse for social reform — for having, as Glazer then put it, "the best society we can manage under the circumstances" — was never put in doubt; nor was it assumed to be doomed by some hypothetical human proclivity for infinite private gain by which Rotarians and Republicans warranted self-regulating markets. Rather, Jews should presume that common plans, educational goals, ecological regulations, and social services need to be developed. That we live decently more by evolving an egalitarian culture in public than by private appropriation.

Nor did *Commentary* fail to ground such democratic ideals in the philosophical and psychological disquisitions democrats periodically need to carry on. Most important, in retrospect, were articles concerning questions we now would include in debates about "intelligence," the impact of social impoverishment on ghetto children, and so forth. *Commentary* seemed to appreciate early on the vital connection between egalitarian ideals and a view of intelligence as cultivated potential. Thus Adolf Portmann in "Beyond Darwinism" (November 1965):

The growing human being is born out of the mother's body into a second uterus in which he traverses the second half of embryonic life; this is the social uterus. Thereby we also characterize the mighty task of society; we see how much the success or failure of the individual life depends on its proper performance during this decisive early epoch.

Of course, Portmann's argument was old hat: it would have seemed obvious to Aristotle. But *Commentary* was implying by such articles what must often be reiterated in democratic societies that, in part, aim to organize themselves according to merit; namely, that the poor performance of the poor cannot be ascribed to the inherent limits of individual minds. Racists and Tories have always been able to marshal empirical evidence against inferior classes but have never acknowledged the extent to which the societies they defend help to produce their evidence.

As with social policy, *Commentary* represented the liberal democratic instincts of American Jews in political and economic matters, publishing scores of articles by such writers as Oscar Gass, Robert Heilbroner, Robert Leckachman, and Dennis Wrong. It similarly pursued a moderate tone on diplomatic questions, running columns by George Lichtheim, Hans Morgenthau, and others who, while by no means indifferent to the fate of democracies abroad, were also concerned about the climate for military adventurism created by evangelical anticommunist sophistry at home. *Commentary* came out against the Vietnam War by 1965, printing a detailed report by David Halberstam, and published a devastating attack by Theodore Draper on the Dominican crisis that same year. Such positions were highly controversial then, aimed to discredit the brinkmanship of Dulles and the domino theory of Rusk, both of which would nevertheless pave the way for foreign disaster.

It seemed appropriate, finally, that the magazine treat Israel and Zionism with strong but equivocal admiration. For one thing, *Commentary* respected cultural fabric and so presumed its readers too ignorant of modern Israel to celebrate it without more basic information. For another, the claims of historic Zionism implied that the tangible, if modest, cultural activities of American Jews, indeed of the magazine, were unlikely or even fraudulent. (*Commentary*'s long-standing indifference to Zionist ideals had provoked the Zionist organizations to launch *Midstream* several years earlier.) Podhoretz therefore printed pieces that aimed to inform American Jews about the culture and politics of the Jewish state, but with the discretion due another country.

The magazine's best writer on Israeli affairs was, after 1967, Amos Elon, whose urbane reports were then unveiling the problems that would fester in the 1970s. But *Commentary* was long before publishing rare, perceptive criticism of rabbinate-state relations (Herbert Weiner, July 1964), of Zionist organizational rhetoric regarding Jewish immigration into Israel, *aliyah* (Ronald Sanders, August 1965), of popular Israeli culture and fiction (Robert Alter, December 1965, and Baruch Hochman, December 1966). Perhaps the best evidence for *Commentary*'s cool and intelligent approach to these issues was the way it handled the Six-Day War, resisting, as no other institution in American Jewish life, the unrealistic euphoria that victory unleashed.

In the August 1967 issue, for example, the magazine published four brilliant pieces on the war and its aftermath. The first two, by Theodore Draper and Walter Laqueur, were about the diplomatic and military implications of the war, and they still seem models of tact and objectivity. Yet the last two now seem even more valuable as the keynotes of a new age. Amos Elon's piece reviewed the events in Israel from May 15 to the climax of the war, but also played the minor chord that Israeli moderates were striking at home. Jerusalem, Elon explained, had been precipitously annexed, and some respectable Israeli leaders were now calling for doing the same to the entire West Bank or for setting up a "puppet state" there, a "Bechuanaland for Arabs." If such thinking prevails, he warned, "the potential fruits of victory may be lost as they were in 1948 and 1956." This was tough talk and was followed, to the end of 1970, by equally tough-minded sequels. The best were by other prominent Israeli intellectuals — Shlomo Avineri and J. L. Talmon — who set out a judicious diplomatic strategy to engage Palestinians on the West Bank in discussions that might lead to a two-state solution.

The final piece, by Arthur Hertzberg, seemed of equal moment. The Six-Day War had, he wrote, suddenly drawn American Jews to a network of claims very different from the ones that had previously been operating with *Commentary*'s support:

The sense of belonging to a worldwide Jewish people, of which Israel is the center, is a religious sentiment, but it seems to persist even among Jews who regard themselves as secularists or atheists. There are no conventional theological terms with which to explain this, and most contemporary Jews were experiencing these emotions without knowing how to define them.

Hertzberg, it must be said, remained equivocal about such narrow political Zionist rhetoric whose triumphant revival he identified: he had, after all, given it short shrift in his book on Zionist ideas. So he could not have known that his article was the harbinger of a trend that would help sink the creative life of the magazine.

BREAKING RANKS

If, as Hertzberg supposed, the 1967 war was a "transforming" event for American Jews, Norman Podhoretz should not have been immune. But the next several years saw the magazine undergo a conversion more complete than any that might have been warranted by the chance to take Israel's part — profess "Zionism" — in the face of the Jewish state's enemies. In fact, the aftermath of the Middle East war coincided with other crucial events affecting the politics of the American left. Podhoretz's literary career also suffered shocks that seemed to provide him with the occasion to "break ranks" (as he's recently put it) with most of the New York writers for whose good opinion he had once so diligently hustled.

His book, *Breaking Ranks,* is intriguing — like all of his didactic memoirs — for what it reveals about his unarticulated images of Jews, gentiles, and power. Only four pages in the book are actually devoted to the subject — to the "movement's" incipient self-hatred or anti-Semitism — but this may be misleading insofar as Podhoretz had already admitted that he could not consider Jewish identity and interests apart from the realpolitik he had claimed to learn in the streets of Brooklyn. In this sense, the entire book is about the reappropriation of his primal view of those interests, about defying "the people in the world who act as if they have nothing to lose": lately, the Soviets, black militants, student radicals, communist insurgents, anti-Zionist Palestinians, and more.

No fair-minded person could fail to appreciate Podhoretz's evolving animus: by the end of 1968, the Soviets had rearmed and incited the Arabs against Israel, had marched on Prague—this, while some American black leaders were composing anti-Semitic and illiberal diatribes, supported openly by thousands of students who violently occupied university buildings or were "into" drugs, and so forth.

Yet, again, his revulsion from the Soviets and the New Left cannot explain Podhoretz's growing distaste for the writers, editors, politicians, and others in the Vietnam peace camp who mainly shared his sentiments. It seems worth recalling that most of *Commentary*'s polemics around 1968 were written by some of the very "radicals" whose presumed fecklessness he meant to expose in writing *Breaking Ranks*: Norman Mailer on the "new politics," Michael Harrington on the Democratic Party, Diana Trilling on the occupation of Columbia University, and Irving Howe on the failure of New York intellectuals to stem the authoritarian instincts of the New Left. These were strong pieces that could hardly be said to be pandering to antidemocratic forces or their apologists.

In fact, Podhoretz was breaking ranks—breaking faith—with those people who were holding to the radically democratic view of politics with which *Commentary* had justifiably tried to identify American Jews for a decade but with which he had himself admitted being at emotional odds since his youth. It is hardly clear just what precipitated the break when it came. Most of the people he would repudiate shared the assumption he suddenly and curiously denied: that the American government's decision to intervene in Vietnam—and the brutal comportment of many American soldiers there—could be traced to some aspects of American political culture.

Perhaps Podhoretz earnestly believed that this was no time to rail against American values, no matter how high-minded the motive, although such concerns did not stop him from opposing the war even when all the reasons for opposing it had not yet become clear. More likely, Podhoretz was confounded by the

wide appeal of those critics, philosophers, and folk singers, also Jews, who invited us to see Vietnam as a product of those particular American values—money, power, fame—which he had just endorsed in *Making It* and with such obvious self-congratulation that "the family" of New York intellectuals could not hide its embarrassment. Of course, it was no short leap from the politics of money, power, and fame to Southeast Asia; it also was not a long one to the new Republican administration, which, Podhoretz must have noticed, had more of all three than even Lionel Trilling.

It is no use dwelling on these motives, but we can hardly ignore their consequences. From 1969 on, *Commentary* gradually revamped the vocabulary by which American Jews were to consider their interests. That's an important word—"interests"—for Podhoretz would invest it with a very different meaning from the one *Commentary* had established during the previous ten years. Where he had assumed American Jews to be an eclectic collection of individuals with incipient purposes—self-criticism, the study of Jewish history and philosophy, democratic ethics—the new *Commentary* had begun to depict us as a corporate entity with overt interests in self-promotion and gain—an "interest group." The magazine now took our consolidation for granted, our material goals as self-evident, and began coaching us, too, on how to make it in America.

To reinforce the determination of American Jews to break ranks along with him, Podhoretz began writing editorials on all sorts of issues—from rock culture to rent control—which invited his readers to consider what seems now "good for the Jews" according to what he began to call "traditional" criteria. I shall consider that new tradition presently, but I first want to comment on two articles by other writers that epitomize the narrow and reckless style of argument by which *Commentary* sought to convince American Jews that it was no longer difficult to figure out what was good for them.

The first, by Emil Fackenheim, set the tone by using the images of catastrophe—of the Holocaust—to contrive a moral climate in which intense American Jewish solidarity could seem plausible without regard to our deteriorating cultural bonds. It also implied the pitiless nature of mankind in general and so seemed to warrant our preoccupation with gain.

It is important to emphasize that this was a new departure for the magazine, which had hitherto treated the mass murders as history so complex one required great modesty to get a grasp of it. For example, while carefully refuting Hannah Arendt's indictment of the *Judenrat*, Podhoretz had himself in 1963 followed her lead in presenting the Nazis' Final Solution not as the basis for some new Jewish cosmology, but as the moral burden of German culture, of Christians, as the material for psychoanalytic reasoning. It was not a Jewish moral problem in any positive sense that may attach to modern Jewish life, but *the* problem for anyone concerned with politics. This is, of course, not to denigrate the sufferings of individual Jews or the loss of the Jewish cultural center in Eastern Europe. Nor should anyone deny traditional and Orthodox Jews the appropriation of the Holocaust as an event unique to the Jews, to be absorbed into the liturgy like former catastrophes. It is to suggest, as Podhoretz put it, that there are no easy lessons to be learned except that "the victims were hopelessly vulnerable in their powerlessness."

Victims cannot claim a privileged vantage point from which to solve political questions, not, at least, just for having been victims. Indeed, what Jewish victims could fail to find in mass murder perfect evidence for the justice of their political philosophy? Liberals, assimilationists, communists, and Zionists — all will have theories about how the world goes wrong that anticipate how to put it right. Podhoretz was not wrong, in 1963, to confess confusion about whether the survival of Jews was worth the hair of an infant. It is not the murderers who solve the existential dilemmas that may have plagued the murdered and continue to perplex their survivors. Yet in August 1968, Fackenheim's article implied just this murderer's inadvertent solution for the Jewish Problem, a modern revelation by which Jews could regain a common purpose, could know and promote each other in public. No *shlemiels* they, the transformed Podhoretz and his fellow editors of the new *Commentary* seized upon it — its preoccupation with the "power" of physical violence — to shrug off almost every serious question that's been raised about Jewish life from the Napoleonic Sanhedrin to the *New York Review*. The death camps, it seems, have given the Jews a new opportunity to "prepare a way for God":

> Auschwitz is a unique descent into hell. It is an unprecedented celebration of evil. It is evil for evil's sake. Jews must bear witness to this truth. . . . They were and still are singled out by it, but in the midst of it they hear an absolute commandment: *Jews are forbidden to grant posthumous victories to Hitler.* They are commanded to survive as Jews, lest the Jewish people perish. They are commanded to remember the victims of Auschwitz lest their memory perish. They are forbidden to despair of man and his world, and to escape into either cynicism or otherworldliness, lest they co-operate in delivering the world over to the forces of Auschwitz. Finally, they are forbidden to despair of the God of Israel lest Judaism perish. A secularist Jew cannot make himself believe by a mere act of will, nor can he be commanded to do so; yet he can perform the commandment of Auschwitz.

Now it is true that traditional Jews are supposed to act as if they too stood at Sinai, but this is something very different. Fackenheim is not asking us to take on some distinct ethical obligations but rather to "stand at Auschwitz" in order to see Jewish survival as an end in itself. Thereby we all—even our suburban children—take on the prestige of victims.

Putting aside the obvious moral difficulties evoked by words like good and evil, Fackenheim's dialectical argument cast the Jews in the role of the purveyors of absolute good and raised the old, ironic concern of our fathers—now Podhoretz's new one—with what's "good for the Jews" to some apparently unambiguous ontological claim.

I've implied that Hitler's main victory to be denied is a view of Jews compatible with fatuous and tribalistic criteria, the obscuring of the serious differences in culture, outlook, and temperament between, say, Anne Frank and Elie Wiesel, Lillian Hellman and A. B. Yehoshua. But this is not the victory Fackenheim had in mind.

The Jews spite the forces of Auschwitz, rather, by staying alert to their interests, by remaining tough-minded and realistic—not "cynical or otherworldly"—and so concerned to augment the material forces of Jewish "power." The greatest Jewish act, he wrote (as if he had never heard of Mussolini), is to have Jewish babies. He once told me in Toronto that, instead of American Jews hearing the slogan "never again" from our leaders, he would have us hear a running tally of the divisions and weapons at the disposal of Israel and the Western powers. And as if such ironies were not sufficient, Jews must also reaffirm Orthodox practice at least insofar as this will ensure our cohesion.

What forces of Auschwitz specifically did Fackenheim expect his united, crusading people to defy? Can it be true that the subjects of this retribution to which he further alludes are *Commentary*'s new foils: the Palestinians, the Soviets, "anti-Semites" of the New Left, and the "appeasers" in America who fail to notice how the world may "be delivered into *their* hands"? Tyrants, terrorists, and Jew-haters are political adversaries that do Fackenheim credit. But no recognition of enemies requires Jews to surrender to apocalyptic demagoguery. It is not the "forces of Auschwitz" that turned Fackenheim into a Cold Warrior par excellence but the poverty of his own moral and historical imagination; and *Commentary* certainly did the political experience of American Jews no justice by running his piece.

We should be truly naive to assume that Fackenheim's article was meant to stand on its own, apart from Podhoretz's new determination to see "Jewish interests" in America as everyone else's gain. This determination obviously inspired Milton Himmelfarb's subsequent article, "Is American Jewry in Crisis?" published in March 1969, just after Nixon and Agnew (and Moynihan) took office. Here Himmelfarb dismissed the Jews' defensible position in politics and social life and advised us to see ourselves as victims worthy of Fackenheim's cosmos. Specifically, he charged that the New York liberal democratic establishment—WASPs and anti-Jewish Jews alike—had conspired, maybe secretly, with black militants to win public concessions that could mainly hurt "ordinary Jews" whose sensible fears he then adumbrated: burgeoning welfare rolls carried by Jewish taxes, places held in universities for black children who inevitably would push out Jewish ones, and so forth. Himmelfarb's main evidence of anti-Jewish conspiracy was the political showdown between the predominantly Jewish New York Teacher's Union and the Oceanhill-Brownsville school board. Some scurrilously anti-Semitic pamphlets were published by anonymous black authors, which seemed to him sufficient reason to sound the shofar.

The tone of Himmelfarb's piece was even more disconcerting than his thesis. As if American Jews were already carrying the mantle of Jewish martyrs, Himmelfarb proceeded with exquisite sanctimony to condemn all "universal" claims—claims that, he guessed, do not specifically recognize Jewish "particularly"—as sham altruisms beneath which Jews leave themselves open to physical attack. Could Jews, for example, expect reciprocal support from the other "ethnics" in the Democratic Party, from the Italians, the Poles? Jews could not: "On aid to parochial schools and smut control, they are for, the Jews are against. The Jews go to college, they do not. They hunt, the Jews do not."

How does *Commentary* propose we deal with such extraordinary isolation and vulnerability? Settling in Israel would seem the obvious answer, but the magazine's Zionism was never strong and remained vicarious. Israel might now be a cause for celebration—the same issue boasted a piece by Gil Carl Alroy suggesting that tough, technological Israel would trounce any combination of Arab armies for a generation—but it was Israel's image, not its culture or problems, that the new *Commentary* wanted. What would "Israel" do if it lived in Brooklyn and not among the Arabs? It would, Himmelfarb suggested, vote Republican, or at least threaten the Democrats with abandonment.

Himmelfarb had in fact begun his piece with what he thought was a revealing bit of polling. Where some 70 percent of well-heeled gentiles had voted against Hubert Humphrey in 1968, 81 percent of all Jews voted for him. This seemed to him serious evidence indeed for an American Jewish hubris to be compared to the utopianism of Rosa Luxemburg. American Jews as a whole, he contended, are in the "highest income bracket," like Episcopalians, yet seem indifferent to their apparent class interests. New Left critics no doubt found it reassuring to see an anticommunist such as Himmelfarb express this approving fascination for class-consciousness, but many readers were offended by the piece. *Commentary*, to its credit, printed angry letters about it. Yet the magazine proceeded undaunted in Himmelfarb's— and Fackenheim's—manner. The time had come to develop elbows.

## TRADITION

Suppose that Himmelfarb's version of American Jews is right: an interest group whose problem it is to secure its élan and income in the face of self-regarding WASPs, radicals (too often Jewish) pliant in the face of "communism," some black free-loaders, many ethnic stiffs, and other anti-Semites. How can Jews throw their weight around in this plural American Republic? What specific policies ought to capture our imagination (or provoke our opposition), what allies are worth having? It seems to me that much of what has subsequently been called the neoconservative position has been evolved as an implicit answer to this bad question and that the answer itself is neither very conservative nor new, except to New York Jews. European conservatives, Hannah Arendt or Leo Strauss, could not have acquiesced in putting the problem so that common material gain would have priority over the intellectual lives of our best. It should rather be granted that Podhoretz, Irving Kristol, and the rest are quite right to call themselves "liberals"—in the British sense of people who view liberty as the protection of life and property from the invasion of others—convinced supporters of the notion that all men incline to be infinite consumers of scarce utilities (such as "money, power, fame"). They claim that unhampered market societies alone accommodate such propensities efficiently and that market incentives are our best cure for social problems, and good for the Jews for obvious reasons.

By 1971 Nathan Glazer, for example, had raised his reservations regarding the proper execution of social politics to a full-scale attack on the principle of social planning. The article—"The Limits of Social Policy" (September 1971)—demanded virtual resignation from the poor and their "radical" champions to the slaps of the hidden hand of the market. By June 1975 Glazer charged that American Jews were particularly "exposed" by the social remedies. Social policies, he assured us, will not work in America, while "traditional" solutions—presumably "growth"—would. Why should social planning not work? Because resources are too limited, programs become disincentives for wholesome work; they are administered typically by professionals who prove "limited and untrustworthy," and tackle problems too complex for the "knowledge we would like to have." The welfare programs, he charged, are especially good examples of government waste, as are those for housing—charges Michael Harrington has specifically refuted but that I'll concede for the sake of argument.

A close inspection of Glazer's claims suggest only two problems that seem really intractable—scarce resources and incentives—and these are the ones Glazer really meant us to consider. The first, however, turns out to be not an assessment of how resources become scarce (through, for example, badly planned but not hopeless entitlement programs such as Social Security, chronic and structural causes of falling productivity, squandered billions of dollars in Vietnam, and so forth) but rather a warrant for our common disinclination to support welfare measures through our taxes. This disposition he correctly hinged on the widespread conviction that these programs do not work (just what he intends us to believe) and on the fear that welfare encourages the shirking of work. So when one comes down to it, Glazer's celebrated insights were also no more or less compelling than the claims of classical liberalism, that laboring men need to fear the pains of idleness more than the pains of work. At least, it is only because such "incentives" for work were built into Nixon's abortive Family Assistance Program that Glazer endorsed it.

But Glazer endorsed precious little besides. What decent people can best do, he suggests, is "prevent the further erosion of traditional constraints that still play the largest role in maintaining civil society"—erosion of our common belief in productive work, respect for property, social reciprocity, which are supported by the "family, but also the ethnic group, the neighborhood . . . the church and the *Landsmannschaft*." The real problem, revealed by his solution, is that the people in the ghettos will not work because they are disaffected from civil life for want of traditions and family life and seem more mired in social decay than conventional welfare measures will cure.

In this sense, the neoconservative position is a powerful obfuscation, one that has been around almost as long as liberalism. Edmund Burke, too, tried to get his readers thinking about the Terror, professing "traditional" loyalty to "our King and Constitution" and to the family, while assuring everyone that such loyalty is best expressed by refraining from "indiscreet tamperings with the trade of provisions." The market, he urged, will solve its own problems given a sufficient amount of time and faith — which is just what those whom Burke described as thrown off the "great wheel of commerce" never seem to have much of. John Stuart Mill rightly observed, anticipating the politics of the Fabians and of the New Deal, that state interventions for the purpose of enhancing equality and regulating growth was therefore a protection of the property rights in which, he thought, some of our democratic liberties were grounded, while laissez-faire ideas menaced them by encouraging class divisions, crime, and despair. Such economic leadership is more urgent today, when, as in Japan and the West European countries, government may have to act to organize credit for major corporations that are retooling or embarking on a new technology; to assure energy conservation, mediate industry-wide wage disputes, set standards for public health, and so on.

But Glazer will not even concede the use of national health insurance:

> We are kept healthy by certain patterns of life . . . by having access to traditional means of support in distress and illness, through the family . . . the school . . . the neighborhood, the informal social organization. We are kept healthy by care in institutions where traditionally oriented occupations (nursing and the maintenance of cleanliness) still manage to perform their functions.

Some of this is merely trite: no one since Pasteur would deny that clean people will stay healthier than filthy people, though we are immeasurably cleaner owing to government actions against open sewers, air pollution, bad nutrition, and so on, than we would otherwise be regardless of how much our mothers carp at us to wash. But his statement is also tendentious, for Glazer properly wants us to care about the condition of family life without identifying its overt dependence on conditions over which it (and the *Landsmannschaft*) can have no control. Schools and hospitals are not "traditional" institutions merely because such "traditional" occupations as teaching and healing are practiced there. They are built by government to serve people who, by the exigencies of the market, were once kept illiterate and sick. Moreover, Glazer's views seem indifferent to thousands of black families that have been broken as a consequence of "neighborhood" prejudices, which denied them entry during the 1940s and '50s, when the economy was expanding at a pace that might well have substantially broadened the black middle class as it did the Jewish. And Glazer's indifference can only be willful since in his book *Beyond the Melting Pot* (co-authored with D. P. Moynihan), he recognized the racism of ethnic neighborhoods.

In fact, does any of this earnest concern for the family — the hinge on which neoconservatism turns — take account of the way a father's love succumbs to self-hatred when he cannot find work? It does not acknowledge that dignified and secure employment will not necessarily exist even for blacks converted to Calvinist notions of work: that, for example, the "traditional" market forces, interpreted by shortsighted management, have wrecked some of the American auto industry, putting hundreds of thousands more blacks and whites out of the jobs they had.

If Glazer were right that the families of our underclass in the great northeastern cities have not been improved by attempted welfare measures, and that this constitutes a danger to the civil society from which Jews and others make their happier lives, he cannot be right that "benign neglect" (as Moynihan put it) is the alternative. The family needs work, medical services, safe streets, clean housing, good schools, day care, public transportation, public libraries and public television, student loans, and many other services over many years. (We certainly need to wage campaigns against illiteracy and commercial TV, more than Midge Decter's mean-spirited ones against the women's movement and homosexuals.) If conventional government action has not been enough to help consolidate families in the ghettos, then unconventional action might: not less spending but much, much more. But there is no use denouncing social policies that fail or seem to fail if the alternative to them is the worse failure of social life such policies were invented to allay.

Now *Commentary* flattened to a hard line on so many corresponding social issues that its once apparent commitment to eclecticism vanished. Podhoretz seemed, for example, far more exercised by affirmative action programs than he had been about the

welfare state. He began publishing piece after piece (by Paul
Seabury, Earl Raab, Martin Mayer, and others) denouncing affirmative action as a new form of discrimination, particularly
against Jews, who now presumably have as great a stake in "traditional" conceptions of merit as they have had in the free play
of market forces: "As it happens, the Jews are at this moment
in an extremely good position to serve the best interests of the
country as a whole by attempting to serve their own."

I do not propose to defend all affirmative action programs,
especially not those setting firm quotas that Thomas Sowell
rightly condemns for patronizing blacks who don't need them
and putting others into jobs and classes they may not be able to
handle. But special efforts to hire or admit nearly qualified people to these jobs and classes, on the assumption that the new
experience will help them transcend the cultural deprivation of
ghetto neighborhoods, is no pernicious form of discrimination.
Generous people will discriminate on behalf of those who are
disadvantaged, but that does not make such people bigots: the
Hebrews would not have left Egypt if God had judged them
then by the criteria He demanded for entering the promised
land.

Podhoretz misleads Jewish parents, who do not need extra
anxieties, in asserting that programs aiming to include a larger
proportion of black students in professional schools are some
kind of anti-Jewish quota just because Jewish students make up
a disproportionately large number of applicants. The Supreme
Court is right to acknowledge that, as a temporary remedy, race
could be used as one of the many criteria admissions committees
should consider when deciding on applications. Ronald Dworkin
has argued that the social benefits attending an increase of black
professionals constitute a compelling claim. By contrast, *Commentary*'s view of merit — presumably, strict comparisons of performance on aptitude tests, teachers' recommendations, and so
forth — seem no more an impersonal standard for merit than
wealth is for guile.

But, since the advent of Milton Friedman's disciple Thomas
Sowell, we do not see advocates of affirmative action like Leon
Higginbotham and Vernon Jordan honorably defended in the
pages of the magazine. What we do see are attacks suggesting
that the very spirit in which affirmative action programs are

mooted is yet another conspiracy of New Class intellectuals, who despise everything "bourgeois" because they are not sufficiently horrified by communism, and quotas. We also see such pieces as Irving Kristol's "Equality," which aimed to reassure us that "the bourgeois conception of equality, so vehemently denounced by the egalitarian, is 'natural' in a way that other political ideas are not," and that the poor, like the rest of us, need spiritual values that no economic system can provide.

I shall consider in a little while the kind of spiritual values this radical, possessive individualism is likely to generate in America, whether Kristol's bourgeois elites will promote the tolerance Jews need. But his distinction between the purposes of the flesh and those of the spirit already concedes more than an American Jew should.

Spiritual consolation is not irrelevant to common opportunities to exert our capacities as creative men and women, to cultivate our appreciation for the works of others. This was called humanism before the Reverend Jerry Falwell turned the word into an epithet. Such opportunities, Kristol surely understood, have some foundation in economic claims—pianos, for example, are not free—which is not to say (what Kristol in fact needs to maintain in order for markets to work) that material interests are the only ones that count.

Still, since Kristol has anointed his contradictory bourgeois concepts as "natural," what can be left to debate? Nothing, or so it seemed from the increasingly strident polemics that Podhoretz was demanding from his writers. Traditionalists are nothing if not consistent. For example, the theory that continuing economic expansion under laissez-faire is impossible—first proposed by Mill in his *Principles of Political Economy*—was not to be merely refuted but must be said, as in a Rudolph Klein piece, to be the work of "enemies." Moreover, a majority of blacks were now in the "middle class" (which Scammon and Wattenberg delicately defined to include anyone not chronically unemployed), and only "liberal" rhetoric calls this progress into question. More recently, the magazine even sought vindication for California's Proposition 13, which Lipset and Raab asserted was mainly directed at the welfare bums Glazer had supposedly identified some years before.

None of these claims against "New Class" assumptions can

match for pure venom the magazine's hopeless campaign to revive the prestige of IQ testing as a basis for explaining inequality and merit, promoting especially the work of social scientists who have attempted to account for the black underclass as if it were, at least in part, determined by biological necessity. Again, the issue of IQ raises profound questions about what educated people mean by intelligence and learning—epistemological questions—which cannot be settled here. The effort to extrude some quantified version of intelligence may itself derive from a simple-minded view of the mind: the disease, as it were, for which it presumes to be the cure. Further attempts to link our performance in society to such criteria as IQ—to show the poor as dumber than the rich—seem a double violation of moral tact.

David K. Cohen stated just this view in the magazine as late as 1972. Yet such sensible opinions were not to last long in a magazine now committed to finding egalitarian ideals utopian and inequalities rooted in nature: for if a certain few social scientists are vilified by the New Class for searching out the genetic roots of inequality, how much more reason to assume them right.

In spite of Cohen's article, *Commentary* published (July 1972) a lively defense of Edward Banfield's book *The Unheavenly City* (which had argued to the nifty proposition: "if the lower class were to disappear . . . the most serious and intractable problems of the city would disappear with it"). Then, as if we did not get the point, *Commentary* eventually published articles by scholars whose vigorous advocacy of IQ testing in relation to racial groups—Richard Herrnstein and Arthur Jensen—have made their work still more notorious than Banfield's. Podhoretz even had Herrnstein review Jensen's latest book, *Bias in Mental Testing*, which aimed to vindicate the theoretical framework by which Jensen had earlier speculated that blacks inherit intellectual inferiorities, especially what he had called "adaptive reasoning." He might at least have asked Sowell to do the review in view of the latter's interesting point that the IQs of Jews have seemed marvelously to rise since the 1920s—since, that is, more Jews have gained the education and affluence their former below-average IQs would not seem to have assured.

Of course *Commentary*'s sanctimonious view of affirmative action, its advocacy of market solutions to social problems, and implied biological warrants for both, were bound to inflame even black moderates in the Urban League and NAACP. Bayard Rustin, who has remained sympathetic to Podhoretz's view on diplomatic issues, once told me that he considered the magazine's line on social questions a dishonor to the relations of blacks and Jews in New York. For *Commentary* is after all a Jewish magazine, one for which the American Jewish Committee must find a $125,000 subvention every year. Black anti-Semitism, particularly the kind that emerged from the Black Power movement associated with the New Left, can never be condoned.

But neither are Jews exempt from demands of propriety and restraint. Of course, as Ruth Wisse's recent Yiddish fables suggest, Jews are not to begrudge themselves the right to inflame others when their vital interests are at issue; we even have the right to be wrong. But when the editors of the most conspicuous Jewish journal are wrong in the most discreditable way, violating common standards of fairness, that is a worthy subject for public debate. Some other American Jews should be expected to respond in public and repudiate the politics that the magazine claims to be pursuing for our "own good."

This expectation is of course also relevant to the question of the magazine's insistence on a Jewish lockstep regarding Israel. While *Commentary* has generally maintained a balanced view of Israel's diplomatic and military options—continuing to publish moderate pieces by Theodore Draper, Walter Laqueur, Hillel Halkin, and others who remained unimpressed by Uri Raanan's diatribes against Egypt that also appeared in the magazine—it has nevertheless printed two angry attacks on American Jewish groups that have attempted to organize support for the Israeli peace camp. The first, by Joseph Shattan, was a most irresponsible hatchet job on Breira in 1977. More recently, Ruth Wisse has adopted a merely patronizing tone to scold the American Friends of Peace Now. Wisse's indictment in fact suggested that public dissent by American Jews about Israeli actions is inherently wrong since we do not take the consequences of that country's diplomatic actions; that, anyway, Jews who speak against the Israeli government are to be compared to the *shlemiels* of

Chelm who tried to curry favor among the goyim by condemning themselves for their suffering, and are insensible to the need for solidarity.

I've never quite understood the delight Ruth Wisse takes in imagining herself the resident of a ghetto. Nevertheless, she seems to have missed what *Commentary* once deeply grasped, that American Jews register approval and dissent as citizens of a democratic country, and in addressing Israeli problems inevitably support some rather than other Israeli politicians. Israelis make such claims as well. Such groups as Friends of Peace Now have aimed to build coalitions of support for Israel by attempting to salvage the progressive American constituency for Israeli moderates. This peace group did not consider it inappropriate for *Commentary* to publish Raanan's article, which would have had Israel disastrously break off negotiations with Egypt long before the Camp David peace process bore fruit. Raanan represented a minority opinion in Israel, and *Commentary*'s editors would also not "have to live" with the war his hawkish policies might have provoked, or the one that views such as Alroy's did help to provoke. Wisse's demurrers that her views are mindful of Israel's need for power, while "the well-known leftists" of Peace Now are not, seem so much affectation: power must be debated and is just not as devoid of opportunities, limits, and complications as her *shlemiels* may suppose.

## THE PRESENT DANGER — AND OURS

The magazine's defense of "bourgeois" civilization for the sake of the Jews has given way to corresponding and false abstractions about the use of American "interests" and power in international conflicts. *Commentary* now specializes in foreign policy articles aiming to promote greater defense budgets and diplomatic militancy. In the past, the magazine did resist the facile anticommunism that helped put half a million Americans into Vietnam in 1965 — yet surrenders to it now that Podhoretz's earlier courage seems so clearly vindicated. Not that the Soviet Union's ambitions were ever to be trusted, or its regime to be admired. But *Commentary* once published Ronald Steele and others who argued that those ambitions are hardly the main problem in formulating U.S. policy toward the leaders of premodern countries and their liberation movements, for whom socialist principles mainly lead to arguable theories of economic development—often learned at Western universities—which are by no means expressions of allegiance to the Soviet empire. China—which, remember, we had intended to foil in Vietnam—may be the most striking example of how careful we must be about such distinctions, but the Egyptian case is also germane.

Nothwithstanding Jeane Kirkpatrick's faith in the strength of old ways and old cultures, when America lavishes arms and aid on old military regimes in trouble, a country will indeed fall like a domino. Events in Iran should have taught us that such a lavishing can lead to megalomania and thus itself become a cause for popular disaffection. By contrast, when America keeps its hands off as in Nicaragua or vigorously pursues democratic solutions as in Zimbabwe-Rhodesia, "revolutionary" regimes may soon be courting Western countries for the economic and technological support they cannot hope to get from the Soviets. Even the Angolans seem hungry for greater ties with American firms —they are already doing a brisk business with European ones and almost none with the Soviets—though Cuban forces remain. These countries will be lost to American interests if the new administration denies them the aid they need—or keeps reading *Commentary* as therapy for our "Vietnam complex."

But Podhoretz's view that our hard-earned moral and diplomatic caution is a kind of nervous disorder, leaving us powerless in the face of ruthless men, seems curiously familiar—though not, as he fancies, reminiscent of Churchill pushing on alone in a nest of appeasers. If anything, Podhoretz's accusations have done wonders for his reputation among the Republican brokers who are now operating behind Ronald Reagan's reassuring shrugs. They already may claim to have quashed the SALT treaty, discredited Kissinger's "détente," and proposed the MX, the neutron bomb, the B-1, the seizing of oil fields, support for any autocratic government that is merely, in Ms. Kirkpatrick's immortal phrase, "moderately repressive."

Too many articles in this vein have appeared in *Commentary* over the last several years by Jeane Kirkpatrick, Robert W.

Tucker, Edward Luttwak, and others to be answered all at once. Some of these, it must be said, have made a very convincing case for greater attention to NATO and to America's conventional forces, for cutting off high technology to the Soviets, and other policies almost every responsible journal has been promoting recently, in part as a result of *Commentary*'s prodding. But two issues stand out as especially neat examples of childhood fears of cowardice masquerading as diplomatic realism, and I shall treat them in turn.

The first and comprehensive issue, which Podhoretz shrewdly calls "the Present Danger," suggests America's "decline" in the world, owing to our presumed decline in strategic weapons, which has itself been precipitated by our "mood of self-doubt and self-disgust" after Vietnam. I think that "decline" and "self-disgust" pertain more suitably to the realm of writers' blocks and difficulties than they describe the reasons for decisions made by secretaries of state about strategic weapons. *Commentary*'s version of "the Present Danger" surely is more dramatic than any proposal or debate in pursuit of a solution guided by conventional thinking — as, for instance, the proposal to institute compulsory national service, which the magazine virtually ignored. Podhoretz's views require the morale to face up to Soviet designs in the Persian Gulf even at the risk of a nuclear exchange.

Aside from its elaborate and dim view of our collective will, *Commentary*'s argument for more strategic forces and militant diplomacy actually reduces to a syllogism about Soviet intentions and capabilities that is vulnerable on many grounds. According to the official version presented by Richard Pipes (July 1977), the argument goes as follows: We and the Russians have counterforce weapons and countervalue weapons. Counterforce weapons are land-based, hence comparatively accurate missiles that can attack and incinerate the other's missiles in hardened silos and kill a mere, say, twenty million people in the assault. Countervalue weapons (quaintly) are only accurate enough to incinerate cities, yet relatively few (300, in fact, of the 10,000 we have) would be enough to kill everybody in either the Soviet Union or the United States. We have fewer counterforce weapons than the Soviets; they think nuclear war is possible and would execute a first strike if they saw vital advantages to the risk.

This, according to Pipes, is the rub. The Soviets already have and are accumulating a sufficient number of counterforce weapons that, if launched in a surprise attack, could destroy enough of the American counterforce arsenal to leave American leaders only the choice between launching some of the thousands of countervalue missiles that remain to SAC or the submarine fleet —a step leading to the extinction of mankind—or capitulating to a Soviet *dictat.* Even if they never launch their strike, our knowledge that they could is enough to crack our will to oppose their power plays, as in the Persian Gulf. It is this latter scenario that Podhoretz has specifically called our impending Finlandization. The Soviets know that we are aware of this, and therefore they may well try any number of moves against us unless we build the "shell game" MX system.

Some further axioms are necessary to make the argument work. The first is that Soviet leaders would willingly risk sacrificing a good many of their citizens in a counterforce exchange —most likely, some of the millions of ethnic Russians who live along the Trans-Siberian railway, where Soviet counterforce weapons are siloed. Soviet leaders cannot, after all, expect that no American counterforce weapons would escape a Soviet first strike since American leaders would have some thirty minutes to retaliate in kind. Nevertheless, Richard Pipes assures us that the Soviets would take the risk, because having lost tens of millions in World War II the Soviet leadership would not value life as we do in the West. (By this logic, Israeli leaders should be even more keen than the Russians on military adventures.)

Pipes's second axiom is that Soviet missile accuracy is fine enough to wipe out most of our counterforce weapons and that Soviet planners can depend on this. No one at MIT, it seems, is ready to concede this point—Kosta Tsipis has in fact pointed out that the Russians would have to control the winds, rain, and gravitational fields over thousands of miles to depend on it— but I shall concede it without even making the case for our superduper cruise missiles as counterforce alternatives in their own right.

Rather, consider the essential quandary Pipes and Podhoretz envision for the American President after the surprise attack: a full twenty million Midwesterners have been killed, but American countervalue weapons remain intact, as do our conventional forces and most of our vastly superior industrial base. The same can be said for Western Europe, China, and Japan, which still can claim the resources of Africa and Latin America even if the Soviets have captured the Persian Gulf. Can the Soviet leadership expect to withstand a conventional, protracted war waged against it by such an alliance? Can it even hope to count on its East European hostages or burgeoning Moslem populations? Granted, the Soviets would still have nuclear weapons to threaten the world's cities, but so would the United States and other nations, and the choice to capitulate or risk ending civilization could well be reversed.

Of course, Podhoretz and Pipes have presented us with a thoroughly eccentric view of American choices and Soviet risks. It assumes what the Soviets cannot, that free people will surrender their freedom at the drop of a bomb while the populations of totalitarian states will fight to the end. Did the Japanese "Manchurianize" the United States by destroying the fleet at Pearl Harbor? And as if Pipes's casuistry were not enough, Podhoretz adds the insinuation that the Japanese and others would now sell themselves to whatever country should supply them oil, even if the Soviets needed nuclear terror to win the right.

What civilized citizens would stand for this, except in the imaginations of writers so cynical about human nature that they consider all moral ideals and restraints a gloss on material gain? Are the people of democratic countries to be compared to Podhoretz's youthful gangs who retreat in the face of anybody who smacks them in the nose? Is making war the same as becoming king of the block? More to the point, is it worth throwing $200 billion or more at our security problem to preempt a diplomatic choice so cynically conceived, especially since those dollars would procure U.S. first-strike capability, which the Soviets will have to match with trip-wire defenses that are far from reliable?

Jews have a special need to consider these arguments, not only because we've defended civilized behavior since Abraham, but because Podhoretz and Edward Luttwak (February 1975) have made support for expansive American strategic power a sine qua non of support for Israel. We cannot realistically expect Israel to get continuing supplies of weapons and aid, they warn, unless the American president and Congress have made an overall commitment of playing it tough with the Russians. Moreover, in their view, converse relations of dependence also hold: so people who remain open to less hawkish solutions to Israel's problems, who would, for example, welcome an end to Israeli settlement on the West Bank and more forthright Israeli negotiations in the Palestinian autonomy talks, are just appeasers. Palestinian claims are to be compared to those of the Sudeten Germans in the Nazi era, and American Jews, they conclude, should encourage all other Americans to appreciate Israel for a toughness the Czechs lacked in pursuing its interests and those of the West. Israel, in short, is nothing less than a strategic asset for the United States (August 1980).

### GOOD FOR THE JEWS?

Let us be clear that support for Israel in the United States has always been led by a coalition of Jewish activists and non-Jewish liberal politicians, progressive journalists, labor leaders, and so forth, who've approved historic Zionist goals because they despise anti-Semitism and have grown increasingly intrigued by Israel's democratic and cooperative institutions. This, despite the knowledge that Israel only complicates American strategic interests in the Middle East, which have historically rested with the Gulf states and their revolving protectors in the Arab world. It was this coalition—from Stephen Wise to Hubert Humphrey—that prevailed upon President Truman to recognize Israel over the strong objections of the State Department and that has actively secured Israel's military and diplomatic requirements in Congress since the Kennedy administration.

*Commentary*'s depiction of Israel as mainly a strategic asset since 1973 has shaken this progressive coalition. If Israel is a strategic asset—as the post-Vietnam generation has been invited to believe by our premier Jewish monthly—then perhaps it is nothing but this. And *Commentary* has made the job of ignoring our ethical responsibilities to the Jewish state even easier. In spite of Moynihan's raising of the issue in 1977, the magazine has lately insisted that "human rights" questions (which reflect badly on Israel's policy of occupation but not on its right to a just survival) perplexed only the naifs of the Carter administration. Worse, Jeane Kirkpatrick and Carl Gershman have implied that traditional dictatorships are not assumed to be comparable to the tyrannies of communism, because the former satisfy their people's "spiritual" needs. This recipe for diplomatic support was meant to justify our support for regimes like South Korea's; but ordinary Americans who read *Time* magazine are clever enough to note its applicability to the Egyptians and even the Saudis.

Moreover, strident arguments about Israel's indispensable power in case America should make a military entry in the Persian Gulf have tended to discredit the Jewish state on campuses and even in the liberal press, where suspicion of cold war rhetoric continues to run high. Rather, disingenuous Palestinian rhetoric about self-determination is increasingly capturing the high ground within America's progressive constituency, just when considerations of Israel's strategic worth—and Robert Tucker's revelations about its nuclear threat—have given many a pretext to become indifferent to Israel's danger.

*Commentary*'s widely publicized turn against the "liberals" also has contributed to the political climate in which combinations of Jews and less well educated people in the labor movement have themselves turned against liberal senators and politicians— against Church, Bayh, Mondale, and others—who have been leading Israel's fight in the Congress for a generation.

What has *Commentary* gained by this? The magazine will point with some pride to the appointments of Kirkpatrick and Gershman to the UN and of Pipes to the Russian desk at the State Department. The former will no doubt use the forum also to rail against the PLO as Moynihan has done. But the choice for America's foreign policy establishment, new and old, has never been between Israel and the PLO, which is why the Camp David accords were conceived. The choice, rather, continues to be between support for Israel and the immediate protection of American interests in the Gulf.

Granted, these options seemed to coincide between 1970 and 1973, after Israel won the War of Attrition on the Suez Canal and seemed the only invincible policeman at America's disposal: Israel, after all, helped save Hussein's regime in September 1970 and might have been enlisted to support the Saudis as well. But this strategic hiatus did not last. The choice between Israel and the more important Arab regimes became distinct again after the 1973 war, when experts as different as Henry Kissinger and George Ball both could see what Sadat openly claimed, that Egypt and the Saudis are more important allies against Soviet expansion in the Gulf than Israel's Phantoms. Those Phantoms, after all, may be useful only in some all-out war that is likely to ruin the oil installations for which war would be waged.

Eliyahu Salpeter, a writer for the Israeli daily *Ha'aretz*, has remarked that most Israelis are smart enough to worry that the Saudi-connected Bechtel Corporation—the recent turf of Caspar Weinberger and George Schultz—Mobil Oil, and others are likely to have more clout in the Reagan administration than the brainy Mr. Gershman. Weinberger's recent noises about stationing American troops in Israel are nothing new and seem more a cover for arming Saudi F-15s with offensive potential than a statement of concern for Israeli lives.

This raises another important problem for Jews produced by *Commentary*'s contribution to wide-scale disillusionment with democratic humanism. Although the magazine will no doubt attack such fundamentalist Christian groups as the Moral Majority and NCPAC in the months ahead, *Commentary* cannot escape its complicity in the far-reaching cultural consequences the New Right has wrought. Just what kind of "spiritual values" did Kristol and Glazer expect from Americans made content by "tradition," but the one, explicitly, that denies God listens to the prayers of Jews? Were our own parents such idiots for promoting the urbane, communitarian values of the democratic left and resisting the amazing grace of market individualism?

A good number of American Jews, in fact, have been deeply demoralized by *Commentary*'s obscuring of the actual political traditions we've had in America since 1881. Our élan has not been in our "interests" but in our roots: the sweatshops, the unions, the *Forward*s, the New Deal, the antifascist leagues, the civil rights movement; and in figures as different as Emma Goldman, Abe Cahan, Aaron Copland, and Justice Brandeis. Their ideals are not made and unmade by income brackets, but have been the stuff of our families' dinner conversations long before we could all speak English. Such ideals entail heroes, sensibilities, moral taste, the civil religion to which we try to make converts by insisting on a sense of history.

And how can *Commentary*'s regulars sensibly speak of the American Jews' traditions while no longer tolerating the writers whom the magazine once acknowledged to be the basic record of our experience? This is not a rhetorical question. *Commentary* has abandoned American Jewish writing to its ideologically primed book reviewers and has virtually stopped publishing the fiction of our best American Jewish writers, who, if Podhoretz's reformed views on Philip Roth are any indication, only serve to reinforce the conceits of the New Class. Ruth Wisse has argued that Arthur Miller, Bernard Malamud, Philip Roth, and the rest have generated merely a literature "about Jews," but not one issuing from "the civilization and religious structure of the Jews" like the work of the talented but permanently obscure Montreal Jewish poet A. M. Klein. To be a Jewish author, one must hold that a "meaningful Jewishness—whether religious, Zionist, ethnic, or any other kind—exists or deserves to exist." This is, I suppose, how the "commandment of Auschwitz" works as literary criticism.

What can American Jews be about if our own public stories are counterfeit? Consider Cynthia Ozick's reaction to Harold Bloom's book on the Kabbalah and compare it to Marc Galanter's poignant defense of Brother Daniel. Dismissing Bloom's claim to be confronting the God of the Fathers, Ozick writes: "The recovery of the Covenant can be attained only in the living out of the living Covenant; never among the shamanistic toys of literature." And Ozick's ungenerous sermon seems hardly unique since *Commentary* has gradually, but surely, reinstated Orthodox Judaism, really a manipulated version of it, lacking in authentic faith, as the only American Jewish practice to match Zionism in inspiring the cohesion necessary for Jews to make their fights. No more articles by anthropologists like Erich Isaac on dietary laws and circumcision. Instead, we see Ruth Wisse's defense of a male-only rabbinate and Haim Maccoby's panegyrics to the Orthodox movement.

Wisse and Maccoby are brilliant polemicists and their pieces should certainly have been published. But can *Commentary* defend its disposition not to publish, except in the letters column, any dissenting voices, especially on questions of orthodoxy? Does it seriously expect American Jews to revive halachic community, or that halachic standards should entirely prevail? Have Podhoretz, Alter, and Wisse been exemplary purveyors of the living Covenant as against the "shamans of literature"? Ruth Wisse may be correct that much of American Jewish literature would seem remote to the ordinary Jews who populate the Yiddish stories she has masterfully retrieved. But then, Americans are now not ordinary Jews and might be appreciated for not having been ordinary hypocrites.

Yet *Commentary* has not even been right about the American Jewish interests for which we are supposed to brush aside American Jewish values. Whatever the experiences of their parents during the post–World War II boom, young American Jews have disproportionately benefited from government spending on welfare, science, and education, because they are disproportionately the young professionals, educators, and administrators the magazine has sought to defend in opposing affirmative action programs. Most of us live in the big northeastern cities whose decay can be reversed only by more federal spending on housing, mass transit, public works, pollution control, and so forth. But there is a corporate Jewish interest in social policy that is even more compelling. In an unpublished report for a major Jewish organization, Arthur Samuelson has noted that in the crucial fields of service (such as health, child care, aid to the elderly), Jewish philanthropic agencies — especially those expanded to serve non-Jews as well — were receiving 51 percent of their funds from government grants. That figure must be considerably higher today. As Samuelson observes, these agencies do more than help the indigent; they "provide the essential organizational and moral backbone" of the Jewish community itself, since fundraising and committee work have become preeminent secular forms of Jewish identification.

Massive cuts to welfare programs, such as the ones now proposed by OMB Director David Stockman, will cause some of these agencies to collapse. Jewish educational institutions will fare no better: YIVO has been saved from bankruptcy for several years by the National Endowment for the Humanities, which seems very high on Stockman's hit list. And how many American universities will agree to participate in the development of Jewish studies programs if further cuts reduce academic operating budgets? How many American Jewish bright but not brilliant students will be able to go to good universities when tuition is almost $10,000 a year and loans for education are drying up? Does Glazer expect the *Landsmannschaften* to pick up this slack? Jewish philanthropic rates have in fact been falling compared to the national average since peaking in the years after the 1967 war. And if American Jews were to revive their welfare institutions with a new flood of cash, would there be enough left to cope with Israel's problems?

*Commentary*'s approving attitudes toward cuts in social spending are also helping to undermine Israel's related and crucial need for foreign aid. Government attempts to "get off the backs" of Americans may dump Israelis on their backsides. The Jewish state today gets three times as much aid directly from the American government as it gets from American Jews. But Stockman has also insisted that foreign aid programs be cut to prepare a balanced budget by 1983. He is not alone. A Yankelovich poll in 1978 ascertained that some 72 percent of all Americans concur with Stockman that aid should be cut. Can they be expected to bail out Israel when Cleveland is permitted to default on its bonds? Does this year's reprieve guarantee next year's aid and that of the year thereafter?

Toward the end of *Making It*, Podhoretz recalls his decision to replace Elliot Cohen as *Commentary*'s editor. He writes,

> Because Elliot Cohen had had something new to say, like it or not, *Commentary* had been charged with vitality for the first ten years which according to Edmund Wilson was the natural life span of a genuine editorial impulse; all *Commentary* had done since . . . was to insist over and over again, and in an endless variety of ways, on points which had already been made, which had already sunk in, which had no further juice in them. The moment had clearly come to say something new, and the possibility of saying it through a monthly magazine was almost certainly there.

There is, I daresay, sound advice in this.

# Sacred and Secular:
# Michael Walzer's *Exodus*

*April 1985*
According to Michael Walzer, the book of Exodus is our first
recorded revolution. Perceptions of its course have influenced
the way various Western religious and political movements have
regarded deliverance from suffering and oppression. The example of Moses meant much to Thomas Aquinas, Judah Halevi,
and John Knox. Flight from Egypt inspired the Zionist Theodor
Herzl, such defenders of Lenin as Lincoln Steffens, and, in our
day, the liberation theologians of Latin America. To get the meaning of the Exodus story just right, Walzer implies, is an important task; it could even save a life. He continues:

> I don't mean to disparage the sacred, only to explore the secular:
> my subject is not what God has done but what men and women
> have done, first with the biblical text itself and then in the world,
> with the text in their hands.

Interpreting Exodus is no academic exercise for Walzer, yet
*Exodus and Revolution* is unmistakably the work of a professional
political philosopher. The book is studded with allusions to the
*Aeneid*, the speeches of Oliver Cromwell, and the categories of
Isaiah Berlin. The key to Walzer's reading is Jean-Jacques Rous-
seau's *Social Contract*, and how many of us have looked at that

A review of Michael Walzer, *Exodus and Revolution* (New York: Basic Books,
1985).

thesis lately? Still, Walzer's prose is pure and sensible, and he leads us without pedantry to exacting conclusions. Between the lines of syllogism, we discern a man's hope for justice, the more welcome at a time when any effort to help unfortunate people in this country is increasingly regarded as an intrusion on private happiness or, for that matter, on Jewish interests.

But *Exodus and Revolution* is most welcome precisely because the question of what makes for American Jewish interests cannot be settled with elbows alone. The secular Yiddish world of Jewish immigrants is gone, and the notion that it can be replaced by vicarious Zionism is going fast. American Jews who persist in the spirit of Eastern European orthodoxy face no serious crisis, but the rest, indeed the majority, have no clear sense of Judaism's future. Can secular Judaism be taught to children? Inadvertently, perhaps, Walzer's book demonstrates that secular Jewish life may yet be possible in America, but only if intellectuals of Walzer's skill and reputation help make Judaism a civil religion; that is, if Judaism's ritual laws and classic literature can be made a part of the American Jew's "ethical" imagination.

Walzer insists that his book is not intended as instruction for any particular religious group in America. Yet, as if conscious of setting an example, Walzer read the entire Pentateuch (not always in translation), the Prophets, the Writings, and the Midrash. He consulted a good many of the most influential rabbinic commentators, including such pre-Enlightenment thinkers as the Vilna Gaon (the Sage of Vilna), and took up the work of contemporary rabbinic scholars such as Nehama Leibowitz and David Hartman. In fact, Walzer shows that some rabbis' concern for ethics aids a secularist reading of the text. To the extent that eschatological questions touch on ethics, he implies, Rousseau may have lacked the "tough realism" of rabbis like Maimonides.

Walzer's clear affinity for Maimonides is particularly appropriate because Maimonides, too, was faced with a crisis of Jewish continuity brought on by the experience of toleration. Maimonides wrote the *Guide of the Perplexed* in Arabic 800 years ago. The perplexed then were Jewish scholars—some, Maimonides' own students—whose reverence for Jewish law had been undermined by the claims of Alexandrian philosophers. By the time he finished writing the *Guide* in 1190, Maimonides had come to the view that a close study of Aristotle's *Ethics* illuminated what Moses intended by law. Have Jews needed Rousseau all along to grasp what Moses intended by freedom?

*Exodus and Revolution* is composed of four chapters whose titles suggest a paradigm for why political revolutions happen (and may be justified), what rhetoric recurs when they do happen, how they are likely to be led, and what their limits are. First, there is "The House of Bondage," where the Israelites are reduced, "crushed down," by the double oppression of hard labor and capricious rule. The Israelites grow disgusted, and fascinated, with the corrupt physical power and sexual abandon of their masters; in dialectical consequence, they yearn for freedom, though only intuitively. It is Moses who organizes victory over Pharaoh; and it is Moses' Levite priests — the revolutionary vanguard — who guide the people's thoughts to the promised land of milk and honey. (Since this is a secularist's reading, Walzer has little to say about the source of Moses' inspiration.)

The rapture of leaving Egypt, like the song of Miriam, is short-lived, however. In his second chapter, "The Murmurings," Walzer shows how at the first sign of hardship — while Moses ascends Mount Sinai to receive the Law — there is dissension among the Israelites. Why, many ask, did Moses bring the people out of bondage only to die in the wilderness? One hears the forlorn hope of returning to Egypt's "fleshpots"; there is the orgiastic worship of the golden calf. Not until Moses descends from Sinai — and his Levite henchmen kill (or, as Walzer allows, "purge") the leaders of the various tribes, some 3,000 men and women — are the people forced to be free. Only then are they prepared to receive the covenant.

How can this covenant be grasped, and in what spirit do the people receive it? The third chapter, "The Covenant," suggests that it might well be understood in ethical terms, as a kind of social contract by which the individual Israelites reach beyond themselves. Walzer's material conforms most clearly to a Rousseauian pattern here, which, remarkably enough, some of the rabbinic literature helps focus.

After Sinai, Moses — the charismatic legislator — evokes a spontaneous commitment from the people to keep to God's laws. The text states that "all the people answered together." Does spontaneous mean voluntary? For Walzer's part, the question is resolved by *Mekilta De-Rabbi Ishmael*, according to which the Israelites all entered into the Sinai covenant consciously: "They did not give this answer with hypocrisy, nor did they get it one from the other, but all of them made up their minds alike."

To be sure, the people did not produce God's laws, but these, in turn, are the product of what Rousseau called the general will, that is, what any reasonable man would will were he informed, cultivated, and able to keep in mind not private advantage but the general welfare. By Walzer's account, the First Commandment — to serve God — seems nothing more than a metaphorical way of expressing the Israelites' huge effort to be reasonable. Thus, the Israelites at Sinai "embody the excellence of man"; and the covenant entails accepting not only the ethical precepts of the Ten Commandments but other laws that make the Israelites "moral equals," "responsible," "radical voluntarists," "communal."

" 'What does the Lord require of thee,' " Walzer quotes the prophet Micah approvingly, " 'but to do justly, and love mercy, and to walk humbly with thy God?' "

In his final chapter, "The Promised Land," Walzer abandons Rousseau for those tough-minded rabbis — again, Maimonides — who teach the limits of messianism. Exodus, Walzer believes, engendered what is properly called historical time. That is its tour de force. Yet the Exodus story has prompted some prophets to imagine what, finally, Rousseau imagined: an era of perfect harmony, unity, serenity, peace — what some have called the end of history. Thus, there is this from the Syriac Book of Baruch:

> And disease shall withdraw
> And anxiety and anguish and
>     lamentation pass from among
>     men. . . .
> And wild beasts shall come from the
>     forest and minister unto men.

Messianic visions are wonderful, Walzer concedes, but they are also terribly dangerous. They insinuate contempt for the here and now for the sake of an unrealizable future. They provide a rhetorical advantage to demagogues who would have us justify cruel means by invoking stirring ends. Besides, they are out of spirit with the terms of the Exodus covenant. In contrast with messianic politics, Walzer poses the ideal of "Exodus politics," which implies an awareness of our unending capacity for "backsliding," of the endless "marching across the desert, teaching, learning, obeying the law":

> And even if the promises were fulfilled, the result would still be a holy community living in historical time, its citizens farming the land, waiting for the rain, watching for foreign enemies, celebrating the seventh day and the seventh year and the jubilee.

The presumption that the best we can hope for includes watching out for enemies—who are enemies, it seems, because they are foreign—may rankle with some. For me, those words conjure not the fulfillment of God's promise so much as an idealized vision of Kibbutz Degania (the first kibbutz) between the world wars. Still, Walzer's distinction between messianic politics and Exodus politics trenchantly expresses his preference for tolerance over perfectionism. Accordingly, Walzer's "Conclusion" defends the Labor Zionist's willingness to partition the Land of Israel over the scripture hawk's will to annex it. Exodus politics also suggests the superiority of the welfare state to the communist *apparat*.

Can anything be wrong with a view of the covenant that gives us so much? At the risk of revamping Walzer's secularist ground rules, I want to return to that word "holy," which, in spite of himself, Walzer cannot avoid using at the climax of his argument. Can "holy community" mean something less than a community struggling to achieve the fear of God? Or, to put this somewhat differently, is it possible to understand how the story of Exodus unfolds without seeing the longing for God as its driving force? There is more at stake here than a difference of opinion regarding the logic of a cherished text.

If, indeed, it is not possible to separate the secular from the sacred in Exodus, to detach Moses' ethics from his call to faith, then perhaps it was also a more difficult matter for the Israelites to enter into the covenant than Walzer, following Rousseau and some rabbis, would have us believe. And if it was Moses' fate to offer a covenant few could undertake, did the revolution of the priests really succeed? Was the book of Exodus an example of Exodus politics or just another messianic tragedy? (The purges, again, come to mind.)

The most direct way to get at what Exodus means by "holiness" is to put the book in its place, that is, between Genesis and Leviticus. Do these books suggest that holiness is ethical grace? Immediately before encountering Moses, we leave the story of Joseph, who suffered at the hands of his brothers—in part because he was his father's favorite and, in any case, because he had dreamt he was above them all. But the text states that Joseph suffered inwardly, and continued to suffer at least until his father's death, simply because he could not get his brothers to see what he saw: purpose in a man's dreams, immanent order out of scattered human wills—indeed, a divine will whose justice is not readily grasped. (Why was Pharaoh's winemaker pardoned and his baker hanged?)

Now, Joseph's brothers were not slavish people; they were the great-grandsons of Abraham, the grandsons of Rebecca, the sons of Jacob. Still, they seemed unable simply to inherit faith in the One God. When Joseph, now Pharaoh's deputy, reveals himself to his brothers for the first time, he reassures them, "Be not grieved, nor angry with yourselves that you sold me hither, *for God did send me before you,* to preserve life." His brothers, it seems, can no more comprehend this explanation as adults than they could put up with his self-centered dreams as youths. Indeed, the last we hear from Joseph is when he and his brothers are accompanying Jacob's remains back to the land of their forefathers; they have just passed the pit into which Joseph had been thrown before being sold, and the brothers, seized by panic, beg Joseph not to take revenge. This drives Joseph to tears. "Am I in the place of God?" he weeps.

Consider, in contrast, the pivotal chapter of Leviticus, titled Kedoshim, "Holy Ones." It is here, as Walzer notes, that Moses explicitly commands the people of Israel to be a holy community. Does a holiness of social contract anticipate what this chapter requires? To be sure, there are a number of ethical injunctions that support Walzer's reading. Moses commands the Israelites to leave gleanings for the poor and pay workers' wages on time. He forbids them to curse the deaf or put a stumbling block before the blind, to favor the mighty or allow a neighbor to be attacked with impunity. Yet the first proscription in Kedoshim (as in the Ten Commandments) is of idol worship, and the major part of the injunctions have to do not with righteousness but with purity:

> Thou shalt not sow thy field with two kinds of seed; neither shall there come upon thee a garment of two kinds of stuff mingled together.... Ye shall not eat with the blood, neither shall ye practice divination nor soothsaying. Ye shall not round the corners of your head, neither shalt thou mar the corners of thy beard.

Indeed, Kedoshim suggests so many ways people might defile themselves before God, especially in perverse sexual acts—and reveals so little mercy for those who lapse—that one leaves the chapter wondering if God is not mocking human beings by insisting we are made in His image.

In subsequent chapters, it must be said, there are the makings of a reconciliation. Having failed to elicit from the people a sense of what is holy by means of animal sacrifice, the priests adopt a more gradual, less shocking way. They take the best part of the bread, of the oil, of the cloth—and of the week—and separate these from the common, treating them as holy. Thus, they imply what the rabbis came to call Halacha, the way of the Law. The cabalists thought of Halacha as fragments of holiness (or Kedusha) for everyday life, as if in acknowledgement that Moses' faith is otherwise unmanageable.

Incidentally, in his *Shemona Perakim*, Maimonides wrote that had the Ten Commandments not been given at Sinai, "it would have been proper for mankind to add them." But the ritual commandments were another matter. These, he thought, were to be obeyed out of awe before God and were the more awesome precisely because it is not unreasonable to violate them: "Were it not for the Law, they would not at all be considered transgressions."

So Leviticus, like Genesis before it, teaches a version of holiness that is, if not incompatible with a secular social contract, then not quite compatible with it either. Holiness is not the satisfaction one gets from doing good, rather it is the condition for *wanting* to do good. Moreover, holiness is always something ecstatic, not — as with ethics — the alleged product of reason. Indeed, holiness seems an intuition that the senses report too little, that something ought to order our lives according to an apprehension of perfect harmony, unity, etc. — the very qualities that, in Walzer's view, make for good poetry and bad politics.

Is holiness, then, something the Israelites aspire to more readily merely for having been purged? Unquestionably, the text implies progress. Yet even after Sinai, Moses continues to seem as frustrated in trying to convey his vision to the people as Joseph was with regard to his brothers. The one time in Exodus the people seem genuinely to share in Moses' exquisite feelings, and act in a way that is unambiguously voluntary, is when they are invited to offer adornment for the sanctuary, the Tent of Meeting where Moses encounters God in the aftermath of Sinai. Then, all bring "a free-will offering unto the Lord," nose rings and earrings and signet rings; "the blue, and the purple, and the scarlet and the fine linen." Sadly, the exercise gets out of hand; the people bring too much. "So the people," the text continues, "were restrained from bringing."

Sadly, again, we are no more initiated into Moses' vision than the people were. The text scrupulously avoids trying to tell us how holiness feels, though it does state that Moses' first encounter with God, at the burning bush, occurs just after the birth of his son Gershom. Nor are we told how holiness can be captured. What we are told are the dimensions and refinements of Moses' sanctuary, and the text uses as many words to describe these as it uses to narrate his confrontation with Pharaoh. We are told, in addition, that the sanctuary was pitched far away from the Israelite camp, that Moses entered alone, and that seeing him enter, all the people worshiped from afar, every man at his own tent door.

In that sanctuary, Exodus concludes, Moses spoke to God "face to face, as a man speaketh unto his friend," and he pleaded with God to pardon "this stiff-necked" people and take them "for His inheritance" in spite of their shortcomings. By the time God and Moses complete their meeting, Moses' face gives off light. He puts on a veil to inform the children of Israel of the terms of the covenant; he takes off the veil when he returns to the sanctuary.

Are revolutions inevitably led by such people — in D. H. Lawrence's words — in whom one detects the Holy Ghost? Is bondage the source of our desire for freedom, or does that source lie in an intuition of an end to history which, inevitably, yields cruelty? Can it be that in embodying the excellence of man, the Israelites are not so much defined by the covenant as afflicted by it? Shrewdly, perhaps, Walzer refuses these questions. Still, it is hard to read through Exodus without wondering if the children of Israel were envious of Moses, entering that tent, emerging with his face beaming. We envy them just for having been there to see him. Is envy a secularist's faith?

# Index of Names